Issues in Business Ethics

Volume 63

The Issues in Business Ethics series aims to showcase the work of scholars who critically assess the state of contemporary business ethics theory and practice. Business ethics as a field of research and practice is constantly evolving, and as such, this series covers a wide range of values-driven initiatives in organizations, including ethics and compliance, governance, CSR, and sustainable development. We also welcome critical interrogations of the concepts, activities and role-players that are part of such values-driven activities in organizations. The series publishes both monographs and edited volumes. Books in the series address theoretical issues or empirical case studies by means of rigorous philosophical analyses and/or normative evaluation. The series wants to be an outlet for authors who bring the wealth of literature within the humanities and social sciences to bear on contemporary issues in the global business ethics realm. The series especially welcomes work that addresses the interrelations between the agent, organization and society, thus exploiting the differences and connections between the micro, meso and macro levels of moral analysis. The series aims to establish and further the conversation between scholars, experts and practitioners who do not typically have the benefit of each other's company. As such, it welcomes contributions from various philosophical paradigms, and from a wide array of scholars who are active within in the international business context. Its audience includes scholars and practitioners, as well as senior students, and its subject matter will be relevant to various sectors that have an interest and stake in international business ethics.

Authors from all continents are welcome to submit proposals, though the series does seek to encourage a global discourse of a critical and normative nature. The series insists on rigor from a scholarly perspective, but authors are encouraged to write in a style that is accessible to a broad audience and to seek out a subject matter of practical relevance.

Mollie Painter • Patricia H. Werhane

Editors

Leadership, Gender, and Organization

Second Edition

 Springer

Editors
Mollie Painter
Responsible and Sustainable Business Lab
(RSB Lab), Nottingham Business School
Nottingham Trent University
Nottingham, UK

Patricia H. Werhane
Center for Professional Responsibility,
Gies College of Business
University of Illinois
Chicago, IL, USA

ISSN 0925-6733   ISSN 2215-1680   (electronic)
Issues in Business Ethics
ISBN 978-3-031-24444-5   ISBN 978-3-031-24445-2   (eBook)
https://doi.org/10.1007/978-3-031-24445-2

This Springer imprint is published by the registered company Springer Nature Switzerland AG
The registered company address is: Gewerbestrasse 11, 6330 Cham, Switzerland

Acknowledgements

This book is the result of its editors' engagement with wonderful colleagues and professionals over many years – too many to mention. We would however like to single out Natalie Toms for her excellent editorial support and patience in preparing this manuscript. We would also like to acknowledge Mollie's wonderful team at The RSB Lab at Nottingham Trent University for allowing her many experiments in leading, and Dean, Baback Yazdani, for his unwavering support. During the preparation of this manuscript, we also took inspiration on how to deal with the challenges of gendered leading from the outstanding leadership model of Dean Danica Purg of the IEDC-Bled School of Management in Slovenia.

We would like to acknowledge the following journals and publishers for granting access to the articles featured. This allowed us, in important ways, to maintain continuity of thought, whilst also progressing the discourse.

Thanks to Bruce Barry, Editor of *Business Ethics Quarterly*, and David Wasieleski, editor of *Business and Society Review*, for graciously extending gratis permission to publish articles from their journals.

Also, a note of thanks to the other publishers who granted us the rights to revisions or reprinting of previously published materials.

Banco Bilbao Vizcaya Argentaria (BBVA)

Journal of Business Ethics, Springer

The Leadership Quarterly, Elsevier

We also extend thanks to all of our authors for their contributions, as well as to Chris Wilby (Associate Editor, Springer) for his dedication and support.

Last but not least, we are indebted to all the women in our lives: mothers, daughters, granddaughters, nieces, employees, students, collaborators, and soulmates, for giving us reasons to write.

Contents

About the Editors

Mollie Painter is an international scholar and public speaker specializing in business ethics, CSR, sustainability, and responsible leadership. She has held academic positions in South Africa, USA, UK, and Slovenia. She currently heads up the Responsible and Sustainable Business Lab (RSB Lab), a Research Centre within Nottingham Business School, Nottingham Trent University, UK, and is an Extraordinary Professor at the Gordon Institute of Business Science, University of Pretoria. From August 2021, she will be serving as co-Editor-in-Chief of *Business Ethics Quarterly*. Between 2015 and 2020, she held the Coca-Cola Chair of Sustainability at IEDC-Bled in Slovenia on a part-time basis, and has been Visiting Professor at HEC, ESCP-Europe, EDHEC, and IAE in France. In partnership with the Academy of Business in Society (ABIS) and African faculty, she developed the African leadership programmes of focusing on developing values-driven leadership on the African continent, with active programmes now running in Egypt, Kenya, and South Africa.

Mollie's most recent research focuses on sustainability, organizational culture, leadership, and ethics within complex organizational environments. As a philosopher by training, her trademark is bringing insights from twentieth century and contemporary philosophy to management and organizational studies. Topics she has published on include leadership and gender, relational accountability, critical perspectives on organizational ethics, and rethinking ethics pedagogies. In addition to *Gender, Leadership and Organization* (Springer, 2011, with Volume 2 forthcoming in 2021), she has also authored *Business Ethics as Practice* (Cambridge University Press, 2008) and Business Ethics and Continental Philosophy, co-edited with René ten Bos (Cambridge University Press, 2011), which has been translated into Dutch as *Bedrijfsethiek. Filosofische perspectieven* (Boom, 2013).

Patricia H. Werhane, Professor Emerita, was formerly Ruffin Professor of Business Ethics at Darden School of Business, University of Virginia and later the Wicklander Chair in Business Ethics at DePaul University. Currently, a Fellow at the Center for Professional Responsibility at the Gies College of Business at the University of Illinois, she is the author or editor of over 30 books and over 100 articles, most prominently in business ethics. She was the founding editor of *Business Ethics Quarterly* and is the Executive Producer of a video series on founding thinkers in business ethics and corporate responsibility.

Introduction

Mollie Painter and Patricia H. Werhane

Abstract Developing themes from the first volume of this collection, in this second edition we again bring together papers that either exemplify the crossing of disciplinary boundaries, or that allow us to do so in and through the conversations they create. The pieces were chosen based on their relevance to similar themes as discussed in the first volume. The first, most central theme of this volume remains 'leadership', which in and of itself continues to develop into an academic field ever more audacious in its ambitions and multidisciplinary in orientation. Many new and exciting perspectives regarding the importance of relationality in leading have crystalized in recent years and offer rich perspectives for rethinking organizational life. The second theme is gender, which finds its academic force in feminism and gender studies, but has become an important part of organization studies, labor relations, political theory, to name but a few, and is also increasingly central to the study of leadership practices. In highlighting their importance, we hope to set the stage for understanding the normative implications of how gender and leadership discourses intersect. We also continue our interest in systemic thinking and complexity theory. A Golden thread that runs through all of these fields, and certainly weaves together the broad variety of perspectives in this volume, is the notion of relationality. Taken together, this variety of theoretical perspectives informed the selection of the papers in this volume.

Keywords Leadership · Interdisciplinarity · Contextualization · Gender · Relationality · Complexity theory · Systems thinking

M. Painter (✉)
Responsible and Sustainable Business Lab (RSB Lab), Nottingham Business School, Nottingham Trent University, Nottingham, UK

Gordon Institute of Business Science, University of Pretoria, Pretoria, South Africa
e-mail: mollie.painter@ntu.ac.uk

P. H. Werhane
Center for Professional Responsibility, Gies College of Business, University of Illinois, Chicago, IL, USA

M. Painter, P. H. Werhane (eds.), *Leadership, Gender, and Organization*, Issues in Business Ethics 63, https://doi.org/10.1007/978-3-031-24445-2_1

Interdisciplinarity is often hailed as the solution to dealing with intractable dilemmas and aporias and describing complex phenomena, yet such research is not always simple to execute, and certainly not easy to publish. Perhaps this is why pursuing interdisciplinary agendas merits book-length projects, with long gestation periods. This specific collection represents a progression, or sequel, to our earlier work, 10 years after our first experiment in putting together an interdisciplinary volume on *Gender, Leadership and Organization*, which was published in 2011. Our first volume included some historical reflections on gender and leadership, followed by papers by a number of scholars reflecting on the emergence of 'relational leadership theory' or 'complexity leadership', plus a discussion of the implications that this has had for understanding the way in which women (and men) lead in organizations. Our first collection aimed to offer some examples of how gender and leadership were being approached in corporations, community organizations, professions, and how women were leading the charge of building responsible businesses globally. In the decade that has passed, contributions to the discussion of gender in organization studies and leadership literatures have proliferated (Eagly and Heilam 2016), employing both qualitative (Seierstad et al. 2017; Nash and Moore 2019; Phillips and Prieto 2020) and quantitative research methodologies (Wang et al. 2019; Geletkanycz 2020). In introducing this 'sequel' of sorts, we thought that it may be helpful to briefly review the chapters of our first volume, gesturing to continuing conversations and remaining impasses.

We opened our first volume with Mary Hartman's piece, which urged us to retrace our steps in providing the necessary context for our deliberations around the impasses in the study of leadership, gender and organization, 10 years into a new millennium. Her reflections on the genesis of feminism since the 1960s allowed us to understand that the feminist movement, if it could still be considered a 'movement' at that juncture, changed dramatically since its beginnings in the 1960s. As we demonstrated in other essays in this first collection, women have attained leadership positions, although not in as great a number as we had imagined. With only 14 women leading the FT global 500 companies at the time of writing (2010), we are still today challenged with empowering women. At the end of 2020 there were 38 women CEOs in the United States Fortune 500 companies, a better but still unacceptable outcome, considering that 50% of the American workforce is women. Globally about 23% of executives in the 100 largest companies are women (Catalyst 2021). The challenge therefore remains as pertinent as ever in a global economy where interrelationships and networks, not single leaders, are emerging as more propitious leadership models. Indeed, in this next volume we will argue that a global networked economy still demands that leadership styles be changed, moving from a hierarchical individualistic model to a more organic, collaborative systemic approach. Our first volume went some way in arguing for this approach.

Judith Rosener's now classic article on women leaders, (included as the second chapter in our first volume), highlighted that a transformative collaborative model of leading is both more typical of women leaders and actually very effective, particularly in large organizations. Although Rosener barely touched on it, a transformational leader is more comfortable in a complex environment of a large multinational corporation, and that style of leadership, in turn, is more conducive to leadership success in global companies. Following up on Rosener's analysis of a transformational style of leadership, Werhane's contribution to our first volume introduced the reader to systems and systems thinking as a methodology for organizational thinking and leadership that challenges the traditional firm-centered stakeholder models and the hierarchical leadership paradigms those models perpetuate. Elaborating on Werhane's introduction of systems thinking, Collier and Esteban's essay proposed that in postindustrial economies, 'systemic leadership', that is, leading from the middle of an organization and managing that system, allowed its human participants to create solid and sustainable communities, despite its paradoxes. The notion of systemic leadership alludes to many diverse disciplinary perspectives and is often called by different names.

Multiple terminologies emerged in the wake of the insights around how complex systems precipitate new ways of leading. Over many years, Uhl-Bien, Marion, and McKelvey (2007) have developed what they call a 'complexity leadership model' which, like Collier and Esteban's (2000) seminal piece on 'systemic leadership', both challenge hierarchical models and takes into account the complex systems in which commerce operates today in a global economy. Their work has remained as relevant now, as 10 years ago, which is why we again include a piece by Uhl-Bien in this volume, hoping to show how this trajectory has led us towards an increasing understanding of the relational dynamics previously alluded to in both systemic and complexity leadership. In our first volume, Painter-Morland's piece on systemic leadership, also drawing on complexity studies, reminded us that leadership models are all socially constructed, and as such subject to revision and change. In this earlier work, she gestured towards a relational systemic model of leadership which could result in a participatory organization, where trust and collaboration prevail. The relationality inherent in systemic leadership has since been articulated more deliberately in various contexts (Cunliffe and Ericson 2011; Painter-Morland and Deslandes 2017; Ospina and Foldy 2020). We now include a piece by Pérezts, Painter & Russon that highlights the ways in which relational leadership reflects non-Western thinking about leadership dynamics. Though this piece does not unpack the gender-dimension of this relationality, it offers an important departure from male-dominated, individualist conceptions of leadership.

Our first volume argued that a departure from individualist essentialist thinking is important in understanding the barriers to relational thinking in organizations. For example, Gremmen and Benschop's analysis acknowledged that much of the literature on leadership argues that the most successful leaders are those who engage in networking through binding relationships throughout an organization. Because women have fewer opportunities to network and fewer such organizations in which to participate, it is often concluded that the paucity of opportunities explains why there are fewer women than men in leadership positions. Gremmen and Benschop questioned the conclusion that networks are always beneficial, and contend that some professional women's networks are not enabling. The general conclusion to be drawn is that not all collaborative systemic approaches are successful, particularly those that revert to power struggles rather than collaboration. Collaboration as such is in fact often not as simple as it seems. Clark and Kleyn's chapter in Volume I helped us understand that just as not all networks, even professional women networks, produce positive experiences, similarly, not all systems create positive climates, particularly for women. In their study of South African women executives, Clark and Kleyn demonstrate how social and cultural conditions in South Africa such as paternalism, and male exclusive networks, lead to the resignation of many very fine women executives. Sadly, the chapters in this volume attest to similar patterns persisting today.

Already 10 years ago, we realized that systemic leadership cannot be understood without acknowledging the cultural and religious dynamics that animate the relationality in organizational settings. Tedmanson argued that in a global setting where the most propitious leadership styles are interactive, systemic and complex, one of the challenges is to deal with the cultural and religious backgrounds of various participants in an organization. These various backgrounds create multi-layered variables that account for differences in leadership style and may conflict with a more Western view of leadership. Tedmanson's study of women from colonized cultures and how they lead both as community leaders and in organizations, helped the reader to understand these systemic challenges and contributions that cultural diversity engenders. McCartney's chapter revealed another important blindspot in leadership studies. i.e. that the literature on leadership almost exclusively focuses on adults. McCartney analyzed the emergence of leadership in girls between the ages of 12 and 23 in community-based organizations that address horrendous challenges in poor communities. These women self-organize and lead within their communities rather than depending on more institutional and top—down interventions, and do so with surprising success. They thus demonstrate the tenacity and capabilities of women even in adverse conditions. Looking back over the past decade, it has become clear that instead of addressing these socio-economic conditions, gendered constructs are still employed in ways that perpetuate inequality. They are entrenched in mental models that remain resistant to change. The relevance of Werhane's thinking about mental models and its applicability to contemporary settings, led us to include a substantial revision of this chapter in this second volume.

We ended the first volume with a study of Dame Anita Roddick, the founder and former CEO of the Body Shop. Roddick is a model for what Collier and Esteban call 'systemic leadership' deriving from what Uhl-Bien, Marion and Kelvey call 'complexity leadership theory'. Roddick also exemplifies what Pless and Maak identified as "responsible leadership," taking into account the global environment in which the Body Shop interacts, providing outlets for indigenous products, and being profitable as well. Pless and Maak argued that Roddick is an exemplar of the female archetype of leadership. While some of the readers may have disagreed with that conclusion, Roddick's 'responsible leadership' seemed to be an appropriate example of a relational type of leadership theory, style and practice.

Since our 2011 publication, the continued interest in these topics has been evidenced by the ongoing use of the first volume's chapters. This brought us to consider a second edition. We had originally planned to simply revise and update some of the pieces. In attempting to do so, we soon however realized that the field has moved on significantly in the past decade, and that many new, perhaps more nuanced perspectives have emerged in this period. What we ended up collating is a completely new volume. We hope to address some of the blind spots that the first volume revealed, especially in terms of how gender identity is defined, and how cultural prejudices and political and capitalist agendas continue to play into how gendered leadership function in organizational settings. We also intend to bridge the first and second volume in this introduction by offering some reflections on some other seminal pieces published in leading outlets, which set the scene for continuing debate and conversation.

Contextualization

Firstly, we offer some reflections on seminal pieces that we believe offer helpful feminist perspectives on ethics. Since these papers are easily accessible in the published domains, they are not included in this volume, but can be accessed via the relevant hyperlinks. In highlighting their importance, we hope to set the stage for understanding the normative implications of how gender and leadership discourses intersect. Departing from Mary Hartman's essay in our first volume, we believe that feminist theories are still too often neglected both in theoretical and practical ethics, as important dimensions for moral decision making. Revisiting these feminist perspectives sets the stage for multidimensional thinking about more inclusive approaches to leadership in this century of globalization, pandemics, and environmental challenges. Together they create a philosophically grounded basis for feminist developments in leadership that challenge some of the traditional approaches to leadership and ethics. For example, Virginia Held's analysis of feminist theories still offers an important point of departure. In contrast to traditional approaches to moral theory and application, Held argues that "the history of ethics has been constructed from male points of views, and has been built on assumptions and concepts that are by no means gender-neutral" (Held 2006). These are allegedly universal constructions that bias our thinking and frame our moral deliberations and judgments from a masculine perspective. These traditional ethical theories also ignore any feminist or indeed, other gender-sensitive perspectives on ethics. Held reevaluates these theories to argue that there is a whole body of feminist thinking that is left out of what is often called "rational decision making." She then presents three new points of view aligned with feminism, which should transform our thinking about moral philosophy and applications (not only to moral theory, but also, from the perspective of this collection), that feminist thinking is the ground for contemporary leadership.

Held's first critique is the long-held view that moral reasoning is just that, rational decision-making from a normative point of view. Even when we bracket Held's finger-pointing at the demeaning of women by many of these philosophers, her more important point is that this rationalism ignores another element of human nature, that is, our emotions, which play important if not central roles in moral thinking and moral judgment. Critiquing both Kantian and utilitarian forms of moral judgments that are preoccupied with rational thinking, these supposedly gender-neutral theories actually ignore the role of emotions and the ways in which women experience the context and particularities where moral issues arise. Thus, Kantian and utilitarian moral philosophies ignore the moral experiences and judgment of at least half of the population. Held argues that a moral theory should "embrace emotion as providing at least a partial basis for morality itself, and for moral understanding." Moreover, Held points out that a feminist perspective on morality includes the idea not of a separate autonomous ego but of an embodied relational self, a self that is not merely self-interested but one that has been developed from, and grounded in, human experiences, contacts with others, and local contexts. This self has been constructed from these abiding relationships and continues to evolve throughout one's lifetime. That aspect of the self cannot be ignored or dismissed, and accounts for our human ability to feel, care and nurture, as well as reason, since our reasoning processes, too, are embedded in these complex evolving relationships. This relational self, we will argue, however embodied in a gender, creates an ability to lead successfully in the global complex political economies in which we find ourselves. Out of this analysis, Held later develops what she calls an ethic of care "meeting the needs of others for whom we take responsibility; valuing emotions alongside rationality; accepting partiality; including the private sphere as a moral terrain; and acknowledging that people are relational and interdependent" (Held 1990, 2006). A simplistic association of feminism with an ethic of care, is however something that we will cautions against in this volume.

The broader reception of feminism in ethics-related fields has unfortunately been disappointing. In an important book chapter, Laura Spence (2016) recounts the personal history of her work in BE and CSR. She writes, "gender awareness and feminist approaches have a disappointingly low profile in CSR." Despite its normative focus, both the BE and the CSR literatures have "failed to embody [feminist] perspectives in our thinking, our organizations, and our judgments....[despite the fact that]in the context of CSR as elsewhere, issues around gender are embedded variously in power, class, race, religion, sexuality, disability, education, sexism, political and cultural traditions... have affected women and men in the private and public spheres." (Spence 2016, paraphrased from Pearson 2007). Spence points out that often a feminist perspective is filtered out in business and politics. This is despite evidence that a feminist point of view can add to our thinking in organizational and institutional theory and economics. Interestingly, however, in her work on small firms, Spence has discovered much more emphasis on a feminist perspective that takes account of relational values, context, and the interactions between those in firms, as well as their respective communities. Spence has hopes that this primarily masculine focus in business and CSR will change over time, but to date, that evolution has been at best, at a snail's pace.

It is unfortunately the case that even attempts at establishing diversity and inclusion at organizational levels at best fall short in meaningfully addressing the problem, and at worst, re-entrench existing divisions and essentialist identity constructs. For example, Dennissen, Benschop and van den Brink (2018) challenged standard diversity management practices as often being one-dimensional, i.e. focused on single-identity categories, thus reinforcing inequalities that they are meant to address. Most of us have multiple identities and to concentrate on one aspect such as gender, color, or ethnicity, simply reinforces these stereotypes and discourages inclusiveness and acceptance of a multiplicity of identities. The result is often a lingering implicit discrimination, and opportunity losses. We hope that this volume may address these problems, and gesture to ways in which the unique particularity of all genders may play a role in leading organizations responsibly in the decades to come. As it stands, we still have a long way to go, despite important developments in leadership theory.

In Volume II, we continue our interest in systemic thinking and complexity theory, acknowledging that some of the terminology has shifted. For example, harking back to Uhl-Bien's chapters in Volume I, Uhl-Bien and Arena's (2018) more recent work draws on their interest in complexity leadership to develop a theory of leadership for organizational adaptability. Their review of the literature calls for leadership scholars to reimagine leadership as organizational adaptability for contemporary global organizations who must continually adapt to the changing economic and political conditions in which they operate. They argue that leadership for organizational adaptability is different from traditional leadership or even the paradigm of leading change. It involves enabling and adaptive processes by creating space for ideas advanced by entrepreneurial leaders to engage in tension with the operational system and generate innovations that scale into the system to meet the adaptive needs of the organization and its environment. Rather than driving change from the top down, they write that "[organizational adaptability] addresses how leaders can position organizations and the people within them to be adaptive in the face of complex challenges. It taps into current requirements for organizations and those within them to be flexible, agile and adaptive in response to changes associated with a volatile and often unpredictable world." In a complex and often unpredictable global set of economies, adaptability is vital for any organization to survive successfully even in a chaotic and unstable environment. This is best achieved through networking systems rather than top-down hierarchical mandates. It has to be reiterated that a relational approach to leadership can be described in many ways and called by many different names. For example, in their analysis of 'collective leadership', Ospina and Foldy (2020) approach relationality from a constructionist perspective, in order to understand how social change organizations foster the kind of connectedness that allows for collective problem-solving to become possible. Describing 'the relational trend' in the emergence of what is called 'collaborative public management' as an important development, they however argue that one should go even further in developing a 'relational lens' on how collaborative change emerge across various organizations. From this perspective, leaders, followers and their relations do not exist separately from the leadership process. As such, interdependence and intersubjective meanings emerge in and through relational dynamics. Ospina and Foldy's (2020) study identifies important relational elements in the meaning-making that takes place, such as prompting cognitive shifts by challenging existing power-relations, naming and shaping identity, engaging in dialogue about difference, creating equitable governance mechanisms, and weaving multiple worlds together through interpersonal relationships, all the while challenging underlying assumptions.

Understanding the complex dynamics of power and privilege is key in challenging existing biases and prejudices, which is why relational thinking is crucial in addressing the intersections between gender, leadership and organization. Our contention is that though relationality has emerged as an even stronger theme within gender and leadership studies over the past decade, much remains to be studied. Despite the growing literature on embodied leadership (Knights and Pullen 2019), and the way in which this problematizes a stereotypical and one-dimensional understanding of how a leader looks and operates, our understanding of gender and organization is still much too binary in nature. Important new perspectives are however emerging. In a comprehensive volume of essays, entitled *Diversity, Affect, Embodiment in Organizing,* Pullen and Fotaki (2019) embrace corporeality as an important avenue by which to recognize the distortions that binary thinking inevitably brings about in considering matters of gender and organization. Their analysis makes it clear that rethinking leadership from an embodied perspective makes it imperative to challenge the male imaginary, which continues to function as an impenetrable ideal type in leadership studies. Persistent binary thinking allows LGBTQ+ individuals to stay adrift at sea when it comes to their functioning in leadership roles. From our perspective, the full implications of relationality for organizing alternative business practices must still be explored. The complexity of pursuing justice and procuring respect for difference continues to raise perplexing questions. It is towards answering these complex questions that this new volume hopes to make a contribution.

Overview of Papers in This Volume

In this collection, we again bring together papers that either exemplify the crossing of disciplinary boundaries, or that allow us to do so in and through the conversations they create. The pieces were chosen based on their relevance to similar themes as discussed in the first volume. In pursuing these as an ongoing conversation, we hope to think through what has been gained from their intersections in the past decade, and to gesture towards what remains to be done. The first, most central theme of this volume remains 'leadership', which in and of itself continues to develop into an academic field ever more audacious in its ambitions and multidisciplinary in orientation. Many new and exciting perspectives regarding the importance of relationality in leading have crystalized in recent years and offer rich perspectives for rethinking organizational life. The second theme is gender, which finds its academic force in feminism and gender studies, but has become an important part of organization studies, labor relations, political theory, to name but a few, and is also increasingly central to the study of leadership practices. In addition, the interface between leadership and gender still raises multiple normative concerns, and as such, this collection operates within the broad purview of Business Ethics, CSR and sustainability, offering perspectives on diversity and inclusion within organizations (Ciulla et al. 2018). Last but not least, a Golden thread that runs through all of these fields, and certainly weaves together the broad variety of perspectives in this volume, is the notion of relationality. As we explained above, the 'relational turn' (Cooper 2005) is by no means a new development, as it has been revealing itself over the past decade in academic contributions focused on relational leadership (Binns 2008), in philosophical arguments positing 'relational subjects' as an alternative to masculine, individualist conceptions of subjectivity, and in ethical accounts arguing for relational accountability as a non-foundationalist normative force in complex organizational environments (Painter-Morland and Deslandes 2015, 2017).

Taken together, this variety of theoretical perspectives informed the selection of the papers in this volume. In the first part of this volume, we again start by tracking certain historical and conceptual developments that gave rise to the rich intersections between gender, leadership and the organizational practices that emerge from it. We highlight the various ways in which feminism has been approached, and reflect on how it has sometimes been inaccurately appropriated in the literature, highlighting the implications this may have for thinking about leadership in organizations. Secondly, we explore the notion of relationality and how it has come to change our thinking about leadership. Again, this is a multidisciplinary story where complexity studies, leadership studies, ethics and gender come together to challenge the ways in which we think about practices of leading. We also highlight the way in which thinking about relationality allows us to rethink leadership in non-Western, and non-binary ways. We conclude the collection by exploring the implications of the interface between leadership and gender, and the particular the ways in which certain organizational dynamics allow for relationality to be nurtured, or in many cases, foreclosed.

In looking at the volume as a whole, a few broad insights emerged, albeit articulated in different ways and with reference to distinct literatures. The first relates to the problem of essentialism and the stereotypical typecasting of male and female that still plagues leadership studies, and organizational practice more generally. Typecasting women as 'caring' or 'relational' often serves to disqualify them from leadership positions, which seem to be reserved for more individualistic, 'strong', and emotionally disengaged individuals. The reality of 'difference' can certainly not be denied, and it is sometimes indeed necessary to highlight it in order to make the case for equal rights and inclusion, but the way in which gendered difference is operationalized in organizations perpetuates inequalities and impoverishes our understanding of leadership.

We therefore start by analyzing the persistent tendency to establish gendered identities as 'difference from', and attempt to challenge in order to disable the essentialism that lies at the heart of it. Viewing women as 'different-from' always casts the female as the inferior opposite of the male archetype, and as such effectively puts women in the position of having to mimic the male leadership archetype in order to gain access to leadership positions. They often do so while at the same time maintaining essentialist feminine traits in order to avoid being accused of 'inauthenticity'. The experience of being 'damned if you do and damned if you don't' is an all too familiar refrain. One however needs to challenge essentialism without losing sight of the distinct inequality that continues to plague organizations and remain committed to political action that challenges injustice wherever it manifests. Painter's (2011) analysis of the distinction that Elizabeth Grosz (2005) makes between "egalitarian feminists" and "difference feminists" is helpful in understanding an important dilemma in dealing with and embracing embodied differences. Defending difference-effacing equality between the genders may come at the price of disabling political action but arguing FOR difference can also take its toll. The persistent and pernicious existence of archetypes and stereotypes negates alterity and plays into established narratives and political agendas that serve to disable the transformation of institutional practices, on micro, meso and macro-levels. In this volume, Painter's chapter challenges us to take the interaction between social constructions and embodied lived experiences seriously in rethinking leadership constructs such as 'vision'. She also insists on the balance between facticity and freedom, and gestures towards the transformative potential that lies in relational ties with others.

The persistent difficulties in escaping gender-stereotypes are by no means a new, which is why debates around feminism remain crucial to Corporate Social Responsibility (CSR) and Business Ethics (BE). Janet Borgerson's chapter helps us appreciate how feminist ethics has been consistently overlooked, misunderstood, and improperly applied within BE and CSR. Unlike many feminist thinkers including Held, Borgerson does not identify all feminist ethics with the ethics of care, which she and others argue may create a dualism in ethics in terms of masculine v. feminine and/or self v. other. Borgerson contends that these dualisms belie the ways in which the self develops only in context with and relation to others. By distinguishing feminist ethics from 'feminine' ethics, Borgerson (2007) reminds us that feminist ethics has preceded BE and CSR into crucial domains that these fields now seek to engage. Indeed, feminist ethics has developed theoretical and conceptual resources for mapping, investigating, and comprehending these complex, often undefined, realms and, moreover, greeting and communicating with the diverse human beings who make their lives there. Borgerson contends that the emphasis upon relationships, responsibility, and lived experience found in feminist ethics could contribute to the realm of business in ways that traditional moral theories may fail to accomplish.

Pullen and Vachhani explore this potential by discussing leadership as a practice based on relationality, intercorporeality and care. Its potential to transform organizational spaces is however curtailed by the continued predominance of binary thinking in our understanding of gender and leadership. Especially in leadership imaginaries, women are still cast as the inferior opposite of the ideal male archetype. Their analysis supports Painter's contention that construing femininity as 'difference-from' creates stereotypical straight-jackets, making an understanding of individuals' unique gendered existence and leadership capacities impossible, while also depicting the strength of women's leadership in very simplistic terms. The female archetype of the 'caring leader' is indeed a double-edged sword, which is helpful in appreciating and articulating alternatives to strong-man archetypes, but which if used in an essentialist way, ultimately fails to cut it in terms of dealing with difference in organizations and allowing all individuals to play to their strengths. The chapter offers a nuanced discussion in the case of Jacinda Ardern as someone who both conforms and fails to conform to feminine stereotypes, offering a glimpse of what radical alterity might look like in practice.

The importance of thinking outside of typical gender-binary cannot be emphasized enough if all individuals are to find their own unique form of leading in organizations. The chapter by Derry offers an historical analysis of intersectionality as a key concept in understanding practices of exclusion and discrimination and unpacks the implications this has for thinking about gender and leadership in organizations. We are challenged to confront the multiple blind spots that lie at the heart of our understanding of gender. Even those feminists committed to gender equality have to revise their earlier positions and acknowledge their own inability to understand the intersectional realities of discrimination that lead to systemic injustice across societal spaces. The chapter reveals the multiple ways in which hetero-normativity filters through various organizational practices, but especially how it manifests in our thinking about leadership. We have not even begun to consider what this means for LGBTQ+ individuals in organizational spaces, and how it makes truly inclusive leadership practices unlikely in most cases. Derry's account challenges all of us to understand the multiple ways in which inequalities disproportionately affect individuals whose identities lie at the complex intersections of gender, race, and class.

It is clear that true inclusivity has not been accomplished, sadly even within values-driven fields such as CSR and BE. Grosser, Moon, and Nelson have conducted an extensive study of BE and CSR literature since 1990 to see whether and how feminist perspectives are or are not integrated into those literatures. The study is thorough and reveals, in brief, that although feminist perspectives were not ignored, there was little in the way of integration of these theories into the mainstream of the BE and CSR literature. This is not an isolated problem. Examining literature from three areas of feminist work, scholarship in psychology, organizational theory and economics (including the literature in feminist economics) they discovered that feminist perspectives are almost never integrated into the mainstream of these literatures. While there were a few studies of gender differences, often they were only in regard to equal opportunity and drew mostly on empirical studies, rather than offering any normative analyses. There was very little notice of feminist relations and feminine equality. Almost all mentions of feminist theory dealt simplistically with the ethics of care, which, as Borgerson point out, is not inclusive all of feminist ethical theories. Alternately, there is little in the feminist literature about the three areas they examined: organizational theory, psychology or economics (and feminist economics), nor any consideration of possible conversations with the BE and CSR literatures. This neglect leaves a residual paternalistic masculinist perspective that ignores feminist perspectives of intersubjectivity, embodied responsiveness and relationality.

As we did in our first volume, we again place a focus on the various ways in which 'relationality' emerged as a salient concept in leadership theory (Uhl-Bien 2006; Uhl-Bien and Ospina 2012). 'Relational leadership' has emerged out of multiple streams of research, and has been described in different ways, drawing on different disciplines. The tendency towards celebrating the relational dynamics that are part of leading has since been described as 'collective leadership' (Ospina et al. 2020), as part of 'blended leadership' (Collinson and Collinson 2009), and the way in which it functions has allowed alternative ways of leading in different cultures to challenge Western, individualist conceptions of leadership. As explained earlier, relational leadersip also has clear links, especially in its early iterations, with complexity science. In Volume I, Uhl-Bien and her co-authors highlighted how relationality has come to function as a central concept within contemporary leadership discussions, and how it brings us further in challenging the masculine imaginaries that continue to dominate the leadership literature. In this volume, we again highlight the various dimensions of leadership that are constructed relationally, as Uhl-Bien' chapter on 'relational leadership theory' makes eminently clear. Leadership is understood as a social change process, rather than as the result of hierarchical, 'great man' behaviours. Leading, from this point of view, is about processes that engage multiple interrelated and networked stakeholders rather than individualistic behaviour. Uhl-Bien emphasizes the interplay between various leadership roles in ways that become inclusive of all genders, races and ethnicities.

It will be evident that the papers in this part of this second volume were not written with gender in mind, nor do they necessarily focus on women in leadership (apart from including some examples of women leaders or gender-based organizations). This is in some ways deliberate because of our commitment to steering clear of essentialism where possible. Arguing that relational leadership is exclusively displayed by women leaders, would not just be in tension with our own beliefs, but it would also be misguided and in many ways, simply false. 'Relational leadership' is practiced by people from all genders, and in some descriptions, goes beyond the individuals involved towards an understanding of relational processes. That said, the ways in which relational leadership theories have developed does offer rich perspectives on alternative ways of leading to those leadership styles idealized by 'great man' theories. This bodes well for the possibility of male, female and LGBTQ+ individuals to embrace their specific leadership style. It also allows us to think beyond the 'leaders' involved, towards practices of 'leading', in which many different individuals and groups can all find their unique voices.

The 'relational lens' is also of great value in studying leadership practices in different cultural contexts. Individualist and masculinist imaginaries often lead to blind spots in terms of how leadership functions in various cultures across the globe. Not surprisingly, research on matriarchal leaders and on communal leadership is vastly under-represented in leadership studies. Overall, cross-cultural perspectives on relational leading are few and far between. Though this volume does not claim to fill this gap, the paper by Pérezts, Russon and Painter describes the way in which relationality lies at the heart of the African notion of 'ubuntu', the belief that one is a human being in and through one's relationship with others. Though 'relationality' is a relatively recent development in Continental European philosophy, it has been central to African philosophies for a much longer time. The paper also illustrates how embracing relationality in a values-driven leadership programme in Africa allowed participants to find ways to act on their values even in the face of systemic pressures to do the opposite. The importance of relationality in ethics as such, is underscored by the insight that unethical leadership ultimately amounts to 'the failure to relate'.

Understanding unethical behaviour as relational failures means that we have to more systematically unpack some of the implications of gendered organizational interactions and functions. Paradoxically, continuing discrimination and inequality is equally present even in organizational initiatives aimed at redressing social and environmental harms and managing ethical risks, such as CSR, ethics management and diversity and inclusion projects. In understanding the various factors that undermine a meaningful integration of gender-related topics, and concern leadership practices in organizations, it is helpful to consider why powerful female voices never seem to penetrate corporate walls. Grosser's analysis of the ways in which women's NGOs have been excluded from multi-stakeholder CSR engagement practices in corporations, reveals multiple barriers with complex origins. In the first place, there seems to be a perception that the feminist agenda is basically antithetical to 'business'. Engaging with business organizations is therefore not a priority. Instead, feminists who are leaders of women NGOs focus their attention on furthering their agendas in the public domain through engagement with government agencies, lobbying public authorities or mobilizing other societal bodies. Another important dimension is resource constraints, both in terms of monetary and capacity-building support. The lack of transparency in terms of how corporations report on gender issues and deal with issues of diversity and inclusion is also mentioned, though it has to be said that more and more initiative has been taken in this regard over the past few years. More fundamental mind-shifts are however required. Grosser and her co-authors mention an example of a Swedish women's group who reframed CSR as 'Corporate Sexual Responsibility', signaling that strategically reframing and redefining of CSR to truly speak to women's issues, is urgently needed. They also calls for 'tempered radicals' to work with and within business organizations in furthering gender inclusivity. Only in this way will organizations be convinced to include marginalized voices who often fail to meet the 'legitimacy' criterion in terms of being selected as salient stakeholders to engage with.

We have also identified another problematic trend in how gender identity is dealt with in organizational discourses, i.e. the instrumental use of gender identities in the interest of a broad range of agendas. Female 'difference' seems to have been co-opted in neoliberal growth agendas and corporate profit-generation. In the leadership realm, diversity and inclusion agendas are often motivated by making 'the business case'. The belief that 'what cannot be measured cannot be managed' generates a preoccupation with generating data that oversimplifies and misrepresents the roles that various genders can play in leading organizations. Underscoring the relationality that pertains to leading as practiced by all genders, rather than just by women, may also help us avoid treating women as 'band-aids' by which to deal with the multiple socio-economic ills that follow in the wake of capitalist growth all over the world. Essentialist stereotypes often misrepresent or mischaracterize women, and in the process, the particular ways in which women live and work are glossed over or deliberately ignored. For instance, a specific understanding of female entrepreneurial skills and capacities for community service can alleviate poverty and generate sustainable livelihoods, but often such projects are implemented without much consideration for women's self-understanding or their own cultures and ways of being. In this respect, CSR is often a blunt instrument that though well-intentioned, that at best incorporates women in projects that they would not have chosen for themselves, and at worst, continues to subjugate them in and through projects that are supposed to empower them. As a result, both women and men are being robbed of their own unique ways of leading and are stunted in terms of the wide variety of contributions they could potentially make to organizational life. McCarthy's Foucaultian analysis reveals how CSR projects aimed at women's empowerment can be met with resistance by precisely those women they are designed to help. She unpacks the interactions between women's engagement in struggles for power and freedom as part of their ongoing process of self-making. In doing so, McCarthy reveals power is a relational force, and as such, key to the ways in which women organized and are organized. The chapter's critical discussion of the notion of empowerment reveals the reasons why it is often unsuccessful. The empowerment discourse is disproportionally focused on economic empowerment, to the exclusion of understanding the broader relational fabric that is key to establishing equality and inclusion. CSR projects directed at women are unfortunately often misconstrued in service of neoliberal agendas, depicting the individuals involved as atomized individuals participating in entrepreneurial activities, fundamentally misconstruing their identities. The women involved are often depicted as 'powerless', and their empowerment viewed as an once-off accomplishment. Instead, understanding power as relational force means that it is an ongoing socio-political process through which women (and men) continually shape their own identities through practices of resistance. This co-construction of identities involves a relational ethic of care, which serves to enable, or foreclose freedom.

Werhane concludes the volume with the more optimistic call to focus on the as yet untapped potential of systems perspectives in the analysis of diversity, gender and leadership. She argues that worn-out mindsets lie at the heart of the ongoing inequality, and that these can be addressed by three overlapping paradigm shifts. i.e. rethinking stakeholder theory, embracing systems thinking, and approaching leadership from a feminist perspective. Werhane goes further in spelling out how a systems approach enables leaders to be successful in complex global organizations, which are part of many complex adaptive systems in which we as individuals, managers and organizations exist and operate in today. As Werhane quotes, "A system is a complex of interacting components together with the networks of relationships among them that identify an entity and/or a set of processes" (Laszlo and Krippner 1998). In terms of its implications for organizing, "a truly systemic view of considers how a set of individuals, institutions and processes operates in a system involving a complex network of interrelationships, an array of individual and institutional actors with conflicting interests and goals, and a number of feedback loops" (Wolf 1999). These definitions lay the groundwork for thinking more inclusively and diversely as leaders in complex organizations, and systems thinking better equips organizations to improve practices of diversity and inclusion, and for leaders to better embed their agendas in global organizations.

In this volume, we have gathered together a collection of papers that introduce new mindsets on leadership, gender and organization. In the interconnected world in which we live, fresh thinking is essential in order to engage in the present volatile global political economies. In contrast to a classical economic concept of the autonomous independent self, we have been introduced to the notion of the relational self, a self constructed by, and interdependent upon others. Additionally, as we learned from the global Covid pandemic and global environmental change, we live in an interconnected planet where there is no place to escape from others, from other cultures and from the ecology of the earth. Because of these inexorable social interconnections, we can no longer degrade differences of race, gender, ethnicity, culture, income differentials, or context. We are all equally part of this global interconnected system, and to ignore or denigrate any individual religion, culture, or society would be to our peril. These three notions: the relational self, a systemic view of global interconnections, and the resulting demand for inclusion, invite new ideas to reconceive leadership as inclusive, contextual and relational.

We hope these papers, or at least some of them, will engage the reader and challenge each of us to refresh and revise prevailing parochial mindsets in order to think broadly about these pressing issues and engage in the cultural, organizational, and global changes necessary to survive and exist comfortably in the twenty-first century. Adopting a relational approach entails changing and broadening one's ingrained mental models to grasp the complexity of the overlapping global environments, and embracing the multiplicity that characterize individual lives. Without this more relational mindset, leading will fail, and more importantly, so will ethical organizing.

References

Binns, J. 2008. The ethics of relational leading: Gender matters. *Gender, Work & Organization,* 15(6): 600–620. doi:https://doi.org/10.1111/j.1468-0432.2008.00418.x

Byrne, J., M. Radu-Lefebvre, S Fattoum, & L. Balachandra. 2019. Gender Gymnastics in CEO succession: Masculinities, Femininities and Legitimacy. *Organization Studies* doi:https://doi.org/10.1177/0170840619879184

Borgerson, J. 2007. On the Harmony of Feminist Ethics and Business Ethics. *Business and Society Review* 112: 477–509.

Calabretta, G., G. Gemser & N. M. Wijnberg. 2017. The interplay between intuition and rationality in strategic decision making: A paradox perspective. *Organization Studies* 38 (3–4): 365–401. doi:https://doi.org/10.1177/0170840616655483

Catalyst, 2021. catalyst.org/research/women-in-management/

Collinson D. & M. Collinson. 2009. Blended Leadership: Employee Perspectives on Effective Leadership in the UK Further Education Sector. *Leadership* 5: 365–380

Cooper R. 2005. Peripheral Vision: Relationality. *Organization Studies* 26: 1689–1710

Ciulla, J. B., D. Knights, C. Mabey, & L. Tomkins. 2018. Guest editors' introduction: Philosophical contributions to leadership ethics. *Business Ethics Quarterly* 28(1): 1–14.

Cunliffe, A & M. Eriksen. 2011. Relational Leadership. *Human Relations* 64: 1425–1449.

Dennissen, M., Y. Benchop, and M. van den Brink. 2010. Rethinking Diversity Management: An Intersectional Analysis of Diversity Networks. *Organizational Studies* 41: 219–40.

Eagly, A. H., & M. E. Heilman. 2016. Gender and leadership: Introduction to the special issue [Editorial]. *The Leadership Quarterly* 27(3): 349–353.

Fotaki, M. and A. Pullen. 2019. *Diversity, Affect and Embodiment in Organizing*. Palgrave

Geletkanycz, M. A. 2020. Social movement spillover: Barriers to board gender diversity posed by contemporary governance reform. *The Leadership Quarterly 31*(6): 101438. doi:https://doi.org/10.1016/j.leaqua.2020.101438

Grosz, E. 2005. *Time Travels: Feminism, Nature, Power*, Duke University Press.

Held, V. 1990. "Feminist Transformations of Moral Theory." *Philosophy and Phenomenological Research. I, supplement*: 321–44.

Held V. 2006. *The Ethics of Care: Personal, Political, and Global*. Oxford University Press: New York

Knights, D. & A. Pullen. 2019. Masculinity: A contested terrain? *Gender, Work & Organization* 26(10), 1367–1375. doi:https://doi.org/10.1111/gwao.12418

Laszlo A. and S Krippner. 1998. Systems Theories: Their Origins, Foundations and Development. In: *Systems Theories and a Priori Aspects of Perception*, ed. J. Scott, 47–74. Amsterdam: Elsevier.

Liu, H. 2019. Just the servant: An intersectional critique of servant leadership. *Journal of Business Ethics* 156(4): 1099–1112. doi:https://doi.org/10.1007/s10551-017-3633-0

Nash, M. & R. Moore. 2019. 'I was completely oblivious to gender': An exploration of how women in STEMM navigate leadership in a neoliberal, post-feminist context. *Journal of Gender Studies* 28(4): 449–461. doi:https://doi.org/10.1080/09589236.2018.1504758

Ospina, S. and E. Foldy. 2020. Building bridges from the margins: The work of leadership in social change organizations. *Leadership Quarterly* 21: 292–307.

Ospina S.M., E.G. Foldy, G.T. Fairhurst, B. Jackson. 2020. Collective dimensions of leadership: Connecting theory and method. *Human Relations* 73(4): 441–463

Painter-Morland, M. J. 2011. Gender, leadership and organization. In: *Values and Ethics for the 21st Century*, ed. John R. Boatright, Joseph Carens, Thomas Clarke et al., 525–559. Madrid: BBVA.

Painter-Morland, M. J. and G. Deslandes. 2015. Rethinking authenticity and accountability - Facing up to the conflicting expectations of media leaders. *Leadership* Online first: DOI: https://doi.org/10.1177/1742715015578307

Painter-Morland, M.J. and G. Deslandes. 2017. Reconceptualizing CSR in the media industry as relational accountability. *Journal of Business Ethics* DOI https://doi.org/10.1007/s10551-016-3083-0

Pearson, R. 2007. Beyond women workers: Gendering CSR. *Third World Quarterly* 28(4): 731–749.

Phillips, M., & A. Willatt. 2020. Embodiment, care and practice in a community kitchen. *Gender, Work & Organization* 27(2): 198–217. doi:https://doi.org/10.1111/gwao.12419

Phipps, S. T. A. & L. C. Prieto. 2020. Leaning in: A historical perspective on influencing Women's leadership. *Journal of Business Ethics*. doi:https://doi.org/10.1007/s10551-020-04566-6

Seierstad, C., G. Warner-Søderholm, M. Torchia & M. Huse. 2017. Increasing the number of women on boards: The role of actors and processes. *Journal of Business Ethics* 141(2): 289–315. doi:https://doi.org/10.1007/s10551-015-2715-0

Smith, W. K., M. Erez, S. Jarvenpaa, M.W. Lewis & P. Tracey. 2017. Adding complexity to theories of paradox, tensions, and dualities of innovation and change: Introduction to organization studies special issue on paradox, tensions, and dualities of innovation and change. *Organization Studies* 38(3–4): 303–317. doi:https://doi.org/10.1177/0170840617693560

Spence, L. 2016. The Obfuscation of Gender and Feminism in CSR Research and the Academic Community, In *Gender Equality and Responsible Business: Expanding CSR* Horizons, 16–46. Ed. Grosser K., L.McCarthy, and M. Kilgor. Sheffield UK: Greenleaf Press.

Uhl-Bien, M. 2006. Relational leadership theory: Exploring the social processes of leadership and organizing. *The Leadership Quarterly* 17: 654–676.

Uhl-Bien, M., R. Marion & B. McKelvey. 2007. Complexity Leadership Theory: Shifting leadership from the industrial age to the knowledge era. *The Leadership Quarterly* 18: 298–318.

Uhl-Bien, M. & M. Arena. 2018. Leadership for organizational adaptability: A theoretical synthesis and integrative framework. *The Leadership Quarterly* 29(1): 89–104.

Uhl-Bien, M. & S.M. Ospina (Eds) 2012. *Advancing Relational Leadership Research. A Dialogue Among Perspectives*. Charlotte, NC: Information Age Publishing.

Wolf, S. 1999. Toward a Systemic Theory of Informed Consent in Managed Care. *Houston Law Review* 35: 1631–1681

Wang, J. C., L. Markóczy, S. L Sun & M. W. Peng. 2019. She'-E-O compensation gap: A role congruity view. *Journal of Business Ethics* 159(3): 745–760. doi:https://doi.org/10.1007/s10551-018-3807-4

Mollie Painter currently heads up the Responsible and Sustainable Business Lab (RSB Lab), a Research Centre within Nottingham Business School, Nottingham Trent University, UK and is an Extraordinary Professor at the Gordon Institute of Business Science, University of Pretoria. Her research is focused on business ethics, CSR, sustainability and responsible leadership. She has held academic positions in South Africa, the USA, the UK, and Slovenia. She also serves as co-Editor-in-Chief of *Business Ethics Quarterly*. Between 2015 and 2020, she held the Coca-Cola Chair of Sustainability at IEDC-Bled in Slovenia.

Patricia H. Werhane, Professor Emerita, was formerly Ruffin Professor of Business Ethics at Darden School of Business, University of Virginia and later the Wicklander Chair in Business Ethics at DePaul University. Currently, a Fellow at the Center for Professional Responsibility at the Gies College of Business at the University of Illinois, she is the author or editor of over 30 books and over 100 articles, most prominently in business ethics. She was the founding editor of *Business Ethics Quarterly* and is the Executive Producer of a video series on founding thinkers in business ethics and corporate responsibility.

Living Gendered Identities: Beyond Essentialism and Constructivism Towards Embodied Relationality

Mollie Painter

Abstract In this chapter, the embodied and institutionalized roots of gender discrimination in the workplace are explored. The chapter draws on a variety of feminist perspectives to discuss the implications that various approaches to gender differences have for thinking about leadership in organizational contexts. It comes to the conclusion that combining insight into the embodied practices of the lived body with an understanding of gender as a socially-constructed notion may yield the best possible model for thinking about gender within institutions. The chapter ends with an analysis of the systemic leadership approach, which may provide a productive space for conceptualizing a more gender-sensitive understanding of a variety of leadership styles and practices. It also argues for a broader understanding of certain leadership characteristics, such as vision.

Keywords Embodiment · Social construction · Essentialism · Systemic leadership

Introduction

In this chapter, the topic of gender discrimination within the realm of organizational leadership is approached in a very specific way. We will not be exploring the various normative frameworks that could support equality in the workplace, such as appeals to basic human rights, social contracts, deontological duties or utilitarian concerns. Instead, we will seek to understand the tacit gender prejudices inherent in organizational practices and the embodied effects of such prejudices for the individuals involved. We will find that despite an overt acknowledgement of equal rights and opportunities, many women and men still experience very real barriers in terms of

M. Painter (✉)
Responsible and Sustainable Business Lab (RSB Lab), Nottingham Business School,
Nottingham Trent University, Nottingham, UK

Gordon Institute of Business Science, University of Pretoria, Pretoria, South Africa
e-mail: mollie.painter@ntu.ac.uk

M. Painter, P. H. Werhane (eds.), *Leadership, Gender, and Organization*, Issues
in Business Ethics 63, https://doi.org/10.1007/978-3-031-24445-2_2

their access to leadership opportunities. In many cases, the so-called "glass ceiling" or as the metaphor has been recast, the "leaking pipe-line" (PricewaterhouseCoopers 2007), cannot be explained by the existence of discriminatory policies. Instead, we will investigate the subtle gendered prejudices and expectations about how women and men lead that lie at the heart of the challenges many individuals face in finding their leadership role in organizations.

We will see that these tacit prejudices and expectations are institutionalized in everyday practices and eventually shape individuals' embodied existence within organizations. This may cause some women, and some men who fail to conform to gender stereotypes, to feel the urge to leave the organization, refuse leadership positions, or take them on with great discomfort and difficulty. In this chapter, the implications that the interplay between gender and organizational practices has for leadership are unpacked, and alternative leadership models and gender inclusive strategies of resistance and change are explored.

Approaches to Sexual Difference and Its Implications for Leadership Theory

Within the feminist literature, there have been a number of approaches to understanding the differences between men and women and addressing matters of equality and opportunity. In this section, we try to draw out the implications that each of these approaches could have for leadership theory. It will become clear that our beliefs about the origins and manifestation of sexual differences has implications for our thinking about the leadership role(s) women and men can play in organizations.

For instance, Elizabeth Grosz (2005: 6) distinguishes between "egalitarian feminists" and "difference feminists." Egalitarian feminists were concerned with exposing the injustices of patriarchal societies, and fighting for equal rights and opportunities for men and women. They exposed the way in which sexist prejudices institutionalized inequality, and perpetuated the marginalization of women in society. They claimed equal opportunities for women by arguing that men and women were the bearers of equal human rights and dignity. The gains that these early feminists have made are evident in the fact that at least on paper, most organizations claim to uphold equality in the workplace and have institutionalized non-discrimination policies on the basis of sex, race, or sexual preference. However, the acknowledgment of equality on the basis of abstract principles of human dignity and respect did not come without a price. In the first place, it made it possible for organizations to overtly claim principled acquiescence with the idea of human rights, dignity and equality, while tacitly perpetuating some of their established practices and prejudices institutionally. Secondly, the fact that the discourse is centred on "equality" made it difficult for women to lobby around issues specific to women in the workplace, out of fear that this might undermine the argument that they are essentially "the same" as men. This approach therefore cannot account for women's unique contributions to their organizations and society in general. Furthermore, the importance of the very real fight against oppression cannot be recognized or acknowledged from this perspective (Ely and Padavic 2007: 1126).

In the leadership realm, the "equality" discourse often confronted women with the challenge to "do as men have always done," or better. As such, they had to adopt leadership practices that existed within the patriarchal organizations in which they found themselves. In the process these female pioneers often unwittingly perpetuated predominantly "male" leadership stereotypes. While these equality-feminists succeeded in making the argument for equal rights and opportunities, their efforts did not allow women to develop their individual leadership styles, nor did they challenge existing stereotypes about leadership.

An alternative approach to feminism is to insist on respect for the differences between men and women, and an appreciation of the unique role that women could play in the workplace. Feminists who have adopted this approach include important figures like Carol Gilligan, Nancy Hartsock and Nancy Chodorow. These women emphasized the social and psychological specificities of the feminine gender identity as well as the way it shapes individuals' perspective on their role in society. They argue that women have their own unique "voice" or perspective that should be included within societal discourses. From the perspective of these "feminists of difference," it was possible to argue that the unique capacities, traits and predispositions of women were "functional" in terms of supplementing gaps that were typically present within the existing leadership corps (Ely and Padavic 2007: 1125).

The problem with this approach is that it tends to set up essentialist dichotomies between men and women. For instance, it contends that women are more caring, more communicative, and more cooperative than men. Surveys, like that used by the International Women's Forum in 1984, tended to solidify existing gender biases in their categorization of traits that respondents identified within themselves. In these surveys, female traits included being excitable, gentle, emotional, submissive, sentimental, understanding, compassionate, sensitive and dependent. Male traits included being dominant, aggressive, tough, assertive, autocratic, analytical, competitive and independent. Being adaptive, tactful, sincere, conscientious, reliable, predictable, systematic and efficient were considered gender-neutral traits (Rosener 2011: 29).

An unfortunate consequence of this essentialist approach is that women are always associated with the inferior characteristic of the binary opposition: women are emotional, not rational, women are impulsive, not goal-directed, etc. Empirical studies suggest that most respondents regard the various stereotypical male leadership traits as typical of the behavior of a "good manager" (Gmür 2006: 116). Out of the number of ideal managerial traits only two "feminine" traits are considered desirable for managers, i.e. being "adept at dealing with people" and "cooperative."

All the other ideal traits, like being analytical, competent, confident, convincing, decisive, efficient, fore-sighted, independent etc. are associated with the male stereotype. We will attend to these gendered stereotypes in more detail in section three.

Unfortunately these prejudices have been uncritically absorbed into some business ethics discourses. This has led to the claim that feminist ethics essentially pursues "care ethics." Borgerson (2007: 485) has commented on the problematic conflation between feminist ethics and care ethics within the business ethics literature. She (2007: 488) points out that business ethics textbooks like that of Crane and Matten (Oxford University Press, 2004), describe "care ethics" as a feminine approach that solves ethical problems through "intuition" and "personal subjective assessment." Though Borgerson does not deny that certain articulations of care ethics display feminist concerns, she argues that the association of care ethics with feminism tends to essentialize the gendered experience. Because of this, a proper understanding of the causes of gender prejudices and marginalizing practices is never developed. She also points out that there are other "caring" ethical approaches, which are not at all feminist in orientation, such as that of Emmanuel Levinas and other philosophers working on what can be described as an "ethics of proximity."

It is clear that both egalitarian feminism and difference feminism fail to address the origins of the stereotypes that exist about men and women. An important question that animated feminist discourses is whether the differences between men and women were the result of nature or nurture, or both. In other words, are men and women determined by their biology or are they shaped by their personal circumstances and their cultural and social milieu? In order to address these issues, many feminists invested considerable energy into making the case for a distinction between sex and gender. While sex refers to those aspects of physiology and anatomy that are biologically determined, gender is not. "Gender" is the result of early childhood experiences, societal dynamics, power interests, organizational politics and the social constructions that are inevitably part of all these spheres of life (Ridgeway and Cornell cited in Ely and Padavic 2007: 1128). The same goes for the distinction between female and feminine. The fact that many individuals are born "female" does not necessarily mean that they will necessarily conform to stereotypically feminine ways of being and operating in the world. The powerful implications of this distinction lie in the fact that though we may all be born with specific biological sexual characteristics, much can be changed in the way our gender predispositions develop as we grow older and function within society.

Social Constructions and "the Lived Body"

Helpful as the distinction between sex and gender, female and feminine may be, acknowledging "gender" as a social construction may not take us far enough. In fact, the distinction between sex and gender may rely on an uncritical acceptance of the dichotomy between nature and culture, which posits the body as a fixed entity. As a result, we may underestimate how institutional practices of socializing and enculturation, i.e. everyday habits, impact on our bodies and our physical experience of our world.

The limits of viewing gender primarily as a social construction lie in its incapacity to acknowledge the material reality of being a woman or a man in an organizational context. Here, the work of feminists such as Judith Butler, Iris Marion Young and Elizabeth Grosz becomes invaluable. They help us understand that though we might readily agree that gender is a social construction solidified through discourses and practices, we should not underestimate the fact that these discourses and practices have very real effects on the body. In *Gender Trouble*, Judith Butler (1990) has convincingly argued that gender is a social performance, and that the sexed body is derived from such social performativity. Gender is therefore not a mere linguistic term that denotes social and cultural perceptions; instead, it is enacted within real-life practices, and as such, physical changes and adjustments in bodily comportment occur incrementally over time.

In her seminal essay "Throwing like a girl," Iris Young (2005) argues convincingly that the way in which women use their bodies, or develop their physical motor skills, has everything to do with how they are physically oriented in the world from a very early age. Girls are often told that they are fragile, may get hurt more easily than boys, that they must seek help when facing physical challenges, or avoid it altogether. As such, they experience the world as a more threatening place, leading to a distinct type of bodily comportment, like keeping their legs close together when sitting or walking, crossing their arms protectively across their breasts, or carrying objects close to their bodies. They also develop patterns of cooperation rather than competition. These practices are not merely social in nature, they lead to real changes in women's bodies and ways of being in the world.

This however need not lead to deterministic or essentialist conclusions about men and women. Young (2005) argues that we have to understand the interplay between facticity and freedom. Facticity refers to those biological traits and predispositions that we are born with and which develop as part of our physical existence over time, whereas freedom involves the projects that we select to pursue throughout our lives. Both are involved in our embodied experience and actions in the world. Young (2004) employs Toril Moi's alternative to the construct of gender: the so-called "lived body." She defines it as: "a unified idea of a physical body acting and experiencing in a specific socio-cultural context; it is the body-in-situation." Moi disputes the clear distinction between nature and culture by arguing that the lived body is always encultured. According to Young each individual has the ontological freedom to respond to her facticity, to construct and express herself through her projects. Through her accomplishments, it becomes possible to transform her surroundings and relationships, often in cooperation with others. However, the unfortunate reality is that many individuals experience situations in which their surroundings make them feel distinctly uncomfortable.

The construct of the "lived body" allows us to make very distinct gains: it undermines the nature versus culture dichotomy and also takes us beyond essentialist gender binaries by creating spaces for ontological freedom that could function in our design of our life project(s). However, Young argues that this does not mean that we should give up the concept of gender, since it plays an important part in social structures and their implications for creating or curtailing people's freedoms to pursue their life projects. "Gender" is a conceptual tool that allows us to describe and diagnose the way in which the differences between men and women, and their relationships with one another, are institutionalized. As such, it also creates the conceptual space from within which these stereotypes can be challenged.

The value of combining the construct of the lived body with the concept of gender is that it allows us to pose a series of questions on various levels. On the one hand, gender constructs help us unpack the assumptions that underpin certain leadership expectations that exist in organizations, as well as the prejudices to which they give rise. What we may discover is that a series of binaries are mapped onto male and female bodies in a way that makes it very difficult for individuals to develop patterns that fall outside the stereotypical gender moulds. However, without the category of gender, it becomes next to impossible to diagnose the problem and describe it in any meaningful way. One has to refer to the gendered male/female stereotypes to describe their operation in practice.

Such descriptions allow resistance to emerge. We may therefore do well to explore the way in which male and female characteristics play out within their institutional leadership roles, in order to explore the assumptions and prejudices that support it. This may allow us to explore different models and practices by which to incrementally modify the lived experience of both men and women.

"Gender" is a conceptual tool that allows us to describe and diagnose the way in which the differences between men and women, and their relationships with one another, are institutionalized.

Gender Constructs in Organizational Leadership and Implications for the Lived Body

One of the central assumptions that have become institutionalized within many organizational practices is the notion that women are society's care-takers. This care-taking takes place primarily as unpaid labour within the private sphere (Young 2005). In the workplace this manifests in the designation of any kind of job that requires care of individuals' bodily, emotional or domestic needs as "female jobs," with a concomitant expectation of it being compensated at a lower level. Since there is general acceptance that leadership positions within organizations typically go beyond care-taking towards roles that require strong direction, control and agency, women may often be excluded from consideration for such opportunities.

It comes as no surprise that gendered modes of leadership are described as either "agentic" or "communal" (Eagly and Carli 2007: 68). Women's concern for treating others compassionately is thought to display a communal orientation, whereas men's agentic orientation makes them more capable of assertion and control. When women display the traits of the communal orientation, such as being affectionate, helpful, friendly, kind, and sympathetic, as well as interpersonally sensitive, gentle, and soft-spoken, they are seen as not agentic enough and hence not capable of leadership. But when they display the agentic behaviours, i.e. aggressive, ambitious, dominant, self-confident, and forceful, as well as self-reliant and individualistic, they are seen as not communal enough, and they tend to be accused of inauthenticity.

In terms of leadership research, a gendered binary also seems to be operative in the distinction between an "entity" approach that offers a "realist" perspective on leadership, and a more "relational" approach that offers a "constructivist" perspective. Uhl-Bien (2011) associates the realism/entity approach as more masculine in orientation and the constructionist/relational approach as more feminine. The "realist" approach focuses on individuals and their views regarding participation in interpersonal relationships. By contrast, the relational perspective is primarily concerned with being-in-relation and moving away from hierarchical control (Uhl-Bien 2011: 67).

A further gendered dichotomy in the leadership realm is that between so-called "transactional" and "transformational" leadership styles. Men's leadership styles are regularly described as transactional, whereas women leaders are often seen as more transformational in orientation. Transformational leadership is described as a relationship of mutual stimulation between leaders and followers, which converts followers into leaders and also has the capacity to make leaders moral agents (Werhane 2011: 44). It has been argued that women's capacity to inspire and motivate staff is a result of their enhanced interpersonal skills. Further characteristics that supposedly make women better transformational leaders than men include their willingness to share power and information, their tendency to encourage participation and inclusion, their propensity to instill a sense of self-worth in others and their ability to get employees energized and excited about their work (Psychogios 2007: 174). Rosener (2011: 28) reports that women are more likely to use power that is based on charisma, work record and contacts than power based on organizational position and the ability to reward and punish others. Women successfully employ interactive leadership strategies, which entail encouraging participation, sharing power and information, and enhancing the self-worth of others (Rosener 2011: 21–24). Unfortunately, the fact that women are considered to be more natural transformational leaders does not always serve them well in organizations. Reuvers et al. (2008) has found that if men display the traits of transformative leadership, it has a far greater effect on innovation than if women display these same traits. Psychogios (2007) comes to the even more disconcerting conclusion that "feminized management" tends to aggravate the exploitation of female labour instead of creating new management opportunities for women. His research shows that if occupations are "feminized" there is a corresponding decline in salaries and wages.

According to Rosener (2011) transformational leadership cannot be exclusively associated with women: some women succeed by adhering to the traditional male model, whilst some men adopt a transformational leadership style. Both men and women describe themselves as having a mix of "female," "male" and "gender neutral" traits (Rosener 2011: 28). However, this does not mean that many women do not identify with gender stereotypes and employ them in their self-descriptions. For instance, further support for associating specific leadership characteristics with the feminine can be found in Nicola Pless's (2006: 248) account of the self-description of Anita Roddick, founder and former CEO of the Body Shop. Roddick personally claimed that: "I run my company according to feminine principles … principles of caring, making intuitive decisions, not getting hung up on hierarchy…".

Unfortunately, many prejudices are perpetuated in and through these gender stereotypes, with real effects on men and women in the workplace. In a recent *Harvard Business Review* article, Hermina Ibarra and Otilia Obodaru (2009), discuss the research finding that women lack "vision." They explore the puzzling fact that studies have shown that women out-perform men on all the leadership attributes considered important by respondents, except when it comes to envisioning. In the INSEAD study on which Ibarra and Obodaru (2009) reported, vision was defined as the skill to recognize new opportunities within the environment and to determine a strategic direction for the organization. In terms of leadership practice it seems as if the intuitive reading of opportunities within the environment becomes less important than the second aspect of the definition, i.e. determining a strategic direction. Ibarra and Obodaru (2009: 67–68) attribute the perception that women are weaker at "envisioning" than men to the fact that women may think differently about "vision." Female executives insist that for them, strategy emerges in and through a commitment to detail and a very hands-on approach to the implementation of action plans. They are less prone to the formulation of lofty ideals and "big ideas," or experiments with "big, hairy audacious goals," as Collins and Porras (2002) refer to it. This may be explained by the fact that many women have a fear of over-promising and under-delivering, whereas men tend not to have the same reservations. Again, girls' early experience of the world as a more threatening place may go some way towards explaining this difference in thinking about what "vision" means. What emerges clearly from this analysis, is an awareness of the tacit gendered assumptions about "vision." In practice, these tacit assumptions may have a very negative impact on how women are perceived as leaders. Holt et al. (2009) explain that the capacity to articulate a clear vision for the organization is strongly associated with the credibility of a leader. If women are not perceived as "visionary" leaders, they may not be perceived as credible either.

Gendered assumptions are also evident in the way people talk about what they expect from their leaders and from themselves as leaders. In a study conducted by Metcalfe and Linstead (2003: 110) the researchers found that the leadership style of one of their female subjects was described by her colleagues and staff as "masculine" and "authoritarian." Not surprising, they argue, if one considers the remnants of the masculinist discourse in words like "man-ager." In her description of herself, Nia displays contradictory views on the role that femininity plays in leadership, which serves to downplay the importance of her feminine traits. Instead, she re-inscribes masculine leadership models in the way she talks about her successes and difficulties. This case demonstrates how difficult it is to develop an alternative discourse on leadership. It also suggests that, in-and-of-itself, a linguistic analysis of this problem is unlikely to precipitate the desired change. More thought needs to be given to how the embodied reality of men and women and their ability to resist the gendered stereotyping of leadership are circumscribed and curtailed by these discourses.

According to Ely and Padavic (2007: 1129) masculinity and femininity are embodied realities as well as belief systems. It is evident in the muscle tensions and body postures that men and women display, and as such, contribute to a further solidification of gender stereotypes. For instance, "style constraints," pertaining to their way of speaking, gestures and appearance, is a reality that many female executives have to deal with (Eagly and Carli 2007: 64). These constraints impact on the way women can communicate and conduct themselves within everyday business interactions. Women often feel that their less assertive speaking style or hand-gestures may be deemed inappropriate. Disconcertingly, 34% of African American women feel that their physical appearance is more crucial in attaining career success than their actual abilities (Hewlett et al. 2005).

It is also interesting to analyze the way in which people's clothing and accessories both express and re-inscribe their own personal reading of the power dynamics and expectations within an institution. Women leaders tend to wear corporate suits to suggest formality and control—traits that are often associated with the stereotypical male leader. Wearing high heels and walking with a certain confident stride suggests the power and competence that are assumed to be the ideal characteristics of leaders. In men, suits and ties are carefully chosen to tap into specific states of mind, based on the theory that certain colours signify confidence and calm composure. In her essay, "Women recovering our clothes," Young (2005) discusses the split image that results from women seeing themselves, while at the same time being aware of others looking at them. This split image often gives rise to a complex self- conception involving several different images—not all of them always of a woman's own making. For instance, a woman might imagine that she is seen in a particular way when wearing certain clothes, which may or may not be how she imagines herself to be. Clothing and accessories become various kinds of prostheses that allow us to fashion ourselves to the dominant aesthetic as we experience it. In effect we extend and amend our embodiment in response to tacit messages about what is considered "appropriate" within organizational contexts. The question is who and what informs this dominant aesthetic, and what are the ethical implications of this fashioning? Some feminists resist the objectifying and fetishizing implications of women living "in the male gaze." However, in the leadership realm, this could have further discriminating effects. Could women's mirroring of male attire in the workplace be a tacit acceptance of the fact that men are more desirable leaders than women, that they are more powerful, more in control, more reliable? If so, everyday dress-code could contain the clues as to why gender prejudices persist in the workplace.

But how is it possible to resist conforming to the tacit expectations we experience in the workplace and to eventually change the stylized practices that perpetuate prejudices? In the next section, we explore alternative leadership models and seek to reconceptualize certain important gendered notions within the leadership realm.

Potential Sites and Visions of Change

In this section, we will investigate whether it is possible to transform leadership theory and practice through an engagement with the many different ways in which both men and women approach their leadership roles in organizations. What seems to be required is leadership models that allow individuals to lead in their own unique ways, instead of conforming to some pre-conceived gender expectations. We will therefore explore theoretical models that may create a framework for understanding and adopting uniquely individual leadership styles. In the process, we hope to recast important leadership notions, such as "authenticity" and "vision," in more gender-inclusive terms.

Systemic Leadership

In the first volume of *Leadership, Gender, and Organizations* (Werhane and Painter-Morland 2011), a number of scholars related recent developments in relational leadership or complexity leadership to the way women lead in organizations. One of the interesting points made by these scholars is that even though complexity leadership seems to describe leadership styles that are associated with the socially constructed "feminine" style of leadership, it is a model that suits many men's leadership preferences as well.

From the perspective of systemic leadership, leadership is not necessarily restricted to individuals appointed to positions of authority. In this respect, it represents a significant departure from so-called "great man theories" about leadership, with their implicit sexist assumptions. Systemic leadership is informed and supported by a variety of discourses—from Peter Senge's work on organizational learning and change to Karl Weick's sense-making theories. The basic contention is that an organization cannot properly learn, change or create meaning without the sharing of information and cooperative agreements. Senge and Kaufer (2000) speak about "communities of leaders," while others make reference to "distributed leadership" (Friedman 2004), or relational leadership (Maak and Pless 2006).

An influential definition of systemic leadership is provided by Collier and Esteban (2000: 208) who describe leadership as "the systemic capability, distributed and nurtured throughout the organization, of finding organizational direction and generating renewal by harnessing creativity and innovation." Understanding leadership as an emergent, interactive and dynamic property allows one to distribute leadership responsibilities and privileges throughout an organization's workforce (Edgeman and Scherer 1999). Systemic leadership involves a number of different leadership dynamics. Uhl-Bien, Marion and McKelvey (2007: 311) describe these as "administrative," "adaptive" and "enabling" leadership. Administrative leaders play the more formal leadership roles of planning and coordinating organizational activities. It is important to note that though systemic leadership functions are understood in more distributed terms, this does not necessarily mean that formal leadership positions and hierarchies become redundant or have to be abolished. In fact, it is very important that gender-sensitivity is encouraged in and through key managerial tasks, such as setting performance targets, conducting performance reviews, and performing mentoring activities. As such, it is important that those appointed to formal leadership positions are gender- sensitive and play an active role in thinking through the gender implications of their everyday business decisions. Guaranteeing flexible work schedules and childcare facilities for both working mothers and fathers can go a long way towards distributing the childcare responsibilities more equitably. Setting realistic performance targets for the promotion and retention of female leaders, committing to a certain number of female candidates for each leadership vacancy, considering the composition of selection teams and communicating leadership opportunities more transparently have all been mentioned as ways in which management buy-in and commitment to women's leadership can be communicated (PricewaterhouseCoopers 2007). Mentoring has also been identified as an extremely important factor in the success of women leaders, and both male and female executives must commit to providing it (PricewaterhouseCoopers 2007).

Important as the role of administrative leaders may be, real change in practices and belief systems requires the acknowledgement and nurturing of other leadership roles. So-called "adaptive" leadership functions as a "collaborative change movement" that allows adaptive outcomes to emerge in a nonlinear fashion as a result of the dynamic interactions of interdependent agents. The direction and priorities that guide an organization's activities therefore develop inadvertently as an unforeseen and unforeseeable consequence of the daily interactions between many different members of the organization instead of emanating from those at the top of the managerial hierarchy. This approach allows any member of an organization to take initiative and responsibility (i.e. assume a leading role) when and where the situation calls for it. It allows individuals to harness their personal strengths to lead in their own, unique ways.

Adaptive leadership does not mimic stereotypical leadership behaviours, but instead requires a unique response tailored to a specific situation and set of relationships. In this respect it allows women leaders more scope to develop their style of leadership. The challenge however lies in acknowledging this kind of leadership, and not exploiting adaptive leaders by appropriating the positive results of their efforts without any recognition or compensations. Unfortunately, this is what often happens to female leaders who fulfil leadership tasks spontaneously without demanding recognition.

The third leadership role that Uhl-Bien et al. (2007) refer to is that of "enabling" leadership, which provides the catalyst to facilitate the emergence of adaptive leadership within organizations. It often involves a complex interplay between administrative and adaptive leadership. Enabling leadership often does require some authority, but also entails an active involvement in the boundary situations that organizational members confront. Enabling leaders must be capable of engaging in cooperative strategies, fostering interaction, supporting and enhancing interdependency and stimulating the adaptive tension that allows for the emergence of new patterns. For instance, Vivienne Cox, the CEO of BP Alternative energies, described herself as a "catalyst," who does not drive change, but allows it to emerge.

Uhl Bien et al. (2007) make it clear that all three leadership roles necessarily coexist within organizations. The question that remains however is how adaptive and enabling leadership can be acknowledged, recognized and remunerated within organizations. Unfortunately, it could easily become the "unpaid labor" that women and men with alternative leadership styles perform without formal recognition. As such, it could inadvertently lead to the exploitation of these individuals in the workplace. Nevertheless, the systemic leadership model is important because it challenges us to rethink certain leadership stereotypes that are often uncritically perpetuated within organizations.

Rethinking Authenticity

"Authenticity" is often associated with the consistent way in which an individual acts in accordance with his or her personal traits and beliefs. In practice however, this can amount to a kind of inflexibility that renders the individual incapable of adapting to different or dynamic situations and relationships. From the perspective of systemic leadership, another understanding is required, namely that leadership roles, and hence leadership responses, are fluid. This idea is well represented in contemporary leadership literature. Porras et al. (2007: 198), for instance, explain that the best leaders realize that their role might change over time: an individual who works under your direction and supervision today might become the person to whom you report on another day. In time the same person could even become a customer or a vendor. It is important to maintain the relationship in a kind of "virtual team" even as roles change. This does not amount to "inauthenticity," but instead requires authentic relational responsiveness. In other words, to be "authentic," an individual has to respond appropriately to the situation as it *really* is at any given point of time. It also involves an acknowledgement that *reality*—both in terms of the relational dynamics between people in an organizational context and in any business environment in general—is not static, but always complex and dynamic.

Many women are accused of being "inauthentic" when they mimic a stereotypical male leadership style, or at least try and conform to tacit expectations about the way in which leaders ought to talk, walk and make decisions. The problem often is that women are damned if they do, and damned if they don't. If they conform to the male leadership stereotype, they are seen as inauthentic, and if they don't, their leadership is either not recognized at all, or considered inferior to that of men (Eagly and Carli 2007: 64). This is why it is so important to reconsider the meaning of "authenticity." Women can respond quite "authentically" to the unarticulated expectations that inform one particular situation while resisting these same expectations in another. This does not amount to a lack of authenticity. Instead, it is a reflection of the institutionalized prejudices to which women are regularly exposed, and the ways in which particular individuals challenge, resist and navigate them. It is important that organizations pay attention to these dynamics in order to get a better sense of the tacit practices of discrimination that inform the interactions between their members, and to look for ways to challenge and change them. From the perspective of adaptive leadership, it is important to allow individuals to draw on their own strengths, sensibilities and perspectives and to adopt their own unique style as they take responsibility and initiative in leadership roles.

The challenge for gender theorists is to simultaneously challenge socially constructed gender stereotypes and essentialist prejudices and advocate the inclusion and consideration of uniquely female perspectives in leadership discourses. To do so they are forced to argue against the rigid oversimplification of gender roles and traits, while simultaneously insisting that women can offer different perspectives and sensibilities when they are allowed to assume positions of leadership. Linstead and Pullen (2006: 1287) draw on the work of Deleuze and Guattari to address the embodied realities and social practices that perpetuate gender discrimination. This allows them to move away from gender as a social construction, while still seeing it as a social process. More specifically, they disrupt the gender binaries by emphasizing individual differences. They argue that the variety of women's experiences must be explored. Each individual is engaged in the process of desiring-production, through which social "reality" is produced. By focusing on different interactions and connections between unique individuals over time, our attention is focused on the multiplicity that results from the conception of desire as a force of proliferation. In terms of leadership theory, this research suggests that it is important to investigate the embodied experience of individual leaders in the workplace, and explore all the different ways in which they lead. We will now proceed to explore this possibility in one specific area of leadership, namely vision, especially since this has been indicated as an area in which male leaders typically outperform their female counterparts (Ibarra and Obodaru 2009).

Rethinking Vision

Previously we discussed a survey that found that many business practitioners thought women leaders lack "vision." In the course of our analysis it was suggested that because of women's propensity for cooperation, sharing information and power, and their fear of over- promising and under-delivering, they often do not claim any grand idea as the product of their own "vision." As such, women leaders may not always get the credit they deserve. One way to solve this problem is to re-conceive leadership "vision" in more gender-inclusive terms.

This could be accomplished, in part, by simply acknowledging the unique visionary contributions of women leaders. This would help to expand the way in which leadership "vision" is defined. For instance, Vivienne Cox's leadership style has been described as "organic" by those who work with her. Apparently, she designs incentives and objectives in such a way that the organization naturally finds its own solutions and structures. She encourages everyone in the organization to be thoughtful, innovative and self-regulating. Her leadership style is collaborative, drawing on thought leaders outside of the organization and executives in other business units. Her "vision" therefore emerges through her engagements with others, rather than by means of sketching a fixed picture of what the future of the organization should look like.

This example suggests that "vision" need not be understood as the representation of an envisaged future. In fact, thinking about vision as some possible future state that must be realized fixes an organization's operations and activities in inflexible terms. This makes it difficult for the organization's members to respond appropriately to present or future opportunities and challenges and to properly appreciate the significance of past events. In fact, instead of "vision" with its focus on clear-sightedness, neat representations and mimetic strategies, we may do well to consider the more embodied intuitiveness that some philosophers associate with creativity and innovation. Drawing on Bergson, Deleuze (2006: 15) explains that it is up to intuition to show to intelligence which questions are not really questions, as opposed to those that deserve a response. It does this precisely because it assumes duration and offers towards this end an analytical matrix and a method to which intelligence has no access.

Visionary leadership, from this perspective, no longer requires only the capacity to be able to change one's perspective on the world, or to change the world to fit one's perceptions of it, but to embrace a radically new conception of time and experience (Linstead and Mullarkey 2003: 1). Reality is not stagnant, and hence leaders have to be capable of being part of, and of processing and engaging with, the qualitative variations of experiences over time and in time. Drawing on Henri Bergson, Linstead and Mullarkey (2003: 9) argue that the "*élan vital,*" the vital spirit which appears within our organizational life, is the human impulse to organize. But since the *élan vital* is a process of creative improvisation, it does not subscribe to the typical organizational strategies of locating, dividing and controlling. These authors (Idem 2003: 6) make it clear that the specialized understanding of time as measurable and representable in homogenous units does not allow us to grasp the conscious experience of duration, which is heterogeneous, qualitative and dynamic. From this perspective, something like "vision" cannot be reduced to the creation of measurable time-driven targets, as each unit of time, seen from the perspective of duration, is multiple, unique, and as such not measurable in bits and pieces.

The kind of traits that are typically associated with inferior leadership, such as being emotional, sensitive, dependent on others, are recast as legitimate ways of operating in the leadership realm. Again here, we can find philosophical support for including these ways of being in the world in our conception of valuable leadership. Deleuze and Guattari (1996: 161) celebrate the unpredictable, uncontrollable overspill of forces that allows us an intuitive grasp of other possibilities of becoming, i.e. different ways of being in the world, and as such, different ways of "leading." Whereas "effective" visionary leadership may direct the course of individuals or organizations to a predetermined goal based on representations, *affective* envisioning draws on that which is not yet evident within the established order, and hence, cannot be represented. This kind of envisioning draws on forces that exist but remain imperceptible. Deleuze and Guattari (1996: 161) often draw on Uexkull's example of the tick, which is blind, deaf and mute, yet is capable of determining its direction quite accurately. The tick is responding to the perceptual signs and significances of its *Umwelt*. There are no direct causal factors that cause the tick to act, but instead a creative response to a complex range of embodied perceptions. A leader's perception of the direction in which his/her organization is moving emerge from her/his immersion in relationships, participation in society, experimentation with multi-disciplinary insights, and an ongoing openness towards what he/she is becoming in the process. What all of this points towards is the need to develop embodied practices of resistance in our organizations that challenge gender prejudices and expand our conception of good leadership.

Conclusion

In this chapter, it has become clear that the origins of discriminatory practices in organizations lie hidden in our everyday practices, habits and interactions. There is no doubt that gender stereotypes are alive and well in organizations, and that addressing these prejudices is by no means an easy task. In the first place, one has to acknowledge the ingrained social practices and beliefs about the capabilities of both men and women, which play a role from a very early age and are solidified in our workplaces. To address these prejudices, we all have to start thinking about the feedback and advice we provide to our children and students in the course of their early development and education. Within organizations, we have to develop new role models and seek out mentors who have found their own unique leadership styles. Most importantly, we have to start paying attention to how specific individuals have been shaped and formed through gendered practices. A large part of the work lies in no longer viewing nature and nurture as two separate processes. Instead, we need to realize that we are constantly shaping and reshaping ourselves as thinking, feeling and perceiving bodies in, and through, our everyday workplace practices.

Addressing gender in organizations therefore requires a unique type of research, i.e. the kind of research that allows us to observe people in their various environments, track their developmental paths, and listen to their self-reflections. We also have to create a space within which different types of leadership practices could emerge. We have seen that systemic leadership models allow for a variety of leadership roles and styles to coexist in an organization. The challenge lies in acknowledging these various roles, and making sure that they do not go unrecognized or uncompensated. In the process, we may find that inspiring stories about people's authentic responses to challenges could be told. We may also notice how men and women intuitively came across visionary ideas and practices in and through their engagement with others. We need organizational environments in which people are free to become the kind of leaders that infuse the world with creative new solutions and practices. It is the possibility of continually becoming a new kind of leader that may allow both men and women to explore the full range of their individual capacities. This will most certainly enable them to serve their organizations, themselves and the broader society to the best of their multiple abilities.

References

Borgerson, Janet. 2007. "On the Harmony of Feminist Ethics and Business Ethics." *Business and Society Review* 112 (4): 477–509.

Collier, Jane, and Rafael Esteban. 2000. "Systemic Leadership: Ethical and Effective." *The Leadership and Organizational Development Journal* 21 (4): 207–215.

Collins, James, and Jerry I. Porras. 2002. *Built to Last: Successful Habits of Visionary Companies.* New York: Harper Business Essentials.

Deleuze, Gilles. 2006. *Bergsonism.* New York: Zone Books.

Deleuze, Gilles, and Felix Guattari. 1996. *What is Philosophy?* New York: Columbia University Press.

Eagly, Alice H., and Linda L. Carli. 2007. "Women and the Labyrinth of Leadership." *Harvard Business Review* 85 (9): 62–71.

Edgeman, Rick L., and Franz Scherer. 1999. "Systemic Leadership via Core Value Deployment." *The Leadership and Organization Development Journal* 20 (2): 94–98.

Ely, Robin, and Irene Padavic. 2007. "A Feminist Analysis of Organizational Research on Sex Differences." *Academy of Management Review* 32 (4): 1121–1143

Friedman, Audrey A. 2004. "Beyond Mediocrity: Transformational Leadership within a Transactional Framework." *International Journal of Leadership Education* 7 (3): 206.

Gatens, Moira. 2000. "Feminism as 'Password': Rethinking the 'Possible' with Spinoza and Deleuze." *Hypatia* 15 (2): 59–75.

Gmür, M. 2006. "The Gendered Stereotype of the 'Good Manager:' Sex Role Expectations towards Male and Female Managers." *Management Review* 17 (2): 104–121.

Grosz, Elizabeth. 1994. *Volatile Bodies. Towards a Corporeal feminism.* Bloomington, IN: Indiana University Press.

Hewlett, S. A., C. B. Luce and C. West. 2005. "Leadership in our Midst." *Harvard Business Review* 83 (11): 74–82.

Holt, S., R. Bjorklund and V. Green. 2009. "Leadership and Culture: Examining the Relationship between Leadership Background and Leadership Perceptions." *Journal of Global Business* 3 (3): 149–164.

Ibarra, Herminia, and Otilia Obodaru. 2009. "Women and the Vision Thing." *Harvard Business Review* 87 (1): 62–70.

Ibarra-Colado, E., S. R. Clegg, C. Rhodes and M. Kornberger. 2006. "The Ethics of Managerial Subjectivity." *Journal of Business Ethics* 64: 45–55.

Linstead, Stephen, and John Mullarkey. 2003. "Time, Creativity and Culture: Introducing Bergson." *Culture and Organization* 9 (1): 3–11.

Linstead, S., and A. Pullen. 2006. "Gender as Multiplicity: Desire, Difference and Dispersion." *Human Relations* 59 (9): 1287–1310.

Maak, Thomas, and Nicolas M. Pless. 2006. "Responsible Leadership. A Relational Approach." In *Responsible Leadership*, edited by Thomas Maak and Nicolas Pless. London: Routledge.

Metcalfe, B., and A. Linstead. 2003. "Gendering Teamwork: Re-Writing the Feminine." *Gender, Work and Organization* 10 (1): 94–119.

Porras, Jerry, Stewart Emery, and Mark Thompson. 2007. *Success Built to Last: Creating a Life that Matters.* Upper Saddle River, NJ: Wharton School Publishing.

PriceWaterhouseCoopers. 2007. "The Leaking Pipeline: Where are our Female Leaders?" Last accessed on January 3, 2011. http://www.pwc.com/gx/en/women-at-pwc/the-leaking-pipeline.jhtml.

Psychogios, Alexandros G. 2007. "Towards the Transformational Leader: Addressing Women's Leadership Style in Modern Business Management." *Journal of Business and Society* 20: 160–180.

Reuvers, M., M. L. van Engen, C. J. Vinkelburg and E. Wilson-Evered. 2008. "Transformational Leadership and Innovative Work Behavior: Exploring the Relevance of Gender Difference." *Leadership and Innovation* 17 (3): 227–241.

Rosener, Judy B. 2011. "Ways Women lead." In *Leadership, Gender, and Organization*, edited by Patricia H. Werhane and Mollie J. Painter-Morland. Dordrecht: Springer.

Senge, Peter, and Katrin H. Kaufer. 2000. "Communities of Leaders or No Leadership at All" In *Cutting Edge: Leadership 2000*, edited by Barbara Kellerman and Larraine R. Matusak. College Park, MD: Center for the Advanced Study of Leadership, James MacGregor Burns Academy of Leadership.

Uhl-Bien, Mary. 2011. "Relational Leadership and Gender: From Hierarchy to Relationality." In *Leadership, Gender, and Organization*, edited by Patricia H. Werhane and Mollie J. Painter-Morland. Dordrecht: Springer.

Uhl-Bien, Mary, Russ Marion and Bill McKelvey. 2007. "Complexity Leadership Theory: Shifting Leadership from the Industrial Age to the Knowledge Era." *The Leadership Quarterly* 18 (4): 298–318.

Werhane, Patricia H. 2011. "Women Leaders in a Globalized World." In *Leadership, Gender, and Organization*, edited by Patricia H. Werhane and Mollie J. Painter-Morland. Dordrecht: Springer.

Young, Iris Marion. 2005. *On Female Body Experience: "Throwing like a Girl" and Other Essays*. New York: Oxford University Press.

Mollie Painter currently heads up the Responsible and Sustainable Business Lab (RSB Lab), a Research Centre within Nottingham Business School, Nottingham Trent University, UK and is an Extraordinary Professor at the Gordon Institute of Business Science, University of Pretoria. Her research is focused on business ethics, CSR, sustainability and responsible leadership. She has held academic positions in South Africa, the USA, the UK, and Slovenia. She also serves as co-Editor-in-Chief of *Business Ethics Quarterly*. Between 2015 and 2020, she held the Coca-Cola Chair of Sustainability at IEDC-Bled in Slovenia.

On the Harmony of Feminist Ethics and Business Ethics

Janet L. Borgerson

Abstract If business requires ethical solutions that are viable in the liminal landscape between concepts and corporate office, then business ethics and corporate social responsibility should offer tools that can survive the trek, that flourish in this well-travelled, but often unarticulated environment. Feminist ethics has preceded business ethics and corporate social responsibility into crucial domains that these fields now seek to engage. Indeed, feminist ethics has developed theoretical and conceptual resources for mapping, investigating, and comprehending these complex, often unarticulated, realms and, moreover, greeting and communicating with the diverse human beings who make their lives there. Nevertheless, feminist ethics has been consistently overlooked, misunderstood, and improperly applied within business ethics and corporate social responsibility. This article provides conceptual clarification, illustrative examples, and furthermore develops a framework for future research.

Keywords Business ethics · Feminist ethics · Feminine ethics · Steven Darwall · Claudia Card · Carol Gilligan · Margaret Urban Walker · Iris Young

Introduction

This article demonstrates that the common and consistent failure in the business ethics context to make basic differentiations between *feminist* and *feminine* ethics, as well as conflating feminist ethics with care ethics has resulted in misapprehension, theoretical misunderstanding, and, most importantly, missed opportunities to benefit from feminist ethics' extensive and flexible assets. 'Feminist ethics', 'feminine ethics', and 'care ethics' each designates potentially fertile, yet at times wholly discrete, realms of philosophical insight. Crucial and fundamental discord exists amongst them.

J. L. Borgerson (✉)
Institute for Business and Professional Ethics, DePaul University, Chicago, IL, USA
e-mail: jborgers@depaul.edu

© The Author(s), under exclusive license to Springer Nature   37
Switzerland AG 2023
M. Painter, P. H. Werhane (eds.), *Leadership, Gender, and Organization*, Issues
in Business Ethics 63, https://doi.org/10.1007/978-3-031-24445-2_3

I argue that feminist ethics has yet to live up to its potential in business ethics and corporate social responsibility in part because many researchers in these fields have failed to recognize four key points:

1. Feminist ethics and feminine ethics are different;
2. All versions of care ethics are *not* founded upon feminine traits and characteristics;
3. Care ethics and feminist ethics are different; and
4. Feminist ethics is not merely a version of 'postmodern ethics'.

Whereas confusion remains around these four basic points in the business ethics literature, a scholarly search can reveal numerous publications over the decades that have clearly differentiated, distinguished, and mobilized the discreet potentials of the diverse positions (e.g., Borgerson 2001, 2005; Derry 2002; Tong 1996; Tronto 1993; McNay 2000; Noddings 1984; Nunner-Winkler 1995). Whereas aspects of care ethics and feminine ethics arguably have potential contributions to make in business ethics research (White 1998), the focus of this essay will remain on *feminist* ethics to elucidate potential resources for business ethics. Throughout the course of this article, I address each misunderstanding in turn in hopes of providing a more accurate and useful rendering of feminist ethics.

After presenting the philosophical background of feminist ethics and feminist ethical theory, I illustrate the four misunderstandings, including a textbook case of the misrepresentation and underestimation of feminist ethics within the domain of business ethics. Then, to begin expressing the harmony of feminist and business ethics, I discuss crucial intersections of interest emerging around concepts of *relationships*, *responsibility*, and *experience*. A research example demonstrates how feminist ethical awareness intervenes in business ethics research, countering the tendency to employ 'gender differences' in the study of 'ethical sensitivity' – defined as 'an ability to recognize that a particular situation poses an ethical dilemma,' and exemplifies intolerance toward unethical behaviours, and a proneness to do the right thing (Collins 2000: 6). In conclusion, I provide examples of three feminist ethicists 'in action' whose investigations into (1) the 'grey zones' of harms; (2) identity and representational conventions; and (3) the enlarging potential of 'asymmetrical reciprocity' provide insight into feminist ethics' analytic power. First, however, I ask 'Why feminist ethics?' and provide an orientation regarding this article's theoretical sympathies.

Why Feminist Ethics?

Feminist ethics calls attention to relationships, responsibility and experience and their cultural, historical and psychological contexts. Strikingly, whereas compelling business ethics scenarios often call for experience in the organization and engagement with the context at hand, traditional ethical considerations that aim at versions of principle-based objectivity and universality often judge such experience and attention 'inappropriately subjective' or 'unworthy of consideration' in solving problems and coming to terms with conflicts of interest. In other words, a gulf sometimes emerges between business ethics discussions and the way dilemmas are actually resolved.

Moreover, in much ethical discourse, notions of responsibility typically function in reference to fulfilling – usually abstract – duties and obligations provoking scarce investigation into the implied relations. The importance of relationships, or sociality, lies at the core of business organization and practices. Nevertheless, responsibility's more comprehensive and insightful modes – as a context for agency based in relationships, developed and borne out intersubjectively, or in conjunction with others – have little hope of emerging within traditional discussions of business ethics and corporate social responsibility, yet become apparent readily in feminist ethics.

The field of feminist ethics simultaneously draws upon and develops theoretical foundations that question and pose alternatives to traditional ontological and epistemological assumptions. Fundamental reflection unveils productive possibilities. To put this another way, feminist ethics engages broad concerns of interest, motivating powerful and novel ways of thinking and, furthermore providing diverse approaches to central issues in business ethics and corporate social responsibility (e.g., Calás and Smircich 1997; Derry 2002). In extending the context for feminist ethical interventions in the areas of business ethics and corporate social responsibility, this essay animates key concepts derived from feminist ethics, and reveals that – far from being limited to discussions based in gender differences – feminist ethics provides pathways for recognizing, evaluating, and addressing ethical problems generally.

Orientating Theoretical Sympathies

Echoing Rosemarie Tong's concerns for bioethics, if business ethics does not want to become 'just a subfield of law – another rule, regulation and policy generating enterprise,' if it wants to encourage and support investigation of and interventions in difficult ethical questions and conflicts, then 'it must make some changes' (Tong 1996: 89). This article is informed by analytic philosophy, including analytic philosophers' work in feminist ethics, but also in some respects by philosophical work in existential phenomenology. As this term may appear unfamiliar to some, let us define it. *Phenomenology*, as the study of the movement of consciousness through time – including *the way things appear to us* – becomes *existential* with an emphasis upon understanding diversities of human experience in the world, including notions of lived experiences' contingency and uncertainty. Moreover, the body and particular conditions of embodiment become lenses for comprehending intersubjectivity, engagement, and relations with others. In short, this article explores the harmony of feminist ethics and business ethics, mobilizing an existential-phenomenological perspective, broadly conceived.

A number of prejudices and habits of thinking may lurk in business ethic's philosophical background – militating against opportunities for Tong's called for 'changes' – and influential Oxford philosopher G. J. Warnock provides a relevant example. In his entertaining commentary on what he undoubtedly views as unfortunate Hegelian influences on late nineteenth century English philosophy, Warnock (1969) insists that most people are *not* wracked with existential concerns, such as, how to live. He writes, "to practice philosophy in the manner of [G. E.] Moore, it is not necessary to have (as most of us doubtless have not) nor pretend to have (as some at least would be unwilling to do) large-scale metaphysical anxieties. It is necessary only to want to get things clear" (Warnock 1969: 42). Clarity, apparently, is not what Warnock found in Hegel – an influential theorist in existential phenomenology's background. Moreover, 'large-scale metaphysical anxieties' are not only rare, but also decidedly pretentious distractions in real philosophy.

Animating a prominent philosophical brand as Warnock does here, calls attention to the delineation of philosophical questions, including the kinds of questions philosophy – and as a result, philosophically informed business ethics – has the potential, or inclination, to raise. This is not to say that analytic philosophy will take business ethics and corporate social responsibility down a dead end road. However, the particular resources displayed thus far arguably have been unsuccessful in wresting business ethics and corporate social responsibility away from those who would indeed turn them into a 'rule, regulation, and policy generating exercise'. Perhaps if these fields are to flourish and philosophy is to play a part, then turning to alternative perspectives such as feminist ethics and, moreover, remaining open to the potential of an existential phenomenological perspective offer a productive opportunity as the impact of global business and corporate social responsibility continues to grow.

Feminist Ethics: Accessing the Field

Feminist ethics places the tendency to value connection – and demonstrate alternatives to traditional notions of autonomy – outside conventional visions of a natural or an essential female-gender based way of being in the world. Feminist ethics turns instead to concrete and particular, yet theoretically elaborated, cultural and historical understandings of diverse marginal or subordinated groups' experience.

Furthermore, tendency to critical inquiry, especially regarding the frequently forgone 'givens' of particular situations marks feminist ethics *not* as a list of essential sex-based ethically relevant traits or a set of pre-determined gender-based applicable principles, but rather as an intervention that calls for active engagement in dilemmas. The following sections elaborate on important aspects of feminist ethics, including a brief discussion of the distinction between sex (female) and gender (feminine).

Feminist Interventions and Investigations

Feminist ethics states a motive for investigating the ethics of an ethos itself. The word ethic, derived from the Greek *ethos*, refers to the disposition, character, or fundamental value peculiar to a specific person, people, culture, or movement, and usually is conceived of as a set of principles of right conduct or a theory or system of moral values. Feminist ethicists have insisted that 'The process by which a community arrives at its standards or moral norms is itself open to moral scrutiny' (Brennan 1999: 864), forcing attention upon the context and structure of moral reflection and judgment and attending to signs of oppression. Such an understanding clearly evokes an array of questions: How does an ethos make itself known? How is the ethos experienced in day to day life? Or in law? Why do some people or groups have one ethos rather than another? Claudia Card, articulating the work of feminist ethics, writes, 'oppressive sexual politics sets the stage for ethical inquiries into character, interpersonal relationships, emotional response, and choice in persistently stressful, damaging contexts' (Card 1991: 5). In other words, the systematically subordinated positions in which women have found themselves – throughout global history – provoke a range of ethical investigations.

In addition, the concerns of feminist ethics exceed women's oppression and engage the welfare of other groups, as well. Feminist ethics often operates against the backdrop of traditional ethical theories' marginalization of females generally. However, feminist ethics articulates, theorizes, and works to understand modes of exclusion, subordination, and oppression – and the damage inflicted by these processes and practices: and females have not been the only segment, nor the private domestic sphere the only arena, marginalized or excluded from the traditional vision of moral theory (Tong 1993: 224). Indeed, as Alison Jaggar argues, the concepts of traditional moral theory were often 'ill-suited to the contexts under discussion', failing to account for the experience of many within those contexts (Brennan 1999: 861). Moreover, writes Susan Sherwin, Feminist ethics proposes that when we engage in moral deliberation, it is not sufficient just to calculate utilities or to follow a set of moral principles. We must also ask whose happiness is increased, or how the principles in question affect those who are now oppressed in the circumstances at hand (Sherwin 1996: 52). In short, feminist ethics pays attention to who tends to benefit from a particular way of viewing, evaluating, and philosophizing about the world, and who tends to bear the burden.

Recognizing the Sex/Gender Distinction

A fundamental theoretical issue must be recognized in this discussion, that is, the distinction between sex and gender. By marking the sex/gender distinction, it becomes clear in what ways a 'female' perspective differs from a 'feminist' perspective. Moreover, a proponent of 'care' ethics may distinguish some aspects of care from stereotypically articulated 'feminine', self-sacrificing caring behaviours, yet nevertheless not take on board a feminist perspective. 'Gender' is 'used as an analytic category to draw a line of demarcation between biological sex differences and the way these are used to inform behaviours or competencies, which are then assigned as either 'masculine' or 'feminine' (Pilcher and Whelehan 2004: 56). To put this another way, behaviours and traits associated with females are often termed 'feminine'; in turn, males' characteristics and behaviours are often termed 'masculine'. Yet, it is clear that masculine and feminine traits are not necessarily connected to males or females.

Stereotypically masculine traits can be prominent in females; and stereotypically feminine traits can describe certain gestures in males. Indeed, many traits and behaviours said to be masculine or feminine have no 'natural' or essential connection to either sexed body. Rather it could be said that male and female human beings learn and adopt these gendered traits, behaviours, and roles depending upon the social and cultural requirements of their families, communities and cultures at particular points in history. Moreover, whereas a color such as blue can be 'gendered' masculine, this is not a claim that blue is a naturally 'male' color.

The distinction between sex and gender allows researchers to separate biological sex difference from traits and characteristics that are often stereotypically gendered. Thus, feminist ethics claims that self-sacrificing caring traits are not naturally occurring female traits, but rather that females in certain places and at certain times for various reasons have had self-sacrificing caring traits forced upon them as appropriate to their sex. As these traits and concomitant roles are enforced and modelled in female lives, the traits and roles are said to be 'natural', an essential part of being female. The concerns with naturalizing traits and roles that damage human lives and the connection of this with feminist ethics will explored in depth below.

Differentiating Feminist Ethics and Care Ethics

Let us explore more specifically the way in which care ethics, and the feminine-trait based ethical positions that followed (e.g., Noddings 1984; Ruddick 1989) diverge from feminist ethics. Tong succinctly articulates the distinction that has emerged between feminist ethics and versions of care ethics: 'any approach to ethics so naïve as to celebrate the value of caring without caring who cares for whom is not feminist' (Tong 1996: 72). Given the common erroneous sense that feminist ethics *is* care ethics, and given the goal of this essay, it will be useful to explicitly differentiate the positions here.

Psychologist Carol Gilligan, routinely recognized as a forerunner in feminist ethics, remains a relevant, though troubled starting point (e.g., White 1998: 11). Focused upon moral development – as exhibited in decision-making around ethical dilemmas – Gilligan's research challenged attributions of moral superiority usually granted to those research subjects who solved the ethical dilemmas by referring to abstract values derived from universal principles (1982). Her work responded to psychologist Lawrence Kohlberg's influential hierarchical scale of moral maturity, based in dominant Kantian notions of rational morality. Gilligan's early studies revealed 'different' approaches, perspectives or voices, including the voice of 'care', in her subjects' ethical deliberations that defied abstract, universal positioning. Kohlberg's scale would judge them inferior, yet Gilligan argued that these voices deserved recognition for mature moral reasoning: a care perspective was different, yet equally capable of morally mature judgment.

These alternative ethical considerations – centred around values of care and heard most often in Gilligan's female subjects' voices – have been misapprehended as expressing an essentially female ethos, or women's natural way of being. In fact, Gilligan never identified the caring voice with the voices of all, and only, women. Whereas sexual dualism – the opposing and hierarchical ordering of male and female – and female gender roles increase the likelihood that a female 'voice' expresses care, great variation persists in who voices care and why.

In later research, Gilligan (1995) made a crucial distinction between a feminine ethic and a feminist ethic. Conceptions of femininity – understood theoretically as the subordinated element in the gender dualism masculinity/femininity – carry meanings derived from often associated essentialized female traits, such as passivity, irrationality, and desire to nurture even at the expense of self. A *feminine* ethic in a patriarchal social order is an ethic of 'special obligations and interpersonal relationships.' Gilligan writes, 'Selflessness or self-sacrifice is built into the very definition of care when caring is premised on an opposition between relationships and self-development' (Gilligan 1995: 122). To put this another way, a relationship informed by so-called feminine traits emerges as fundamentally unequal – a one-sided concern with the well-being and development of others that demands prior assumption of female sacrifice made unproblematic by essentialist claims. In other words, combining traditional modes of femininity with notions of responsibility and caring puts into play a particularly debilitating permutation of ethical agency, where agency is understood as action that 'transcends its material context' (McNay 2000: 22). In short, the ability to act suffers under a feminine ethos, or feminized way of being.

Alternatively, by remaining reflective upon potential sites of oppression and subordination, feminist ethical theory informs care ethics' focus on relation differently. A *feminist* ethic 'begins with connection, theorized as primary and seen as fundamental in human life' (Gilligan 1995: 122). In this context, 'disconnection' and expectations of autonomy appear as problems. Such a perspective shares certain conceptual points with Emmanuel Levinas' model of responsibility; but as I argue later, adaptations of Levinas' ethical model often underestimate feminist ethics' fundamental contribution. Feminist ethics bears witness to intersubjectivity – or the interrelatedness of subject positions – yet maintains, or develops, 'the capacity to manage actively the often discontinuous, overlapping or conflicting relations of power' (McNay 2000: 16–17).

Whereas some versions of care ethics take up this feminist perspective, others do not. Sherwin writes, "some feminists have argued that if we are to recommend a place for caring in ethics, we do so only in conjunction with a political evaluation of the role of caring in our moral deliberations, and others have rejected caring outright as the central element of feminist ethics" (Sherwin 1996: 51). She continues, "I do not believe it is appropriate to characterize the ethics of care as specifically feminist. It does not capture the dimensions that I regard as distinctively feminist" (p. 51). Many, if not most, researchers in feminist ethics concur with Sherwin, and considerable work has been done to explicate precisely why this is so. Hence, care ethics and feminist ethics are different, though at times certain articulations of care ethics may express feminist concerns.

In attempting to bring together insights manifested in light of such perspectives, focus and reflection on embodied experience of marginalized existence often produces observations on – and new understandings of – living with, enduring, and attempting to resist forms of exclusion, subordination, and oppression; and furthermore may generate instances of previously unrecognized diversity and variation, frequently evoking, demonstrating, and elaborating alternative ontological and epistemological mappings that provoke rethinking of typical mainstream understandings of meaning, being, interaction, and theorizing, itself. By motivating an investigation of feminist ethics' theoretical foundations, a stronger and expanded contribution from feminist ethics will be forthcoming.

Feminist Ethical Theory

Generally, feminist ethical theories are those that aim 'to achieve a theoretical understanding of women's oppression with the purpose of providing a route to ending women's oppression [and] to develop an account of morality which is based on women's moral experience' in the sense that, previously, women's experience has been excluded (Brennan 1999: 860). However, this attempt to gather and comprehend varieties of experience in particular contexts – that formerly remained beyond philosophical ethics' consideration – is not a claim about how women naturally, and hence necessarily, experience the world. Indeed, what we want to be cautious of in the present endeavour is that 'in our efforts to explain various realities that are saturated with the weight of the interests that created them, we often present 'neat' versions of reality to suit our agendas' (Gordon 1995: 133).

Tong has condensed the most important feminist ethical contributions into what she calls 'challenges to the assumptions of traditional ontology and epistemology' (Tong 1993: 49–77). Ontologically, the dualism of self versus other, or individual versus community – in which the discrete existence of each element is linked to conceptions of autonomy - becomes a question of relationships between self and other and responsibilities of self to the other, and visa versa, in particular contexts. That is, feminist ethical theory attempts to account for intersubjectivity, or interrelations between moral agents even as the boundaries between these become blurred. These interactions include situations of inequality, and power, rather than contracts among assumedly equal partners. In addition, traditional oppositions in epistemology, such as, abstract versus concrete knowledge, universal versus particular standpoints, impartial judgment versus partiality, and reason versus emotion also fall under scrutiny.

The epistemological shifts in feminist ethical theory require a sensibility that maintains a closer contact with practice and the particular and, hence, remains receptive of concrete experience's details and insights. Investigations undertaken from a feminist ethical perspective are less likely to accept elements and structures of a dilemma as given. To put this another way, feminist ethical theories often spur expansion of the contexts in which problems are to be understood, allowing a broader range of problem recognition, possible solutions, and, moreover, pre-emptive work (see Dienhart 2000: 263; Weston 1992). So, for example, whereas research in business ethics has explored the phenomenon of 'ethical sensitivity' (e.g., Collins 2000: 11) as a gender difference issue that expresses aspects of apparently natural female, or sex-based, virtues, feminist ethics refuses to essentialize, or treat as naturally occurring, so-called 'women's experience,' thus provoking productively alternative inquiries into 'ethical sensitivity.' As Card argues, feminist ethics calls upon us to interrogate the very occurrence and manifestation of such 'sensitivity.'

Misunderstanding Feminist Ethics: A Textbook Case

The following discussion – focused upon one main textual example – illustrates the impetus to collapse the field of feminist ethics into a 'theory' that reduces to a common ontological trope of essentialized female traits and characteristics assumedly drawn upon in ethical 'consideration'. *Business Ethics* (Crane and Matten 2004, 2007), an influential business ethics textbook published by prestigious Oxford University Press provides an obvious, yet not inconsequential, site of analysis for relevant confusions regarding feminist ethics. Interestingly, Fischer and Lovell's textbook (2003) place a brief, uncritical, yet reasonable discussion of care ethics under a broader section on virtue ethics – pairing care with 'wisdom' (pp. 74–75). Velasquez (2002) provides a superior discussion of care ethics in his well-established textbook. Whereas he does not elaborate on feminist ethics at all, nevertheless he provides an informed and useful articulation of care ethics which avoids conflating feminist ethics and care ethics.

Although presenting the familiar ethical perspectives arguably relevant for business ethics – utilitarianism and deontology – Crane and Matten also include short sections on 'virtue,' 'feminist,' 'discourse' and 'postmodern' ethics. Business ethics desperately needs this augmentation. Nevertheless, the text inaccurately reduces feminist ethics to 'care ethics,' mistakenly grounds care ethics in a 'feminine approach', and moreover states that a feminist ethical perspective solves ethical problems by 'intuition' and 'personal, subjective assessment' (Crane and Matten 2007: 112). Such a set of misunderstandings and conceptual confusions explains much about the remarkable underestimation of feminist ethics in business ethics.

Feminist ethics, a field of philosophical research in itself, appears somewhat misleadingly within both the first and second editions of *Business Ethics* under the heading of 'contemporary ethical theories' (Crane and Matten 2004: 95; 2007: 110) – defined as those theories that include 'consideration of decision-makers, their context, and their relations with others as opposed to just abstract universal principles' (2004: 95). In short, such a theory would offer consideration for ethics emerging from concrete positions and particular situations, rather than prescribe preordained principles or duties in choosing, or judging, the good or right thing to do. Thus, traditional ethical theories, and more recent versions derived from them (e.g. Rawls 1971), are set against contemporary ethical theories. Indeed, contemporary ethical theories often retain aspirations for seeing the bigger picture yet, at the same time, seriously consider details that traditional ethics' approaches have been known to distain and disregard. Nevertheless, various contradictions arise in attempting to generalize 'effects' of a certain ethic, or ethos, on all others and in all situations.

Moreover, this understanding obscures the provocative and fundamental tenuousness that feminist ethics locates in notions of essentialism, necessity, and universality. In the wake of feminist ethics' ontological and epistemological shifts, the impact of such essentialist assumptions would emerge as a site for critical analysis. In the short 'Feminist Ethics' section (Crane and Matten 2004: 97–8; 2007: 111–113), 'male approaches' are directly contrasted with 'feminist perspectives'. This ill-conceived opposition suggests a lack of understanding around the distinction between sex and gender basic to thinking in feminist theory and feminist ethics. Employing coherent concepts in the explication of feminist ethics as a contemporary ethical theory would require marking masculinity's distinction from the male and femininity's distinction from the female. Indeed, given that essentialist notions of 'being' male or female are rejected in feminist ethics, it is a theoretical error to speak of a universally recognizable male or female mode of ethical reflection, response or action as the text does.

As discussed earlier, the 'feminist' term in 'feminist ethics' designates a theoretical position distinct from both a 'female perspective' or a 'feminine perspective'. Indeed, a more accurate introduction to feminist ethics would interrogate why aspects of stereotypical femininity, such as, being passive, emotional, other-focused, or 'sensitive' – often expected of, imposed upon, and developed in female bodies in certain groups, times, and places, including contemporary Western society – are more likely to coordinate with and express a 'care ethic', than are corresponding 'masculine' aspects. This likelihood of embodied females taking on, exhibiting, and acting out – often subordinating – feminine traits in a sexist context is recognized as a problem with which feminist ethics has been particularly concerned.

In addition, notions of female 'intuition' – presented by the textbook as a source of feminist ethics' ethical response – reduces 'feminist ethics' to an informal process of applying feminized female common sense. For example, 'Feminism rather proposes a particular attitude toward ethical conflicts that is more within the framework of what women would allegedly do by intuition anyway' (Crane and Matten 2007: 112). Of course, 'feminism' does not concern only women. Furthermore, this glaring gaffe marks a fundamental misunderstanding and reiterates dualist notions of men as rational and women as 'intuitive'. As Jean Grimshaw puts it, 'the view that women do not act on principle, that they are intuitive and more influenced by 'personal' considerations, has so often been used in contexts where women have been seen as deficient that it is well to be suspicious of any distinction between women and men which seems to depend on this difference' (Grimshaw 1994: 43). This diminutive characterization exacerbates the underestimation of feminist ethics. Moreover as these misunderstandings have been reproduced in the new edition of the textbook, the impact on students and others who turn to this source will be witnessed for years to come.

Not All Caring Relationships Are Feminist: Facing Levinasian Ethics

The debate over which characteristics are crucial for ethical agency, including appropriate approaches to responsibility, has been around for some time; yet the attempt to privilege so-called feminine virtues, for example certain forms of 'caring', without careful consideration of their context defies the wisdom of centuries of anti-sexist work (Wollstonecraft 1792/1985; Young 1990: 73–91). Feminist criticisms of feminine trait-based ethics have raised crucial questions about damaging relationships, desirable boundaries and ethical agency under oppressive conditions (e.g., Borgerson 2001).

In western patriarchal culture and in other cultures as well, *being* has traditionally been divided into two. This binary mode has given rise to well-recognized, hierarchically ordered dualisms of meaning and being: the self/other, white/black, heaven/earth, civilized/primitive, rational/irrational, finite/infinite dichotomies that Val Plumwood finds implicated in the 'logic of colonialism' (1993: 51–55). The field of feminist ethics recognizes that processes of ontological 'othering' have perpetuated and reinforced historically evident privileging of the male, the white, and the rational (Goldberg 1993).

Traditionally philosophers have granted ethical superiority to traits and behaviours arising from a stereotypically masculine way of being. Kant, for example, in his *Observations on the Feeling of the Beautiful and the Sublime* insists upon maintaining the 'charming distinction that nature has chosen to make between the two sorts of human beings' (1960: 77). In this context, males exemplify capacities for depth, abstract speculation, reason, universal rules and principles. Females are said to be modest, sympathetic, sensitive, and capable of particular judgments, but not principles. In Kant's philosophical universe, this 'charming distinction' leaves women unilaterally unable to attain full ethical agency. Feminist ethics has attempted to confront the impact of such sexist dualisms.

However, given this traditional underestimation should not feminist ethics welcome the opportunity to award female contributions and feminine characteristics their long overdue recognition of moral or ethical worth? After all, the re-evaluation of ghettoized caring traits has opened up discussions of the role of care-taking and relationships with others within ethics generally, including a much-heralded challenge to notions of disembodied, contextless, autonomous agents. Moreover, women's experience of relationships seem to suggest the permeable nature of boundaries between individual beings, self and other, pointing out possibilities for communication between persons, rather than contracts (Held 1993: 28).

Nevertheless, designations of 'typical' feminine or masculine habits of deliberation, no matter how apparently virtuous, maintain a troublesome and damaging sexist dualism not extinguished even as the value of traits shift. Socialized female and stereotypical feminine traits have long been valued by philosophers as 'charming distinctions' appropriate to women's ways of being, yet this valuing has not changed the overall judgements of female ontological and epistemological potential (see e.g., Card 1996: 49–71; Sherwin 1996: 49–54). Thus, in the field of ethics, and western philosophy generally, the legacy of hierarchical dualism dominates, even in the work of those who in other contexts seem extraordinarily concerned with power, subordination, and marginality.

For example, Levinas-inspired ethicists elaborating responsibility for, and response to, the Other – in ways that echo a feminine version of caring – have not listened to the feminist call for full consideration of histories of subordination both in theory and lived experience. In *Closeness: An Ethics* (Jodalen and Vetlesen 1997), philosophers working in the 'ethics of proximity' reassert a kind of essential human responsiveness in the face of the Other, but disconnect the apparently related human traits from sexist and racist dualisms.

Caring – in particular, feminine trait-based caring – often opposes concern for self with concern for other (Card 1996), evident when a self-forgetting caring response is held in contrast to alternative modes of being. The ethics of closeness, or proximity, emerge from a phenomenological conceptual lineage, especially from the apparent move beyond phenomenology by Levinas. From this perspective, human beings express their freedom in their response to the Other, not in a cognitive process, of willing or 'taking' responsibility, not as a matter of contract or reciprocity, but as a pre-condition to being human (Jodalen and Vetlesen 1997: 1–19). They write, 'Responsibility means to respond, to respond to the call for responsibility issued wordlessly from the Other and received pre-voluntarily by the subject' (1997: 9). This formulation, an example of 'having' responsibility, raises an interesting paradox. The manner of response that a Levinas-inspired intimate ethic lauds is precisely the kind of response demanded of subordinate being, evoking a traditional feminine caring or mothering model (see e.g., Gilligan 1982; Noddings 1984).

Yet, Levinasian responsibility is proposed as simply human (cf. Nietzsche 1998: 36–37; Borgerson 2001: 82–84). The lack of reflection upon such essential 'responsibility' and, moreover, the failure to acknowledge the shared oppressions of subordinated peoples leaves crucial domains of ethics untouched by the 'bare givenness of intersubjectivity', or a Levinas-inspired vision of human relation (Jodalen and Vetlesen 1997: 7). To put this another way, the one who must answer *the call* becomes uncritically *feminine* invoking the interrelations of oppressions that share position and characterization in semiotically and existentially relevant dualistic hierarchies.

Indeed, work in feminist theory and philosophy of race suggests that other-centeredness will be recognized most readily in semiotically associated oppressed groups (Gordon 1997; Stack 1993). In ignoring the critical discourse from, specifically, the field of feminist ethics, proponents of ethical closeness have steered clear of acknowledging the relation between the mode of being they celebrate and the actual circumstances of those who have modelled and still model – willingly or not – those behaviours, regardless of whether there is anything essentially ethical about them (Bell 1995: 17–48). In other words, the 'proximity ethics' interpretation of Levinas – and arguably Levinas himself – fails to incorporate insights from feminist ethics into the notion of responsibility based in uncompromising intersubjectivity, ignoring the ethical implications of being a particular human being, or kind of agent, in contexts of marginalization, subordination, and oppression. In the following section, I return to the notion of ethical sensitivity and demonstrate in what ways a feminist ethical analysis may be better equipped than a traditional one to illuminate obscured aspects.

Feminist Ethics Is Not Merely a Version of Postmodern Ethics

Many of the insights credited to 'postmodern ethics' (Gustafson 2001: 21 cited in Crane and Matten 2004, 2007: 115–118) could be derived from work in feminist ethical theory – as will be discussed later – and indeed often emerged earlier within feminist thought. In equally relevant exclusions, critical race theory (e.g., Gordon 1997) and disability studies (e.g., Shildrick 2005) raise crucial, complex issues of identity, intersubjectivity, and agency, and – this should be obvious – not only as a result of specific engagement and ideological agreement with post-structural theory or thinkers. Insights that have emerged from the experiences, innovations, and theorizations of marginalized groups – such as women, racial minorities, and the disabled – often are ascribed solely to what is known as postmodern theory and post-structural theorists. Such careless attribution both reveals and breeds ignorance (and worse) and serves to reintroduce the marginalization such theory often seeks to acknowledge.

Whereas feminist ethical theory does share some fundamental assumptions with post-structural theory – a ground for so-called postmodern ethics – this emerges not because all feminist theory, and therefore feminist ethics, is derivative. Rather, many feminist philosophers and theorists, as well as their critical race theory and disability studies colleagues, have trained in similar intellectual traditions – philosophical phenomenology, epistemology, and semiotics – as, for example, have Foucault, Deleuze, and Derrida (Borgerson 2005a). Sharing, then, academic heritage and disciplinary genealogies, feminist ethical theory has, in some instances, exploited derived tools to develop conceptual and practice-based contributions often along lines of gender, theoretically understood (Alcoff 1988; Diprose 1994; Walker

1998). Such work includes attention to the intersecting meanings, instantiations, and functionings of hierarchical dualisms in lived human experience, and thus has implications beyond gender difference (Borgerson 2001).

Considerable development in various disciplinary territories has been cultivated with insights derived from theorizing multiple and particular experiences of living in divergent societies, places, times and bodies. Yet, recognition of such fundamental data tends to vanish in attempts to maintain the status of an abstract and authoritative voice. Given this observation, it is not surprising that a certain kind of discourse intimately connected to, and privileged by, this 'tradition' continues processes of exclusion and marginalization. Focusing upon feminist ethics as a feminine trait-based ethic of care concerned with 'harmonious and healthy social relationships', and relying upon 'personal, subjective reasoning' (Crane and Matten 2004: 98), underestimates and undermines the critical power of feminist ethic's analytical examinations and philosophical arguments around unequal power relations, agency and identity formation, and systemic subordination. We turn, now, to three key concepts that emerge from feminist ethics.

Insights from Feminist Ethics

Recognizing, of course, that conceptual foundations and debates are as diverse in feminist ethics as in other fields of philosophy, for present purposes three theoretical signposts will be indicated as fundamental to feminist ethical terrain. These include attention to responsibility in conjunction with the recognition of the primacy of relation – including aspects of co-creative intersubjective agency – and a focus upon particular experience in context. Whereas alternative aspects of feminist ethics' rich genealogical conceptual heritage could also inspire us here, feminist ethical theories' reframing of responsibility, relationships, and experience adequately exemplifies new possibilities for the impact, complexity, and potential of business ethics.

Robbin Derry, in particular, has argued that feminist ethical theory, and related research methods, 'could significantly extend the scope of issues addressed and the depth of learning from research in the field of business ethics' (Derry 2002: 81). As a brief example, consider elements of an 'ethical decision-making process' offered for business decision-making (e.g., Hartman 2001: 6). Firstly, 'identify the dilemma'. Secondly, 'obtain unbiased facts'. Next, identify a variety of choices; identify stakeholders; then 'identify the impact of each alternative on each stakeholder and the stakeholders' resulting impacts on you and your firm' (Hartman; 6); and so on.

At each of these steps, rich understandings from feminist ethics – of relationships, responsibility, and experience, as explicated in the following sections – could provide resources for spurring crucial inquiry in these ethical investigations. Readers are encouraged to reflect upon the way in which aspects of relationships, responsibility, and experience would expand and in some cases rearticulate responses to each step of such an ethical decision-making process checklist (cf. Weston 1992: 12–36).

Relationships

Traditionally, relationships might be hypothesized as between autonomous individuals (agents); or between agents who themselves are the products of relations and therefore, represent some modified version of autonomy. Arguments have been made in business ethics stating that autonomy must be the basis for ethical action and reflection – with a focus on recognizing the sight of agency, decision-making, and, of course, blame tending to minimize incidences of multiple influence, manipulation, and chance. However, reflection on relationships and intersubjectivity's interference with autonomy models has provoked alternative articulations of autonomy (Lippke 1995). For example,

> The idea is not that we should involve others in our deliberations because they will help us come to the right decision. Rather, because the question is always what to do in light of the various relationships we have to others, there is no way of specifying the right decision independent of others' input. And since the relevant relationships are often reciprocal, appropriate deliberation must often be collective. (Darwall 1998: 224)

Stephen Darwall points to the distinction between acknowledging the fundamental role of relationships and accepting a more vulgar understanding of an almost democratically compromised autonomy.

In a theoretical model of co-creation and development, these relationships could be understood as formed between the self, or subject, and some other, in and across a hypothesized gap that separates these agents and protects their status as independent, responsibility-bearing decision-makers. The interactions and exchanges form the basis of subject, and self, formation and the development of relationships over time. Feminist ethical notions of self/other relations – as Tong's notion of ontological shifts suggests – are largely intersubjective and interdependent in just this way: that is, self and other are conceived of as developing in relation with each other.

Indeed, calling attention to intersubjectivity and interdependence raises varying degrees of doubt about the very nature of the distance that supposedly separates self and other, and this provides a critical context for interrogating autonomy. In ethical theory, relationships have often appeared threatening to autonomy and moral integrity because of the role strict boundaries in individual rational decision-making and choice have played in making one's decisions one's own (see Card 1996: 21–48). Feminist ethical theory faces this threat to the perceived site of agency, examining and observing revealed contradictions and emergent insights, yet acknowledging that relationships – actual or imagined, lived or theoretically conceptualized – form the foundation for notions of responsibility.

Paying greater attention to the fundamental role of relationships in human existence invokes notions of responsibility to and for others beyond traditional moral contract-based and principle-justified duties and obligations. Furthermore, human agents may be conceived of as 'having' or 'taking' responsibility. Manifestations of this discussion are wide-ranging and complex, and will be developed later in the next section.

Responsibility

As Darwall notes above, human embeddedness in relationships, our intersubjectivity, cannot be disregarded in discussions and elaborations of responsibility. Card writes:

> The challenge is to show how the importance and point of responsibility can survive the realization that the quality of our character and our deeds is not entirely up to us as individuals. (Card 1996: 22)

Responsibility is often understood to describe an ability to respond to a situation – whether this involves another person, a group, or simply a scenario in which one acts to accomplish an action – and may take the form of recognizing or refusing ties, duties, or obligations that we have in relation to this world around us. Such a notion may also be expanded to include possibilities of responsibility to self.

Alternatively, Levinas turns to being-in-relation's inescapable sociality, a scenario in which the challenge is to recognize and accept, as human being, responsibility for the other in a pre-existing relation (Levinas 1985). This is a case of what Card would call 'having' rather than 'taking' responsibility (Card 1996). For Levinas, this response scenario is demanded by ethics, the foundational mode of intersubjectivity, a 'face to face' relation of responsibility for the Other that Levinas calls the 'curvature of intersubjective space' (Levinas 1969: 290–291, cited in Oliver 2001: 204). In this sense, each must choose to recognize their responsibility, yet there is no choice about entering into the relationship itself as this has emerged in 'the bare giveness of intersubjectivity'. Ethics, the condition of the always already existing intersubjectivity, sets the stage for appropriate modes of responsibility. Whereas, Levinas offers a complex vision of responsibility, its lack of feminist reflections embeds a troubling lack of boundaries, as discussed earlier. For now, Card's notion of 'taking' responsibility shall be the focus.

Card (1996) argues that whereas someone or something may *have* responsibility for a set of situations or actions, *taking* responsibility requires a centre of agency, a choosing to act or follow through in a certain way. This has implications in a feminist ethical context in that females and other subordinated groups may be perceived as having less agency if they have not chosen their responsibilities. In other words, being unable to choose one's responsibilities, having them thrust upon one, may have ontological implications. In short, over time certain groups may be perceived as unable to 'take' responsibility. Diverse scenarios exist: 'We may be given responsibility, assigned it, inherit it, and then accept or refuse it' (Card 1996: 29). Card continues, 'Agents are more responsible when they take responsibility in a sense that shows more initiative than when they do not' (p. 29). As Larry May has argued, tracing 'initiatives' and hence responsibility in groups requires understandings of realms in which shared actions take place and attitudes and values are transformed (May 1992).

Card designates four different senses of taking responsibility each with its own related accomplishments (Card 1996: 28):

1. *Administrative* or *managerial* – estimation and organization of possibilities, deciding which should be realized and how
2. *Accountability* – being answerable or accountable, either through specific agreement or 'finding' oneself such, for something and following through
3. *Care-taking* – a commitment of support or backing of something or someone, and holding to the commitment
4. *Credit* – taking the credit or blame for something that did or did not happen, 'owning up'

Administrative or managerial responsibility clearly involves decision-making, setting out boundaries, and suggesting the form that various organizational processes will take. Being responsible in the sense of being 'accountable' reflects the position to which others will turn when decisions have been made, outcomes are under scrutiny, or results are in. Care-taking here invokes a commitment, perhaps a promise, to put resources or support behind a person or project and seeing this through to an end. In other words, one does not withdraw support from a person or project that is expecting such, even if perceived outcomes have changed. Taking responsibility in the sense of credit or blame may evoke not the decision-making process or following or supporting something through to an end; rather credit or blame may fall to one outside the general workings of organizational or institutional processes.

For Card, 'having' responsibility cannot generate the same sense of agency as 'taking' it, perhaps undermining the very means by which responsible actions are produced. In this way, contexts that encourage 'having' rather than 'taking' responsibility, may provide support for unethical behaviours and attitudes. Taking responsibility requires an active willingness: and what kind of agent manifests such willingness becomes an issue for investigation. Of course, some people, or agents, may not be willing to 'take' responsibility in these ways if as a result they incur more burdens or blame than they would have had otherwise. There is, then, a potential flight from responsibility – or bad faith – that remains troubling. Levinas, for example, engages this concern, attempting to place ethics and relations of responsibility beyond human choice. Feminist ethics, instead, tends to elaborate on being a certain kind of agent, and, thus, having particular kinds of experiences.

Experience

Knowledge gained through experience in situations not generally regarded as morally relevant nevertheless generates ways of functioning and modes of decision-making that have broad ethical import. Feminist ethics has taken a special interest in the understandings acquired by particular, often marginalized, groups and individuals. Ethical investigations that include such perspectives require listening to other's voices and emphasizing a broader acknowledgement of human interaction and attention to the lives people lead.

As Iris Marion Young has noted, descriptions of experience express 'a subject's doing and undergoing from the point of view of the subject' (Young 1990: 13). Therefore, 'talk about experience expresses subjectivity, describes the feelings, motives, and reactions of subjects as they affect and are affected by the context in which they are situated' (Young: 13). Vikki Bell discusses experience in conjunction with the notion of embodiment (Bell 1999: 113–138): In the sense that in the past, notions of embodiment were understood as invoking an essentialist stance, Bell argues that 'being 'anti-essentialist' need not be a reason not to consider the phenomena and import of embodiment' (Bell: 132). She suggests theorizing 'the body in a way that captures the import of the proximity of the body, the debt of identity to the body' (Bell 1999: 132). Echoing this recognition of the impact of particular histories and position on a subject's perspective, Grimshaw writes, 'Ethical concerns and priorities arise from different forms of social life' (Grimshaw: 42). Experience emerges through and with diverse and nonsubstitutable modes of embodiment.

Feminist ethical theory may push us to critically reflect on a phenomenon rather than simply assume its merits, and hence interrogate the emergence and effects, for example, of 'ethical sensitivity'. May has argued that sensitivity to the lives of others and their particular experiences can serve as an opening to acting ethically in relation (May 1992). Whereas sensitivity to others has often been understood as feminine gender's domain, May does not find such an essentialized limitation necessary, rather regarding sensitivity a basic human capacity that can be cultivated.

Recalling Hobbes' statement in *Leviathan*, May points out that the opportunity to learn and develop from experience is one of the fundamental equalities that exists in the state of nature (May 1992: 130). Clearly, such an opportunity is altered by prevailing experiential circumstances: and ultimately, some people seem to learn more than others from the lessons of their lives and even succeed in applying these to solve future dilemmas. Moreover, there is no guarantee that the lessons learned point toward 'ethical' behaviour and actions, sensitive or otherwise, as life is not an ethically reliable teacher.

Focus on acknowledgement of lived experience and learning invites a distinction between the 'natural' and 'unnatural' conditions under which people make choices, including recognition of how histories of oppression circumscribe the contexts in which relationships and responsibility emerge. Card writes, 'It is not enough to confront the inequities of the 'natural lottery' from which we may inherit various physical and psychological assets and liabilities. It is important also to reflect on the unnatural lottery created by networks of unjust institutions and histories that bequeath to us further inequities in our starting positions and that violate principles that would have addressed, if not redressed, inequities of nature' (Card 1996: 20). Being born into a situation may be a 'natural fact,' but how the nation or race into which one is born has been treated historically and how various effects emerging from these historical variables will place a newborn are not natural facts. Contingent – though not necessarily accidental – historical circumstances, shaped and held in place by systems of power and status, may be ascribed to the just and unjust functioning of 'institutions': Such institutions may be as intimately related to an individual as her family relations, her skin colour, and her gender. The following section explicates the impact these insights from feminist ethics could have on research in business ethics.

Shared Research Concerns: Revisiting 'Ethical Sensitivity'

To explore further feminist ethics' potential to impact research being done in the field of business ethics, I turn to the example of 'ethical sensitivity'. The *Journal of Business Ethics* has given witness to the role that ethical sensitivity plays in ethical dilemmas in business contexts (Collins 2000). As suggested in the introduction to this essay, feminist ethical theory opens understanding around the issue of 'ethical sensitivity', offering insight into, and tools to address, the concern that 'many gender studies lack a theoretical framework that predicts when and why women are more ethically sensitive than men' (Collins 2000: 11). The emphasis upon relationships, responsibility, and lived experience found in feminist ethics provides penetration into the realm of business that traditional moral theories may fail to accomplish.

Ethical sensitivity has often been examined in terms of gender differences, in particular, an interest in whether women's so-called feminine characteristics, including caring traits, form the foundation for greater ethical sensitivity. As Collins has noted, the results and conclusions have been mixed (see e.g., Shultz and Brender-Ilan 2004: 305–6). However, conceptual innovations and analysis motivated by feminist ethics suggest that ethical sensitivity could be studied as a matter of attention to certain details, more obvious, compelling, and relevant to some ethical agents than to others.

Recall that feminist ethical conceptualizations support the conclusion that context matters. To put this another way, feminist ethical theory encourages us to explore why it is that agents with experience of certain kinds – for example, a lived awareness of intersubjectivity and particularity arising in daily life practices and culturally socialized ways of being still regularly expected of and manifested in women in contemporary Western cultures – are more likely to be ethically sensitive. (What such agents ultimately do, of course, is a different question.)

The contributions of feminist ethics push us beyond an essentialist view of gender difference – that bases female predilection for ethical sensitivity in an unfathomable natural, 'intuitive' or even cognitive, difference – to conceive, perceive, and construct alternative, and supplementary, understandings that can be mobilized, theorized, and applied in future scenarios. Thus, the phenomenon of ethical sensitivity emerges as an outcome of specific epistemological and ontological assumptions and cultural preconceptions that play out in lived experience of being female, or conversely male, at a historically specific time and place. In short, ethical sensitivity derives from experience generally and, further, out of experience in relationships of responsibility with others. Such critical reflection gives us a depth of perspective regarding ethical tendencies and traits. The next section investigates three feminist ethicists in action.

Feminist Ethics in Action: Three Examples

As suggested above, feminist ethics in many ways preceded business ethics into areas now recognized as of concern to business ethics and corporate social responsibility, such as complex relations of power between unequal parties. Feminist ethicists drew upon theoretical insights derived from bringing to bear notions of responsibility, relationships and experience informed by the challenging, shifting, and reformulating of basic ontological and epistemological assumptions. Examples from the work of three prominent feminist ethicists, Claudia Card, Margaret Urban Walker, and Iris Marion Young are offered to demonstrate the way feminist ethical insights inform analysis, articulation, and intervention in the world – past, present, and future.

The context and depth of these philosophers' theoretical work is far greater than can be expressed in brief here. Readers are encouraged to seek out the writings of these and other feminist ethicists on their own. Moreover, insofar as bioethics engages critical contours of business and organizational practices the works of feminist bioethicists such as Tong, Sherwin, and Wolf are indispensable (e.g., Sherwin 1996; Wolf 1996; Tong 1997).

Claudia Card: Harm and 'Grey Zones'

Card, a student of John Rawls, demonstrates in *The Atrocity Paradigm* (2002) philosophical strengths gleaned from charting and developing the concepts, dimensions, and ultimately the field of feminist ethics. She defines 'evil' most basically as 'foreseeable intolerable harms produced by culpable wrongdoing' (Card 2002: 3). She writes, 'One reason that many evils go unrecognized is that the source of harm is an institution, not just the intentions or choices of individuals (many of whom may not share the goals of the institution, even when their conduct is governed by its norms). Another is that the harm is the product of many acts, some of which might have been individually harmless in other contexts. Victims are more likely than perpetrators to appreciate the harm. But when the source is an institution, even victims can be hard-pressed to know whom to hold accountable' (Card 2002: 24–25). Particularly in situations in which privilege meets disadvantage, wealth meets poverty, or power meets constraint – constantly emerging for example in globalized labour, or international health research practices (Borgerson 2005b) – decision making processes to avoid real harms in the face of apparent benefits become ever more opaque.

'Feminists', writes Card, 'have long struggled with the question of how ethically responsible agency is possible under oppression, given that oppressive practices are coercive' (Card 2002: 234). In her discussion of 'the grey zone', Card elaborates on 'the complex and difficult predicaments of some who are simultaneously victims and perpetrators'. Such a situation might be seen arising in a rural community adjusting, for example, to the presence of new outsourced factory work in which some people come to hold the means of survival for others, perhaps suddenly, perhaps with nearly impossible demands from those farther up the supply chain. What Card argues is that, 'evils may be prevented from perpetuating themselves in a potentially unending chain as long as victims who face grim alternatives continue to distinguish between bad and worse and refuse, insofar as possible, to abdicate responsibility for one another' (Card 2002: 26). Some of her analysis specifically addresses social institutions; nevertheless discussions of 'institutions' might as well suggest the organization or corporation. Card argues that institutions that create 'grey zones', sometimes intentionally, are particularly culpable.

Margaret Urban Walker: Moral Understandings and Representational Practices

Walker contends that the assumption that people are a kind or type is propagated and created by representational practices, which 'are among those that construct socially salient identities for people' (Walker 1998: 178). She argues that if practices of representation 'affect some people's morally significant perceptions of and interactions with other people, and if they can contribute to those perceptions or interactions going seriously wrong, these activities have bearing on fundamental ethical questions' (p. 179). That is, a person influenced by such images may treat members of the represented group as less than human or undeserving of moral recognition.

Drawing upon and developing such insights allows marketing communications scholars to articulate the way in which representations are part of lived experience. Representations from advertising images, film, and the internet inform and co-create notions of reality. Mobilizing an 'ethics of representation' can sensitize international marketing campaigns to their interactions with, and impact upon cultural difference, global race relations, and the constitution of the consuming subjects (Ahmed 2000; Chouliaraki 2006; Borgerson and Schroeder 2002, 2005; Schroeder and Borgerson 2005).

Philosophers concerned with ethical norms and behaviour have traditionally proceeded as through all problematic situations of moral recognition could be countered in three ways: through constructive definitions of personhood, through formal requirements of universality or universalizability, and through substantial demands for impartial or equal consideration (Walker 1998). From Walker's feminist ethical perspective these three formulations lack sufficient conceptual strength to handle representations that characteristically manipulate and damage the identity of subordinate groups. Moreover, these prescriptions fail to provide sufficiently complex considerations to deal with problems of representation and, worse, damaging representations often fail to even qualify as ethical or moral problems.

Not surprisingly, then, we find in Robert Solomon's chapter on business ethics a discussion of 'consumer intelligence and responsibility' including issues of advertising. The use of 'sex' – apparently referring to displayed sexuality – to lend appeal to products and 'the offensive portrayals of women and minorities' become a 'lack of taste': But, asks Solomon, is it 'an ethical issue'? What Solomon utterly misses here is advertising's role beyond appeal, information, and persuasion, its perpetual representation of an entire vision of life and the world around us, often provoking responses and consequences equivalent to and as 'serious' as 'outright lying in advertising' (Solomon 1994: 362; cf. Borgerson and Schroeder 2002, 2007; Schroeder and Borgerson 2005; Vaver 2007).

Iris Marion Young

Young addresses the issue of attempting to understand 'the point of view of others before drawing conclusions about what is right or just', for example in encouraging a more privileged group to fairly consider the importance of some benefit to a less privileged group. Believing in the potential for dialogue between people that happens 'across difference without reversing perspectives and identifying with each other', Young finds the common sense thought experiment of 'putting yourself in the place of the other' not only misleading and politically suspect, but reinforcing 'subjective understanding of issues', disregarding the 'nonsubstitutable relation of moral subjects' and disrupting opportunities for what she calls enlarged thought (Young 1997: 39).

This response to work on theories of communicative ethics invokes 'asymmetrical reciprocity' based in a subject's unique temporality and position, and moreover recognition of asymmetry of power, opportunities, and understandings. Young writes, 'with regard to the Hegelian ontology of self and other, each social position is structured by the configuration of relationships among positions. Persons may flow and shift among structured social positions, and the positions themselves may flow and shift, but the positions cannot be plucked from their contextualized relations and substituted for one another' (Young 1997: 52). Work in business ethics and corporate social responsibility that requires 'efforts to express experience and values from different perspectives' – as discussions between corporations and countries do – may take note of the dangers of collapsing diverse perspectives and experiences into 'shared' expectations. Furthermore, recognition of inequalities, and the opportunities they offer, may help build understandings, for example, of the way trust works, or does not, in corporate and organizational environments (e.g., Gustafsson 2005).

This article has sought to clarify what business ethics can learn from feminist ethics – understood in a robust way that makes an educated exploration of resources beyond care ethics and uncritical notions of femininity. The introduction of three feminist ethicists in action attempts to bring to light notions that business ethics and corporate social responsibility might find useful. Nevertheless, this is only a brief sketch, and the true benefits of engaging with feminist ethics, as with most areas of philosophy, may only emerge with further reading and reflection.

Conclusion

As has been suggested here, feminist ethics in many ways preceded business ethics into areas of concern that business ethics and corporate social responsibility now seek to engage. This includes the work of feminist ethics in developing theoretical and conceptual resources for charting courses through these complex, often unarticulated, realms.

Feminist ethics does more than displace traditional ethical voices, only to assert a 'different' voice with alternative concerns. As illustrated in the preceding discussions, simply asserting the primacy of relationships, recognizing the existence of permeable boundaries between the self and the other, and questioning the site of agency may fail to attend to the existential-phenomenological realities of intersubjectivity and responsibility – including issues of power – that shed light on business ethics and organizational environments. This requires noting both in theorizing, and in day-to-day life experience, that lack of boundaries between self and other – as evoked in the case of Levinas' ethics, but also often in some care ethics and feminine ethics – may have dangerous effects and, moreover, forms the typical situation of oppressed groups.

Furthermore, an insistence on residing closer to understandings of lived experience may have a particular attraction challenging – yet making sense to – those who work in business contexts, and who can be expected to invoke on-site experience-based insights that traditionally trained business ethicists may lack. The underestimation of feminist ethics in business ethics could be viewed as in unfortunate continuity with modes of privileged, traditional philosophical discourse that have ignored, excluded, and subordinated marginalized alternative views of identity, society, and the world for centuries. However, business ethics, a field with its own shadowed subordinations and feminized margins, may well defy the underestimation of feminist ethics, recognizing powerful philosophical opportunities and conceptual innovations in the potentially harmonious landscape of feminist ethics and business ethics.

References

Ahmed, S. (2000) *Strange Encounters: Embodied Others in Post-Coloniality*. London: Routledge.

Alcoff, L. (1988) 'Cultural feminism versus post-structuralism: The identity crisis in feminist theory' *Signs*, 13(3): 405–436.

Bell, L. (1993) *Rethinking Ethics in the Midst of Violence: A Feminist Approach to Freedom*. Lanham, MD: Rowman and Littlefield.

Bell, V. (1999) *Feminist Imagination*. London: Sage.

Borgerson, J. L. (2001) 'Feminist ethical ontology: Contesting the "bare givenness of Intersubjectivity"' *Feminist Theory*, 2(2): 173–189.

Borgerson, J. L. (2005a) 'Judith Butler: On organizing subjectivities' *Sociological Review*, 53(October): 63–79.

Borgerson, J. L. (2005b) 'Addressing the Global Basic Structure in the Ethics of International Biomedical Research Involving Human Subjects' *Journal of Philosophical Research*, special supplement: 235–249.

Borgerson, J. L. and Schroeder, J. E. (2002) 'Ethical Issues in Global Marketing: Avoiding Bad Faith in Visual Representation' *European Journal of Marketing* 36(5/6): 570–594.

Borgerson, J. L. and Schroeder, J. E. (2005) 'Identity in marketing communications: An ethics of visual representation' in A. J. Kimmel, (ed) *Marketing Communication: New Approaches, Technologies, and Styles.* Oxford: Oxford University Press: 256–277.

Brennan, S. (1999) 'Recent work in feminist ethics' *Ethics*, 109(July): 858–893.

Butler, J. (1987/1999) *Subjects of Desire: Hegelian Reflections in Twentieth-Century France.* New York: Columbia University Press.

Calás, M. B. & L. Smircich. (eds.) (1997) 'Predicando la moral en calzoncillos. Feminist Inquiries into business ethics' in A. Larson & R. E. Freeman, *Business ethics and women's studies.* Oxford, England: Oxford University Press.

Card, C. (1991) *Feminist Ethics.* Lawrence: University Press of Kansas.

Card, C. (1996) *The Unnatural Lottery: Character and Moral Luck.* Philadelphia: Temple University Press.

Card, C. (2002) *The Atrocity Paradigm: A Theory of Evil.* Oxford: Oxford University Press.

Chouliaraki, L. (2006) 'The aestheticization of suffering on television' *Visual Communication* 5(3): 261–285.

Collins, D. (2000) 'The quest to improve the human condition: The first 1500 articles published in *Journal Of Business Ethics' Journal of Business Ethics*, 26: 1–73.

Crane, A. and D. Matten (2004) *Business Ethics: A European Perspective.* Oxford: Oxford University Press.

Crane, A. and D. Matten (2007) *Business Ethics: Managing Corporate Citizenship and Sustainability in the Age in Globalization*, Second ed. Oxford: Oxford University Press.

Darwall, S. (1998) *Philosophical Ethics.* Boulder, CO: Westview.

Derry, R. (2002) 'Feminist theory and business ethics' in R. Fredrick (ed.) *A Companion to Business Ethics.* Oxford: Blackwell: 81–87.

Dienhart, J. (2000) 'Just caring, caring justice' *Business and Society Review*, 105(2): 247–267.

Diprose, R. (1994) *The Bodies of Women: Ethics, Embodiment and Sexual Difference.* London: Routledge.

Fisher, C. and A. Lovell (2003) *Business Ethics and Values.* Harlow: Prentice-Hall.

Gilligan, C. (1982) *In A Different Voice: Psychological Theory and Women's Development.* Cambridge, MA: Harvard University Press.

Gilligan, C. (1995) 'Hearing the difference: Theorizing connection' *Hypatia*, 10(2): 120–127.

Goldberg, D. (1993) *Racist Culture: Philosophy and the Politics of Meaning.* Oxford: Blackwell.

Gordon, L. (1995) 'Rethinking ethics in the midst of violence: A feminist approach to freedom' *Sartre Studies International*, 1(1&2): 133–150.

Gordon, L. (1997) *Her Majesty's Other Children: Sketches of Racism from a Neocolonial Age.* Lanham, MD: Rowman and Littlefield.

Grimshaw, (1993) 'The idea of a female ethic' in P. Singer (ed.) *A Companion to Ethics.* Oxford: Blackwell: 491–499.

Gustafsson, C. (2005) 'Trust as an example of asymmetrical reciprocity: An ethics perspective on corporate brand management' *Business Ethics – A European Review*, 14(2): 143–150.

Hartman, L. (2001) 'Technology and ethics: Privacy in the workplace' *Business and Society Review*, 106(1): 1–27.

Held, V. (1993) *Feminist Morality: Transforming Culture, Society, and Politics.* Chicago: University of Chicago Press.

Jodalen, H. and A. Vetlesen (eds.) (1997) *Closeness: An Ethics.* Oslo: Scandinavian University Press.

Kant, I. (1960) *Observations on the Feeling of the Beautiful and the Sublime*, trans. J. T. Goldthwait. Berkeley: University of California Press.

Levinas, E. (1985) *Ethics and Infinity*, trans. R. Cohen Pittsburgh, Duquesne University Press.

Lippke, R. (1995) *Radical Business Ethics.* Lanham, MD: Rowman and Littlefield.

May, L. (1992) *Sharing Responsibility.* Chicago: University of Chicago Press.

McNay, L. (2000) *Gender and Agency: Reconfiguring the Subject in Feminist and Social Theory*. Cambridge: Polity.

Nietzsche, F. (1998) *On the Genealogy of Morality*, trans. M. Clark and A. Swensen. Indianapolis: Hackett.

Noddings, N. (1984) *Caring: A Feminine Approach to Ethics and Moral Education*. Berkeley: University of California Press.

Nunner-Winkler, G. (1993) 'Two Moralities?: A Critical Discussion of an Ethics of Care and Responsibility versus an Ethic of Rights and Justice' in M. J. Larrabee (ed.) *An Ethic of Care*. New York: Routledge.

Oliver, K. (2001) *Witnessing: Beyond Recognition* Minneapolis, MN: University of Minnesota Press.

Pilcher, J. and Whelehan, I. (eds.) (2004) *50 Key Concepts in Gender Studies*. London: Sage.

Plumwood, V. (1993) *Feminism and the Mastery of Nature*. London: Routledge.

Rawls, J. (1971) *A Theory of Justice*. Cambridge, MA: Harvard University Press.

Ruddick, S. (1989) *Maternal Thinking: Toward a Politics of Peace*. Boston: Beacon Press.

Schroeder, J. E. (2007), 'Brand culture: Trade marks, marketing and consumption' in J. Ginsburg, L. Bently, and J. Davis (eds.) *Interdisciplinary Perspectives on Trade Marks*. Cambridge: Cambridge University Press, in press.

Schroeder, J. E. and Borgerson, J. L. (2005) 'An ethics of representation for international marketing' *International Marketing Review*, 22: 578–600.

Sherwin, S. (1996) 'Feminism and bioethics.' in S. M. Wolf (ed.) *Feminism and Bioethics: Beyond Reproduction*. Oxford: Oxford University Press.

Shildrick, M. (2005) *Dangerous Discourses: Disability Studies, Subjectivity, and Sexuality*.

Shultz, T. and Brender-Ilan, Y. (2004) 'Beyond justice: Introducing personal moral philosophies to ethical evaluations of human resource practices' *Business Ethics – A European Review* 13(4): 302–316.

Solomon, R. (1993) 'Business ethics' in P. Singer (ed.) *A Companion to Ethics*. Oxford: Blackwell: 354–365.

Stack, C. B. (1993) 'The culture of gender. Women and men of color' in M. J. Larrabee (ed.) *An Ethic of Care: Feminist and Interdisciplinary Perspectives*. New York: Routledge.

Tong, R. (1993) *Feminine and Feminist Ethics*. Belmont, CA: Wadsworth.

Tong, R. (1997) *Feminist Approaches to Bioethics: Theoretical Reflections and Practical Applications*. Boulder, CO: Westview.

Tronto, J. (1993) *Moral Boundaries: A Political Argument for an Ethic of Care*. New York: Routledge.

Vaver, D. (2007) 'Images in brand culture: Responding legally to Professor Schroeder's paper' in J. Ginsburg, L. Bently, and J. Davis (eds.) *Interdisciplinary Perspectives on Trade Marks*. Cambridge: Cambridge University Press, in press.

Velasquez, M. G. (2002) *Business Ethics: Concepts and Cases*, Fifth ed, Upper Saddle River, NJ: Prentice-Hall.

Walker, M. (1998) *Moral Understandings: A Feminist Study in Ethics*. New York: Routledge.

Warnock, J. G. (1969) *Contemporary Moral Philosophy*. New York: St. Martin's Press.

Weston, A. (1992) *Toward Better Problems*. Philadelphia: Temple University Press.

Whitbeck, C. (1983) 'A different reality: Feminist ontology' in C. C. Gould (ed.) *Beyond Domination*. Totowa, NJ: Rowman & Allenheld.

White, T. (1998) 'Sexual harassment: Trust and the ethics of care' *Business and Society Review*, 100/101:9–20.

Wolf, S. (ed.) (1996) *Feminism and Bioethics: Beyond Reproduction*. Oxford: Oxford University Press.

Wollstonecraft, M. (1975) *A Vindication of the Rights of Woman*. London: Penguin.

Young, I. M. (1990) *Throwing Like A Girl and Other Essays in Feminist Philosophy and Social Theory*. Bloomington: Indiana University Press.

Young, I. M. (1997) *Intersecting Voices: Dilemmas of Gender, Political Philosophy, and Policy*. Princeton: Princeton University Press.

Janet L. Borgerson is Senior Wicklander Fellow at the Institute for Business and Professional Ethics at DePaul University. She earned a BA in Philosophy from the University of Michigan in Ann Arbor and a PhD in Philosophy from the University of Wisconsin, Madison. She completed postdoctoral work in philosophy, gender, and religious studies at Brown University. She holds an MSc in Islamic Studies from the University of Exeter in England. Borgerson writes at the intersections of philosophy, cultural studies, and business studies with an overarching focus on how identity forms and functions within organizations, markets, and consumption contexts. She is also author of Caring and Power in Female Leadership: A Philosophical Approach (Cambridge Scholars Press, 2018).

Feminist Ethics and Women Leaders: From Difference to Intercorporeality

Alison Pullen and Sheena Vachhani

Abstract This paper problematises the ways women's leadership has been understood in relation to male leadership rather than on its own terms. Focussing specifically on ethical leadership, we challenge and politicise the symbolic status of women in leadership by considering the practice of New Zealand Prime Minister Jacinda Ardern. In so doing, we demonstrate how leadership ethics based on feminized ideals such as care and empathy are problematic in their typecasting of women as being simply the other to men. We apply different strategies of mimesis for developing feminist leadership ethics that does not derive from the masculine. This offers a radical vision for leadership that liberates the feminine and women's subjectivities from the masculine order. It also offers a practical project for changing women's working lives through relationality, intercorporeality, collective agency, ethical openness with the desire for fundamental political transformation in the ways in which women can lead.

Keywords Difference · Ethics · Feminine · Feminism · Gender · Intercorporeality · Leadership

Introduction

Women leaders are persistently scrutinised and disadvantaged by systemic discrimination in theory and practice. Despite decades of research investigating the gendered nature of leadership, the gender bind that Joyce Fletcher (2004) raised our

A. Pullen (✉)
Macquarie University, Macquarie Park, NSW, Australia
e-mail: alison.pullen@mq.edu

S. Vachhani
Centre for Action Research and Critical Inquiry in Organisations (ARCIO), School of Management, University of Bristol, Bristol, UK

© The Author(s), under exclusive license to Springer Nature
Switzerland AG 2023
M. Painter, P. H. Werhane (eds.), *Leadership, Gender, and Organization*, Issues in Business Ethics 63, https://doi.org/10.1007/978-3-031-24445-2_4

attention to, remains intact. That is, women are understood only in relation to men rather than on their own terms, women will continue to be subordinate in leadership practice and thought. Public and academic interest has focused on women leaders in terms of what difference women bring to organizations and their leadership roles. Women leaders experience disproportionate visibility due to their gender (Bell and Sinclair 2016b). They are scrutinized on issues as broad ranging as their suitability and capabilities to perform leadership roles, the advantages and disadvantages that women bring to leadership, and the structural inequalities they suffer from (Calás and Smircich 1991; Eagly and Karau 2002; Eagly and Heilman 2016; Heilman 2012; Stainback et al. 2016).

Not surprising, gendered stereotypes surrounding women's leadership abound, deriving largely from women's *difference to* men. Women are commonly seen as subordinate and lacking in the gendered symbolic order, with this ordering shapes the language, ideologies and assumptions of leadership. Practically, women are located in the impossible position of being required to perform the masculine, rational order of leadership whilst still being subject to feminine ideals (Fletcher 2004). Any independent notion of womanhood is a simply 'a threat to organizations' such that in practice women are subjected to 'the therapeutic imperative of [masculine] rationality as the price of membership and of "success"' (Höpfl and Matilal 2007: 198).

To think of women outside of this gendered symbolic order (see Fotaki 2013) with this paper we shift our analysis of women's leadership away from our difference to men, and towards our own embodied realties as experienced by ourselves and with others. Our purpose is to disrupt the dominant tendency for feminine leadership to be reduced to a system that oppresses women's autonomy. We reflect on women's leadership as a site of ethical practice based on relationality, intercorporeality and care. We also contribute a discussion of feminist leadership as an alternative way of thinking about leadership and ethics. Whilst leadership ethics has surfaced the importance of ethics and morality in leadership studies (Ciulla 2005; Ciulla and Forsyth 2011), we contribute by considering a feminine leadership ethics arising from relations between living, breathing bodies (cf. Ladkin 2008, 2012; Sinclair 2005a). This intercorporeality (literally, subjectivity arising from the relation between one's body and the bodies of others) casts leadership as relational (Uhl-Bien 2006) as well as embodied. This allows for a consideration of women's subjectivity within a 'system of intercorporeality' (Diprose 2002: 90; see also Painter-Morland and Deslandes 2014) wherein bodies in interaction with and dependence on other bodies create political and ethical possibilities for leadership. It is within these relations that open, ethical and embodied relations (cf. Knights 2015) becomes possible. We put forward that this harbours the potential to liberate the feminine from patriarchal authority and influence.

Feminism has long showed us that changing the culture which frames our subjectivity and our negation is a necessity for emancipation. Nevertheless, the question remains: How can women act? In considering this question, we are reminded of Luce Irigaray's radical political vision and notion of agency: an ethics of sexual difference which enables us to contest how the feminine comes to be defined through the masculine and thus only ever able to represent one subject, the masculine, at the expense of the other, the feminine. It is such a politics that we align with in this paper. In the first section of the paper we discuss leadership ethics with a focus on exposing how feminist concepts such as care have been narrowly conceived in opposition to the masculine. To address this, we explore feminist ethics as a political and practical intervention that can liberate women from subordinate and controlled positionings in gender hierarchies. This enable us to rethink leadership ethics towards, ethical openness, intercorporeality, care and connections. Next, we consider the leadership of Jacinda Ardern, Prime Minister of New Zealand, to illustrate the tensions that arise when women leaders are othered. We also explore how femininity becomes constructed in ways that both renders and downplays difference. This focus on difference forms the basis for our advocacy for ethical openness based on relationality and intercorporeality. We draw on the work of Luce Irigaray's writing, together with Miri Rozmarin's (2013) development of Irigaray's notion of agency, to advance a practical, political approach to initiate alternatives for women leaders that traverse the classic gender bind that limits the feminine to being the other of the masculine (Fletcher 2004). Further we consider Rozmarin's (2013) strategies of mimesis, the speaking Other, parody and body language as a way of breaking the bind of how the feminine is constructed. Finally, we draw together the implications of our discussion for developing feminist leadership ethics based on relationality and intercorporeality.

From Leadership Ethics to Feminist Ethics

The very concept of leadership is a morally laden social construction with normative connotations of what a good leader should be (Ciulla 1998). Leadership and ethics are closely intertwined (Ciulla et al. 2018a; Eubanks et al. 2012) and commentators have questioned whether there is something ethically distinctive about leadership (Ciulla 2005). In their recent editorial, Ciulla et al. (2018a: 2) note that 'sometimes leadership is required for someone to take moral action, which is one reason why leadership ethics serves as a companion to business ethics'. Further, 'leadership is something that almost everyone engages in at one time or another. It consists of more than a position or a person' (Ciulla 2013, cited in Ciulla et al. 2018a: 1–2). Commonly research and theory in leadership ethics focuses on individual action, virtue or the application of rational and normative regulative ideals (Ciulla and Forsyth 2011). Indeed, as Plumwood (1991: 9) notes, rationalism and the prestige of reason 'have influenced not only the concept of what morality is… but of what is central to it or what count as moral concepts'.

Critical research on leadership ethics has discussed the role of an ethics of care, trust, responsibility and duty (Borgerson 2018; Ciulla et al. 2013; Knights and O'Leary 2006; Munro and Thanem 2018; Rhodes and Badham 2018) where the ethical archetype of a caring leader looms large (Gabriel 2015). Within this frame, however, care has been very much generalised so as to not pay attention to the importance of political categories of difference such as gender and race. Also under-represented in any exposition or challenge to the privileged material and symbolic positions afforded to white, able-bodied, heterosexual male leaders (Ciulla et al. 2018a). The cultural association of rationality with both masculinity (Lloyd 1984) and leadership (Ciulla and Forsyth 2011) and as being understood in oppositional relation to feminine emotionality is especially limiting and prejudicial. Val Plumwood (1991: 9) writes, 'concepts such as respect, care, concern, and so on are resistant to analysis along lines of a dualistic reason/emotion dichotomy, and their construal along these lines has involved confusion and distortion (Blum 1980). They are moral "feelings" but they involve reason, behavior and emotion in ways that do not seem separable.' (Plumwood 1991: 9). The gendered assumptions that underpin ethical and political concepts such as care, relationality and responsibility are, therefore, largely over-looked (see Borgerson (2007, 2018) for notable exceptions).

In an important study which questioned gender binaries in leadership, Jackie Ford et al. (2008) suggest that leadership creates significant anxieties for women managers. It does so by putting them in the contradictory position of having to be both masculine and feminine at one and the same time. An inability to do this means that so whatever they do is unacceptable to the organizational status quo. where the masculine has long been privileged. Additionally, the problem of not identifying with discourses of masculinity/femininity often give rise to androgynous images of leadership that are also constructed as problematic (Kark et al. 2012; Korabik 1990; Pullen and Vachhani 2017). Altogether this means that the overarching assumptions ascribed to women leaders are problematic for women's career choices, their lack of agency and the ways that choice is enacted.

Janet Borgerson (2018: 3) notes that the normalised and normative gendered assumptions invoked by female and feminine leadership approaches, such as care and empathy:

> create disadvantage in contexts which stage leadership as importantly constituted by male-embodied, but also stereotypically masculine, practices that historically have proceeded with no mention of care [...] Simply put, for females, social, intersubjective, and organiza-tional engagement often includes the manifestation of so-called caring traits, which con-trasts with varied notions and practices of power, a traditional path to organizational advancement. [In addition] stereotypical feminine notions—such as emotional attachment and self sacrifice, often embedded in care ethics—potentially undermined female agency, that is, the ability to make things happen. (Borgerson 2018: 2)

Imagining positive constructions of femininity as cooperation, empathy and care suited to effective leadership styles can also be read as a response to urges for women to take responsibility for themselves and their lives. This reflects a neolib-eral feminist ideology promoted by pro-managerial feminists to identify with lead-ership and thus receive legitimation in some form or another. Alternatively, as Angelika von Wahl (2011: 393) notes, 'female leaders may perceive that acting on behalf of women will make them seem "weak" or only supportive of "special inter-ests" and will therefore shy away from being identified too closely with women's issues'. It is clear that the gender bind in leadership is being reinforced by a bind that juxtaposes emotion against rationality, rationality being privileged in leadership.

Feminist ethics provides us with philosophical inspiration for enriching debates about women's leadership (Borgerson 2007; Ford 2005). Alison Jaggar (1989: 91) states that feminist ethics:

> seeks to identify and challenge those ways, overt but more often and more perniciously covert, in which western ethics has excluded women or rationalized their subordination. Its goal is to offer both practical guides to action, and theoretical understandings of the nature of morality that do not, overtly or covertly, subordinate the interests of any women or group of women to the interests of any other individual or group

By identifying and problematizing subordination and oppressions, feminist ethics offers an opportunity to reimagine leadership ethics by focusing on women's agency and on care, nurturing and networks. Following Rosemarie Tong (1993) it can also identify how feminine approaches to ethics resonate with the moral experience of women in ways that conventional and traditional ethical theory fails to do. The communal focus of feminine and feminist approaches revise, reformulate, or rethink traditional ethics and their deprecation and devaluation of what is understood as women's (moral) experience (Jaggar 1992).

If we map characteristics of care onto leadership ethics we see that it has become a valuable component. Yiannis Gabriel (2015), for example, explores the archetype of a caring leader which encompasses frequently going beyond the call of duty, displaying compassion, being giving and displaying concern and empathy for the well-being of others. In short, love is the *sine qua non* of the caring leader (Parry and Kempster 2014, cited in Gabriel 2015: 321). Gabriel considers an ethics of care by drawing on using feminist writers such as Carol Gilligan (1977), whose work expresses connectedness, relationality with others, equity and reciprocity alongside care (see also Benhabib 1992, in Binns 2008). Gabriel (2015: 323) sees a ethics of care not as an attitude or virtue, but as a practice (cf. Noddings 1986; Tronto 1993). What Gabriel does not capture, however, is the political effects of care ethics, where leaders are expected to be caring and go 'beyond the call of duty', for example. Empathy, which Gabriel especially valorises within care ethics, becomes a feminised attribute of leadership and translates into the expectations for feminine performances of leadership.

Politically, a significant concern is that there is an unspoken feminine in leadership ethics, understood through features such as care, empathy, humanity and nurturing that attempt to control and serve to further oppress women's subjectivity through its appropriation of the feminine within the dominant masculine (Irigaray 1993a). The stereotypical images of femininity and care in leadership ethics risk perpetuating inequalities that feminist ethics has long worked to undo. Forms of discrimination are likely to be reproduced or neglected in leadership ethics when what is focused on is who and what is different, thus reproducing gender binaries, instead of exploring a non-subordinate feminine. Political critique of instrumentalised masculinity and the appropriation of femininity in leadership is required (cf. Fletcher 2001; Binns 2008; Ford 2006). It is this that can liberate women and the feminine from subordinate status as leaders (cf. Ford 2005; Fotaki 2013; Knights 2015; Pullen and Vachhani 2013; Plumwood 1991).

A Different Leader? Prime Minister Jacinda Ardern

Women's leadership often focuses on the distinctiveness of female leaders, women's proclivities for particular styles of leadership such as more participation-orientated approaches, or how gender is not a factor in leadership 'effectiveness' at all (Stempel et al. 2015). For others there is a novelty value in seeing women in leadership positions, especially in visible spaces such as politics. The promotion of women is part of a broader dynamic that wields femininity as ideological cement for capitalists where women leaders are 'required to maintain the soft, tender caregiver image on the outside while needing to be tough, brutal and cut-throat on the inside to get to the top' (Miller 2016: n.p.). The visibility and prominence of women leaders also relates to appraisals of their authenticity and scrutiny of their leadership. Indeed, it has been noted that displaying an inauthentic gender performance can have dire consequences for women's success (Ford and Harding 2011; Ladkin and Taylor 2010).

A unique case lauded as exemplifying caring and compassionate leadership is Jacinda Ardern who was elected as Prime Minister of New Zealand in 2017. Despite challenges to her political interventions, Jacinda Ardern received considerable positive news coverage for her compassionate and heartfelt approach to leadership following the Christchurch shootings in New Zealand in 2019 where 51 people died. Heralded for feeling deeply (Roy 2019) and acting with sympathy, love and integrity (Moore 2019), Ardern's vision for a better world gained global attention at a time when world leaders were facing scrutiny and criticism. It also enacted a distinctive a combination of strength and compassion by a woman leader at a time when women leaders were often charged with either being heartless and ruthless or overly caring and compassionate. Jacinda Ardern is a leader who took swift action to tighten gun laws, to not name the terrorist by their name. She showed a steely determination not to foster and fuel any Islamophobic sentiment arising from the terrorist attacks (Manhire 2019). During the coverage of the event Ardern was pictured hugging those affected by the attacks, holding hands and showing empathy, not afraid to show sorrow and emotion.

The integrity of Ardern's approach exemplifies not only a different form of leadership, but a valuing of that which is different in itself. It has been said that she 'sees difference and wants to respect it, embrace it and connect with it' (Moore 2019: n.p.). In so doing, it has also been recognised that 'she has shown a quiet, strong leadership, and been very focused on looking after the people who are most affected straight away.' (Roy 2019: n.p.). Ardern's approach has also been praised for showing intuition (Manhire 2019) and compassion. This prompted *The New York Times* to ask, 'Can women save the world?' (Brown 2019). Also noteworthy is that Ardern not only had her first child in office, but took her daughter to the United Nations General Assembly (Moore 2019). This act led her to being constructed as an exemplary working mother in the public eye. Ardern can be see to embody an ethics of care, trust and responsibility at the heart of ethical leadership (Ciulla et al. 2013). Further, she has not abided by the imperative to downplay femininity and perform the masculine as a marker of good leadership. Ardern, in part, has escaped the classic bind of performing femininity in a way that is reduced to solely a therapeutic, care imperative and is elevated to being an exemplary leader with the credibility needed for public leadership (Dick 2019).

Despite her exemplarity, the established stereotypes of women and women leaders are not irrelevant to Arden's political position. When Ardern falls short of public expectations in her decision-making and actions, as a woman leader she is often criticized because she fails to enact a version of femininity expected of her. Her female body is caught up in gendered expectations from the global public because she offers an alternative model of leadership such that Ardern's feminine leadership (caring and compassionate) is employed as a strategy which differentiates her from masculine leadership and ethics (Krewel and Karim 2019). In contrast to other women leaders such as Angela Merkel, Ardern is always represented in the political and popularist media as a feminine leader. Her leadership is judged in relation to her female body, especially motherhood (The Guardian 2019). She is othered, differentiated and deferred, even as a global leader. This pattern of othering continued throughout the COVID-19 pandemic of 2020 as Ardern demonstrated decisive leadership on her own terms. She enforced strict lockdowns in advance of other countries, gave a broadcast to children at Easter where she talked of her own daughter, and was proactive in cutting her cabinet's salary by 20%. Ardern demonstrates relational leadership (Uhl-Bien 2006), whilst being repeatedly open, honest and authentic in her reporting and constantly relating and engaging diverse, local communities.

Jacinda Ardern has been included in media comparisons of women politicians outperforming their male counterparts during the pandemic recognising women responding faster in terms of crisis and health management rather than in the interest of the economy (Campbell 2020; Wittenberg-Cox 2020). Despite this, it is commonly her qualities of care and compassion which are the public focus, as if the only thing that really matters is that she make people feel that from the remoteness of a television screen she can 'hold you close in a heart-felt and loving embrace' (Wittenberg-Cox 2020). This is a clear example of how, despite leadership success, women continue to be othered in relation to the masculine and reduced to having only caring qualities. How then might we celebrate leaders such as Arden so as to liberate the feminine and female body towards ethical possibilities rather than reinforce gender binaries which perpetuate women's difference to men?

From Othering and Difference to a Radical Encounter of Alterity for Leadership

To consider the possibility of a feminine leadership that is not reduced to a shadow of men's leadership, we turn to the work of Luce Irigaray. Of special value us Irigaray's explication of how discourse and language have only been able to bear one subject, the masculine subject, rendering the feminine 'other' (Fotaki et al.

2014; Vachhani 2012) as well as how this can be overcome. Irigaray's ethical philosophy (Irigaray 1985a, b) asserts an ethics that enables women to become subjects themselves rather than holding the position of objects construed as other to men. As we have stated before, feminine attributes of leadership are almost exclusively defined in relation to the existing binary of masculine/feminine where the masculine dominates. In opposition to this, Irigaray allows us to ask whether we might 'seek modes of being which cultivate the sexuate, or whether we obliterate the articulations of sexual difference under the demand of sameness' (Jones 2011: 6).

An ethics of sexual difference is relevant for leadership ethics in two ways: First, for Irigaray, if we were simply to start valuing the feminine over the masculine this would amount only to a reversal which does not realise an ethically grounded feminine subjectivity outside of its relation to masculinity. Such a strategy renders the feminine the same as masculinity, in an inverted sense. In the case of Jacinda Ardern, regardless of her successful leadership, for many observers she is woman, unmarried and mother first. Her leadership practice or effectiveness is never free of her feminine subjectivity. Ardern is often reminded of her difference in relation to her male colleagues. As she commented in interview

> I get asked: 'Do you compare yourself to X or Y politician?' and I'll then get a string of male politicians from around the world – mostly, to be fair, because there aren't too many females. And my response to that? I wonder if they get asked the same question. 'Do you liken yourself to Jacinda Ardern?' And my bet is that no one would. So I actually think that, in New Zealand, we do things our own way. (Manhire 2019)

Feminist philosophy provides a means to break the bind of gendered binaries and the gendered assumptions founded in feminine approaches to leadership ethics. For Jacinda Ardern, this binding is articulated by Manhire (2019) as follows:

> At the UN in New York last September, Ardern made the case for action on climate change, and for 'kindness and empathy' in politics – a message amplified by the fact her partner and baby daughter were sitting next to her. US Vogue dubbed her 'the anti-Trump'.

Empathy, compassion, tolerance, peace and love are assigned to Ardern as a woman and amplified by her status as a mother (Moore 2019; Cowie 2019); Indeed, in New Zealand, she is often referred to as 'mother of the nation' (Buchanan cited in Roy 2019). In practice, however, there is much more to Ardern's leadership that this. Ardern's leadership is often seen as contradictory, in traditional terms. She is often depicted so that 'inclusiveness' and feeling issues 'deeply' are often juxtaposed with 'clarity and decisiveness'. Her warmth is balanced by a steeliness. Roy (2019) explicitly invokes Ardern's feminine leadership as an alternative to addressing injustice:

> It is a leadership style that particularly suits New Zealand. New Zealand does have a serious dark side, it does have racism. But what she is doing is giving us a moment to confront these demons, this darkness and change our ways.

Ardern's leadership can be understood in relation to Irigaray's political vision of a lived feminism. In this life, individual agency is:

an embodied possibility of utilizing precisely these repetitions as a political site for trans-formation. An explicit account of agency would therefore be required to explain how it would be possible for individuals to act not in accordance with the regularities of social power that constitute their subjectivity, and how such transgressive actions would affect the acting individual and her/his world. (Rozmarin 2013: 470)

This agency is a political way of life that emerges through a lived and embodied ethics that places women as actors of their own life, challenging the symbolic and material practices that violate them. With such an ethics, men and women are required to go through 'deep transformations' to 'meet each other in new ways and create a more humane and just culture (Rozmarin 2013: 470). This ethics can be seen in the way that Ardern is able to transcend the political role assigned to her as a woman by connecting, relating and building community in different ways.

Irigaray's philosophy invokes 'modes of action which individuals reshape their social and symbolic positioning and this actively reshapes their subjectivity'. In turn this allows for a 'recuperation of the feminine within the logic that maintains it in repression, censorship, non-recognition' (Irigaray 1985a: 78 cited in Rozmarin 2013: 470). This possibility of recuperation is especially salient where women's cultural symbolic position in leadership has long reduced them to a 'mere echo of masculine existence' (Rozmarin 2013: 471) giving rise to women having to 'mimic subjectivity' by either repeating their cultural position as opposite of the subject or attempting to be recognised as men. Ardern refutes such mimicry and any urge to become like her male colleagues.

Irigaray employs mimesis as a political strategy to undermine dominant and repressive gender norms and stereotypes. This mimesis is a form of aberrant repeti-tion that draws attention to and undermines the structure women's subordination and incorporation. It is 'a tool for unsettling… and creating the conditions for new practical and theoretical forms of subjectivity' (Rozmarin 2013: 471). Following this strategy, woman has to 'recover the place of her exploitation by discourse, with-out allowing herself to be simply reduced to it' (Irigaray 1985a: 78, cited in Rozmarin 2013: 471). Mimesis creates unique positions for women which can be applied to leadership. In seeking such an application we gain inspiration from the three strategies of mimesis developed by Miri Rozmarin (2013): the speaking Other, parody and body language prevent women repeating oppressive gender norms.

First, creating a distinct space for the position of the speaking Other is required to critique the reduction of difference to a dichotomy, where '"femininity" is the negation of subjectivity' (Rozmarin 2013: 472; see Irigaray 1993b). Speaking Other illuminates the incompleteness of male centred culture, which centres the masculine at the heart of the social world. This strategy is especially valuable for challenging leadership ethics as it creates alternative speaking positions which fracture leader-ship masculinity. Subjectivities for women that arise elsewhere than from their negation become possible as alternatives to dominant masculine leadership and multiple, agentic feminine subjectivities surface. As Rozmarin (2013) explains, 'the position of the speaking Other reflects woman's status as object, a silent mirror reflecting the male subject' (p. 472). This 'silent mirror can become self-reflective and self-assertive' (ibid: 472) and we suggest enables the deconstruction of feminine leadership as it is developed from the male centred foundation upon which leadership rests. Developing Irigaray's speaking mirror suggests that 'undoing phallocentric culture demands articulating, in different media, its various manifestations in women's life' (ibid: 472), and which involves talking about women's subordination, vulnerability, victimisation and silencing.

Leadership ethics sustains specific utterances, practices, relations and moments that mark women's alternative leadership subjectivities. For Jacinda Ardern, resisting the pressure to align with dominant leadership norms and feminine leadership expectations that are assigned to her is central. 'New sites of clash' (Rozmarin 2013) that extend further than what is considered 'natural or obvious' involve resisting ideal images of femininity/feminine leadership (cf. Helgesen 1995). This speaking out does not aim to render the subject fixed but rather, after Irigaray, is a transformative practice through which relations amongst femininity and leadership are challenged. As an example, in the third US presidential debate during the 2016 election campaigns, Donald Trump named Hilary Clinton a 'nasty woman'. Women developed the linguistic strategy via the hashtag '#nastywoman' as a means to launch a speaking position - speaking the other. Nasty women, therefore, does not just challenge Trump's misogyny, but rather establishes sites of clash which subsequently uncovers the harms of women's experiences and restores individual subjectivity in relation to these experiences. Rozmarin says that, 'self-enunciation qua woman paves the way to experience femininity as a different and autonomous aspect of one's life' (Rozmarin 2013: 473), and for us this is a necessary part of the transition of resisting assignment to gender binaries inherent in leadership and having agency on one's own terms.

The second strategy is 'parodic imitation of discourses of the "feminine"' (Rozmarin 2013: 473). Here Rozmarin traces Irigaray's 'essentialist-like rhetoric' to illustrate 'the ways in which essentialist thought blocks the possibility of thinking about difference as a basic relation, and obliterates the possibility of alternative subjectivities'. For parody to work, the feminine voice is exaggerated (as in the case of the political 'nasty woman'), even made grotesque, to comprehend what has been excluded from the feminine. Leaders deliberately play with gendered codes, such as dress, that do not conform to phallocentric ideals of femininity, and attempts to queer leadership with a strategic emphasis on excess (Atkin et al. 2007; Pullen and Vachhani 2013). As an example, Pussy Riot's 2016 song about female sexuality 'Straight Outta Vagina' was a direct response and resistance to politicians who praise strong, authoritarian leadership and self-celebrated misogyny. As they sang:

My pussy, my pussy Is sweet just like a cookie
It goes to work, it makes the beats, it's C.E.O., no rookie
From senator to bookie, we run this shit, got lookie
You can turn any page, any race, any age, from Russia to the States
We tearing up the place.

The song exemplifies a parody that involves 'blunt and bitter speech that expresses a culturally silenced truth about the relationship between men and women, thus making this truth explicit and unbearable' (Rozmarin 2013: 473). This mimetic parody establishes a gap between woman and her social identity – woman becomes separated from her leadership identity – and it is in the creation of this gap that different affects are produced and politically utilised which mark a break in the identification with the social position of femininity. Parody is a practice of self-transformation, and women 'become agents of their own annihilation, their reduction to a sameness that is not their own' (Rozmarin 2013: 474).

Rozmarin's third strategy is body language. Amanda Sinclair (2005b, 2011, 2014) considers physicality and how leadership is practised through bodies to demonstrate the pressures women face to manage their bodies towards the masculine and how their physical performances are more tightly regulated and subject to heightened scrutiny (see also, Bell and Sinclair 2016a, b). The pressure to 'do gender' in expected ways (Martin 2003) involves cultural norms that prescribe the bodies considered appropriate for leadership (Fletcher 2004). The feminine body is therefore reduced, othered and for Irigaray's body language 'women need to undo the ways by which their embodiment of cultural constructions of femininity cut them from their embodied sensual experiences' (Rozmarin 2013: 474). Irigaray urges women to 'cross the boundaries of "proper" speech that severs them' and to 'challenge the boundaries of their self-representation' (Rozmarin 2013: 474). Cultural inscriptions on women's bodies and their representation as leaders must be spoken and challenged (cf. Meriläinen et al. 2013). The presentation of women's embodied experiences and their public roles are required to be made visible, including the 'hurt, abused, objectified body, as well as the normative sexed body' (Rozmarin 2013: 475). This strategy symbolises the history inscribed onto women's bodies that 'create new ties between their bodies and their sense of self' (Rozmarin 2013: 474; Sinclair 2005b). This focus on embodiment casts women's bodies centrally in leadership and promises to be an important way in which an ethics of woman's leadership can be developed, as we explore in the next section.

Toward Feminist Leadership Ethics

Recent leadership ethics research has attended to the character of moral responsibility associated with the practice of leadership and claims to offer 'insights into leadership that will be useful for understanding how to better promote ethical leadership and prevent unethical leadership' (Ciulla et al. 2018b: 249). Some academic commentators have asked whether women make more ethical leaders (Lämsä and Sintonen 2001) which may be a possible response to the lack of leadership ethics of corporate men (for example, Knights 2015, 2016).

Despite welcomed philosophical work that interrogates leadership in relation to ethics, this space is dominated by the ethical theories of male philosophers and the absence of feminist philosophers. Noting the inherent masculine nature of leadership and ethics, Ciulla et al. (2018a) observe how both leadership and ethics have been addressed in:

linear, rational, and individualistic manner such that leaders are seen to possess agency and power, display high levels of certainty and decisiveness, and exhibit a masterly control of all that they survey. Equally, ethics has been dominated by masculine, technical approaches regarding practical reason (Kant), normative rules and regulations (deontology), calculations of consequences (utilitarianism), and the elevation of "good" individual character (virtue) (pp. 6–7).

Recent critical writers raise issues of responsibility for the other (Rhodes and Badham 2018) and the nature of affective leadership (Munro and Thanem 2018) demonstrating that that relational and embodied approaches have been called for in leadership ethics. Mary Uhl-Bien (2006) and Joyce Fletcher (2012) conceptualised relational leadership where leadership surfaces in the relations between leaders and follows and effects social change. Arguably what emerges 'is a less individualistic, more relational concept of leadership, one that focuses on dynamic, interactive processes of influence and learning intended to transform organizational structures, norms, and work practices' (Fletcher 2004: 648). Thus, ethics surface in the relations between people. Nicholson and Kurucz (2019) propose relational leadership necessary for sustainability with an ethics of care essential for unpacking the moral dimensions of relational leadership. For us, focusing on an ethics of care (Gilligan 1982) 'in' relational leadership, is a feminist ethics. As we have discussed, care is often appropriated, de-gendered and decoupled from feminist ethics, or care is employed as a feminine leadership requirement, reduced to the bodies that they are attached to and becomes feminine care (Vachhani 2014).

In this paper have contested pervasive, normative and normalised gender assumptions that underpin much writing on leadership and ethics. To develop feminist leadership ethics, we envisages a new feminine symbolic, after Irigaray, that contests masculine sameness reproduced in leadership ethics. Moreover, we see Jacinta Ardern's leadership as a significant development of this in practice. Marianna Fotaki et al. (2014: 1245) remind us that to resist 'an alternative feminine symbolic order, or a new economy of sexual difference, that opens up spaces for feminine sensualities' is required. To pursue this thinking, an ethics which emerges from relations between bodies, an intercorporeality has political potential. This politics focuses on 'the subject's productive and active engagement with the world' and 'an explicit account of agency is a necessary aspect of any philosophical vision of political transformation.' (Rozmarin 2013: 469). This political transformation is an ethical encounter renders ethics not as rational and calculable prescriptions to social actions but recognition of others – to people and their bodies. For Irigaray, bodies are active and enable corporeality and addresses how 'powerful dimensions of women and women's subjective experiences routinely get left out of leadership; and how ways of doing leadership continue to oppress' (Sinclair 2011: 127).

Feminist leadership ethics emerges as intercorporeal through the relationships between individuals including leaders and followers. The key challenge for leadership is recognising the complexity of the intersections between gender, ethics and leadership. Rosalyn Diprose (2002) develops Irigaray's account of ethics to put forward the idea that ethics are not just about rules, rationality and reasoning, but rather originate with a pre-rational and generous openness to the other. Such ethics are infused with and informed by affect characterised by encounters with others and otherness made in and through the body. Leadership too is a relational phenomenon characterised by 'affective openness and response to difference' (Pullen and Rhodes 2010: 246), and political potential emerges from affective leadership (Munro and Thanem 2018). For Diprose politics are founded in an ethics of radical generosity that opens up difference manifest neither in the 'self-serving collection of debts nor in an expectation of unconditional self-sacrifice in the service of the other but in the indeterminacy of generous acts that lie somewhere in between' (Diprose 2002:187; cf. Pullen and Rhodes 2014). This entails leadership enacted without an economy that expects from others in return for your leadership behaviour. It is with this practical and political position that the potential for rethinking leadership ethics as a feminist leadership ethics begins.

Defining leadership in terms of types and archetypes, such as the heroic leader, or particular virtues negates alterity because it limits, controls and rationalises expected moral action. For women, this binds them in a set of relations that symbolically and materially violates them. There is a need to acknowledge this closure to the other through rigid perceptions that render the other as 'finished' (Diprose 2002: 177). A feminist leadership ethics orientated around ethical concepts such as care whilst recognising an ethics of difference would need to break with the notion that femininity can only be interpreted through its relationship with masculinity and individual agency. In place we propose a feminine agency and ethics that is intercorporeal and relational so as to engender collective agency.

Feminist leadership ethics challenges the dominance of reason in ethics in favour of a 'welcoming of the alterity of the ethical relation' (Diprose 2002: 140). Such ethics rests on collective agency through intercorporeality where ethical leadership is a responsibility we take on in relation with each other, regardless of sexual difference and associated gendered inscriptions. Ardern's relational leadership practice can be understood as a site through which ethics emerges and becomes possible through intercorporeality. From our observations, as Ardern relates to others, she connects and works not only with individuals but transforms the ways in which politics is enacted and leadership is captured anew, not withstanding, critique. Her openness can be read in the ways in which she carries her ethics through her embodied relational practices, from wearing the korowai (traditional Maori cloak) to respect for the traditional owners of the land, to wearing a black head scarf to meet members of the Muslim community after the Christchurch shootings. Whilst symbolic, these embodied gestures carry agency which shifts the focus from the individual leader and the responsibility attributed to them, to what she can inspire collectively, thus carrying ethical and political significance.

Conclusion

Feminist ethics challenges the individualism, universality, difference and rationalism found in leadership ethics. This radical approach addresses leadership ethics at the site of intercorporeality and relationality. Feminist leadership ethics lies in a radical vision for leadership which liberates the feminine and women's subjectivity from the masculine order and offers practical implications for changing women's working lives through ethical openness and fundamental political transformation (Rozmarin 2013). The notion of care in leadership ethics is often promoted as 'humanizing' the workplace through practices of empathy, relatedness and cooperation primarily associated with the feminine (Edlund 1992) and is understood in terms of what is 'effective' for organisations. Such demarcations of difference have political effects in relation to the legitimation or instrumental rationalisation of feminized traits but neglects the complexities of different individual and collective subjectivities. The very concept of feminine ideals of leadership become problematic, and the conflation of 'humanization' and the 'feminine' only seeks to rehearse and reify narrowly defined gender differences in leadership research and practices outmoded categories of feminine and masculine leadership.

With a practical politics in mind, and in alignment with Irigaray's radical political vision, collective agency becomes important in pursuing our vision for feminist leadership ethics, as witnessed by the case of Jacinda Ardern. Rozmarin's (2013) development of Irigaray's notion of agency helps us to develop different modes of women's transformation in leadership by facilitating ethical openness rather than foreclosing ethics as an application of moral philosophy that limits differences such as gender or race. A focus on ethical relations rather than the individual leader is necessary in leadership ethics where timely light can be shed on the intercorporeal features of leadership relations that form collective agency. Feminist leadership ethics encompasses the relationship between leaders and followers but extends to wider conceptions of how leadership is accomplished communally. It is here where the feminine within leadership can be undertaken on the grounds of ethics or equality and intercorporeal relationality in leadership can bring about social change and political transformation through collective agency. Intercorporeal leadership relations addresses the current lack of attention to differences between groups of women and men within their historical or cultural contexts, and shifts attention from the regulative, normative ideal and already ascribed categories of femininity (Due Billing and Alvesson 2000) in leadership ethics to subjective, varied embodied experiences.

Equality for women's leadership relies on redefining a feminine symbolic of leadership and which holds the potential to break the disadvantage women leaders experience when they are designated as fulfilling a care function in leadership. This inverts problematic gendered dualisms and as Borgerson (2018: 3) notes, 'caring characteristics and caring interactions when embodied by women at work, and in everyday life, appear to undermine positive perceptions of female agency, reinforcing a general underestimation of female potential, as well as blocking access to true leadership opportunities.'

It is through ethical openness (Pullen and Rhodes 2014) that the oppression of difference can be identified and problematized. This leads to it being practically addressed and politicised. Normative leadership ethics further marginalises the political potential for women's equality. Our practical intent is that instead of being considered 'a threat to organizations' (Höpfl and Matilal 2007: 198) feminist leadership ethics casts men and women, masculine and feminine, in relation with each other, rather than at the expense of one another. Otherness, alterity and difference become ever present, and opportunities for women's advancement ever available rather than subjected to the 'imperative of rationality as the price of membership and of "success"' (Höpfl and Matilal 2007: 198). The crucial and pivotal moment for change rests on a radical vision for leadership ethics that liberates the feminine and women's subjectivity from the masculine order affording the opportunity for changing women's working lives. Such embodied ethics enables leaders to become who they are through the people they have interactions with (cf. Painter-Morland and Deslandes 2014). Yet feminist leadership ethics based on relationality, collective agency and intercorporeality constitutes organizational transformation, beyond the leader. Intercorporeality casts leadership as relational (Uhl-Bien 2006) and the consideration of women's radical alterity within a 'system of intercorporeality' (Diprose 2002: 90; see also Painter-Morland and Deslandes 2014) wherein bodies in interaction with and dependence on other bodies create political and ethical possibilities for leadership. It is within these relations that women leaders can be seen outside of patriarchal authority, instead collective relationships sustain women's agency. It may be utopian, but we start somewhere, both practically and politically.

References

Atkin, I., Hassard, J. and Wolfram Cox, J. (2007) Excess and Mimesis in Organization Theory: Emancipation from Within? *Culture and Organization*, 13(2): 145–156.

Bell, E. and Sinclair, A. (2016a) 'Bodies, sexualities and women leaders in popular culture: from spectacle to metapicture', *Gender in Management: An International Journal*, 31(5/6): 322 – 338.

Bell, E. and Sinclair, A. (2016b) 'Re-envisaging leadership through the feminine imaginary in film and television', in C Steyaert, T Beyes and M Parker (eds) The Routledge Companion to Reinventing Management Education. London: Routledge.

Binns, J. (2008) The Ethics of Relational Leading: Gender Matters. *Gender, Work and Organization*, 15(6):600–620.

Borgerson, J. (2018) *Caring and Power in Female Leadership: A Philosophical Approach.* Cambridge: Cambridge Scholars Publishing.

Borgerson, J. (2007) On the Harmony of Feminist Ethics and Business Ethics. *Business and Society Review*, 112:4 477– 509.

Brown, T. (2019) What Happens When Women Stop Leading Like Men - Jacinda Ardern, Nancy Pelosi and the power of female grace. *The New York Times*, 30th March 2019. https://www. nytimes.com/2019/03/30/opinion/women-leadership-jacinda-ardern.html?fbclid=IwAR2Q 8IOwm8DvoZ26oW5KUzB6kB8UWn%2D%2Dyr8D77%2D%2DvhHNvLmSU8kH56s7 a3I. Date accessed: September 1st 2019.

Calás, M. and Smircich, L. (1991) Voicing seduction to silence leadership. *Organization Studies*, 12(4): 567–601.

Campbell, A. (2020) Jacinda Ardern's coronavirus plan is working because unlike others, she's behaving like a true leader. *The Independent*. April 11.

Ciulla, J.B. (1998) (ed) *Ethics – The Heart of Leadership Second Edition.* Boston: Praeger.

Ciulla, J.B. (2005) The state of leadership ethics and the work that lies before us. *Business Ethics: A European Review*, 14(4):323–335.

Ciulla, J.B. (2013) 'Introduction: Theoretical Aspects of Leadership Ethics', in Ciulla, JB, Uhl-Bien, M and Werhane, PH (eds) (2013) *Leadership Ethics*. Pp. xxv-xxxvii. Los Angeles: Sage

Ciulla, J.B. and Forsyth, D.R. (2011) 'Leadership Ethics' in A. Bryman, D. Collinson, K. Grint, B Jackson, M Uhl-Bien (eds) *The Sage Handbook of Leadership*. London: Sage.

Ciulla, J.B., Knights, D., Mabey, C. and Tomkins, L. (2018a) Guest Editors' Introduction: Philosophical Contributions to Leadership Ethics. *Business Ethics Quarterly*, 28(1): 1–14.

Ciulla, J.B., Knights, D., Mabey, C. and Tomkins, L. (2018b) Guest Editors' Introduction Philosophical Approaches to Leadership Ethics II: Perspectives on the Self and Responsibility to Others. *Business Ethics Quarterly*, 28(3): 245–50.

Ciulla, J.B., Uhl-Bien, M. and Werhane, P.H. (eds) (2013) *Leadership Ethics*. Los Angeles: Sage.

Cowie, T. (2019) 'A Beacon of Tolerance, Love and Peace': Jacinda Ardern mural to be painted on Brunswick silos. *The Age*. 22rd April 2019. https://www.theage.com.au/national/victoria/a-beacon-of-tolerance-love-and-peace-jacinda-ardern-mural-to-be-painted-on-brunswick-silos-20190422-p51g7t.html?fbclid=IwAR3s8n3bwGRYgDeKecfpXcMjd2h4q7sO6haX9Inn ZMenpmjLXCjoP-z4MAw. Date accessed: June 17th 2019.

Dick, S. (2019) Australia's most trustworthy politicians are all women, research says. *The Age*. 8th May 2019. https://thenewdaily.com.au/news/national/2019/05/08/women-politicians-trustworthy/?fbclid=IwAR0z-Sx0NQFlAv9Nr2SAq6_JfCL7KaWJ3g0d5x5ACy94fwLHQtzS JfLL1_I. Date accessed: September 1st 2019.

Diprose, R. (2002) *Corporeal Generosity: On Giving With Nietzsche, Merleau-Ponty and Levinas,* New York: SUNY.

Due Billing, Y. and Alvesson, M. (2000) Questioning the Notion of Feminine Leadership: A Critical Perspective on the Gender Labelling of Leadership, *Gender, Work and Organization*, 7(3): 144–157.

Eagly, A. H., & Karau, S. J. (2002) Role congruity theory of prejudice toward female leaders. *Psychological Review*, 109, 573–598.

Eagly, A.H. and Heilman, M.E. (2016) Gender and leadership: Introduction to the special issue. The Leadership Quarterly, 27: 349–353.

Edlund, C.J. (1992) Humanizing the Workplace: Incorporating Feminine Leadership, in M.T. Bailey and R.T. Mayer (Eds.) *Public Management in an Interconnected World*, pp. 75–88. Westport: Greenwood Press.

Eubanks, D.L., Brown, A.D. and Ybema, S. (2012) Leadership, Identity, and Ethics, *Journal of Business Ethics*, 107: 1–3.

Fletcher, J.K. (2001) *Disappearing Acts: Gender, Power, and Relational Practice at Work.* Cambridge, Mass: MIT Press.

Fletcher, J.K. (2004) The paradox of postheroic leadership: An essay on gender, power, and transformational change, *The Leadership Quarterly*, 15: 647–661

Fletcher, J. K. (2012) The relational practice of leadership. In M. Uhl-Bien & S. M. Ospina (Eds.), *Advancing relational leadership: A dialogue among perspectives* (pp. 83–106). Charlotte, NC: Information Age Publishing Inc.

Ford, J. (2005) Examining leadership through critical feminist readings'. *Journal of Health Organization and Management.* 19 (3), 236–251.

Ford, J. (2006) Discourses of leadership: gender, identity and contradiction in a UK public sector organization. *Leadership* 2(1): 77–99.

Ford, J. and Harding, N. (2011) The Impossibility the 'True Self' of Authentic Leadership: A Critique through Object Relations Theory. *Leadership*, 7(4): 463–479.

Ford, J., Harding, N. and Learmonth, M. (2008) *Leadership as Identity – Constructions and Deconstructions*. Basingstoke: Palgrave.

Fotaki, M. (2013) No Woman is Like a Man (in Academia): The Masculine Symbolic Order and the Unwanted Female Body. *Organization Studies*, 34(9): 1251–1275.

Fotaki, M., Metcalfe, B.D. and Harding, N. (2014) Writing materiality into management and organization studies through and with Luce Irigaray, *Human Relations*, online first DOI: https://doi.org/10.1177/0018726713517727.

Gabriel, Y. (2015) 'The caring leader – What followers expect of their leaders and why?', *Leadership* 11(3):316–334.

Gilligan, C. (1977) In a Different Voice: Women's Conceptions of Self and of Morality. *Harvard Educational Review*, 47(4): 481–517.

Gilligan, C. (1982) *In a different voice: Psychological theory and women's development.* Cambridge, MA: Harvard University Press.

Heilman, M. E. (2012) Gender stereotypes and workplace bias. *Research in Organizational Behavior,* 32, 113–135.

Helgesen, S. (1995) *The Female Advantage: Women's Ways of Leadership*, Currency/Doubleday, New York.

Höpfl, H. and Matilal, S. (2007) "The lady vanishes": some thoughts on women and leadership. *Journal of Organizational Change Management, 20*(2):198–208.

Irigaray, L. (1985a) *This Sex Which is Not One*. Trans. C. Porter. New York: Cornell University Press.

Irigaray, L. (1985b) *Speculum of the Other Woman*. Trans. G.C. Gill. New York: Cornell University Press.

Irigaray, L. (1993a) *An Ethics of Sexual Difference*. Trans C. Burke and G.C. Gill. London: Athlone.

Irigaray, L. (1993b) *Je, Tu, Nous – Toward a Culture of Difference*. Trans. A. Martin. London: Routledge.

Jaggar, A.M. (1989) 'Feminist Ethics: Some Issues for the Nineties', *Journal of Social Philosophy* 20(1–2):91–107.

Jaggar, A.M. (1992) *Encyclopedia of ethics*, Garland Press: New York.

Jones, R. (2011) *Irigaray*. Cambridge: Polity Press.

Kark, R., Waismel-Manor, R. and Shamir, B. (2012) Does valuing androgyny and femininity lead to a female advantage? The relationship between gender-role, transformational leadership and identification. The Leadership Quarterly, 23: 620–640.

Knights, D. (2016) The Denial of Ethics: Leadership and Masculinity in the Financial Sector. In J. Storey et al (eds) *The Routledge Companion to Leadership*. London: Routledge.

Knights, D. (2015) Binaries need to shatter for bodies to matter: Do disembodied masculinities undermine organizational ethics? *Organization*, 22(2): 200–216.

Knights, D. and O'Leary, M. (2006) Leadership, Ethics and Responsibility to the Other. *Journal of Business Ethics*, 67:125–137.

Korabik, K. (1990) Androgyny and leadership style. *Journal of Business Ethics*, 9(4–5): 283–292.

Krewel, M and Karim, S (2019) Is there a 'feminine' response to terrorism? *The Conversation*, 29th April 2019. https://theconversation.com/is-there-a-feminine-response-to-terrorism-115873. Date accessed: 15th September 2019.

Ladkin, D. (2008) Leading Beautifully: How Mastery, Congruence and Purpose Create the Aesthetic of Embodied Leadership Practice. *The Leadership Quarterly*, 19 (1): 31–41.

Ladkin, D. (2012) Perception, Reversibility, "Flesh": Merleau-Ponty's Phenomenology and Leadership as Embodied Practice. *Integral Leadership Review, January.*

Ladkin, D., and Taylor, S. (2010) Enacting the 'True Self': Towards a Theory of Embodied Authentic Leadership. *Leadership Quarterly*, 21(1): 64–74.

Lämsä, A-M. and Sintonen, T. (2001) A discursive approach to understanding women leaders in working life, *Journal of Business Ethics*, 34: 255–267.

Lloyd, G. (1984) *The man of reason: "Male" and "female" in western philosophy*. London: Methuen & Co. Ltd.

Manhire, T. (2019) Jacinda Ardern: 'Very little of what I have done has been deliberate. It's intuitive'. *The Guardian*. 6th April 2019 https://www.theguardian.com/world/2019/apr/06/jacinda-ardern-intuitive-courage-new-zealand?CMP=fb_gu&fbclid=IwAR0vXw7oFU3gpVaTW_7aVrqXaWx7Mfugv4hA3CQcd5_3cxJiQsgcrErRS3g Date accessed: September 15th 2019.

Martin, P.Y. (2003) "Said and done" versus "saying and doing" gendering practices, practicing gender at work. *Gender & Society, 17*(3): 342–366.

Meriläinen, S, Tienari, J and Valtonen, A (2013) Headhunters and the 'ideal' executive body, *Organization*, 22(1): 3–22

Miller, S. (2016) Trump and Women: A Marxist Critique. *Jacobin*, published 14th October 2016. Available at: https://www.jacobinmag.com/2016/10/donald-trump-women-sexism-clinton-ivanka/?utm_campaign=shareaholic&utm_medium=email_this&utm_source=email. Date accessed: October 25th 2016.

Moore, S. (2019) Jacinda Ardern is showing the world what real leadership is – sympathy, love and integrity. *The Guardian*. 18th March 2019 https://www.theguardian.com/commentisfree/2019/mar/18/jacinda-ardern-is-showing-the-world-what-real-leadership-is-sympathy-love-and-integrity. Date accessed: September 15th 2019.

Munro, I., & Thanem, T. (2018) The ethics of affective leadership: Organizing good encounters without leaders. *Business Ethics Quarterly, 28*(1), 51–69.

Nicholson, J. & Kurucz, E. (2019) Relational Leadership for Sustainability: Building an Ethical Framework from the Moral Theory of 'Ethics of Care'. *Journal of Business Ethics*, 156(1): 25–43.

Noddings, N. (1986) *Caring: A feminine approach to ethics & moral education.* Berkeley: University of California Press.

Painter-Morland, M. & Deslandes, G. (2014) Gender and visionary leading: rethinking 'vision' with Bergson, Deleuze and Guattari. *Organization, 21*(6), 844–866.

Plumwood, V. (1991) Nature, Self, and Gender: Feminism, Environmental Philosophy, and the Critique of Rationalism, *Hypatia*, 6(1):3–27.

Pullen, A. and Rhodes, C. (2010) 'Revelation and Masquerade: Gender, Ethics and The Face', in R. Simpson and P. Lewis (Eds.), *Concealing and Revealing Gender*, pp. 233–248, Basingstoke, Palgrave.

Pullen, A. and Rhodes, C. (2014) Corporeal ethics and the politics of resistance in organizations. *Organization, 21*(6): 782–796.

Pullen, A. and Vachhani, S. (2017) Examining The Politics of Gendered Difference in Feminine Leadership: The Absence of 'Female Masculinity. In S Adapa and A Sheridan (eds) *Inclusive Leadership – Negotiating Gendered Spaces*. Basingstoke: Palgrave Macmillan

Pullen, A. and Vachhani, S. (2013) The Materiality of Leadership, *Leadership*, 9(3):315–319.

Rhodes, C. & Badham, R. (2018) Ethical irony and the relational leader: grappling with the infinity of ethics and the finitude of practice. *Business Ethics Quarterly, 28*(1), 71–98.

Roy, E.A. (2019). Real Leaders do exist: Jacinda Ardern uses solace and steel to guide a broken nation. *The Guardian*. https://www.theguardian.com/world/2019/mar/19/real-leaders-do-exist-jacinda-ardern-uses-solace-and-steel-to-guide-a-broken-nation. Date accessed: September 15th 2019.

Rozmarin, M. (2013) Living Politically: An Irigarayan Notion of Agency as a Way of Life. Hypatia, 28(3): 469–482.

Sinclair, A. (2014) On knees, breasts and being fully human in leadership. In D Ladkin and S Taylor (eds) *The Physicality of Leadership: Gesture, Entanglement, Taboo, Possibilities*. Emerald. P. 177–197

Sinclair, A. (2011) 'Leading with Body', in E Jeanes, D Knights and P Yancey Martin (eds) *Handbook of Gender, Work and Organization*. Chichester: Wiley.

Sinclair, A. (2005a). *Doing Leadership Differently*. Melbourne: Melbourne University Press.

Sinclair, A. (2005b) Body Possibilities in Leadership. *Leadership* 1(4): 387–406.

Stainback, K., Kleiner, S. and Skaggs, S. (2016) Women in Power Undoing or Redoing the Gendered Organization? *Gender & Society, 30*(1): 109–135.

Stempel, C.R, Rigotti, T. and Mohr, G. (2015) Think transformational leadership – Think female? *Leadership*, 11(3):259–280.

The Guardian, (2019) Jacinda Ardern grilled over motherhood plans on first day. https://www.theguardian.com/world/video/2017/aug/02/jacinda-ardern-grilled-over-motherhood-plans-on-first-day-video) *The Guardian*, 2nd August 2017. Date accessed: 15th September 2019.

Tong, R. (1993) *Feminine and Feminist Ethics*. Belmont, CS: Wadsworth.

Tronto J.C. (1993) *Moral boundaries: A political argument for an ethic of care.* New York: Routledge.

Uhl-Bien, M. (2006) Relational Leadership Theory: Exploring the social processes of leadership and organizing. *The Leadership Quarterly*, 17(6): 654–676.

Vachhani, S.J. (2012) The subordination of the feminine?: developing a critical feminist approach to the psychoanalysis of organisations. *Organization Studies*, 33(9): 1237–1255.

Vachhani, S.J. (2014) 'Working The Grey Zones: Feminist Ethics, Organisational Politics'. in: A Pullen and C Rhodes (eds) *The Routledge Companion to Ethics, Politics and Organization*. London: Routledge.

Von Wahl, A. (2011) A 'women's revolution from above'? Female leadership, intersectionality, and public policy under the Merkel government, *German Politics*, 20:3: 392–409.

Wittenberg-Cox, A. (2020) Lessons on Q2 Leadership from Jacinda Ardern & Cinema's Leading Ladies. Linked-In 2020.

Alison Pullen is Professor of Management and Organization Studies at Macquarie University, Australia and Otto Mønsted Visiting Professor at Copenhagen Business School, Department of Organization. Over the course of her career, Alison's work has been concerned with analyzing and intervening in the politics of work as it concerns gender discrimination, identity politics, and organizational injustice. In the course of pursuing this agenda, Alison has become a prolific contributor to leading journals in the fields of organization theory, gender studies, and management studies. Alison is joint Editor-in-Chief of *Gender, Work and Organization*, Associate Editor of *Organization* and sits on the editorial board of *Organization Studies* among other journals.

Sheena Vachhani is a Reader in Work and Organization Studies and Co-director of the Centre for Action Research and Critical Inquiry in Organisations (ARCIO) at the School of Management. Her work centres around ethics, politics and difference in work and organization. She has an interest in how systems and structures of inequality, including those reified by climate change and narratives of sustainability, offer new insights into business, politics and society. She is co-editor (with Emma Bell) of the book series 'Feminist Perspectives on Work and Organization', published by Bristol University Press. She publishes in journals such as: *Organization Studies; Human Relations; Work, Employment and Society; Journal of Business Ethics* and *Organization* amongst others and am Associate Editor and editorial board member for *Gender, Work and Organization*.

An Intersectional Perspective on Gender and Leadership

Robbin Derry

Abstract The concept of intersectionality has emerged as a powerful metaphor for understanding the simultaneous experience of multiple forms of oppression. Although intersectional perspectives have become commonplace in sociology, psychology, and health sciences, among other fields, they are rarely applied in management theory or business ethics. In this chapter I argue that an understanding of intersectionality is critical for developing leadership theories that will provide guidance in establishing greater workplace equity of all kinds. Early studies in this domain describe how intersectional leadership may be enacted and the challenges such leaders face. The willingness to recognize the interaction of oppressions and to engage constructively in systemic critique are essential skills of intersectional leaders.

Keywords Intersectionality · Systemic critique · Workplace inequity · Radical inclusion

Introduction

Intersectionality is the study of how multiple forms of inequality interact and the systemic practices that perpetuate these inequities. The term intersectionality has made its way into the lexicon of social justice research, and the realms of diversity, equity, and inclusion work. While it has become a familiar and widely used concept in a range of social sciences, it is still unfamiliar to many researchers who study business ethics and management theory, with notable exceptions, such as work published in the journal, *Gender, Work and Organization* (e.g. Pullen et al. 2019;

R. Derry (✉)
Dhillon School of Business, University of Lethbridge, Lethbridge, AB, Canada
e-mail: robbin.derry@uleth.ca

M. Painter, P. H. Werhane (eds.), *Leadership, Gender, and Organization*, Issues in Business Ethics 63, https://doi.org/10.1007/978-3-031-24445-2_5

Rodriguez et al. 2016). Intersectionality generally refers to an approach or perspective in which multiple aspects of identity are seen to interact, thereby shaping access to privilege, power, and resources, or the lack thereof. For example, race, class, and ability/disability interact in many societies to determine where people are able to live and raise their families. Gated communities, prestigious condominium buildings, housing projects, suburban neighborhoods and urban neighborhoods are frequently inhabited by populations clearly distinguishable by race and class. In other arenas, gender, ethnicity, and religion interact to constrain or enable what political role a person may engage in. In many work environments, the roles of gender and race have been contested for centuries, as people around the world have struggled to decide whether to legislate equal access to jobs and workplace protections, and how best to achieve employment equity for all persons.

When health care researchers talk about working from an intersectional perspective, it implies that they are striving to look at unique experiences at the intersections of multiple axes of oppression (Collins and Bilge 2016). The questions they are asking are not exemplified by: "how are women's surgery experiences different than men's surgery experiences?", but more like: "how are income level, race, gender, and disability related to surgical outcomes?" As scholars have acknowledged the interactive effects of these categories, there has been an increased recognition that none of these operate independently in our lives. Therefore, our analysis of social challenges, recognition of marginalization, and proposals of solutions must go beyond single axis assessment and policies, e.g. those simply addressing gender, racial, class, or disability status as stand-alone considerations.

In addition to looking carefully at experience at the intersections of identity categories, intersectional thinking also pushes us to ask deeper systemic questions. What are the benefits of the systems that perpetuate the unequal distribution of rights and privilege? To whom do those benefits accrue? What needs to be questioned and challenged in order to disrupt the patterns of inequality? What beliefs and entitlements enable the continued entrenchment of inequities?

This chapter provides a brief background on the history and emergence of intersectional thinking. It is a concept that is frequently discussed in reference to race, class, and gender analyses, although the meaning of gender is too often narrowly described. I advocate for a critical understanding and embrace of gender as complex and socially constructed. The application of intersectionality to management and organization theory has lagged behind equity work in many other social sciences (Jean-Marie et al. 2009; Liu 2019; Richardson and Loubier 2008). I offer here strong encouragement to attend to the essential components of intersectional thinking in future contributions to much needed work in gender, leadership and ethics.

Emergence

The first formal descriptions of the concept of intersectionality came from critical legal theorist Kimberle Crenshaw (Crenshaw 1989, 1991). She used the term 'metaphorically' (Collins 2019) to describe the discrimination faced by Black women working at General Motors in 1976. In an economic downturn, Black women were being laid off first, but General Motors claimed that they were not discriminating on the basis of race, evidenced by the fact that they were not laying off Black men, and they were not discriminating on the basis of gender, evidenced by the continued employment of white women. A court decision ruled that the Black women could not successfully claim they were experiencing a unique combination of race and gender discrimination, because that would be essentially double dipping – trying to benefit twice from anti-discrimination laws. Crenshaw pointed out that by this judicial decision, Black women were excluded from legal protection due to their lives being at the intersection of the axes of race and gender.

> The court's refusal in *DeGraffenreid* to acknowledge that Black women encounter combined race and sex discrimination implies that the boundaries of sex and race discrimination doctrine are defined respectively by white women's and Black men's experiences. Under this view, Black women are protected only to the extent that their experiences coincide with those of either of the two groups. Where their experiences are distinct, Black women can expect little protection as long as approaches...which completely obscure problems of intersectionality, prevail. (Crenshaw 1989: 142–143)

Crenshaw's argument made plain the reality that social policies, even those that are ostensibly designed to address inequities in society, frequently overlook the reality and complexity of individual lives. The term "overlook" frames it in benign terms. For many people experiencing continuing harm and barriers to basic rights and security, being thus "overlooked" translates into intentional and long-lasting systemic violence. By limiting our definitions and understanding of oppression to that which is experienced by the largest, loudest, most visible, or most (relatively) privileged groups, we are often denying the experience of others, and therefore our proposed solutions do not acknowledge or meet their needs.

Over the ensuing three decades, the concept of intersectionality has become widely applied by scholars around the world. A few examples serve here to demonstrate the broad range of intersectionality's relevance for research. Sociologist Mary Pattillo's celebrated work on race and class in the settling of Chicago neighborhoods (2007) challenges facile assumptions of racial homogeneity by describing the process of Black gentrification. Lifestyle, income, and education, all play into class distinctions and shape the spatial politics of neighborhoods, determining who is able to reside in which communities. Attempts to convey this social history simply on the basis of race OR class would be inadequate to portray the dynamic interaction of these various factors.

A further example highlights the lack of intersectionality in many quantitative research methods. Lisa Bowleg critiqued her own positivist research approach in two studies of Black lesbians that overlooked the interactions of sexual orientation, gender, and race (Bowleg 2008), pointing out that treating these identity aspects as distinct and additive implied that they could be isolated and ranked. Quantitative methods with assumptions of linearity and uncorrelated factors "…do not reflect the real-world complexities of intersections of race, sex/gender and sexual orientation. In short, we need new analytical tools and strategies…", Bowleg argued (2008: 320). Scrutinizing her own research practices, Bowleg demonstrated the limited ability of so-called objective research methods to accurately portray the lives and experiences of her subjects.

A recent collection of writings searching for more inclusive approaches to gender and activism, *Can We All Be Feminists?*, provides descriptions of young feminists' experiences in the UK, South Asia, and Africa, confronting cultural norms and exclusions related to European colonialism, disability, skin color, class, and immigration (Eric-Udorie 2018). For many of these young people, their early encounters with feminist messages were full of promise, but also full of rejection. It seemed that white European and American women could be emancipated, but these women of color could not, raising questions of who counted as women and who was represented by the most visible feminist movement. These essays ask: why are the enormous burdens of immigration not central to feminism? (2018: 193); why are cosmetic companies not held accountable for promoting the imperial standard of fair skin to "solve Blackness"? (2018: 188); why are the deep links between misogyny, homophobia, and transphobia not acknowledged? (2018: 160). The writers and images of second wave feminism were predominantly white women, writing about the needs and interests of white women to the exclusion of South Asian and African women, immigrant women, transgender women, disabled women, and women in poverty. Intersectional feminism confronts these exclusions and demands a broader vision and strategy to speak up for equity for all, not just for a narrow segment of women.

These examples show the broad reach of intersectional thinking in contemporary research and activism. However, it is important to acknowledge that Crenshaw gave a name to an experience that was already familiar to women of color, many of whom had written and spoken out over centuries about the mix of oppressions they faced as women and as racialized minorities (Hull et al. 1982; Carbado 2013; Moraga and Anzaldua 2015; Hancock 2016).

Roots of Intersectionality

African American women whose words and writings are preserved from the nineteenth century spoke out about the double penalty of gender and race. Sojourner Truth, an enslaved woman freed in New York in 1827, did not have the opportunity to learn to read or write, but she was a passionate feminist-abolitionist. Her speech, "Ain't I a Woman", delivered in 1851 at the women's rights convention in Akron, Ohio, is a revered record, challenging the idea that Black women were not deserving of the rights and respect of white women (Guy-Sheftal 1995: 36).

As Black women gained opportunities for education in the North, and during reconstruction in the South, many took up teaching careers and journalism. Mary Church Terrell was educated at Oberlin College, served as the founding president of the National Association of Colored Women in 1896, and travelled throughout Europe, lecturing on the remarkable achievements of Black women, and confronting myths about Black women in that era (Guy-Sheftal 1995). Ida Wells-Barnett founded newspapers, reporting the horrific scale and details of lynching's. When her publishing offices were burned in Memphis, she moved north, teaching, writing and continuing activism for women's suffrage. Despite her long commitments and public visibility, she was relegated by white women leaders to the back of suffrage marches in Chicago in the 1890s (Silkey 2015).

Anna Julia Cooper, Claudia Jones, Pauli Murray, Angela Davis, Michelle Wallace, bell hooks, and Audre Lorde were among dozens of women who documented the unique injustices and oppression in the lives of Black women in America (Guy-Sheftal 1995). Through the 1970s and '80s, the voices of these women gained visibility and began to lay a claim to feminism and recognition in the civil rights movement, calling out their exclusion by white women as well as by Black men. The Combahee River Collective, an activist group of Black feminists in Boston, issued a now famous manifesto in 1974:

> ...we are actively committed to struggling against racial, sexual, heterosexual, and class oppression and see as our particular task the development of integrated analysis and practice based upon the fact that the major systems of oppression are interlocking. The synthesis of these oppressions creates the conditions of our lives. As black women we see black feminism as the logical political movement to combat the manifold and simultaneous oppressions that all women of color face. (in Guy-Sheftal 1995: 232)

Voices and writings of women in Asia, Europe, Africa, and South America contributed to this groundswell of recognition that class, ethnicity, sexuality, gender, and other identity factors were not just additive, but interactive contributions to these 'simultaneous oppressions'. Crenshaw's articulation of the fact of intersecting oppressions was powerful in its reach and impact, but it was not a new idea.

While white feminists in the U.S. marched in the early 1900s for the vote and protested in the 1960s and '70s for access to jobs and equal salaries, their women's organizations were frequently cool to women of color and lesbians. As with so many social justice or freedom movements, "equal rights for women" turned out to be "equal rights for people like us" where "us" meant the people with the most power and voice within that particular rights movement.

In these key moments of feminist history, the experience of white, educated, middle class women was one of increasing empowerment, while the experiences of Black women, other women of color, girls and women in poor or working class families, the experiences of women with little access to education, and women with disabilities were continued marginalization and many more hurdles to gain access to jobs, universities, or economic security (Guy-Sheftal 1995; Hooks 1981; Moraga and Anzaldua 2015). Oppression is a collection of experiences along many axes: racial, sexual, economic class, social caste, religion, and others (Collins and Bilge 2016). Intersectional theory points out that privilege shifts between the intersections of the matrix of these oppressions because each of us experiences the simultaneous impact of who we are in these categories. If we are unconscious of how our individual identities affect our experience, it is likely that our privilege buffers us from that awareness. Those people who suffer higher levels of oppression or marginalization are not unaware of how their identity affects their opportunities and place in society.

Need for Systemic Scrutiny

Beyond recognizing the unequal distributions of privilege and advantage in society, intersectional theory demands that we look carefully at the institutional structures, patterns and practices that perpetuate these inequities (Cho et al. 2013; Collins and Bilge 2016; Dill and Kohlman 2011). The increasing calls to investigate systemic racism demonstrate the need for finding solutions that go beyond simply diversifying the workforce. It is not enough to notice that in North America and Europe positions of authority are most often filled with white people, or that more people of color are targets of police violence, or that women's complaints of harassment and assault often go uninvestigated. Consider more broadly which women, in which neighborhoods and at what income levels are more quickly protected, and whose fears and complaints are 'overlooked' or dismissed. Singer Tracy Chapman's line comes to mind: "The police always come late, if they come at all."

In order to change these destructive patterns, we need to understand the factors that contribute to such outcomes and why these practices and cultures are maintained. Collins and Bilge (2016) identify four interconnected "domains of power" (2016: 7): interpersonal, disciplinary, cultural, and structural. They use these domains to analyze the role of power and the inequities of privilege in particular cases and organizations. This kind of analysis is an essential component of intersectionality as critical inquiry. But, as many of the examples above demonstrate, intersectionality is about critical praxis as well. Scholarly research and reflection are valuable for developing the conceptual framework, but progress toward social justice needs to occur in practice, not on paper. Collins and Bilge (2016: 47) suggest that the groundwork for more widespread understanding and application of an intersectional approach must be laid in undergraduate and graduate education, so that it becomes part of the road map for pursuing a field of professional study and action.

While critical inquiry is central to intersectionality as a social theory (Collins 2019), I believe it is both a major barrier to intersectionality's further integration into organizational theory and also a significant window of opportunity for management scholars. Although many management educators and business ethics professors claim to be concerned about social justice and perhaps even about systemic racism, they are hesitant to explore questions about who actually benefits from systemic racism and the ongoing injustices created by our current economic and social structures. Incentive systems, hiring practices, admissions criteria, performance assessments, and definitions of 'merit', are potential sites of institutional bias and discrimination where scrutiny is warranted. An unwillingness to engage in careful scrutiny blocks a deeper understanding of the methods of racism, sexism, and other forms of harmful prejudice. Victor Ray points out that organizational theorists generally presume bureaucratic structures to be race-neutral, overlooking the racializing practices that make whiteness a credential and legitimating the unequal distribution of resources (Ray 2019). Equity initiatives in business and in organizational scholarship are on the rise, but they still largely embrace a diversity and inclusion paradigm, emphasizing an additive approach, rather than a critical one. We will not be able to dismantle oppression without recognizing the incentives for its continuation, and the tools of its success.

Yasmeen Abu-Laban and Christina Gabriel (2011) persuasively argue that as the discourse of globalization took over labor market equity debates, the initiatives to manage diversity in ways that created bottom line benefits "effectively displace[d] issues of systemic discrimination" (2011: 158). The diversity, equity and inclusion movement has provided corporations and governments with tools to improve their image and indeed, to diversify their workforces, but it has not embraced questions of redress or structural harm. In order to find solutions to systemic injustice, researchers must first be willing to ask questions about who is invested in maintaining things as they are and why. Whose interest is being served? What will it take to serve the interest of equality rather than the interest of the already privileged? Many scholars have argued that capitalism, in its increasingly dominant neoliberal form, prioritizing private wealth accumulation over widespread social benefits, is fundamentally at odds with goals of equity and equality (Hancock 2016; Mohanty 2003). Further arguments highlight the enduring links between global consumerism and economic coloniality, the suppression of sub-altern voices, and "the failures of democratic institutions in an increasingly marketized world" (Faria and Hemais 2020).

The application of an intersectional perspective to management and organizational theory is just beginning, perhaps due to its critique of and challenge to institutional structures. Seeking to identify and alter the systems that exploit and harm the least advantaged has been outside the mainstream agenda of many business schools. Exceptions to this generalization can be found outside of the US, in Europe and the British Commonwealth, where broader approaches to capitalism are less threatening to the hegemony of business school curricula (e.g. Andrews and Grant 2020; Jones et al. 2005). Protests against harmful social impacts of business, whether environmental, economic, or equity issues, have largely been dealt with ad hoc, by researchers as well as by administrators. Intersectionality asks for more: the recognition that some people are systematically harmed by our institutions: educational, for profit businesses, not for profit organizations, judicial, governance, electoral, recreational, entertainment, familial, and religious institutions, to name a few. All of these have been seen at times to create systematically harmful impacts, while engaged in their routine activities. An intersectional lens for organizational leadership would help to identify the sources and disparate effects of this harm and to pursue broad structural solutions.

Beyond the Gender Binary

In working towards greater gender equity, the debates around transgender identities cause us to revisit the questions that have been raised in various waves of the women's movement. Who is included and who is excluded in the ongoing struggle for equality of opportunity and equal rights? The goal of 'freedom and justice for all' rings hollow if your 'all' only includes the people who are most like yourself, in gender, race, sexual orientation, class, religion, nationality, or physical/mental ability.

Research studies in management and organizational literature that purport to be about gender, are nearly always about women, and more precisely, cisgender women (often shortened to cis women) – women whose personal gender identity aligns with the sex and gender they were assigned at birth (e.g. Fotaki and Harding 2018; Grosser et al. 2016; Werhane and Painter-Morland 2011). Occasionally 'gender' in research refers to a study of women compared to men, who are generally assumed to be cis women and cis men. For example, a study of gender and leadership might predictably be a study of the traits of women leaders compared to the traits of men leaders (e.g. Madsen 2017). The authors do not mention that as far as they know, they studied exclusively cis women and cis men. Further, they would likely have assumed that they were studying traits that are innate to women and men, without wondering or asking about gender nonconforming, nonbinary, or transgender identification. Contemporary assumptions about a gender binary create a hegemonic understanding of gender identity that marginalizes gender nonconformity.

It is hard to find research in management literature about the experience of transgender people in the workplace, let alone as leaders (Jones 2020; Kollen 2016). Research and teaching about queerness are now widely discussed topics in the academic world: the history of homosexual liberation as part of human rights struggles; the portrayal of queer relationships in theater and film; drag competitions in popular media; and gay literature, to name a few. While 'queer' has recently become an umbrella term for a range of gender identifications and sexual orientations, many people, even within the gay and lesbian community, see transgender people as outliers. Transmen, transwomen, and non-binary individuals, who are slightly more visible than in previous decades, are the current 'not like us' group, in popular culture, as well as in much of academic research.

Celia Harquail cogently points out (2020) that the politics of patriarchy assert that biology determines gender, and then mandates and socializes gender performances, essentializing bodies and roles. The evolution and necessity of these gendered roles for industrial and modern society is thoroughly documented (Federici 2014; de Beauvoir 1949/2011). Gender is seen by many as a distinction of power, a political category, and a social indicator more than a representation of individual identity (Lindemann 2006).

> Therefore, if we understand that 'woman' is a political category and not an objective biological category, it helps us see that there are several criteria – some biological, some relational, some social, some even arbitrary – that are used to sort humans into the political class of 'women' to be subordinated by men. (Harquail 2020: 38).

An increasing number of people are publicly acknowledging that they do not belong in nor do they accept the gender category that was assigned to them at birth. Further, some may not identify with either of the two predominant and presumed gender categories society offers. As young and old individuals come out as transgender or gender nonconforming, they are finding communities and solidarity as well as resistance, disbelief, and backlash (Rajunov and Duane 2019; Shultz 2015).

Intersectional feminism is an opportunity to recognize and include those who have been 'othered' for any reason. Gender work is no longer just about increasing the numbers of women in an industry or workplace. Nor is it only about including and supporting women of color, although this is essential. It is also about problematizing understandings of gender as binary, which serve to perpetuate constrained social, emotional, physical, and political roles. It is important to ask again and to recognize the harms of limited answers: who counts as a woman and who counts as a man? For what purpose does gendering, and more specifically binary gendering matter?

The debates about who belongs in which bathrooms, who can play on which sports teams, who can participate in "women only" events, who is eligible and welcome in women's shelters - these are quandaries that have challenged the rules of schools, sports leagues, service providers, and resulted in antagonistic camps arguing for and against broadening our understanding of gender.

Broader questions now facing feminism and gender studies include these: who gets to define what is oppressive and what is emancipatory? Who is being served and who is excluded by the current struggles for equality and equity? Even within the gender and racial justice movements it is useful to apply a reflective intersectional lens and ask what bias and harms are entrenched in our own longstanding assumptions and practices. We must look beyond the second wave focus on more women in the workforce and equal pay, although these have not yet been widely achieved. The feminism our society needs now is a commitment to work against all hegemonic normativities and systems that create inequality. This vision of transversal alliances in feminism reaches back to the Combahee River Collective (Pullen et al. 2019) and also forward to next wave of equality movements that strive for radical inclusion and collaboration (Eric-Udorie 2018).

Leadership Wisdom: Whose Is Valued?

In the study of gender and leadership we can use intersectional thinking to engage in critical inquiry about the kinds of research questions that dominate this field, and consider what questions are being overlooked or neglected. What do popular questions about gender and leadership tell us about the distribution of privilege and power? What do they tell us about our assumptions about gender? Whose work on leadership is most visible and what perspectives are we missing?

Last year, in preparing to teach an undergraduate course on Gender, Race, and Leadership, I visited the large, newly reconstructed public library in the major city where I live, in Western Canada. I aimed to find inspiring books on leadership that I could share with my students. Identifying the stacks on leadership, I began perusing the shelves. Within a few minutes I started to scan more quickly, getting skeptical, and then angry. Ninety-nine percent of the books I saw were authored by men: white men, describing the experience of other white men who they admired. Nearly all of their examples were men who were military leaders, men who were politicians, men who were successful CEOs, or wealthy consultants; men who provided aspirational goals for the authors and their readers. Every so often, Oprah or Indra Nooyi, former chairperson, and CEO of PepsiCo, would be celebrated. But they were clearly token representatives in these books, conveniently providing checkmarks in two diversity boxes. I found one shelf of books by women, clearly segmented off into a "women's leadership" section. Presumably, these books were identified as guidance specifically for women who might need help navigating what was still assumed to be a men's world of management and organizations.

Interestingly, another distinction seemed to be that men could write and publish books with titles such as *Do Nothing! How to Stop Overmanaging and Become a Great Leader* (Murnighan 2012), while women-authored books included these titles: *How to be Successful without Hurting Men's Feelings* (Cooper 2018)[1]; *The Velvet Hammer* (Allison 2015); *Leading from the Front: No Excuse Leadership Tactics for Women* (Morgan and Lynch 2017). Leadership books targeting women often reinforce the stereotypes that women are not natural leaders, that they must fight their way into organizational roles, while making sure to ease the pain of their existence for the men who struggle with equity. Whereas leadership books by and about white men can boast a cover of one man in military uniform, or a business suit, and that seems to be sufficient to justify a claim to wisdom and authority, even if their advice is basically to do nothing.

It was an instructive experience. Who gets published, what books are well reviewed and purchased by libraries, who is cited and quoted in such books, who is celebrated as a worthy leader, all these reflect and contribute to widespread perceptions of what makes a good leader. This collection of books conveyed a strong message that model leaders are cis white men. From the representation on these shelves, this same demographic appears to be the most knowledgeable about leadership. These leaders don't have disabilities, nor do they face racial barriers; they are not transgender. Apparently, they do not feel the need to include any of these social justice considerations in their leadership wisdom, perhaps because these men, as authors or exemplars, never had to face such challenges in their own lives.

Nicole Ferry and Eric Guthey documented this phenomenon in their study of leadership literature (2020), which tracks the rise of the 'women's leadership' discourse. They note that the counterpoint of women's leadership is not men's leadership, but just leadership – presented as a gender-neutral concept. But there are obvious and stark contrasts, seen in the topics covered, e.g. maintaining work-family balance is always addressed in women's leadership, but rarely in the 'regular'

---

[1] A spoof, by the very talented comedienne Sarah Cooper

leadership books; and also in the advice given, e.g. the need to seek mentoring vs. the value of being a mentor. Being a woman is clearly treated as a situation that needs to be fixed in order to achieve strong leadership roles and respect from followers.

Early Work on Intersectional Leadership

The development of theories of intersectional leadership is in its infancy. The potential for intersectionality to contribute to a greater understanding of effective leadership is both significant and understudied (Ospina and Foldy 2009). One area of intersectional insight is in the evaluation of leaders. Using a case study in Australia, Liu (2019) pointed out that the concept of servant leadership when applied to Asian leaders was reduced to 'just the servant', as the subordinates tended to evaluate the qualities associated with the roles of immigrant Asians as servants, while discounting their leadership skills and achievements. The dominant perceived feature described by subordinates was the frame of ethnicity and race, in which gender performance and management ability were assessed in comparison to hegemonic leadership styles of white heterosexual cis men.

Intersectional theory has been further applied to examine subordinates' perception of leader behavior, accomplishments, and efficacy, based on their leaders' gender, race, context, and professional experience. In a study designed to compare the leadership styles of a male and a female university president, subordinates identified differences attributed to educational background, prior business and leadership experience, cultural values, and their vision of the future as more salient than gender (Richardson and Loubier 2008). This explicitly intersectional study gathered observations from a cross section of faculty, about their perceptions of the interactions of gender with leadership style, inclusiveness, authoritarianism, financial competence, prior leadership roles, and strategic vision. By looking at the interaction of these identity factors, the authors were able to move beyond stereotypes and assumptions about gender differences, recognizing the other factors that influenced subordinates' comparative assessments.

The leadership experiences of people of color are frequently absent in leadership literature (Ospina and Foldy 2009; Sanchez-Hucles and Davis 2010; Moorosi et al. 2018). Several key gaps in knowledge result from this neglected inclusion. There is little discussion of how race-ethnicity shapes engagement with power, governance, and decision making. The experiences of people of color are often seen as a "special case rather than as a potential source of theorizing" (Ospina and Foldy 2009: 877). Studying the leadership of Oprah, or Martin Luther King, or Nelson Mandela recognizes and celebrates these individuals, but such research does not acknowledge the many rich contexts, nor the complexity of leadership work done by Black people, Indigenous people, and many other people of color in the Americas, in Europe, Africa, or globally.

Leadership researchers could remedy this exclusion by explicitly collecting multiple aspects of leaders' identity information and including this as part of their analysis (Sanchez-Hucles and Davis 2010). This inclusion may also push researchers to be more conscious and intentional about diversity within their research design variables; further, it may serve to move leadership research beyond a study of the "master identity" (2010: 178).

A stream of intersectional research has emerged over recent decades studying the experience of women leaders in education. Moorosi et al. (2018) collected life history interview data from three Black women school principals, working in England, South Africa, and the United States. Each participant discussed the gendered & racialized barriers they had navigated in their specific workplaces, while also coming to terms with the historical impact of apartheid, colonialism, and slavery on their students, their communities, and themselves. Moorosi et al. advocated for more honest dialogue about racism within the schools, pointing out that the standards-based school leadership preparation in each of these countries does not address the effects of gender and race on educational leaders or on the dynamics between principals, teachers, the students and their families. While intersectionality is a valuable tool for researchers to see the interaction of identity categories in how subordinates assess leaders (Richardson and Loubier 2008), it is described as a survival tool for Black women, striving to build their leadership strengths, while also recognizing the hurdles they face in higher education (Davis and Maldonado 2015).

In a qualitative study of 130 British women of different racial and ethnic backgrounds, in senior management positions, gender and ethnicity were salient in how participants defined the challenges they faced in enacting leadership (Showunmi et al. 2016). Not surprisingly, white women described gender and class barriers, while Black, Asian, and other racialized women described barriers linked to their ethnic and religious identities. An intersectional lens in this study enabled examination of the interaction of gender, ethnicity, and religion in the leadership experiences of these women.

In 1993, Christine Williams theorized the 'glass escalator' to describe situations in which men received advantages for leadership in so-called women's professions (Williams 1993). Her model was widely acclaimed and frequently cited. Twenty years later, Williams published a subsequent critique of her own work for its lack of intersectional perspective. This critique created a valuable example of intersectional leadership within the academic environment: a well-known researcher publicly acknowledged her own failures to theorize the interactions of race, sexuality, and class. Williams identified groups of people she had overlooked and thus excluded in her theorizing. In her later article, she argued for the design of a more inclusive model, despite the academic and pedagogical popularity of the glass escalator, suggesting that "...new concepts are needed to understand workplace gender inequality in the 21st century" (Williams 2013: 609). In advocating for intersectional perspectives in knowledge construction, Williams admitted that while she recognized in her original research that her theory did not apply to gay men or racial/ethnic minority men, she simply described them as 'different' and therefore exceptions outside the 'normal' model of heterosexual white males. She had not bothered to question how the social privilege for those at the center was produced by the same institutional forces that marginalized the non-white, and/or gay men.

These examples demonstrate the value of intersectional approaches in making research more inclusive, and in recognizing that simultaneous oppressions affect how leaders are seen and assessed. An understanding of intersectionality may also enable leaders to gain awareness of the ways their leadership approach has been devalued. With this, they may better develop a leadership style building on their own experience, rather than following the examples established by the norms and expectations of hegemonic white male leadership.

However, these applications of intersectional theory have mainly limited themselves to drawing on the identity feature of intersectionality – recognizing the interaction of multiple categories of identification in their analysis (e.g. also considering race-ethnicity, class, or sexuality along with gender), but failing to engage in critical scrutiny of the systems that perpetuate the hazards for people at these intersections. While these are a step beyond simplistic attributions of male and female leadership styles, they are a weak form of intersectional analysis (Dill and Kohlman 2011).

In the integration of intersectionality into leadership studies, there is still a need to engage in systemic scrutiny. What would intersectional leadership look like? How would it be enacted? What steps could be taken to identify and dismantle the institutional structures that perpetuate the injustices of power, unequal opportunities, barriers to full participation, and the myth of meritocracy? These questions need to be fully explored and addressed.

Enacting Intersectional Leadership

There are a number of tools available to look carefully at systemic components. One of these is Life Cycle Assessment (LCA), used extensively by organizations to evaluate their supply chains, operations, distribution, and service systems for sustainability assessments (Dauvergne and Lister 2013). By looking at each stage of their sourcing, production, labor management, and delivery of goods or services, businesses can identify more precisely where they are contributing to harmful environmental impacts. This kind of mindful scrutiny of the value chain components of business operations, with an eye for honest recognition of harmful exclusions and social impacts, could interrupt the 'way business has always been done' and find opportunities to create anti-racist and anti-sexist practices that are inclusive of the needs and interests of those who have been 'othered'. An important aspect of LCA is that it must go beyond a simple sustainability audit. It is not enough to simply keep track of environmental impacts over time.

Similarly, it is not enough to just keep track of how many women or how many people of color are hired or promoted. Systemic change requires more than celebrating representation numbers. Systemic change requires identifying problems, dismantling the sources of those problems, and finding new solutions. This is true for reducing environmental impact and it is true for reducing systemic racism. True intersectional leadership would include such steps as: building collaborative processes with those that have been silenced or excluded, reimagining training messages, re-defining merit, and co-creating goals and the pathways to achieve those goals. Life Cycle Assessment, utilized as a tool of intersectional leadership would look carefully at each stage of a business's operation to ask who is valued and who is not valued? Who is heard and who is not? In sustainability work, companies may look at their stages of growing, harvesting, manufacturing, delivery, and waste reduction or recycling to identify their overlooked impacts. In intersectional work, companies could similarly assess each stage of their value chain to identify impacts on overlooked neighborhoods, communities, identity groups, or people at unrecognized intersections in the matrix of oppression.

Intersectionality as a critical social theory teaches us to be attentive to those who have been overlooked, erased, silenced. It also tells us to look at the systems perpetuating those exclusions. How can we identify who benefits and who is harmed by the current distribution of privilege and power? A popular instrument for identifying which stakeholders 'count' most and therefore are most salient for managerial decision making was developed by Mitchell, Agle, and Wood, using the criteria of power, urgency, and legitimacy (1997). This could become a useful tool for recognizing who *doesn't* count and why. It describes whose concerns don't matter to managers, or when used prescriptively, whose concerns *shouldn't* matter to managers, the most powerful decision-makers and resource controllers in the corporate scenario. This instrument has been widely used in strategy textbooks to instruct business students about who matters and who they should prioritize as managers – who should get the most resources or the most immediate attention.

However, for our purposes, this indicator of 'salience' could also serve to reveal who doesn't matter, who clearly lacks in legitimacy, power, and urgency. As several researchers have argued, this is a model that effectively asserts that managers implicitly have the authority to determine which stakeholders have power and legitimacy (Banerjee 2000). In doing so, it reifies economic colonialism. It does not challenge implicit bias, it does not enable the voices of outsiders, or marginalized stakeholders (Derry 2012). I do not advocate the use of this instrument for instructing managers who to attend to, but it may be useful for identifying who is most readily overlooked, silenced, and excluded.

In the Mitchell et al. model, those stakeholders who are identified with urgency and power, but not legitimacy are classified as dangerous. As Banerjee (2000) points out, those dangerous stakeholders would include civil rights activists, labor activists, and radical environmentalists. Classifying groups who are demanding equal rights, or attention to urgent causes that have not been recognized as legitimate by those in power, as dangerous, is a political tool used to further silence and discredit marginalized people. The violent police response to Black Lives Matter protestors communicated this classification of 'dangerous' to vigilante inclined citizens, creating the false belief that peaceful protestors deserved brutal treatment; that in giving voice to the violence they experienced on a daily basis, these protestors became a threat to other members of society rather being recognized as expressing a legitimate plea for equality and security. This model of stakeholder identification and salience centers corporate or established power. It provides a means to assess the power of claimants and to distance and dismiss those who are irritants and whose urgent claims can readily be ignored (Mitchell et al. 1997: 875).

In contrast, intersectional leadership would teach us to decenter the voices of power and of privilege to better hear and understand the voices of those who have been oppressed. To address systemic racism under intersectional leadership, we need to decenter white voices. White people will not be able to adequately recognize and address our structures of racist practices by strategizing with other white people. People who benefit by the existing systems of privilege are buffered by these same systems from experiencing their disparate harmful impacts. To decenter white, male, cis, or able-bodied perspectives, those who are currently in the center of the circles of power must be willing to step aside and rethink the 'we' at the center of the stakeholder map. As Audre Lorde famously said, "The master's tools will never dismantle the master's house" (Lorde 1979/2015: 95).

Intersectional leadership asks us to listen more broadly, not to dismiss as illegitimate those whose voices can be represented as dangerous. We need to learn to listen to the experiences of those who have been harmed by oppressive practices of our many institutions, not ignore those marginalized in hopes of maintaining a false stability. The stakeholder attributes of power, legitimacy and urgency are contingent, not inherent attributes. To whom they are assigned is entirely dependent on relative context, shifting political pressures, and managerial beliefs about what constitutes such terms.

The intersections of social class, race, and even gender have proven to be relevant to the risks and impact of the Covid-19 pandemic (Oppel et al. 2020). In addition to the disparities of who became infected, who could afford to safely self-isolate, and who recovered more quickly, the attributed legitimacy of health experts as salient stakeholders was also a significant factor in how resources were distributed, and therefore a factor in who received needed care, or went to work with adequate protection. In an environment where medical researchers were respected as authoritative, a demand by the U.S. Center for Disease Control for the rapid production and distribution of N-95 masks to health care workers would have been considered urgent, legitimate, and powerful. However, in an environment where the scientists were dismissed as less knowledgeable and authoritative than political leaders, such a request was set aside as neither urgent, nor powerful, and its legitimacy was questionable as the CDC was overruled by members of the Trump administration narrowly focused on the economy. Those voicing the realities of viral transmission and risks to public health were deemed less urgent, powerful, or legitimate by the men in the central circle of power (Gibney 2020). The resulting devastation to the most vulnerable communities: seniors, people with pre-existing conditions, people with lower incomes, people of color in the U.S., people with precarious employment, is still being calculated. Nine months after the first documented Covid-19 infection in the US, the spread of the virus exceeds that of any other country. When stakeholder attributes of urgency, legitimacy, and power, are assigned by fiat of governors or managers who hold the greatest economic or political power, we should be careful not to confuse such clout with either factual or moral accuracy. Intersectional leadership may be employed by those with economic and political responsibilities, if they are guided by a deep and honest commitment to human rights for all people, not merely for those whose salience is justified by political or economic ends.

Pullen, Rhodes, McEwen and Liu (2019) propose a transformative approach to intersectional leadership for diversity by engagement with the radical politics demonstrated by the Combahee River Collective and the leaders of the Idle No More movement. These activist feminist groups, separated by 50 years and a national border, relied on similar processes. Each built on transversal alliances among women from differing social and racial positions, who shared the experience of being silenced and sidelined by social, political, and intellectual leaders. Both groups used their alliances to push for a more radical democracy where they would be recognized as legitimate stakeholders and the urgency of their concerns would be heard. Pullen et al. argue that transversal alliances formed in the interest of radical democracy could serve to create powerful movements for progressive change within organizations. Such movements would be a significant departure from the current methods of diversity and inclusion, which reinforce the interests of the corporation rather than challenging it at the essential center.

> …the focus on managing diversity provides a way to redirect attention away from the political activism and praxis that would question and contest dominant institutional structures…[thus] pre-existing political, commercial, and managerial agendas remain intact, albeit for the addition of some politically correct window dressing which may, or may not, foster organizational social responsibility. (Pullen et al. 2019)

The intersectional approach to leadership proposed by Pullen et al. demonstrates a commitment to systemic critique and organizational transformation rather than simply striving for greater inclusivity. Perhaps further lessons can be learned about intersectional leadership from the grassroots initiatives of the Combahee River Collective and Idle No More. As evidenced by the books on the library shelves on leadership, we rarely turn to the experience and strategies of the disenfranchised to instruct us, but when we are searching to understand persistent structural oppressions, the insights of those who have experienced them directly may offer the greatest wisdom.

Conclusion

The concept of intersectionality demonstrates that social advantages and disadvantages are not distributed between simple dichotomous categories. Who has privilege and who faces disadvantages in labor markets, educational institutions, interactions with police, and the interactions of everyday life, are not comprehensively described by a single axis analysis of gender, race, age, class, or ability. Instead, these and other identity factors, combine to create a divergent range of hurdles, access, open and closed doors due to social biases about who is capable, who is meritorious, and the implicit worth of different peoples. These have become embedded in our applied theories and resulting systems, even in the systems for strengthening diversity and inclusion. If we are serious about eliminating systemic racism, sexism, and other forms of structural injustice, we would be wise to decenter the perspectives of privilege and power as presumptions for leadership. Assessing organizational practices with an intersectional lens would enable leaders to recognize institutionally created disparate harms and to build structures that value equity, critical self-scrutiny, and the voices of the disempowered.

Acknowledgements I gratefully acknowledge the research assistance of Winfred Gachigi, as well as her constructive insights and helpful critique.

References

Abu-Laban, Y. & Gabriel, C. (2011). *Selling diversity: Immigration, multiculturalism, employment equity, and globalization.* Toronto: University of Toronto Press.

Allison, E. (2015). *The velvet hammer: PowHERful leadership lessons for women who don't golf.* Vancouver: Positive Presentations Plus.

Andrews, N. & Grant, J. A. (Eds.) (2020). *Corporate social responsibility and Canada's role in Africa's extractive sectors.* Toronto: University of Toronto Press.

Banerjee, S. B. (2000). Whose land is it anyway? National interest, indigenous stakeholders, and colonial discourses: The case of the Jabiluka uranium mine. *Organization & Environment, 13*(1): 3–38.

Bowleg, L. (2008). When Black + woman + lesbian =/ Black lesbian woman: The methodological challenges of qualitative and quantitative intersectionality research. *Sex Roles, 59*: 312–325.

Carbado, D. (2013). Colorblind intersectionality. *Signs: Journal of Women in Culture and Society, 38*(4): 811–845.

Cho, S.K., Crenshaw, K. & McCall, L. (2013). Toward a field of intersectionality studies: Theory, applications, and praxis. *Signs: Journal of Women in Culture and Society, 38*(4): 785–810.

Collins, P.H. (2019). *Intersectionality as critical social theory.* Durham, NC: Duke University Press.

Collins, P. H. & Bilge, S. (2016). *Intersectionality.* Malden, MA: Polity Press.

Cooper, S. (2018). *How to be successful without hurting men's feelings: Non-threatening leadership strategies for women.* Kansas City, MO: Andrew McMeel Publishing.

Crenshaw, K. W. (1989). Demarginalizing the intersection of race and sex: A Black feminist critique of anti-discrimination doctrine, feminist theory and anti-racist politics. *The University of Chicago Legal Forum,* 1989, article 8.

Crenshaw, K. W. (1991). Mapping the margins: Intersectionality, identity politics, and violence against women of color. *Stanford Law Review, 43*(6): 1241–1299.

Dauvergne, P. & Lister, J. (2013). *Eco-business: A big brand takeover of sustainability.* Cambridge, MA: MIT Press.

Davis, D. R. & Maldonado, C. (2015). Shattering the glass ceiling: The leadership development of African American women in higher education. *Advancing Women in Leadership, 35*: 48–64.

De Beauvoir, S. (2011). The Second Sex. (C. Borde & S. Malovany-Chevallier, Trans.). Vintage Books. (Original work published 1949).

Derry, R. (2012). Reclaiming marginalized stakeholders. *Journal of Business Ethics, 111*: 253–264.

Dill, B. T. & Kohlman, M. H. (2011). Intersectionality: A transformative paradigm in feminist theory and social justice. In S. N. Hesse-Biber (Ed.), *The handbook of feminist research: Theory and praxis* (2nd ed.) (pp. 154–174). Thousand Oaks, CA: Sage Publications.

Eric-Udorie, J. (Ed.). (2018). *Can we all be feminists?* New York: Penguin Random House.

Faria, A. & Hemais, M. (2020). Transmodernizing management historiographies of consumerism for the majority. *Journal of Business Ethics*. https://doi-org.ezproxy.uleth.ca/10.1007/s10551-020-04528-y

Federici, S. (2014). *Caliban and the witch: Women, the body and primitive accumulation.* Brooklyn, NY: Autonomedia.

Ferry, N. & Guthey, E. (2020). There is no *Lean In* for men. Presented at the Academy of Management Annual Conference.

Fotaki, M. & Harding, N. (2018). *Gender and the organization: Women at work in the 21st century.* London: Routledge.

Gibney, A. (Director). (2020). *Totally Under Control* [Film]. Yellow Bear Films.

Grosser, K., McCarthy, L., & Kilgour, M. A. (Eds.). (2016). *Gender equality and responsible business: Expanding CSR horizons.* Sheffield, UK: Greenleaf Publishing.

Guy-Sheftal, B. (Ed.) (1995). *Words of fire: An anthology of African-American feminist thought.* New York: The New Press.

Hancock, A. (2016). *Intersectionality: An intellectual history.* New York: Oxford University Press.

Harquail, C.V. (2020). *Feminism: A key idea for business and society.* New York: Routledge.

Hooks, B. (1981). *Ain't I a woman: Black women and feminism.* Boston: South End Press.

Hull, G. T., Scott, P. B., & Smith, B. (Eds.). (1982). *All the women are white, all the Blacks are men, but some of us are brave.* New York: The Feminist Press.

Jean-Marie, G., Williams, V. A., & Sherman, S. L. (2009). Black women's leadership experiences: Examining the intersectionality of race and gender. *Advances in Developing Human Resources, 11*(5): 562–581.

Jones, C., Parker, M. & ten Bos, R. (2005). *For Business Ethics.* London: Routledge.

Jones, S. E. 2020. Negotiating transgender identity at work: A movement to theorize a transgender standpoint epistemology. *Management Communication Quarterly, 34*(2): 251–278.

Kollen, T. (Ed.). (2016). *Sexual orientation and transgender issues in organizations: Global perspectives on LGBT workforce diversity.* New York: Springer.

Lindemann, H. (2006). *An invitation to feminist ethics.* New York: McGraw-Hill.

Liu, H. (2019). Just the servant: An intersectional critique of servant leadership. *Journal of Business Ethics, 156*: 1099–1112.

Lorde, A. (1979). The master's tools will never dismantle the master's house. In Moraga, C. & Anzaldua, G. (Eds.) *This bridge called my back* (4th ed.) (pp. 94–97). Albany, NY: State University of New York.

Madsen, S. (Ed.). (2017). *Handbook of research on gender and leadership.* Northampton, MA: Edward Elgar.

Mitchell, R. K., Agle, B. R. & Wood, D. J. (1997). Toward a theory of stakeholder identification and salience: Defining the principle of who and what really counts. *Academy of Management Review, 22*(4): 853–886.

Mohanty, C. T. (2003). *Feminism without borders: Decolonizing theory, practicing solidarity.* Durham, NC: Duke University Press.

Moorosi, P., Fuller, K. & Reilly, E. (2018). Leadership and intersectionality: Constructions of successful leadership among Black women school principals in three different contexts. *Management in Education, 32*(4): 152–159.

Moraga, C. & Anzaldua, G. (Eds.). (2015). *This bridge called my back* (4th Ed.). Albany, NY: State University of New York.

Morgan, A. & Lynch, C. (2017). *Leading from the front: No excuse leadership tactics for women.* New York: McGraw-Hill.

Murnighan, J. K. (2012). *Do nothing! How to stop overmanaging and become a great leader.* New York: Portfolio/Penguin.

Oppel, R. A., Gebeloff, R., Lai, K. K. R., Wright, W. & Smith, M. (2020). The fullest look yet at the racial inequity of Coronavirus. *New York Times*, July 5.

Ospina, S. & Foldy, E. (2009). A critical review of race and ethnicity in the leadership literature: Surfacing context, power and the collective dimensions of leadership. *The Leadership Quarterly, 20:* 876–896.

Pattillo, M. (2007). *Black on the block: The politics of race and class in the city.* Chicago: University of Chicago Press.

Pullen, A., Rhodes, C., McEwen, C. & Liu, H. (2019). Radical politics, intersectionality and leadership for diversity in organizations. *Management Decision.* https://doi.org/10.1108/MD-02-2019-0287

Rajunov, M. & Duane, S. (Eds.). (2019). *Nonbinary: Memoirs of gender and identity.* New York: Columbia University Press.

Ray, V. (2019). A theory of racialized organizations. *American Sociological Review, 84*(1): 26–53.

Richardson, A. & Loubier, C. (2008). Intersectionality and leadership. *International Journal of Leadership Studies, 3*(2): 142–161.

Rodriguez, J. K., Holvino, E., Fletcher, J. K., & Nkomo, S. (2016). Theory and praxis of intersectionality in work and organisations: Where do we go from here? *Gender, Work and Organization, 23*(3): 201–222.

Sanchez-Hucles, J. V. & Davis, D. D. (2010) Women and women of color in leadership: Complexity, identity, and intersectionality. *American Psychologist 65*(3): 171.

Showunmi, V., Atewologun, D. & Bebbington, D. (2016). Ethnic, gender and class intersections in British women's leadership experiences. *Educational Management Administration & Leadership.* 44(6): 917–935.

Shultz, J. W. (2015). *Trans/Portraits: Voices from transgender communities.* Hanover, NH: Dartmouth College Press.

Silkey, S. L. (2015). *Black woman reformer: Ida B Wells, lynching & transatlantic activism.* Athens, GA: University of Georgia Press.

Williams, C. L. (1993). The glass escalator: Hidden advantages for men in the "female" professions. *Social Problems, 39*: 253–267.

Williams, C. L. (2013). The glass escalator, revisited: Gender inequality in neoliberal times. *Gender and Society, 27*(5): 609–629.

Werhane, P. & Painter-Morland, M. (Eds.). (2011). *Leadership, Gender and Organization.* New York: Springer.

Robbin Derry is an associate professor in strategy at the Dhillon School of Business at the University of Lethbridge in Alberta, Canada. Her current research builds a bridge between Intersectional theory and Business Ethics, exploring topics related to social justice and critical assessments of organizational practices. Robbin has published on gender and moral reasoning, sexual harassment in the workplace, tobacco industry strategies, improving sustainability through complexity thinking, and challenging the marginalization of stakeholders. Robbin earned her BA at Dartmouth College, her MBA and PhD at the University of Massachusetts, Amherst. Prior to joining the University of Lethbridge, Robbin served on faculties at Clarkson University, the Wharton School of the University of Pennsylvania, Appalachian State University, and the Kellogg School of Northwestern University.

Gender, Business Ethics, and Corporate Social Responsibility: Assessing and Refocusing a Conversation

Kate Grosser, Jeremy Moon, and Julie A. Nelson

Abstract This article reviews a conversation between business ethicists and feminist scholars begun in the early 1990s and traces the development of that conversation in relation to feminist theory. A bibliographic analysis of the business ethics (BE) and corporate social responsibility (CSR) literatures over a twenty-five-year period elucidates the degree to which gender has been a salient concern, the methodologies adopted, and the ways in which gender has been analyzed (by geography, issue type, and theoretical perspective). Identifying significant limitations to the incorporation of feminist theory in these literatures, we discuss how feminist scholarship relating to behaviour (through psychology and related fields), organizations (through feminist organization studies), and economics (through feminist economics) could be integrated. We suggest that a better integration of feminist theory would strengthen BE/CSR research, and point to new research directions and agendas arising from our approach.

Keywords Business ethics · CSR · Feminism · Gender

Introduction

A conversation between business ethicists and feminist scholars was begun in the early 1990s. How has this conversation developed since then, and how have ensuing debates related to—or failed to relate to—developments in feminist theory? This

K. Grosser (✉)
RMIT University, Melbourne, VIC, Australia
e-mail: kate.grosser@rmit.edu.au

J. Moon
Copenhagen Business School, Frederiksberg, Denmark

J. A. Nelson
University of Massachusetts Boston, Boston, MA, USA

© The Author(s), under exclusive license to Springer Nature   103
Switzerland AG 2023
M. Painter, P. H. Werhane (eds.), *Leadership, Gender, and Organization*, Issues
in Business Ethics 63, https://doi.org/10.1007/978-3-031-24445-2_6

article seeks to answer these questions in regard to the business ethics (BE) and corporate social responsibility (CSR) literatures. Through it we advance the illumination and integration of feminist theory in BE/CSR scholarship (Arnold 2016). The article proceeds as follows: We begin by defining our terms with respect to gender, feminism, business ethics, and CSR, in section I. In section II we outline the origins of the intersection between BE/CSR and feminism. Then in Section III, by means of a bibliographic analysis of the BE/CSR literature, we map the development of conversations about gender since the early 1990s. In particular, we map the salience of gender as a concern, the methodologies adopted, and the ways in which gender has been brought into focus in BE/CSR literature, and point to limitations in the way that feminist theory has been used in the field. We concentrate on the core concerns of feminist scholarship, namely gender relations and gender equality, as these focal points provide the base from which feminist theory contributes to any field. In section IV we draw upon three specific kinds of feminist scholarship, relating to behavior (through work in psychology and related fields), organizations (through feminist organization studies), and economics (through feminist economics). We suggest ways in which each of these theoretical perspectives can be better integrated to advance BE/CSR scholarship, and how such integration might inform new research directions and agendas. Section V discusses wider implications for the field of BE/CSR, notes the limitations of our analysis, and identifies further research opportunities.

Defining Terms

Gender and feminism are highly contested concepts, making the relationship between the two particularly complex, variable, and contextual. The term "gender" is most commonly used to refer not only to the socially constructed norms, values, roles, and identities accorded to human beings on the basis of their (assumed) sex, but also to the opportunities and threats associated with these. While bodies and identities play significant roles in the construction of gender, institutional and social practices, and power, play important—though often less recognized—roles as well. Indeed, gender is an integral part of all organizational, social, political, and economic practices and processes: Gender is relational and is performed and renegotiated through everyday interactions (Acker 2004; Butler 2004; West and Zimmerman 1987). Moreover, the intersection of gender with other systems of social inequality and difference, including race, class, and sexuality, are increasingly shown by feminists to be fundamental to the way in which contemporary organizations and societies function and are sustained (Acker 2004; Calás and Smircich 2006; Gherardi 2010). Gender also plays a role at the level of cognition and epistemology, as gendered associations—for example, cultural associations of the sphere of business and the project of science with masculinity (as contrasted to the relatively feminine associations made with the home and the humanities)—can shape the ways we perceive our social world, and the techniques we choose to analyze it (Harding 1986; Keller 1985).

"Feminism is about the social transformation of gender relations" (Butler 2004: 204), and about the quest for justice through reducing gender inequality by advancing the diverse interests of women (Walby 2011), as well as achieving equity through structural change. The study of women continues to be important in gender studies, however, increasingly the literature also addresses "men as men" (Collinson and Hearn 1994: 2), exploring how different kinds of masculinity are constructed, normalized, and maintained in organizations and societies. The cognitive and epistemological dimension of gender means that feminism also questions masculine biases in how things (e.g., business, ethics, responsibility) are defined, thought-about, framed, and investigated. In addressing gender relations and equality, feminism engages with the concept of power: "Feminist theory is a critique of the status quo and therefore *always political*," however, "the degree of critique and the nature of the politics vary" leading to agendas that range from fixing individuals and "reforming organizations; to transforming organizations *and* society; to transforming our prior understanding of what constitutes knowledge" in the field (Calás and Smircich 2006: 286, emphasis in the original).

Turning to the other voice in the conversation, we see business ethics and corporate social responsibility as related and overlapping, if reflecting somewhat different assumptions and purposes. Whilst the ethical principles and challenges, and peculiar responsibilities, of business are a long-standing societal concerns evidenced from ancient philosophies of East and West (Moon et al. 2017) to social movements against slavery (Knudsen and Moon 2017: chapter 5), their status as part of the management and business academic curriculum is rather more recent. However, they have emerged as distinctive but overlapping fields with professional associations and journals.

Business ethics is concerned with the identification and evaluation of the right thing—and all too frequently, perhaps, the wrong thing—to do in business. To some extent this entails the application of more general ethical concepts and principles to business situations (e.g. Kantianism, utilitarianism). But it has also generated its own ethical frameworks such as stakeholder theory (Donaldson and Preston 1995; Freeman et al. 2004) and integrated social contract theory (Donaldson and Dunfee 1994, 1995). The field of business ethics can apply to individuals and organizations within or engaged with business.

Corporate social responsibility has had a more recent status as an academic field. It has been variously defined. Some definitions limit the responsibility to actions independent of regulation or market interest. Davis defined CSR as "the firm's consideration of, and response to, issues beyond the narrow economic, technical, and legal requirements of the firm" (1973: 313), and McGuire contends that "the idea of social responsibilities supposes that the corporation has not only economic and legal obligations but also certain responsibilities to society which extend beyond these obligations" (1963: 144). Other definitions presume that CSR should be integral to the whole business: "CSR refers to the integration of an enterprises' social, environmental, ethical, and philanthropic responsibilities towards society into its operations, processes, and core business strategy in cooperation with relevant stake-holders" (Rasche et al. 2017: 6). Yet others frame an inductive definition such as the formative author Bowen who defined CSR as "the obligations of businessmen to pursue those policies, to make those decisions, or to follow those lines of action which are desirable in terms of the objectives and values of our society" (1953: 6).[1] More recently, anticipating the significance of context, Matten and Moon defined it as "policies and practices of corporations that reflect business responsibility for some of the wider societal good. Yet the precise manifestation and direction of the responsibility lie at the discretion of the corporation" (2008: 405). These more inductive definitions enable account to be taken for the roles that corporations now play in societal governance, and their associated responsibilities, both at a domestic (Moon 2002) and at an international level (Scherer and Palazzo 2011).

Many scholars regard CSR as being heavily influenced by business ethics (e.g., Garriga and Melé 2004) and Carroll's fourfold typology includes ethical responsi-bility (referring principally to business conduct) as one of its elements, along with economic, legal, and philanthropic responsibility (1979). However, CSR can also be distinguished from business ethics in several ways. First, its focus is upon the responsibilities of the corporation by virtue of its distinctive ownership and gover-nance structures, although CSR has also broadened to include concern with the responsibilities of other forms of business organizations, whilst the responsibilities of individuals remain more in the ambit of business ethics. Secondly, this concern with the responsibilities of corporations is not solely motivated by concerns of the right thing to do but may also be motivated by the strategic interests of corporations (e.g. McWilliams and Siegel 2001) and by the relationships of business responsibil-ity to wider systems of governance by which corporations are regulated and in which corporations also assume governance roles (e.g. Knudsen and Moon 2017; Matten and Crane 2005; Scherer et al. 2016). As noted, however, for present pur-poses, unless otherwise specified, we consider business ethics and CSR as a single voice in the conversation with feminism, hence BE/CSR.

Origins of the Intersection of Business Ethics/CSR and Feminism

A conversation between business ethics and feminism was begun in earnest in 1990 at a conference held at the University of Virginia's Darden School, as part of the Ruffin Series in Business Ethics. This brought scholars from women's studies together with those from BE to explore the significance of gender in the ethical management of business organizations (the field of CSR barely existed at that time).

---

[1] Bowen's (1953) book was entitled *Social Responsibilities of the Businessman*. Carroll (1999: 269) notes that "there apparently were no businesswomen during this period, or at least they were not acknowledged in formal writing" and adds that "it is interesting to note that the phrase 'busi-nessmen' was still being used [in the CSR literature] even in the mid-1960s" (p. 269).

Four overarching feminist themes emerged from this conference (Larson and Freeman 1997), broadly reflecting developments in feminist organization studies at that time (Acker 1990). First, contributors pointed out that "corporations are presented as socially constructed organizations that assume, in their practice and ideology, that men are the standard of measurement" (Larson and Freeman 1997: 4). Workers are conceived of as having few caring responsibilities that encroach on the workplace (e.g., Acker 1990). Acknowledging this reality, it was claimed, helps make visible "cognitive and gendered biases" (Larson and Freeman 1997: 4) that limit our under- standing of business institutions, and leads us to question assumptions that, for example, organizations are merit based. Second, contributors highlighted "the power of feminist critiques to bring gender into focus as a central organizing principle of economic life" (p. 4), along with race and class. For example, Martin and Knopoff (1997: 49) note the dependence of organizations on women's unpaid labour in the home to support and reproduce workers, and argue that, although invisible to many, as a result "bureaucracies will continue to rationalize, legitimate, and perpetuate gender inequality—whether they intend to or not—until that time when men carry a full share of home and dependent-care responsibilities."

A third theme problematized the role of "unexamined frames," as in dominant views that are reified and naturalized, and that order our thinking and "govern us," such that "alternative ways of thinking" about business "are silenced" (Larson and Freeman 1997: 5). The feminist theorists at the conference attempted to bring such frames into focus by viewing business institutions from the periphery, adopting the point of view of those who are frequently left out of the centre, and in particular through the standpoint of women (p. 5). Ferguson (1997) develops this argument with reference to the variety of different perspectives from the periphery that can inform the debate. She argues that while "liberal feminism's reforms often enhance the opportunities available to those classes and colors of women who can claim access to traditional institutions" (1997: 82), the perspectives of women who operate further out on the periphery of organizations are important in enabling us to see, and alter, "the structures that produce global gender inequities" (1997: 83).

Finally, in making gender visible, a fourth theme in the conversation explored how "business ethics is portrayed as feminized in its subordinate position relative to the more central and dominant areas of business management (e.g. finance and accounting). Yet, at the same time business ethics is seen as in collusion with management ideology" creating "business ethics arguments that will find acceptance within traditional business school environments" (Larson and Freeman 1997: 5).

It is clear that inviting "outsiders" from the periphery, in this case women's studies scholars, to contribute to the discourse on business ethics led to a number of creatively disruptive interjections and challenges, particularly from poststructuralist feminist perspectives. Yet as the dialogue progressed, it appears that the focus of debate narrowed, and, it may be argued, in some cases derailed (below we discuss non-feminist research on gender and BE/CSR).

The immediately ensuing conversation, much of which took place in BEQ, focused in particular on the ethics of care (Burton and Dunn 1996; Derry 1996;

Dobson and White 1995; Liedtka 1996; Wicks 1996; Wicks et al. 1994). Gilligan (1982), a psychologist, had previously identified "different voices" in moral reasoning, demonstrating that both an ethic of justice, based on principles, and an ethic of care, based on relationships, often inform moral judgments. Using psychoanalytical theories popular at the time, Gilligan associated justice ethics with masculine-associated notions of individuality and independence, and care ethics with a more relational understanding of the world more commonly associated with women's upbringing. Business ethicists adopted the concepts of care and relation- ality to advance a discussion about the moral grounding of stakeholder theory, and to reinterpret this theoretical perspective with a focus on the relationships that constitute the corporation (Burton and Dunn 1996; Dobson and White 1995; Wicks 1996; Wicks et al. 1994). Some of these works (including Derry 1996; Wicks et al. 1994) were careful to point out that both men and women use the voices of care and justice, and that both voices contribute importantly to business ethics. Many scholars, however, identified care ethics as a distinctly women's perspective, or even as *the* feminist perspective. Studies hypothesizing and emphasizing differences between men and women in the handling of ethical dilemmas in business began to proliferate (White 1992).

The limitations of conflating care ethics with feminist ethics were explored, early on, by Wicks et al. (1994) and Derry (1996), and more recently by Borgerson (2007) and others. Gilligan's ethic of care and related works represent only a small, if significant, segment of scholarship which attends to gender issues. In particular, the BE/CSR literature on gender following the Darden conference rather sidelined feminist concerns relating to gender relations, and gender equality. Derry (1996: 106) pointed to the fact that there has been less discussion of feminist ethics of justice which "explicitly attempts to solve the inequities of discrimination rather than finding in women's skills a fortuitous tool to economic efficiency." Borgerson (2007) asserts the need to ensure that the gender equality concerns of feminist theory remain on the business ethics agenda. This point is raised also by Kelan (2008: 427) who, taking her lead from organisational theory and business ethics research which analyses representations of gender in management texts, argues that "there is little space within this web of discourses for an awareness of the continued inequalities experienced by women in relation to men to be voiced." Not only does the emphasis on a "feminine" care ethics tend to sideline concerns with gender inequality, it may even exacerbate it by reinforcing hackneyed stereotypes and limiting the types of business roles available to women and men (Derry 1996: 105). Stereotyping based on presumed gender differences can cause people to be pigeonholed by, for example, giving women only "caring" jobs and men only "risk-taking" ones. This approach ignores individual capabilities, usually to the further detriment of women as a group. Thus, in revisiting the conversation we are interested in how the core concerns of gender relations and inequality in feminist theory can be better advanced in BE, and non-feminist approaches that reinforce stereotypes avoided (see below). Finally, we note Borgerson's (2007) appraisal of the relationship between feminist and business ethics, which called for greater attention not only to relationships, and responsibility, but also to a focus on experience, agency, and power.

The origins of the conversation between gender studies and CSR is more recent than the conversation between gender studies and BE, since the emergence of CSR as a significant field is itself more recent. CSR expanded as a field of research only around the turn of the twenty-first century. This built on earlier but rather isolated studies from the early 1950s (e.g. Bowen 1953, often regarded as the foundational work; Carroll 1979; Davis 1960; Preston and Post 1975). Lockett, Moon, and Visser (2006) trace CSR's somewhat iterative growth between 1992 and 2002, and judge its academic salience to be roughly comparable to that of entrepreneurship by 2002. If anything, the field has further burgeoned since then, with leading journals of management and of business publishing special issues, review articles, and single papers extending empirical and theoretical knowledge on the topic.

It is in this context that scholarship on gender and CSR emerged. Much of the latter has focused on gender equality per se, exploring this issue not just with reference to corporate boards (e.g. Bear et al. 2010), but also in the workplace (e.g., Grosser and Moon 2005; Larrieta-Rubın de Celis et al. 2015), in corporate supply chains(e.g. Barrientos et al. 2003; Prieto-Carron 2008), with reference to the community impacts of corporations, in the mining sector for example (Keenan et al. 2014; Lauwo 2016), and through corporate run microfinance and entrepreneurship programs targeted at women (e.g. Dolan et al. 2012; Johnstone-Louis 2017; McCarthy 2017; Tornhill 2016). In addition, attention has been drawn to gender equality in stakeholder relations (Grosser 2009), and in CSR as a process of governance (Grosser 2016). Attention to gender equality in CSR research is driven in part by CSR practice, where numerous initiatives now focus exclusively on this issue, as, for example, the Women's Empowerment Principles[2] (developed as a partnership between the United Nations Global Compact and UN Women). Many other initiatives attempt to integrate consideration of gender equality within wider CSR programs of work, such as the Global Reporting Initiative's[3] gender reporting criteria (informed by a gender working group), and work on gender equality in the Ethical Trading Initiative.[4] Having stimulated the interest of feminist researchers from a number of disciplines, it is increasingly argued that feminist theory is needed for analysis of such initiatives, although such theory is not often explicitly referenced in this body of work (Grosser and Moon 2017). Next we trace the development of the intersection of BE/CSR and feminism on the basis of a bibliographic analysis of the literature.

---

[2] http://www.weprinciples.org/

[3] https://www.globalreporting.org/Pages/default.aspx. For GRI gender reporting see also https://www.globalreporting.org/search/Pages/default.aspx?k=Gender

[4] http://www.ethicaltrade.org/

Development of the Intersection of Business Ethics/CSR and Feminism

This section explores the way in which gender has been treated in the BE/CSR business and management academic literature over a quarter of a century period between 1991 and 2015. Drawing upon quantitative and qualitative bibliographic analysis (see the Appendix for methodological details and descriptive findings),[5] we explore (1) the salience of gender in BE/CSR research; (2) methodologies used therein; and (3) the focus of gender in terms of geographical region and issue type. We then explore gender perspectives as represented in the BE/CSR literature. This part of our analysis finds extensive reference to gender differences, in ethical decision making for example, coupled with a significant lack of research on gender equality and gender relations. Thus, the core concerns of feminist theory, which were reflected in the conversation that began at the Darden School in 1990 (discussed above), have subsequently become obscured, thereby limiting the integration of feminist theory in BE/CSR.

Salience

A key question of interest is whether gender has been a conspicuous research topic, or whether as it been a "non-issue." We investigate, first, the changing salience of the topic of gender in the BE/CSR literature. This enables us to answer the basic questions about how much attention it has received (in proportionate and absolute terms), whether this salience has been uniform over twenty-five years, and, if not, how its salience has varied.

We find that over the twenty-five-year period gender-related papers accounted for 4.8% of the articles published in the BE/CSR in management literature (See Table 1).

It is hard to know whether this is intrinsically a high or low score. However, when compared to other bibliographical analyses of BE/CSR over the same time period, reference to gender issues, including the study of women in all parts of the world, is scarcer than reference to other categories of interest/constituencies, as for example Asian topics (6%) (Kim and Moon 2015: 355). The proportion of gender papers published has fluctuated somewhat, and declined in the last five years of our analysis. It is unclear what significance to attach to this. It should be noted, first, that

---

[5] Our bibliographic analysis follows that used to investigate the salience, methodologies, and focus of the CSR literature overall (Lockett et al. 2006), and of the CSR in Asia literature (Kim and Moon 2015). Our approach differs from the bibliographic analysis by Johnstone-Louis (2017) – Appendix A – mainly by surveying a narrower set of high-quality journals and including all papers that focused on issues of gender, whether or not they had a specifically feminist analytical focus.

Table 1 Gender Articles as a Proportion of All Articles Published in BE/CSR Journals, 1991–2015

Period	% of Articles
P1 1991–1995	4.6% (38)
P2 1996–2000	7.2% (83)
P3 2001–2005	5.9% (84)
P4 2006–2010	5.3% (110)
P5 2011–2015	3.4% (126)
Total	4.8% (441)

Note. Raw numbers in parentheses

the BE/CSR agendas have expanded dramatically over the last decade (represented by P4 and P5 in Table 1) and it is possible that newer issues (e.g. those raised by sustainability more broadly, climate change in particular, shared value, global governance) have crowded out the gender issues.[6] Secondly, despite the proportionate fall of gender's salience in significance in BE/CSR management journals, the actual number of papers published has continued to rise (from 38 in P1 to 126 in P5), suggesting that the issue has not been sidelined in the context of BE/CSR research.

Methodology

We next examine the methodologies deployed in the analysis of gender in the BE/CSR literature. It is important to know, in as much as gender is a feature of the literature, what the nature of the knowledge has been therein.

We distinguish articles according to the empirical or theoretical methodologies that have been deployed in the analysis of gender, and divide these respectively into quantitative and qualitative; and normative and non-normative (e.g. using conceptual or positive analysis) methodologies. We find that the literature has been dominated by empirical research (85% of papers over the whole twenty-five-year period), with this trend rising in the three most recent periods of our analysis (Table 2). The majority of these empirical articles use quantitative methodologies (85%). This focus on quantitative research appears to reflect the fact that the majority of papers on gender in the BE/CSR journals investigate gender differences in ethical orientations or behaviour (see below), relating to decision making for example, where quantitative methods are particularly applicable.

The remaining 15% of the papers in this twenty-five-year period can be classified as reflecting theoretical research. Whereas there was a relative balance of non-normative and normative theoretical papers in the first five-year period of our

---

[6] However, in this context, research suggests that companies may prefer to focus on environmental issues in the context of CSR rather than more marginal, as they see it, gender issues (Grosser 2016).

Table 2 Methodological Focus of Gender Articles on BE/CSR Journals, 1991–2015

Period	Empirical			Theoretical		
	Total	Quantitative	Qualitative	Total	Non-Normative	Normative
P1 1991–1995	68% (26)	65% (17)	35% (9)	32% (12)	58% (7)	42% (5)
P2 1996–2000	71% (59)	88% (52)	12% (7)	29% (24)	71% (17)	29% (7)
P3 2001–2005	88% (74)	86% (64)	14% (10)	12% (10)	80% (8)	20% (2)
P4 2006–2010	95% (104)	85% (88)	15% (16)	5% (6)	67% (4)	33% (2)
P5 2011–2015	89% (112)	86% (96)	14% (16)	11% (14)	79% (11)	21% (3)
Total	85% (375)	85% (317)	15% (58)	15% (66)	71% (47)	29% (19)

Note. Raw numbers in parentheses

analysis, subsequently non-normative papers (usually conceptual) have tended to dominate. This might be considered broadly consistent with a Kuhnian scientific paradigm in which theorising initially dominates a new field (Kuhn 1962) and subsequently this is complemented by increasing empirical research, initially qualitative to frame knowledge and then quantitative to substantiate it (see Lockett et al. 2006, for an extended discussion of the CSR literature and Kuhnian conceptions of science). A principal concern with empirical matters might be considered the prerogative of business and management journals, given the significance of substantive issues for the field. However, feminist researchers point to the need to unearth the experience of women and others on the margins of society in order to reframe the key questions in our field and in this respect, further qualitative studies need to be encouraged. Overall, conclusions as to the nature of knowledge at the BE/CSR interface appear premature given the rather narrow issue focus of the gender related BE/CSR literature (see below).

Moreover, when feminist theory is utilised in the gender papers in the BE/CSR field, we note that these draw predominantly upon feminist ethics of care (we will have more to say about this below). While other feminist theoretical work is referenced, its potential is rarely explored in depth.

Geography and Issue Type

Exploring gender analysis in terms of geographical region and issue type is important because it enables us to contextualize the analysis of gender in this literature. We can then ascertain whether, for example, gender is addressed in its various international contexts, or whether it is considered particularly in some regions (e.g. the global North) and neglected in others (e.g. the global South). Secondly, we can assess whether the gender analysis is concerned with social, environmental, ethical,

Table 3 Geographical Focus of Gender Articles in BE/CSR Journals, 1991–201

Period	Europe, North America, Australasia	Asia	Africa	South/Central America	No focus	Multi-region focus
P1 1991–1995	26	0	0	0	12	0
P2 1996–2000	54	6	0	0	23	1
P3 2001–2005	62	9	0	0	14	2
P4 2006–2010	77	17	2	3	16	3
P5 2011–2015	78	20	2	1	17	12
Total	297 (65%)	52 (11%)	4 (1%)	4 (1%)	82 (18%)	18 (4%)

Note. The figures presented do not represent a count of papers; they represent a count of the references to the regions (see Appendix). Percentages in the "total" row indicate total proportions of references to geographical regions. No focus = articles with no clear geographical focus. Multi-region focus = articles with focus on two or more areas.

or stakeholder issues.[7] Thirdly, we also investigate the perspective on gender that the papers take, distinguishing those papers whose principal focus is on the issue of gender equality and its significance as a normative standard or objective, as compared to those whose principal focus is on gender difference and its significance for explaining business behavior, for example.

Regarding geographical region, findings reveal a domination of focus on Europe, North America, and Australasia with some growth in those papers that focus on Asia (Table 3). This is consistent with the wider CSR findings (Kim and Moon 2015). However, Africa and South/Central America barely figure in the BE/CSR and gender literature. Feminist postcolonial and transnational theory, as applied in the gender and management journals, would suggest that this finding reflects the focus of the majority of Western scholarship, including feminist scholarship, which often fails to explore the voice of the "other" (e.g., Grosser and Moon 2017). Finally, there has also been a steady representation of papers with attention to no geographical focus.

Following Kim and Moon (2015), we investigate the issue focus of papers by distinguishing among social, environmental, ethical, and stakeholder issues. The papers on gender in the BE/CSR journals overwhelmingly focus on the issue of ethics (63% of our total sample of papers – see Table 4). This reflects the pre- dominance of ethics in the literature. However, in the last five years of our analysis, this

---

[7] Whilst it might be objected that all gender issues are "social," our point is to follow a distinction in the BE/CSR literature between those issues which are about social context, causes, and consequences from the more particular ethical (i.e., the right thing), the environmental (i.e. concerning ecological considerations), and the stakeholder (i.e., regarding a particular relationship with companies) perspectives on gender (see Lockett et al. 2006: 117–118)

Table 4 Issue Focus of Gender Articles in BE/CSR Journals, 1991–2015

Period	Social	Environmental	Ethics	Stakeholders
P1 1991–1995	13% (5)	3% (1)	79% (30)	5% (2)
P2 1996–2000	16% (13)	3% (3)	81% (67)	0% (0)
P3 2001–2005	34% (29)	0% (0)	61% (51)	5% (4)
P4 2006–2010	24% (26)	0% (0)	70% (77)	6% (7)
P5 2011–2015	43% (54)	2% (3)	41% (52)	14% (17)
Total	28% (127)	2% (7)	63% (277)	7% (30)

Note. Raw numbers in parentheses

orientation changed quite dramatically with the ethics-focused papers falling off to about 40% of the total. This decline was compensated for with greater focus on CSR as opposed to business ethics, as the gender and CSR literature began to emerge, with greater attention to social and stakeholder issues.

Gender Perspectives

We now turn our attention to gender perspectives within BE/CSR literature, and especially how the core concerns of feminist theory, namely gender relations and gender equality, are addressed. Here we find that these concerns are the focus of a relatively small minority of papers: over the twenty-five-year period studied, just 21% of papers in our sample had a primary focus on gender relations and gender equality. It thus appears that the integration of feminist theory in this field of scholarship remains quite limited.

In contrast, 48% of our sample treat gender as a variable, focusing in particular on gender differences in ethical decision making. These studies address responses to ethical dilemmas by, for example, university students, business managers, CEOs, accountants, and consumers, categorized by gender. Others discuss gender differences in attitudes towards CSR issues, such as environmental issues. Beyond this group of papers (and not included in this 48%), others address the impact that gender diversity has on ethical decision making in business organizations. What this analysis tells us is that the field of gender and BE/CSR has been, until recently, heavily focused on a very narrow set of research questions about gender differences.

In sum, we find a growing number of papers addressing gender issues in the BE/CSR literature, but that proportionately this focus is declining in the key journals in our field. We have witnessed an increase in empirical over theoretical papers, and in particular those using quantitative methodologies. The theoretical articles in our sample are mostly non-normative. We identify significant space for future research on gender and BE/CSR in developing country contexts in particular. While the overwhelming focus in the gender papers in BE/CSR journals has been on ethics, we are currently seeing a rise in such research addressing social and stakeholder issues, as the field expands from business ethics to a greater focus on CSR. In this context we see a move beyond individual ethics and responsibility, to more structural issues relating to corporations and their impacts upon gender equality/inequality at a societal level, in line with a similarly broad focus in the CSR literature more generally. Thus, while only a small proportion of research in this field over the twenty-five-year period studied focuses on gender equality per se, this may be changing. Finally, while our analysis focused on the BE/CSR journals, we also investigated the extent to which the gender and management journals address BE/CSR. We find that while many of the workplace issues addressed are of relevance to BE/CSR, explicit discussion of these fields of research is almost invisible therein, where only 0.4% (13) of all papers published in three gender economics, organization, and society journals over the twenty-five-year period, refer to BE/CSR. This suggests a lack of interdisciplinary dialogue, for example between those researching gender and organizations, where there is a focus on gender equality per se (see section on Feminist Organization Theory and BE/CSR below), and BE/CSR (see Appendix). In the next section we return to our focus on clarifying and further integrating feminist theory in BE/CSR.

Feminist Theory Integration: Behavioral Studies, Organization Studies and Economics

This section illustrates how key cognate literatures for BE/CSR—behavioral studies, organization theory, and economics—have been deployed by feminist scholars. We argue that renewal of the conversation between gender and BE/CSR research depends upon, among other things, further illumination and integration of feminist theory, and we illustrate this point with reference to these three areas of feminist scholarship.

Feminist Behavioral Studies

Whilst the investigation of gender differences in attitudes or behavior has become a popular mode of research across a number of disciplines, it often leads to misleading conclusions. What can be—at most—statistically confirmed from studies using gender as a variable is a difference between the *average* scores of men and women on some respective measure. Yet such average differences are mostly quite small, especially in comparison to what is generally quite substantial intra-group variation, and these results do not permit conclusions to be drawn about the behavior of any *individuals* or about the unobserved underlying "essence" or "nature" of a group. Often, statistically significant differences are not found at all. For example, Jaffee and Hyde (2000) completed a meta-analysis of 113 studies of moral reasoning that had been inspired by Gilligan's insights concerning care and justice orientations. Contrary to the many claims about women's presumably distinct ethical orientation, they found that over two-thirds of the samples failed to yield a statistically significant association between moral orientation and gender. While the remaining studies tended to find, overall, a small *average* tendency for men to favor a justice orientation and women to favour care, the results were also consistent with considerable use of both orientations by individuals of both sexes. Nelson (2015) found similar results in a meta-analysis of studies about risk preferences.

Yet "gender difference" studies are often misrepresented as reflecting fundamental biological differences between men and women—ignoring potential effects of socialization, context, and/or group dynamics—and generally fail to report the degree of similarity between the genders (Fine 2010; Hyde 2005; Nelson 2014). Moreover, there is evidence that studies that find gender difference in a stereotypically-expected direction may be more likely to be published than those that do not (Nelson 2014). Moving from the individual level to the company level, studies examining the gender composition of boards of directors are often compromised by the false assumption that men and women represent distinct behavioural categories, the implausible assumption that men and women on boards are drawn randomly (rather than highly selectively) from their respective populations, and/or the assumption that gender composition directly impacts board behavior rather than perhaps being jointly causally determined.

Hence—and this is the key point here—the large literature on gender differences in ethical styles (as well as management styles, risk-taking, competitiveness, etc.) in which differences are exaggerated is, by the definition adopted at the start of this chapter, non-feminist. Better quality empirical work that accurately portrays similarity as well as difference, and looks at social as well as biological reasons for differences in behaviour, should of course still be welcomed. However, for the most part, this body of research fails to contribute to the illumination and integration of feminist theory into BE/CSR research.

Feminist Organization Theory

The importance of integrating feminist organization theory (FOT) in CSR scholarship is addressed by Grosser and Moon (2017). These authors illustrate how six strands of feminist theory—liberal, radical, psychoanalytical, socialist/gendered organizations, post-structural, and transnational/(post)colonial—are deployed in feminist organization studies, and how each has informed, at least implicitly, the gender and CSR literature. Mapping these approaches with reference to six strands of CSR theory (ethical, instrumental, stakeholder, political, institutional, and critical), Grosser and Moon (2017) point to new research directions for each. Here we build upon that mapping exercise with reference to ethical approaches in particular as these are most commonly used at the BE/CSR interface. We consider how revisiting the 1990 conversation at Darden, and our bibliographic analysis of the literature since then, extend our understanding of how to better apply FOT in the context of BE/CSR.

With respect to ethical approaches to CSR, Grosser and Moon (2017) draw upon liberal feminism to suggest a need for increased scholarship on equal opportunities, with respect to involvement in ethical decision-making for example. Our bibliographic analysis confirms that attention in the BE/CSR gender literature is focused on gender differences in ethical decision making rather than equal opportunities therein. Thus the latter remains a significant research gap which, if addressed, could advance integration of FOT in BE/CSR.

In addition to exploring representation and voice in business ethics decision making as gendered phenomena, we would suggest that research could better articulate the relationships between gender equality and business ethics. Such research could be framed with reference to literatures on hypernorms and business ethics, human rights, or inequality in business and management. Research here might build upon the conversation that emerged from the Darden conference, in particular Derry (1996: 106–7), who referenced three normative goals deriving from the work of Tong (1993) and Jagger (1992) in particular:

1. To articulate moral critiques of actions and practices that perpetuate women's subordination;
2. To prescribe morally justifiable ways of resisting such actions and practices;
3. To envision morally desirable alternatives that will promote women's emancipation.

By implication, "feminist approaches to ethics are actively committed to social change by means of critically recognizing subordination, creating resistance, and envisioning alternatives" (Derry 1996: 107). Applying these goals to business organizations, Derry (1996: 107) then imagines what a "feminist firm" would look like, identifying challenges relating to workplace practice, marketing, and investment, for example. We note that the gender and BE/CSR literature has begun to address such issues as they relate to the workplace in particular (e.g. Bear et al. 2010; Grosser and Moon 2005; Larrieta-Rubin de Celis et al. 2015; Prieto-Carron 2008; Terjesen and Sealy 2016), but less so with respect to marketing and investment, and that many opportunities remain for further investigation of these agendas within a literature on gender equality and BE/CSR.

With respect to FOT, Grosser and Moon (2017) find that psychoanalytic feminist theory, focusing on the difference between women and men, and the articulation of supposedly feminine values relating to the ethics of care and relational leadership, for example, has had a major impact upon ethical research in CSR. Our bibliographic analysis of BE/CSR gender research confirms and substantiates this finding with respect to the fact that such perspectives predominate in approximately half of the papers in this analysis. As noted above, we see a future for empirical work that accurately portrays similarity as well as difference, and that looks at social as well as biological reasons for differences in attitudes and behaviour between men and women. Yet, given that such research can reinforce gender stereotypes, we argue that this not a good avenue for integrating feminist theory in BE/CSR.

Radical FOT affirms the importance of women-centred knowledge, defined as knowledge that is generated as far as possible outside patriarchal structures (Calás and Smircich 2006; Grosser and Moon 2017), via women-only focus groups, for example. Grosser and Moon (2017) argue that this theoretical perspective could bring insights and contributions to BE/CSR relating to stakeholder issues and methodologies employed (e.g. McCarthy and Muthuri 2016). Yet, despite the fact that the gender and CSR literature has begun to explore the contribution of women's NGOs to CSR (Grosser 2016), our bibliographic analysis serves to confirm Grosser and Moon's (2017) assertion of little reference to this body of theory in BE/CSR.

One of the main contributions of FOT is that it moves us beyond the study of individual women and men to address the ways organizations, and organizational theories, are themselves gendered (Calás and Smircich 2006; Gherardi 2010; Grosser and Moon 2017). One of these approaches adopts socialist feminist/ gendered organization theory and suggests a need for ethical analysis of the gendered nature of organizations, and its implications for gender equality and social justice. Such organizational level approaches to gender are not novel to the BE/CSR literature. For example, the conversation begun at the Darden conference led to interrogation of "'masculinist' assumptions" (Wicks et al. 1994: 475) in business ethics itself, particularly stakeholder theory. Rhodes and Pullen, drawing on both FOT and critical business ethics, interpret business ethics as part of a "masculine drive for public greatness" on the part of patriarchal corporations (2017: 11). We consider that the extension of such approaches will be important in facilitating further integration of FOT into the BE/CSR literature. We note also that such contributions to BE/CSR have hitherto usually stopped short of returning to the issue of gender equality. We consider that their impact on the field can be enhanced by doing just this. Researchers may take a lead here from the gender and organization literature, where, for example, Phillips (2014: 443) utilizes eco-feminist theory to explore the "'logic of patriarchy' based on interrelated and cross-cutting dualisms that support the subordination of nature and other oppressed groups," including women.

FOT reveals that organizations are also gendered through their reliance on unpaid care work, done predominantly by women. The disadvantaging of workers with caring responsibilities which effectively support and sustain organizations and societies undermines merit-based workplace practice, and limits our overall understanding of business organizations and what makes them work well. This issue is a focus of attention in feminist economics also. Yet, despite the fact that Martin and Knopoff (1997) highlight this in the debate following the Darden conference, our bibliographic analysis reveals that little literature addresses this issue.

Although poststructuralist/postmodern feminist theory as witnessed in FOT (Grosser and Moon 2017) was presented at the Darden conference (e.g. Martin and Knopoff 1997), our bibliographic analysis reveals that such approaches have not been prominent in the BE/CSR literature since then. We consider that a return to these perspectives and associated methodologies would facilitate the integration of feminist theory in BE/CSR by offering potential to increase reflexivity on the part of researchers and to bring missing voices and perspectives to the conversation. In addition, the finding in our bibliographic analysis that most gender and BE/CSR research focuses on Europe, North America, and Australasia supports Grosser and Moon's (2017) arguments that considerable work needs to be done to integrate transnational/(post)colonial FOT in BE/CSR. This would bring perspectives from Third World women to defining and applying ethical norms, and CSR, in relation to business, a process that appears particularly relevant in the context of globalization. In sum, our return to the conversation at the Darden conference, and our analysis of the literature since then, serve to confirm a number of suggestions regarding the potential to integrate feminist theory in BE/CSR (Grosser and Moon 2017), and to add to these. In particular we point to the need for better articulation of the relationship between gender equality and business ethics; extending interrogation of masculinist assumptions in business ethics theory and practice, and relating this analysis back to concerns about gender equality itself; ethical analysis of the contribution of unpaid care work to business organizations as it relates to gender equality; revisiting feminist textual deconstruction analysis as a research methodology in BE/CSR; and focusing more energy, resources, and attention to bringing the voices and perspectives of Third World women to processes that define and apply ethical norms in relation to business.

Feminist Economics

At about the same time the Darden conference was raising challenges to BE/CSR, feminist economists were challenging the conventional definitions, models, and methods of the field of economics. In the volume *Beyond Economic Man: Feminist Theory and Economics* (Ferber and Nelson 1993), contributors pointed out the distortions that a one-sided view had created in the image of the economic actor, in theories of the household, in empirical research, and in policy making. When conventional economics treats people as autonomous, self-interested, and rational agents, the contributors pointed out, they ignore the equally important interdependent, social, and emotional dimensions of human life—dimensions that are more closely culturally associated with women and women's traditional roles. "Work" is usually defined in the economics discipline as paid work only, excluding unpaid work, much of which is done by women. Women are often missing as subjects of study, and policy options of particular interest to women (e.g., concerning inequalities within households, or childcare) are often given short shrift. Many of these discussions of the exclusion of women and women's roles in economics developed parallel to— though largely in isolation from—similar discussions in the BE/CSR and feminist organization studies fields.

The *Beyond Economic Man* volume also began to set out an epistemological and methodological critique of the economics discipline that has perhaps even more far-reaching implications for the field of BE/CSR. As mentioned earlier, the fourth theme that arose at the Darden conference pointed to two issues. One is that BE/CSR often seems to occupy a "feminized" and subordinate position relative to areas of management deemed more central, such as finance. According to mainstream economic doctrine, the purpose of a firm is to maximize profits or shareholder wealth. Many scholars have discussed how writings during the 1970s by economists (Friedman 1970; Jensen and Meckling 1976) gave a large boost to this idea's academic and popular respectability. This doctrine, they point out, has increasingly come to permeate management education, the business media, and even the executive suite itself, as well as academic studies (Applebaum and Batt 2014; Bratton 2011; Ghoshal 2005; Smith and Rönnegard 2016; Stout 2012). Against the backdrop of this economist-supplied belief, BE/CSR is often considered to be at best a weak addition to, or at worst a distraction from, the underlying "principles" of capitalism and business. Only when making a "business case" for ethics and responsibility (by which is meant showing that they increase profits), does the BE/CSR field, from this viewpoint, address central management concerns.

The second issue mentioned at the Darden conference is that BE/CSR is often observed by those on the academic left, including a number of feminists (e.g. Calás and Smircich 1997; Ferguson 1997; Pearson 2007; Rhodes and Pullen 2017; Roberts 2015), as insufficiently critical of systemic issues and therefore in collusion with central management profit-oriented interests. That is, it is said to merely provide window-dressing on a fundamentally oppressive capitalist system. Consideration within BE/CSR of epistemological insights from feminist economics, however, could help the field move past these limiting views.

Feminist economists working in the 1990s drew on feminist studies of science from the 1980s in order to analyze their own discipline. Feminist scholars of science (e.g., Harding 1986; Keller 1985) had pointed out that since its beginnings in the sixteenth and seventeenth centuries, European science had been based on notions of separation, detachment, and reason. Ideas of connection, relationship, and emotion— associated with notions of a lesser-valued femininity—were emphatically excluded. Feminist economists noticed that such an analysis, applied to economics, provided a systematic explanation for biases in models and methods, in addition to biases concerning the chosen subjects of study.

Feminist scholars of science demonstrated how such a one-sidedly masculinist conception of science leads to serious biases and only "weak objectivity," as contrasted to "strong objectivity." To be reliable, knowledge should be as free of bias as possible and provide insights into real world phenomena. They showed how such strong objectivity can only be attained as a social project, through carefully examining findings from multiple points of view (Harding 1986; Keller 1985). Thus the use of mathematics in economics, for example, while often taken as a sign of cool detachment from the object of study and therefore of scientific rigor, can at most provide a model with internal consistency, not objectivity.

In a follow-up volume to *Beyond Economic Man* published ten years later (Ferber and Nelson 2003), the implications of a feminist critique for the theory of the firm were explored (Nelson 2003). The idea that firm performance is always, naturally, and perhaps exclusively about profitability is, it turns out, no more than an invention by economists who wanted to make their discipline seem more like physics and therefore more "scientific" and masculine (Nelson 2011; Stout 2012). While making a profit is one goal (of possibly many), businesses are not, in fact, legally required—not even in the United States, much less in Europe and elsewhere—to earn every single dollar of profit that might be possible. Neither, in many real-world markets with powerful firms, does market competition enforce profit-maximization (Bratton 2011; Nelson 2011; Stout 2012). Many, including some more open-minded economists, now recognize that businesses could not survive if populated only by opportunistic "economic man": cooperation, trust, and social and emotional motivations clearly play as great a role in economic organizations as they do in any other social organization (Bowles 2016; Fehr and Falk 2002; Stout 2012). That is, an unmerited belief in universal "principles" and "laws," propagated by economists in work that is underpinned by masculinist biases, has served to veil the highly varied and intrinsically social nature of businesses, markets, and capitalist economies. This belief underlies both the marginalization of business ethics by those who make financial concerns central, and its demonization by those who see BE/CSR as a merely a tinkering with oppressive capitalist practices (Gibson-Graham 1996; Nelson 2006).

Getting away from sexist biases allows us to looks at firms as entities that are both (inherently) relational and (potentially) value-creating. Feminist economics further reveals that the tendency—in the main business literatures, business education, the media, and increasingly in corporate leadership itself—to sideline issues of ethics is itself a result of sexist biases in the formation of the economics discipline. Recognition of the gendered origins of the shareholder wealth maximization ideology could help the field of BE/CSR as a whole—both when it explicitly deals with gender issues and when it does not—claim its place in the core of management scholarship and practice.

Discussion and Conclusion

We have revisited the origins of the conversation between BE/CSR and feminism, and conducted a bibliographic analysis of the literature over the twenty-five-year period since then. Identifying gender relations and gender equality as the central concerns of feminist theory, we have assessed the field of BE/CSR gender research and found it somewhat lacking in its attention to these core tenets of feminism. We note that while research on gender equality has become more prominent in the field in recent years in the context of CSR, it remains a relatively minor focus therein. In order to advance the field with respect to the integration of feminist theory we have clarified insights arising from three closely related bodies of work: feminist studies of behavior, feminist organization studies, and feminist economics. In illuminating these we have shown how they raise challenges for BE/CSR, and simultaneously, point to new avenues for research with the potential to further our understanding of gender inequality in business itself, and at the business-society interface. They also help us address other intersecting inequalities. Moreover, the feminist theoretical perspectives discussed here have wider implications for BE/CSR in that they lead us to rethink a number of core concepts relating to business, business ethics, and CSR.

Examination of feminist studies of behavior, drawn from psychology and related fields, should encourage a re-evaluation of the frequent focus on gender differences that has arisen, particularly, in the BE literature. A more sophisticated approach— both in terms of feminist understanding, and in terms of the appropriate use of statistics—would generate and interpret empirical findings more carefully and so avoid reinforcing false stereotypes.

The implications arising from further integration of FOT in BE/CSR are to encourage research that focuses on gender equality itself, and that investigates business ethics as a gendered phenomenon. This could clarify the numerous ways in which gender equality can be understood as an issue of ethics in business: through discussion of hypernorms, human rights, the contribution of unpaid care work to business organizations, and inequality more broadly. Research on the ways in which women experience CSR interventions is also encouraged by FOT, and both of the articles in the special section make contributions in this regard. In particular, FOT leads us to focus more energy, resources, and attention to bringing the voices and perspectives of Third World women to processes that define and apply ethical norms in relation to business, and to further our understanding of CSR initiatives that focus on women. Through their analysis of women's entrepreneurship programs, and women's empowerment initiatives, in the context of CSR, where women in the global South are the objective and supposed main beneficiaries of CSR, the articles in the special section both advance knowledge in this respect. FOT also has implications for research methodologies in BE/CSR beyond exploring the voice of the "other," extending to research that interrogates masculinist assumptions in our field, through revisiting feminist textual deconstruction analysis for example, which is an area where future research could focus.

The feminist re-evaluation of economic orthodoxy demonstrates the sexist biases underlying core economic theories, and invites BE/CSR researchers to be more careful about deferring to economistic arguments. It points out that the idea of profit maximization has its origins in masculinist pretensions rather than scientific investigation. This recognition could free BE/CSR both from its marginalization within management studies and from its too-easy dismissal by many who seek transformative change. If BE/CSR scholars were to point out, at every opportunity, the dogmatic and misleading nature of the shareholder value maximization doc- trine, the field could become both more central and more effective in analyzing and advocating for justice and care. One way to do this would be for gatekeepers of BE/CSR scholarship to stop treating favorable views of shareholder wealth maximization or narrow business-case arguments as acceptable default assumptions. Dissertation advisors, reviewers, and journal editors could require authors to, at a minimum, engage with the literature arguing for a broader and less gender-biased theory of the firm, if not reject these lines of argument entirely. Scholars critical of capitalism who rely on profit-maximization assumptions could be likewise challenged. BE/CSR scholars could work to challenge the narrow theory of the firm within general management journals as well. Lastly, business education could be redesigned towards spending less time on stale and misleading theories imported from the economics department, and more on issues of ethics.

We do wish to mention a few limitations of our approach. With respect to the bibliographic analysis, first, our sample of literature is derived from only the leading BE/CSR journals. Second, given that policies for usage of abstracts and key words vary among journals and over time, it was not possible to apply our key-word-search method uniformly. Accordingly, judgements of the research assistant and authors played a greater role for papers where there were no key words or abstracts. However, standard practices intended to ensure coding reliability were applied (see the Appendix). Finally, in moving to further integrate feminist theory in our field we have been limited to summaries of key contributions of three fields of feminist research. Clearly there are further insights to be gleaned from interdisciplinary research informed by a wider range of feminist theory.

Appendix: Bibliographic Analysis Details

In this Appendix we present methodological details of a bibliographic analysis aimed at capturing and summarizing how gender has been treated in the BE/CSR academic literature over the period between 1991 and 2015.

Our approach broadly follows that used to investigate the salience, methodologies, and focus of the CSR literature overall (Lockett et al. 2006), and of the topic of CSR in Asia in leading CSR journals and in Asian business and management journals (Kim and Moon 2015). Thus we are able to make some broad comparisons of the treatment of gender in the field with other treatments of BE/CSR literature. Moreover, the evaluative criteria of salience, methodologies, and focus offer the basis for specific insights into the question of the treatment of gender in this literature.

The analysis was undertaken in two main stages: the creation of the database, and the further coding of those articles selected for the database.

Creation of Article Database

We first selected journals to represent the BE/CSR field. These were the four leading BE/CSR journals as rated by the Chartered Association of Business Schools (CABS 2015), each rated at CABS 2 or higher on a five point scale of 1–4/4*.

These are *Business Ethics: A European Review* (CABS 2); *Business Ethics Quarterly* (CABS 4), *Business and Society,* (CABS 3), *Journal of Business Ethics* (CABS 3).

Second, search terms for articles in the selected journals were identified: *women, woman, feminist, feminism, gender.*

Third, we searched for articles published in the selected journals during the period from 1991–2015, applying the identified search terms to article titles, abstracts, and keywords. In cases where neither abstracts nor keywords were available, the search terms were applied to the full article text.

In general terms our approach to creating the database was an expansive one, designed to capture as much literature as possible rather than to delimit overly the initial search. The first list of potential articles was then subject to further scrutiny. The preliminary dataset was reviewed and decisions were made on inclusion or exclusion of what seemed to be marginal or ambiguous cases. The decisions to exclude papers were made for a variety of reasons. For example, the initial search yielded many papers whose concern is individual ethics or ethics of organizations that are not businesses. Likewise the initial search yielded many papers that refer to women but do not focus on issues of gender and organizations or business, or BE/CSR specifically. Book reviews, review articles, editorials, and bibliographies were also excluded.

Coding and Classification

The second stage involved analyses of the selected journal articles in order to identify qualitative attributes of each paper related to its study of gender. This consisted of analyses of:

1. The methodology of the papers, mainly empirical or theoretical:

   (a) If empirical, whether they were mainly quantitative or qualitative.
   (b) If theoretical, whether they were mainly normative or non-normative (e.g. conceptual, explanatory).

2. The focus of the papers:

   (a) By geographical region: focused on Europe, North America, Australasia, Asia, Africa, South/Central America, with no geographical focus, or with a multi-regional focus. In this case, the count was of references to different geographical regions in each paper, rather than counting a single geographical region as the focus of the papers (e.g., a paper focusing on countries from two different regions was scored for each region).
   (b) By issue: social, environmental, ethical, or stakeholder.
   (c) By gender perspective: gender equality, gender difference, or neither.

A number of measures were taken to maximise the reliability of the article selection and subsequent coding. First, a researcher was appointed who brought experience with this form of analysis of academic literature. She was the main coder for Kim and Moon (2015)'s analysis of CSR in Asian business and management journals and of discussion of Asia in CSR journals. Second, the researcher provided feedback on preliminary analysis, engaging two of this article's authors to inform final selection criteria and search terms. To assure reliability in selection and coding of articles, the two authors reviewed the initial database of papers, the decisions about what to include and what to exclude from the final data base, and also the final database created by the research assistant. Discussions were held between the researcher and the two authors to resolve the small number of papers where there were initial differences of interpretation or where the research assistant was unsure of how to code the methodology or focus of the papers.

The initial search of the literature yielded 3587 journal articles. After closer analysis and review, 441 of these were deemed substantively relevant to our research objectives. These articles were then divided into the respective five-year periods in which they were published (P1: 1991–1995; P2: 1996–2000; P3: 2001–2005; P4: 2006–2010; P5: 2011–2015), allowing us in the main analysis (Tables 1, 2, 3, and 4) to consider trends over time.

Using a similar methodology we also investigated the extent to which the gender and management journals address BE/CSR. We selected three leading gender journals: *Gender, Work & Organization*; *Feminist Economics*; and *Gender & Society*. *Gender, Work & Organization* and *Feminist Economics* both feature on the CABS journal index, and are rated CABS 3 and CABS 2 respectively (*Feminist Economics* rated CABS 3 in 2010 and 2009). *Gender & Society* is not ranked on the CABS list but is ranked A* on a four point scale of C–A/A* in the most recent edition of the Australian Business Deans Council Journal Quality list (ABDC 2016) in the management research field. For the creation of this database we used the search terms *corporate social responsibility*, *corporate responsibility*, *sustainab**, and *ethic**. In view of the extremely low salience of BE/CSR in these journals (accounting for only 0.4% of papers [n = 13] over the twenty-five-year period), further analysis was precluded.

References

ABDC (Australian Business Deans Council). 2016. *ABDC releases new journal quality list*. September 6. http://www.abdc.edu.au/news.php/100/abdc-releases-new-journal-quality-list

Acker, J. 1990. Hierarchies, jobs, bodies: A theory of gendered organizations. *Gender and Society*, 4(2): 139–158.

———. 2004. Gender, capitalism and globalization. *Critical Sociology*, 30(1): 17–41.

Appelbaum, E., & R. Batt 2014. *Private equity at work: When Wall Street manages main street*. New York: Russell Sage Foundation.

Arnold, D. G. 2016. Three models of impactful business ethics scholarship. *Business Ethics Quarterly*, 26(4): ix–xii.

Barrientos, S., C. Dolan, & A. Tallontire. 2003. A gendered value chain approach to codes of conduct in African horticulture. *World Development*, 31(9): 1511–1526.

Bear, S., N. Rahman & C. Post. 2010. The impact of board diversity and gender composition on corporate social responsibility and firm reputation. *Journal of Business Ethics*, 97(2): 207–221.

Borgerson, J. L. 2007. On the harmony of feminist ethics and business ethics. *Business and Society Review*, 112(4): 477–509.

Bowen, H. R. 1953. *Social responsibilities of the businessman*. New York: Harper & Row.

Bowles, S. 2016. *The moral economy: Why good incentives are no substitute for good citizens*. New Haven: Yale University Press.

Bratton, W. W. 2011. At the conjunction of love and money: Comment on Julie A. Nelson, Does profit-seeking rule out love? Evidence (or not) from economics and law. *Washington University Journal of Law and Policy*, 35: 109–115.

Burton, B., & C. Dunn. 1996. Feminist ethics as moral grounding for stakeholder theory. *Business Ethics Quarterly*, 6(2): 133–148.

Butler, J. 2004. *Undoing gender*. London: Routledge.

CABS (Chartered Association of Business Schools). 2015. Academic journal guide 2015. https://charteredabs.org/academic-journal-guide-2015/.

Calás, M. B., & L. Smircich. 1997. ¿Predicando la moral en calzoncillos? Feminist inquiries into business ethics. In A. Larson & R. E. Freeman (Eds.), Women's studies and business ethics: Toward a new conversation: 50–79. New York: Oxford University Press.

———. 2006. From the "Woman's Point of View" ten years later: Towards a feminist organization studies. In S. Clegg, C. Hardy, W. Nord, & T. Lawrence (Eds.), Handbook of organization studies (2nd ed.): 284–346. London: Sage.

Carroll, A. B. 1979. A three-dimensional conceptual model of corporate performance. *Academy of Management Review*, 4(4): 497–505.

Collinson, D. & J. Hearn. 1994. Naming men as men: Implications for work, organization and management. *Gender, Work and Organization*, 1(1): 2–22.

Davis, K. 1960. Can business afford to ignore social responsibilities? *California Management Review*, 2(3): 70–77.

———. 1973. The case for and against business assumption of social responsibilities. *Academy of Management Journal*, 16(2): 312–322.

Derry, R. 1996. Toward a feminist firm: Comments on John Dobson and Judith White. *Business Ethics Quarterly*, 6(1): 101–109.

Dobson, J. & J. White. 1995. Toward the feminine firm: An extension to Thomas White. *Business Ethics Quarterly*, 5(3): 463–478.

Dolan, C., M. Johnstone-Louis & L. Scott. 2012. Shampoo, saris and SIM cards: Seeking entrepreneurial futures at the bottom of the pyramid. *Gender and Development*, 20(1): 33–47.

Donaldson, T. & T. W Dunfee. 1994. Toward a unified conception of business ethics: Integrative social contracts theory. *Academy of Management Review*, 19(2): 252–284.

———. 1995. Integrative social contracts theory: A communitarian conception of economic ethics, *Economics and Philosophy*, 11(1): 85–112.

Donaldson, T. & L. E. Preston. 1995. The stakeholder theory of the corporation: Concepts, evidence, and implications. *Academy of Management Review*, 20(1): 65–91.

Fehr, E. & A. Falk. 2002. Psychological foundations of incentives. *European Economic Review*, 46(4–5): 687–724.

Ferber, M. A., & J. A. Nelson (Eds.). 1993. *Beyond economic man: Feminist theory and economics*. Chicago: University of Chicago Press.

———. 2003. Feminist economics today. Chicago: University of Chicago Press.

Ferguson, K. E. 1997. Postmodernism, feminism, and organizational ethics: Letting difference be. In A. Larson & R. E. Freeman (Eds.), *Women's studies and business ethics: Toward a new conversation*: 80–91. New York: Oxford University Press.

Fine, C. 2010. Delusions of gender: How our minds, society, and neurosexism create difference. New York: W. W. Norton.

Freeman, R. E., A. C. Wicks & B. Parmar. 2004. Stakeholder theory and "The Corporate Objective Revisited." *Organization Science*, 15(3): 364–369.

Friedman, M. 1970. The social responsibility of business is to increase its profits. *The New York Times Magazine*: Sept 13.

Garriga, E. & D. Melé. 2004. Corporate social responsibility theories: Mapping the territory. *Journal of Business Ethics*, 53: 51–71.

Gherardi, S. 2010. Feminist theory and organization theory: A dialogue on new bases. In H. Tsoukas & C. Knudsen (Eds.), *The Oxford handbook of organization theory*. Oxford: Oxford University Press.

Ghoshal, S. 2005. Bad management theories are destroying good management practices. *Academy of Management Learning & Education*, 4(1): 75–91.

Gibson-Graham, J. K. 1996. *The end of capitalism (as we knew it): A feminist critique of political economy*. Oxford: Blackwell Publishers.

Gilligan, C. 1982. *In a different voice*. Cambridge, MA: Harvard University Press.

Grosser, K. 2009. Corporate social responsibility and gender equality: Women as stakeholders and the European Union sustainability strategy. *Business Ethics: A European Review*, 18(3): 290–307.

———. 2016. Corporate social responsibility and multi-stakeholder governance: Pluralism, feminist perspectives and women's NGOs. *Journal of Business Ethics*, 137(1): 65–81.

Grosser, K. & J. Moon. 2005. Gender mainstreaming and corporate social responsibility: Reporting workplace issues. *Journal of Business Ethics*, 62(4): 327–340.

———. 2017. CSR and feminist organization studies: Towards an integrated theorization for the analysis of gender issues. *Journal of Business Ethics*. https://doi.org/10.1007/s10551-017-3510-x.

Harding, S. 1986. *The science question in feminism*. Ithaca, NY: Cornell University Press.

Hyde, J. S. 2005. The gender similarities hypothesis. *American Psychologist*, 60(6): 581–592.

Jaffee, S. & J. S. Hyde. 2000. Gender differences in moral orientation: A meta-analysis. *Psychological Bulletin*, 126(5): 703–726.

Jagger, A. 1992. Feminist ethics. In L. Becker & C. Becker (Eds.), *Encyclopedia of Ethics*: 363–364. New York: Garland Press.

Jensen, M. C., & W. H. Meckling. 1976. The theory of the firm: Managerial behavior, agency costs and ownership structure. *Journal of Financial Economics*, 3(4): 305–360.

Johnstone-Louis, M. 2017. Corporate social responsibility and women's entrepreneurship: Towards a more adequate theory of "work." *Business Ethics Quarterly*, 27.

Keenan, J., D. Kemp & R. Ramsay. 2014. Company–community agreements, gender and development. *Journal of Business Ethics*, 135(4): 607–615.

Kelan, E. K. 2008. The discursive construction of gender in contemporary management literature. *Journal of Business Ethics*, 81: 427–445.

Keller, E. F. 1985. *Reflections on gender and science*. New Haven, CT.: Yale University Press.

Kim, C. H. & J. Moon. 2015. Dynamics of corporate social responsibility in Asia: Knowledge and norms. *Asian Business & Management*, 14(5): 349–382.

Knudsen, J. S. & J. Moon. 2017. *Visible hands: National government and international CSR*. Cambridge: Cambridge University Press.

Kuhn, T. S. 1962. *The structure of scientific revolutions*. Chicago, IL: University of Chicago Press.

Larrieta-Rubín de Celis, I., E. Velasco-Balmaseda., S. Fernández de Bobadilla & M. del Mar Alonso-Almeida, 2015. Does having women managers lead to increased gender equality practices in corporate social responsibility? *Business Ethics: A European Review*, 24(1): 91–110.

Larson, A. & R. E. Freeman. 1997. Introduction. In A. Larson & R. E. Freeman (Eds.), *Women's studies and business ethics: Toward a new conversation*: 3–8. New York: Oxford University Press.

Lauwo, S. 2016. Challenging masculinity in CSR disclosures: Silencing of women's voices in Tanzania's mining industry. Journal of Business Ethics. https://doi.org/10.1007/s10551-016-3047-4.

Liedtka, J. M. 1996. Feminist morality and competitive reality: A role for an ethic of care? *Business Ethics Quarterly*, 6(2): 179–200.

Lockett, A., Moon, J. & Visser, W. 2006. Corporate social responsibility in management research: Focus, nature, salience and sources of influence. *Journal of Management Studies*, 43(1): 115–136.

Martin, J. & K. Knopoff. 1997. The gendered implications of apparently gender-neutral theory: Rereading Max Weber. In A. Larson & R. E. Freeman (Eds.), *Women's studies and business ethics: Toward a new conversation: 30–49*. New York: Oxford University Press.

Matten, D. & A. Crane. 2005. Corporate citizenship: Toward an extended theoretical conceptualization. Academy of Management Review, 30(1): 166–179.

Matten, D. & J. Moon. 2008. "Implicit" and "explicit" CSR: A conceptual framework for a comparative understanding of corporate social responsibility. *Academy of Management Review*, 33(2): 404–424.

McCarthy, L. 2017. Empowering women through corporate social responsibility: A feminist Foucauldian critique. *Business Ethics Quarterly*, 27.

McCarthy, L. & J. N. Muthuri. 2016. Engaging fringe stakeholders in business and society research: Applying visual participatory research methods. *Business & Society*. https://doi.org/10.1177/0007650316675610.

McGuire, J. W. 1963. Business and Society. New York: McGraw-Hill.

McWilliams, A. & D. Siegel. 2001. Corporate social responsibility: A theory of the firm perspective. *The Academy of Management Review*, 26(1): 117–127.

Moon, J. 2002. Business social responsibility and new governance. *Government and Opposition*, 37(3): 385–408.

Moon, J., Murphy, L. & J-P. Gond. 2017. Historical perspectives on CSR. In A. Rasche, M. Morsing, & J. Moon (Eds.), *Corporate Social Responsibility: Strategy, Communication and Governance*: 31–62. Cambridge: Cambridge University Press.

Nelson, J. A. 2003. Separative and soluble firms: Androcentric bias in business ethics. In M. A. Ferber & J. A. Nelson (Eds.), *Feminist economics today: Beyond economic man*: 81–99. Chicago: University of Chicago Press.

———. 2006. *Economics for humans*. Chicago: University of Chicago Press.

———. 2011. Does profit-seeking rule out love? Evidence (or not) from economics and law. *Washington University Journal of Law and Policy*, 35(69): 69–107.

———. 2014. The power of stereotyping and confirmation bias to overwhelm accurate assessment: The case of economics, gender, and risk aversion. *Journal of Economic Methodology*, 21(3): 211–231.

———. 2015. Are women really more risk-averse than men? A re-analysis of the literature using expanded methods. *Journal of Economic Surveys*, 29(3): 566–585.

Pearson, R. 2007. Beyond women workers: Gendering CSR. *Third World Quarterly*, 28(4): 731–749.

Phillips, M. 2014. Re-writing organizational environmentalism: Ecofeminism, corporeality and the language of feeling. *Gender, Work & Organization*, 21(5): 443–458.

Preston, L. & J. E. Post. 1975. Private management and public policy: The principle of public responsibility. Englewood Cliffs, NJ: Prentice Hall.

Prieto-Carrón, M. 2008. Women workers, industrialization, global supply chains and corporate codes of conduct. Journal of Business Ethics, 83(1): 5–17.

Rasche, A., M. Morsing & J. Moon. 2017. The changing role of business in global society: CSR and beyond. In A. Rasche, M. Morsing, & J. Moon (Eds.) *Corporate social responsibility: Strategy, communication and governance*: 1–28. Cambridge: Cambridge University Press.

Rhodes, C. & A. Pullen. 2017. Critical business ethics: From corporate self-interest to the glorification of the sovereign pater. *International Journal of Management Reviews*. https://doi.org/10.1111/ijmr.12142.

Roberts, A. 2015. The political economy of "transnational business feminism." *International Feminist Journal of Politics*, 17(2): 209–231.

Scherer, A. G. & G. Palazzo. 2011. The new political role of business in a globalized world: A review of a new perspective on CSR and its implications for the firm, governance, and democracy. *Journal of Management Studies*, 48(4): 899–931.

Scherer, A. G., A. Rasche, G. Palazzo & A. Spicer. 2016. Managing for political corporate social responsibility: New challenges and directions for PCSR 2.0. *Journal of Management Studies*, 53(3): 273–298.

Smith, N. C., & D. Rönnegard. 2016. Shareholder primacy, corporate social responsibility, and the role of business schools. *Journal of Business Ethics*, 134(3): 463–478.

Stout, L. 2012. *The Shareholder value myth: How putting shareholders first harms investors, corporations, and the public*. San Francisco: Berrett-Koehler.

Terjesen, S., & R. Sealy. 2016. Board gender quotas: Exploring ethical tensions from a multi-theoretical perspective. *Business Ethics Quarterly*, 26(1): 23–65.

Tong, R. 1993. *Feminine and feminist ethics*. Belmont, CA: Wadsworth.

Tornhill, S. 2016. The wins of corporate gender equality politics: Coca-Cola and female micro-entrepreneurship in South Africa. In K. Grosser, L. McCarthy, L. & M. A. Kilgour (Eds.), *Gender equality and responsible business: Expanding CSR horizons*: 185–202. Saltaire, UK: Greenleaf.

Walby, S. 2011. *The future of feminism*. Cambridge: Polity.

West, C. & H. Zimmerman. 1987. Doing gender. *Gender & Society*, 1(2): 125–151.

White, T. 1992. Business, ethics, and Carol Gilligan's "two voices." *Business Ethics Quarterly*, 2(1): 51–61.

Wicks, A. C. 1996. Reflections on the practical relevance of feminist thought to business. *Business Ethics Quarterly*, 6(4): 523–531.

Wicks, A. C., D. R. Gilbert, Jr. & R. E. Freeman. 1994. A feminist reinterpretation of the stakeholder concept. *Business Ethics Quarterly*, 4(4): 475–497.

Kate Grosser is a Senior Lecturer at RMIT University (Melbourne) School of Management, and Co-Director of RMIT's Business and Human Rights Centre. She has pioneered research that critically engages with Corporate Social Responsibility (CSR) theory and practice from feminist perspectives, including new scholarship on gender, business and human rights. She is particularly interested in the contribution of feminist theories; CSR as a process of governance; and the role of feminist social movements. Her work appears in, among others: *Business Ethics Quarterly; Journal of Business Ethics; Organization; Gender, Work and Organization; Business Ethics: A European Review*. She sits on the Distinguished Advisory Board at *Gender, Work & Organization*, and has a strong focus on research engagement and impact, having acted as advisor to the UN Working Group on Business and Human Rights, and numerous other international and national bodies.

Jeremy Moon is Professor of Sustainability Governance, Copenhagen Business School and was Professor and Founding Director of the International Centre for Corporate Social Responsibility, University of Nottingham. He held visiting positions at: Trinity College, Melbourne; Institute for Advanced Studies, Princeton; Churchill College, Cambridge; European University Institute, Florence. His paper 'Implicit and Explicit CSR' (with Dirk Matten) won the 2018 *Academy of Management Review* Paper of the Decade Award. Recent publications include 'Corporate Social Responsibility and Government' (with Jette Steen Knudsen), *Business Ethics Quarterly*.

Julie A. Nelson, Professor Emerita, University of Massachusetts Boston, currently conducts research on feminism and economics, with special interests in methodology and in implications for social and environmental policies. She has also published in the areas of ethics, the teaching of economics, and the empirical analysis of household and individual behavior. She has served as a Research Economist at the U.S. Bureau of Labor Statistics, an Assistant and Associate Professor of Economics at the University of California-Davis, an Associate Professor of Economics at Brandeis University, a Visiting Associate Professor at Harvard University, a Fellow at the Center for the Study of Values in Public Life at Harvard Divinity School, and as the Visiting Sowell Professor of Economics at Bates College. Professor Nelson is the author of *Economics for Humans* (2006) and *Feminism, Objectivity, and Economics* (1996), co-author of several other books and textbooks, and author of articles in journals ranging from *Econometrica* and the *Journal of Political Economy, to Signs: Journal of Women in Culture and Society* and *Ecological Economics*.

Relational Leadership Theory: Exploring the Social Processes of Leadership and Organizing

Mary Uhl-Bien

Abstract Relational leadership is a relatively new term in the leadership literature, and because of this, its meaning is open to interpretation. In the present article I describe two perspectives of relational leadership: an *entity* perspective that focuses on identifying attributes of individuals as they engage in interpersonal relationships, and a *relational* perspective that views leadership as a *process of social construction* through which certain understandings of leadership come about and are given privileged ontology. These approaches can be complementary, but their implications for study and practice are quite different. After reviewing leadership research relative to these two perspectives I offer Relational Leadership Theory (RLT) as an overarching framework for the study of leadership as a social influence process through which emergent coordination (*e.g.*, evolving social order) and change (*e.g.*, new approaches, values, attitudes, behaviors, ideologies) are constructed and produced. This framework addresses relationships both as an outcome of investigation (*e.g.*, How are leadership relationships produced?) and a context for action (*e.g.*, How do relational dynamics contribute to structuring?). RLT draws from both entity and relational ontologies and methodologies to more fully explore the relational dynamics of leadership and organizing.

Keywords Relational leadership · Entity perspectives · Relationality

> We consider the relational perspective and [the approaches within it]... to be at the forefront of emerging leadership thrusts The relational focus is one that moves beyond unidi-rectional or even reciprocal leader/follower relationships to one that recognizes leadership wherever it occurs; it is not restricted to a single or even a small set of formal or informal leaders; and, in its strongest form, functions as a dynamic system embedding leadership, environmental, and organizational aspects. (Hunt and Dodge 2000: 448)

While the concept of relationship-oriented behavior has been around since the earliest formal studies of leadership in organizations (Stogdill and Coons 1957), the

M. Uhl-Bien (✉)
Institute for Innovative Leadership, University of Nebraska, Lincoln, NE, USA
e-mail: muhlbien@unlnotes.unl.edu

M. Painter, P. H. Werhane (eds.), *Leadership, Gender, and Organization*, Issues in Business Ethics 63, https://doi.org/10.1007/978-3-031-24445-2_7

term *relational leadership* is surprisingly new (Brower et al. 2000; Drath 2001; Murrell 1997; Uhl-Bien 2003, 2005). Because of this, its meaning is still uncertain. In traditional management discourse, the term relational means that "an individual likes people and thrives on relationships" (Lipman-Blumen 1996: 165). Traditional research on leadership examines behavioral styles that are relationship- oriented (Likert 1961), meaning considerate and supportive (Stogdill et al. 1962) or leadership behaviors focused on developing high quality, trusting, work relationships (Brower et al. 2000; Graen and Scandura 1987; Graen and Uhl-Bien 1995; Uhl-Bien et al. 2000).

In recently developing discourse (Drath 2001; Hosking 2007; Murrell 1997), however, the term relational is being used to describe something quite different for leadership – a view of leadership and organization as human social constructions that emanate from the rich connections and interdependencies of organizations and their members (cf., Bradbury and Lichtenstein 2000; Hosking et al. 1995). In contrast to a more traditional orientation, which considers relationships from the standpoint of individuals as independent, discrete entities (i.e., individual agency) (Bradbury and Lichtenstein 2000; Hosking et al. 1995), a "relational" orientation starts with processes and not persons, and views persons, leadership and other relational realities as *made* in processes (Hosking 2007).

The more traditional orientation, which can be called an *entity* perspective because it focuses on individual entities, is consistent with an epistemology of an objective truth and a Cartesian dogma of a clear separation between mind and nature (Bradbury and Lichtenstein 2000). It assumes that: (a) individuals have a "knowing mind," (b) individuals have access to the contents of their mind (mind contents and knowledge are viewed as properties of entities, as individual possessions), and (c) these entities can be distinguished from other entities (i.e., people) and the environment (Dachler and Hosking 1995). As such, the "knowing" individual is understood as the architect and controller of an internal and external order which makes sense with respect to the array of their personal "possessions" (their mind contents) (Dachler and Hosking 1995). This view approaches relationship-based leadership by focusing on *individuals* (e.g., leaders and followers) and their perceptions, intentions, behaviors, personalities, expectations, and evaluations relative to their relationships with one another (e.g., Hollander 1978; Lord et al. 1999; Uhl- Bien et al. 2000). Dachler and Hosking (1995) call this approach a "subject-object" understanding of relationships: "Social relations are enacted by subjects to achieve knowledge about, and influence over, other people and groups" (p. 3).

The second, and less well-known, *relational* perspective views knowledge as socially constructed and socially distributed, not as "mind stuff" constructed or accumulated and stored by individuals: "That which is understood as real is differently constructed in different relational and historical/cultural settings" (Dachler and Hosking 1995: 4). Taking a relational orientation means recognizing that organizational phenomena exist in interdependent relationships and intersubjective meaning: "... [K]nowing occurs between two subjects or phenomena simultaneously, therefore we must attend to the multiple meanings and perspectives that continuously emerge.. ." (Bradbury and Lichtenstein 2000: 552). From this perspective, knowing is always a process of relating; relating is a constructive, ongoing process of meaning making – an actively relational process of creating (common) understandings on the basis of language; meaning can never be finalized, nor has it any ultimate origin, it is always in the process of making; and meanings are limited by socio-cultural contexts (Dachler and Hosking 1995). Applied to leadership (Dachler and Hosking 1995; Hosking 2007), a relational orientation does not focus on identifying attributes of individuals involved in leadership behaviors or exchanges, but rather on the social construction processes by which certain understandings of leadership come about and are given privileged ontology (cf., Meindl 1995).

In the sections below I review leadership theory relative to these two perspectives. As we will see in this discussion, although both *entity* and *relational* approaches view leadership as a social process, what they mean by process, particularly with respect to their ontology and epistemology, is quite different. The former views relational processes as centered in individuals' perceptions and cognitions as they engage in exchanges and influence relationships with one another, while the latter views persons and organizations as ongoing multiple constructions *made "in"* processes and not the *makers "of"* processes (Hosking 2000). As will be described later in the article, these different ontologies result in very different ways of conceptualizing and operationalizing relational leadership, with the former adopting primarily a variable-based approach and the latter more of a constructionist approach.

Following this review, I present an overarching framework for the investigation of relational leadership. I identify relational leadership as a social influence process through which emergent coordination (i.e., evolving social order) and change (e.g., new values, attitudes, approaches, behaviors, and ideologies) are constructed and produced. This perspective does not restrict leadership to hierarchical positions or roles. Instead it views leadership as occurring in relational dynamics throughout the organization; as will be discussed below, it also acknowledges the importance of context in the study of these relational dynamics (cf., Osborn et al. 2002). Since space does not permit a detailed discussion, I provide some examples of the kinds of questions raised by a Relational Leadership Theory (RLT) framework, and discuss how these questions could be addressed and tested considering the potential contributions of both entity and relational perspectives. I suggest that we are best served not by arguing over whether entity or relational offers the "best" way, but rather by considering how our perspectives will be informed if we view these issues from multiple orientations (cf., Fairhurst and Putnam 2004; Hosking 2007).

The Entity (Individual Reality) Perspective

As described above, entity perspectives assume individual agency – that "organizational life is viewed as the result of individual action" (Hosking et al. 1995: x). Individuals are thought of as "entities," with clear separation between their internal selves and external environments. These individuals are seen as possessing "the capacity to reason, to learn, to invent, to produce, and to manage" which serves as the basis for assumptions that "the 'reality' of management is understood as individual creation and control of order" (Hosking et al. 1995: x). Studies that align with this perspective explain relationships on the basis of the properties and behaviors of interacting individuals or organizations (Dachler and Hosking 1995).

The predominant entity perspectives exploring relational leadership issues are the "relationship-based" approaches to leadership research (Graen and Uhl-Bien 1995). From this perspective, leadership can be seen as a two-way influence relationship between a leader and a follower aimed primarily at attaining mutual goals (Brower et al. 2000; Graen and Scandura 1987; Graen and Uhl-Bien 1991, 1995; Hollander 1978, 1979). In relationship-based approaches, the focus is on interpersonal relationships, most often among leader-member dyads (Graen and Scandura 1987; Uhl-Bien et al. 2000), but also leadership relationships that occur between a leader and a group (Hollander 1964; Howell and Shamir 2005) or among triads (Offstein et al. 2006) or larger collectivities (Graen and Graen 2006; Graen and Uhl-Bien 1995; Balkundi and Kilduff 2005). Relationship-based perspectives view relationships in a traditional sense of the word – a relationship as *a particular type of connection existing between people related to or having dealings with each other* (American Heritage Dictionary 2000) – and relational processes are considered relative to individual characteristics that leaders and followers bring to their interpersonal exchanges.

Leader-Member Exchange Theory

The most prominent relationship-based approach is leader-member exchange (LMX) theory (Gerstner and Day 1997; Graen et al. 1982; Graen and Uhl-Bien 1995; Liden et al. 1997). According to Graen and Uhl-Bien (1995), the central concept of LMX theory is that leadership occurs when leaders and followers are able to develop effective relationships (partnerships) that result in incremental influence (i.e., leadership, see Katz and Kahn 1978) and thus gain access to the many benefits these relationships bring (Gerstner and Day 1997). The theory describes how effective leadership relationships develop (Liden et al. 1997; Uhl-Bien et al. 2000) among dyad "partners" (e.g., leaders and members, teammates, peers) to generate bases of leadership influence (Graen and Uhl-Bien 1991, 1995), as well as demonstrates the benefits of these leadership relationships for organizational outcomes (Gerstner and Day 1997).

LMX is an entity perspective because it focuses on the properties and behaviors of individuals as they engage in interactions with one another (cf., Dachler and Hosking 1995). Uhl-Bien et al. (2000) describe the relationship development process as beginning with two individuals, who engage in an interaction or exchange sequence (a series of interactions). The nature of these interactions depends on several things:

> First, it depends on the characteristics each individual brings to the relationship, including their personal, physical, and psychological makeup that remains relatively stable and disposes them to approach interpersonal situations in a certain way (Phillips and Bedeian 1994). Second, it depends on the individuals' expectations of the exchange, which are developed based on past experience, outside information about the other, and implicit leadership theories or "schemas" (Lord and Maher 1991). Third, it depends on their assessment of and reaction to the exchange both while it is occurring and in retrospect (Blau 1964; Homans 1961; Jacobs 1971; Uhl-Bien et al. 2000: 146–147)

In accordance with Dachler and Hosking (1995), this is a "subject-object" understanding of relationships and an entity perspective: "When a person is understood as a knowing individual s/he is being viewed as a subject, distinguishable from the objects of nature. The latter implicitly are viewed as passive, as knowable and malleable only by the subject" (p. 3). In this case, the subject is the individual, and the object is the relationship, which lies in the mind of the individual: "Relations are considered only from the point of view of the entity [the individual] considered as the subject in that relationship" (Dachler and Hosking 1995: 3).

Hollander's Relational Theory

Another prominent relationship-based approach to leadership is that provided by Hollander (1964, 1978). Hollander was one of the earliest scholars to adopt a focus on leadership as a relational process (Hollander 1958), a two-way influence and social exchange relationship between leaders and followers (Hollander 1979). According to Hollander and Julian (1969), (1) leadership is a process involving an influence relationship (2) the leader is one among other participants in this relationship, and (3) there are "transactions" (i.e., exchanges) that occur between leaders and followers, basic to which is the belief that rewards will be received for benefits given (cf., Homans 1974; Jacobs 1971).

Hollander's model is relational and focuses on process, but considers this process from the standpoint of individuals – making it an entity approach. For example, in the idiosyncrasy credit (IC) model of innovative leadership, leaders are given latitude for innovative behavior in a "credit-building" process that is a function of the followers' perceptions of the leader's competence and loyalty displays that engender follower trust in the leader (Hollander 1958, 1979, 1992).

> The essential point of the IC model is that leadership is a dynamic process of interpersonal evaluation: Individuals earn standing in the eyes of present or eventual followers and then have latitude for associations, including innovations associated with the leader role, that would be unacceptable for those without such status. (Hollander 1992: 72–73)

Moreover, while Hollander (1995) says that leadership is "a shared experience, a voyage through time" and the leader is not a sole voyager, he also says that "a major component of the leader-follower relationship is the leader's perception of his or her self relative to followers, and how they in turn perceive the leader" (p. 55). Hence, consistent with an entity perspective, this model describes processes that are located in the perceptions and cognition of the individuals involved in the relationship.

Charismatic Relationships

A third entity perspective of relationship-based leadership is offered in views of charisma as a social relationship between leaders and followers (Jermier 1993; Klein and House 1995; Kark and Shamir 2002; Howell and Shamir 2005; Shamir

1991; Weierter 1997). This work began by considering the qualities of followers that lead them to identify with (Shamir 1991) and react to leaders as charismatic (Shamir et al. 1993; Klein and House 1995). It progressed into a consideration of the relationships that foster the perception of the leader as charismatic. For example, Weierter (1997) suggested that objective social forces define and set the potential for charismatic relationships and provide the framework within which subjective relationships are possible. Within his framework, different characteristics of followers (e.g., self-monitoring and self-concept clarity) establish the role of personal charisma and the charismatic message of the leader in varying types of charismatic relationships (socialized, personalized, and social contagion) and affect the extent to which the charismatic relationship is maintained or re-created.

Building on Weierter (1997) and others, Howell and Shamir (2005) integrate self-identity theory with two types of charismatic relationships – socialized and personalized – to develop propositions about how followers' self-concepts influence the type of relationship they form with the leader. They consider how followers may affect various stages of the charismatic relationship process, including susceptibility to charismatic leadership, responses to charismatic influence, empowerment of the leader, and consequences of the relationship.

Relational and Collective Self

A similar perspective to the one just described is offered in work applying social cognition and identity to leadership (Hogg 2001; Lord et al. 1999; Shamir et al. 1993; van Knippenberg et al. 2004). This work focuses on *social* self-concept – the extent to which individuals define themselves in terms of their relationships to others (Andersen and Chen 2002; Brewer and Gardner 1996; Lord et al. 1999). Within social self-concept are two distinct constructs: *relational self*, which emanates from relationships with significant others, and *collective self*, which is based on identity with a group or social category.

Relational Self According to Brewer and Gardner (1996), "At the interpersonal level, the *relational self* is the self-concept derived from connections and role relationships with significant others" (p. 84). It is defined in terms of relationships with others in specific contexts – the sense that the self is construed from the responses and satisfaction of the other person in the relationship. Self-worth comes from the feeling that one is behaving appropriately and acceptably with respect to the other (Brewer and Gardner 1996). This idea is further developed by Andersen and Chen (2002), who describe the self as "relational – or even entangled – with significant others" which "has implications for self-definition, self-evaluation, self- regulation, and most broadly, for personality functioning, expressed in relation to others" (p. 619).

Andersen and Chen (2002) suggest that an individual's overall repertoire of relational selves stem from all of his or her relationships, and serves as a major source of the interpersonal patterns the individual enacts and experiences in the course of everyday interpersonal life. Specifically, each individual has a relational self that is an embodiment of the unique self one experiences in relation to given significant others (i.e., a "significant-other representation"); when a significant-other representation is activated, the relevant relational self is activated accordingly. This infuses the working self-concept with knowledge that is a reflection of the self in relation to the significant other, setting into motion a "transference" of the significant-other representation to the individual who triggered it (Andersen and Chen 2002).

In a specific application of these concepts to leadership, Ritter and Lord (2006) explore the issue of transference in leader-follower relationships by examining whether representations of relationships with former leaders that are cognitively stored by followers influence the perceptions of an incoming leader. In two studies, they demonstrate the existence of leader transference, with findings showing that leader effects on motivation and performance differ for individuals encountering a new leader who is similar versus one who is non-similar to previous leaders. Variables transferred from a similar leader are more likely to influence regulatory aspects of follower self-identity and goal setting than non-transferred variables.

Based on these results, the authors suggest that because transferred variables include information regarding how we see and feel about ourselves, the motivation to maintain positive self-views or eliminate negative self-views may be the underlying mechanism driving subsequent judgments and behavioral responses. The findings imply that leader transference processes may serve as a very early bias in the formation of such relationships, such that followers of leaders who activate a negative significant-other representation may be quickly turned off to relationship development attempts, while followers of a new leader who triggers a positive significant-other representation may be predisposed to form a beneficial exchange relationship with that leader (Ritter and Lord 2006).

Consistent with Ritter and Lord (2006), van Knippenberg et al. (2004) call for more research on *relational self-construal*, or the extended sense of self that is based on the individual's role relationships with the leader. Such relational self-construal "renders mutual benefit and mutual interest more salient, and motivates the individual to take the other's interest to heart" (van Knippenberg et al. 2004: 828). Variables of interest for relational leadership based on self-construal might include motivations (self-interest versus other-interest, cf., Uhl-Bien and Maslyn 2003), affect (cf., Boyd and Taylor 1998), and evaluations (i.e., whether feedback is reinforcing of relational self-worth or disconfirming, Lord et al. 1999). Moreover, van Knippenberg et al. (2004) suggest that personal identification with the leader may motivate followers to be loyal to the leader, and cause followers to experience the leader's interest as a shared interest, enhancing leadership effectiveness. Relational self-construal may also play a role in dyadic leadership processes, offering a different perspective to relationship development and formation than the role-making (Graen and Scandura 1987) or social exchange (Liden et al. 1997; Uhl-Bien et al. 2000) explanations currently offered by LMX theory.

Collective Self Contrary to *relational* self-identities, which emanate from relationships with significant others, *collective* social identities do not require personal relationships among members (Brewer and Gardner 1996). Instead they come from identification with a group, an organization, or a social category. At the collective level, identification implies "a psychological 'merging' of self and group that leads individuals to see the self as similar to other members of the collective, to ascribe group-defining characteristics to the self, and to take the collective's interest to heart" (van Knippenberg et al. 2004: 828). This results in a "depersonalized" sense of self, "a shift towards the perception of self as an interchangeable exemplar of some social category and away from the perception of self as a unique person" (Turner et al. 1987: 50, as quoted in Brewer and Gardner 1996: 83). Important at this level are the cognitive processes that help reinforce and promote the collective welfare of the group (Lord et al. 1999).

Hogg (2001) uses the concept of collective self to develop what he called a "Social Identity Theory of Leadership." Recognizing gaps in prior leadership theorizing that neglects consideration of the effects of larger social systems within which individuals are embedded, he offers a view of leadership as a "relational property" within a group: "Leaders exist because of followers and followers exist because of leaders" (Hogg 2001: 185). Considering that *leader* and *follower* are interdependent roles embedded within a social system bounded by common group or category membership, he presents a model of leadership dynamics grounded in social identity cognitive processes of "self-categorization" and "depersonalization." Specifically, he proposes that leaders emerge, maintain their position, and are effective as a result of basic social cognitive processes among group members that cause them to: (a) conceive of themselves in terms of an ingroup (i.e., self-categorization or identification with an ingroup prototype) (b) cognitively and behaviorally assimilate themselves to the ingroup prototypical features (i.e., cognitive and behavioral depersonalization, which produces normative or stereotypic attitudes and behavior), and (c) to perceive others through the lens of ingroup and outgroup prototypes rather than as unique individuals (i.e., perceptual depersonalization of others, producing homogenization) (Hogg 2001). The implication is that if leadership is produced by these social psychological processes, then for an individual to be effective as a leader he/she must display the prototypical or normative characteristics of an ingroup member.

While the concepts of collective identity and collective self in the preceding paragraphs may sound like they more closely approximate a *relational* than *entity* perspective, they are included here because the processes described are primarily considered to occur in the "minds" of the individuals involved in the collectivity rather than in the social dynamic. In this way they appear more consistent with a *constructivist* (e.g., entity) than a *constructionist* (i.e., "relational") perspective. As described by Bouwen and Hosking (2000), in a social *constructivist* perspective, "internal" processes are understood to be influenced by social relations, whereas social *constructionism* centers communication processes as the vehicle in which self and world are in ongoing construction.

Social Networks

More recently, relationship-based leadership theory has begun to move beyond a focus on manager-subordinate exchanges to consider other types of leadership relationships that can occur in the broader organization (Balkundi and Kilduff 2005;

Graen and Graen 2006; Offstein et al. 2006; Sparrowe and Liden 1997, 2005; Uhl-Bien et al. 2000). Although these approaches consider relationships in the context of larger collectivities, they are still entity perspectives in that they focus on individual perceptions of relational quality and relational ties, rather than a socially constructed reality (Hosking et al. 1995).

In a much overdue integration of social network theory and leadership, Balkundi and Kilduff (2005) describe the key role that networks play in either supporting or negating the actions of individual leaders (whom they define as individuals who may or may not hold formal supervisory positions, cf., Bedeian and Hunt 2006). According to Balkundi and Kilduff (2005), network theory has four core principles: the importance of relations between organizational actors; actors' embeddedness in social fields; the social utility of network connections (i.e., social capital); and the structural patterning of social life (Kilduff and Tsai 2003). Building upon these principles, and particularly the importance of understanding interactions between actors rather than a focus solely on the attributes of actors, they present a model that allows one to "zoom" in and out (Ibarra et al. 2005) between individual level cognitions and the larger collectivities in which individual leaders function and interact. This model uses as a starting point cognitions in the minds of leaders, and then expands to consider the broader social structure of the organization and the interorganizational realm (Balkundi and Kilduff 2005).

This approach is an entity perspective because of its grounding in "cognitions in the mind of the leader" (p. 944), though at times the language used to describe the theoretical underpinnings sounds more *relational*:

> An early treatment of network research on organizations stated that "the social network approach views organizations in society as a system of objects (e.g., people, groups, organizations) joined by a variety of relationships" (Tichy et al. 1979: 507), whereas a more recent survey represented organizational network research as a movement "away from individualist, essentialist and atomistic explanations toward more relational, contextual, and systemic understandings" (Borgatti and Foster 2003). The importance of understanding relationships as constitutive of human nature was stated as follows in a recent book: "Human beings are by their very nature gregarious creatures, for whom relationships are defining elements of their identities and creativeness. The study of such relationships is therefore the study of human nature itself" (Kilduff and Tsai 2003: 131). Our network approach locates leadership not in the attributes of individuals but in the relationships connecting individuals. (Balkundi and Kilduff 2005: 942)

Despite the relational tone in this quote, network theory has still not approached the *relational* (social reality) perspective described by Hosking and others (Hosking 1988; Dachler 1992). From a relational orientation, network theory would focus on the dynamic interactions through which relational networks are enacted, including those that occur between people as well as those between people and other social constructions (e.g., constructions of natural and "man-made" things and events, such as markets, fair trade, etc.) (cf., Hosking 2007). Until now, network theory has appeared to be concerned with description (e.g., who talks to whom, who is friends with whom) and taxonomy (e.g., friendship network, advice network, ego network) of relational links, focusing primarily on "mapping" network interconnections (e.g., identifying the number and types of links that occur among individual actors), rather than on how relational processes emerge and evolve – e.g., how these interpersonal relationships develop, unfold, maintain, or dissolve in the context of broader relational realities (including other social constructions).

LMX-MMX Sharing Network Theory In another integration of network theory and leadership, Graen (2006) offers a transformation of LMX theory to what he is now calling the "new LMX-MMX theory of Sharing Network Leadership" (p. 277). In this extension, he moves into what Graen and Uhl-Bien (1995) called "Stage 4" LMX research: expansion of dyadic partnerships to group and network levels. Building upon earlier work viewing organizations as systems of interdependent dyadic relationships, or *dyadic subassemblies* (Graen and Scandura 1987), this approach recognizes the importance of both formal and informal influences on individual, team and network flows of behavior (cf., Katz and Kahn 1978). Describing two different types of working relationships, he calls for researchers to move beyond the more limited focus on manager-subordinate relationships to consider informal leadership that occurs outside formal reporting relationships – to address both LMX and MMX, with "LMX being vertical and MMX is every direction but vertical" (p. 276).

Triads Consistent with Graen's (2006) extension of LMX theory, Offstein et al. (2006) propose extending LMX research beyond the dyad by introducing the triadic level of analysis. Using recently developed statistical models from network analysis (such as $p*$), they develop a theoretical framework that not only allows for ways to identify and analyze triads but also go beyond network theory to explain why particular triads form and how they function. Specifically, they develop and explore the constructs of competitive and collaborative interdependence and introduce the notion of multiplexity within LMX triads, which suggests that the structure of a triad may be predicated on the content and nature of the relations that exist (Offstein et al. 2006). They suggest that triads are formed and exist to fulfill either competitive or collaborative motives, and depending on which of these tensions dominates, the management and outcomes of those triads are distinctly different. Moreover, they draw from Simmel (1950), Heider's (1958) balance theory, and Krackhardt's (1999) concept of Simmelian ties to describe how triad interactions differ from those in dyads, due to the more complex interactive dynamics that accompany the introduction of an additional person to the relational exchange.

Rost's Postindustrial Leadership

Finally, another perspective that sees leadership as relationship-based, and also considers these relationships in the broader context of the organization, is Rost's (1991, 1995) definition of "postindustrial" leadership. Rost (1995) defines leadership as not what leaders do but what leaders and collaborators do *together*:

> Leadership is an influence relationship wherein leaders and collaborators influence one another about real changes that reflects their mutual purposes. Leaders compete with other leaders for collaborators. Collaborators develop a relationship with leaders of their own choosing, not necessarily those who have authority over them. Leaders and collaborators may change places. There may be a number of leadership relationships in one organization, and the same people are not necessarily the leaders in these different relationships. The intended changes reflect the purpose or vision that leaders and collaborators have for an organization. That purpose is usually not static but is constantly changing as leaders and collaborators come and go, as the influence process works its effects on both leaders and collaborators, and as circumstances, environment, and wants and needs impact on the relationship and the organization. (Rost 1995: 134)

In this way, Rost (1995) sees leadership as a multidirectional influence relationship (i.e., it can act in any direction, not just from top down) in which leaders and collaborators are the actors in the relationship: "If leadership is what the relationship is, then both collaborators and leaders are all doing leadership. There is no such thing as followership" (p. 133). He does not suggest that all actors in the relationship are equal in influence (he says this can almost never be the case); the influence patterns are inherently unequal, and reflect intended real changes that reflect the mutual purposes of the leaders and collaborators. Moreover, he sees these relationships as operating within a larger context of the organization in which multiple influence relationships are interacting with one another.

Summary of Entity Perspectives

In sum, *entity* perspectives approach relational leadership from the standpoint of relationships lying in individual perceptions, cognition (e.g., self-concept), attributes, and behaviors (e.g., social influence, social exchange). They view leadership as an influence relationship in which individuals align with one another to accomplish mutual (and organizational) goals. These perspectives assume and center a realist ontology. They presume an individually constituted reality, which conveys a view of leadership as a more individually-based, causal set of factors in the design and development of organizations (Dachler 1992). Moreover, they have primarily focused on leadership as manager-subordinate exchanges under the condition of already "being organized" (Hosking and Morley 1988). Emerging work in relationship-based leadership, however, is beginning to call for expansion of relationship-based approaches beyond the manager-subordinate dyad (Balkundi and Kilduff 2005; Graen 2006; Offstein et al. 2006; Uhl-Bien et al. 2000), as well as recognition that leadership can occur in any direction (Rost 1991, 1995) and that leadership is a relational property of a group (Hogg 2001).

In contrast to *entity* approaches, *relational* perspectives (Hosking et al. 1995) see leadership as a fundamentally social-relational process of organizational design and change (Dachler 1992). According to Dachler and Hosking (1995), because the focus in the individual *entity* perspective is on properties and behaviors of interacting individuals or organizations, *relational processes* are left largely untheorized:

"What usually gets ignored are the social processes by which leadership is constructed and constantly in the making" (p. 15). Relations, "are given little explanatory power beyond an unexplicated view that influence results from relationships between certain properties possessed by interacting entities" (Dachler and Hosking 1995: 3–4). To explain what they mean by this, I turn next to a discussion of "relational" (multiple realities) perspectives.

The "Relational" (Multiple Realities) Perspective

A relational perspective assumes that social reality lies in the context of relationships – it "takes as primary the nexus of relations.. .., rather than focusing on discrete, abstracted phenomena" (Bradbury and Lichtenstein 2000: 551). Such a perspective is skeptical of the validity of mental models or inner representations – rather, it assumes that any formulations of thoughts and assumptions have to be understood in the context of ongoing conversations and relations (Holmberg 2000):

> Whereas more traditional approaches... emphasize the interplay between the outer world and how this is represented in the minds of actors in ways that lead to more or less effective behaviour, a relational understanding is an opportunity to focus on processes in which both the actor and the world around him or her are created in ways that either expand or contract the space of possible action. (p. 181)

Relational perspectives do not adopt traditional organizational and management language of "structures" and "entities"; instead, they view organizations as elaborate relational networks of changing persons, moving forward together through space and time, in a complex interplay of effects between individual organizational members and the system into which they enter (Abell and Simons 2000; cf., Sayles 1964). In this way, organizations change as a result of the "co-ordination" of people's language and actions in relation to each other *at all levels* and to the ever-changing larger socioeconomic environment (Abell and Simons 2000). Moreover, power is not a commodity, concentrated within certain individuals, but is distributed throughout the social field (Foucault 1977).

Applied to leadership, a relational perspective changes the focus from the individual to the collective dynamic (e.g., to combinations of interacting relations and contexts). It sees an appointed leader as one voice among many in a larger coordinated social process (Hosking 2007). "Within a relational perspective appointed leaders share responsibility with others for the construction of a particular understanding of relationships and their enactment... leaders and those with whom they interact are responsible for the kinds of relationships they construct together" (Dachler and Hosking 1995: 15). Whereas entity approaches focus their attention on the quality and type of interpersonal relationships that occur among interacting individuals and groups, relational perspectives emphasize the *relational* (i.e., *"in relation to"*) – they view multiple realities of self and other as coevolving, or constructed "in relation" (Hosking 2007).

Relational Constructionism

The most prominent work on relational perspectives in leadership is that of Hosking, Dachler, and colleagues (Dachler 1988, 1992; Dachler and Hosking 1995; Hosking 1988; Hosking and Fineman 1990; Hosking and Morley 1988; Hosking et al. 1995). Calling for a change in leadership research strategy that switched attention from leaders, as persons, to leadership as process, Hosking (1988) argued that *"we need to understand leadership, and for this, it is not enough to understand what leaders do* [emphasis added]" (p. 147). Instead, we must focus on processes – the influential acts of organizing that contribute to the structuring of interactions and relationships. In these processes, interdependencies are organized in ways which, to a greater or lesser degree, promote the values and interests of the social order; definitions of social order are negotiated, found acceptable, implemented and renegotiated (Hosking 1988).

Similarly, Dachler (1992) argued that the main focus of leadership, management and organization research would be better directed at *social processes* rather than specific content issues (e.g., leader behaviors, contents of employee motivation), since such content issues are "not 'facts of an objective organizational reality', but an emergent reflection of socially constructed realities in constant change" (p. 171; cf., Rost 1991). Both Hosking (1988) and Dachler (1992) see leadership as a process of organizing that breaks down the traditional distinction between "leadership of people" and "the management of organization." Rather than searching for traits, behavioral styles, or identifying particular types of leaders or people management techniques, a relational ontology raises different questions for leadership. For example, it asks how the processes of leadership and management in organizations emerge – e.g., how realities of leadership are interpreted within the network of relations; how organizations are designed, directed, controlled and developed on the bases of collectively generated knowledge about organizational realities; and how decisions and actions are embedded in collective sense-making and attribution processes from which structures of social interdependence emerge and in turn reframe the collectively generated organizational realities (see Dachler 1992: 171).

The key difference between relational and entity perspectives is that relational perspectives identify the basic unit of analysis in leadership research as *relationships*, not individuals. However, relationships have a quite different meaning from entity perspectives:

> By relationships we do not refer to the still dominating paradigmatic conception of basically instrumental and influence-based notions of interpersonal, intra-group, inter-group and other forms of relationships that are still for the most part implied in current theories and practice of relational phenomena.. .. Relationships are inherently communicative... [They are] subject to multi-meanings since they are produced and heard by others within a multitude of interdependent contexts.. .. [and] *embedded...* in complex multiple and simultaneously activated relational networks. (Dachler 1992: 173)

As described by Hosking (2007), the reference to relating should not be construed as a reference to one person communicating in face-to-face relations with another. *Relational* researchers are not speaking of inter-personal or intrapersonal processes between already known actors, but instead of the "relating of written and spoken language, as well as the relating of nonverbal actions, things, and events" (Hosking 2007).

Consistent with this idea, the focus of relational perspectives is on processes of interaction, conversation, narrating, dialoguing, and multiloguing (Dachler and Hosking 1995). As described by Abell and Simons (2000), relational perspectives adopt a narrative metaphor that engenders:

> A shift in our understanding of organizations as "things" towards experiencing them more as an array of stories, always in the act of construction whose meaning and relevance is context-dependent. Meaning is constantly negotiated and renegotiated in the relational act of conversation, deriving its meaning within the context of its particular sociocultural location. The world is seen as being brought into being via our collaborative "storying" of our experience, implying that as humans, we can actively intervene in constructing the societies and organizations we'd like to see emerge. (p. 161)

Hence, in a relational constructionist perspective, what is and how we know it are viewed as ongoing achievements constructed in sequences of acts/events (Hosking 2000).

Sayles (Lateral Relationships)

Although not purely a *relational* approach, Sayles (1964) description of organizations as systems in which the actions of the manager are embedded not only in an organizational and environmental context but within a dynamic and unfolding history of role-bounded interpersonal relationships (Osborn 1999) are more consistent with relational orientations than traditional entity perspectives. As described by Sayles, because the manager does not have a neatly bounded job but rather is placed in the middle of a stream of relationships, much, if not most of a manager's time is spent on lateral relationships (Ashforth 1999). Management is an iterative and messy interpersonal process in which planning and decision-making are not separate managerial activities but rather a social process that is shaped by interactions with others (Stewart 1999). "To the outsider, the organization may appear to be a stable monolith, but to the insider it more closely resembles a loosely coupled federation of departments" (Ashforth 1999: 22). The organization is actively held together not by its policies and rules and procedures, but the web of interpersonal relationships that is built through ongoing interaction: "The one enduring objective [of managers] is the effort to build and maintain a predictable, reciprocating system or relationship" (Sayles 1964: 258 as quoted in Ashforth 1999: 23).

Drath and Murrell's "Relational Leadership"

The relational perspective is consistent with what Drath (2001) and Murrell (1997) individually refer to as *Relational Leadership*. According to Drath (2001), leadership is not personal dominance (the more traditional leader-centric models) or interpersonal influence (the two-way influence process described by LMX and Hollander's exchange theory) but rather a process of *relational dialogue* in which organizational members engage and interact to construct knowledge systems together. Leadership is generated by bringing in increasing numbers of increasingly responsible people to produce an unfolding of ever more involving and complex knowledge principles. This *relational dialogue* enhances the capacity of a system to accomplish leadership tasks at various levels of complexity. In this way, "the very idea of leadership – what it is and how it works and even how people even know it when they see it – is in the process of changing Nothing less than a revolution of mind is required, a shift in order of thought, a reformation of how leadership is known" (Drath 2001: 124).

Murrell (1997) sees leadership as shared responsibility: "Leadership is a social act, a construction of a "ship" as a collective vehicle to help take us where we as a group, organization or society desire to go" (p. 35). He describes a model of relational leadership in which the focus is broadened to include "more parties to the process than just the leader," and "more than just the leader-follower exchange relationship" (p. 39). His approach moves past what he calls the hero myth that focuses on the behaviors and characteristics of the individual leader to understanding the collective act of leadership (Murrell 1997):

> Relational leadership puts the emphasis of study squarely on human processes of how people decide, act, and present themselves to each other. In this study it is possible to see relationships other than those built from hierarchy and those in which nurturing and supporting roles could be legitimized as means of influence. It is also possible... to envision transformational phenomenon where the social change process occurs well outside the normal assumptions of command and control. (p. 39)

Similar to Drath's (2001) view, Murrell states that by looking more deeply into the relational dynamics of organizations we may be on the verge of a completely new way of seeing leadership. He argues that by studying leadership that occurs relationally, researchers have an opportunity to account for many more of the social forces working to influence group and organizational behavior.

Summary of Relational Perspectives

In summary, relational perspectives view leadership as the processes by which social order is constructed and changed (Hosking and Morley 1988). In a relational perspective, self and other are not separable but coevolving in ways that need to be accounted for in leadership research (cf., Bradbury and Lichtenstein 2000). As described by Hosking (2007), a relational discourse does not view process as "intra" or "interpersonal" or as individual cognitions and acts, but rather as "local-cultural-historical" processes that are moving constructions of what is "real and good" (see also Gergen 1984). Because of this, relational perspectives do not seek to identify attributes or behaviors of individual leaders but instead focus on the communication processes (e.g., dialogue, multilogue) through which relational realities are "made" (Hosking et al. 1995). They share an emphasis on communication and on language as a means of communication (Fairhurst and Putnam 2004); they see dialogue as a dialectical movement between and among human (and nonhuman) phenomena in which true interaction or real meaning emerges in the "space between" (Bradbury and Lichtenstein 2000). A relational perspective views leadership as social reality, emergent and inseparable from context (Dachler and Hosking 1995; Hosking 1988) – an iterative and messy social process that is shaped by interactions with others (Sayles 1964).

Comparing Entity and Relational Perspectives of Relational Leadership

In comparing these two approaches, we can see common themes emerging across entity and relational perspectives that have important implications for leadership research and practice. The most basic underlying theme is the emphasis of both perspectives on relationships, though the meaning of relationship differs across the perspectives. Entity perspectives (e.g., relationship-based leadership) emphasize the importance of interpersonal relationships, while relational perspectives (e.g., relational constructionism) emphasize the importance of "relating" and relatedness (i.e., the processes and condition of being in relation to others and the larger social system in constructing the meaning and reality of leadership). The former focuses primarily on leadership in conditions of already "being organized" while the latter considers leadership as "a process of organizing" (Dachler 1992; Hosking and Morley 1988).

A second theme is the call for leadership to be considered as separate from management and beyond the manager-subordinate dyad (Balkundi and Kilduff 2005; Dachler 1992; Graen 2006; Hosking 1988; Uhl-Bien 2003). Relational leadership approaches allow for consideration of leadership relationships more widely than the traditional focus on the manager-subordinate dyad (Balkundi and Kilduff 2005; Graen 2006; Offstein et al. 2006; Seers 2004; Uhl-Bien et al. 2000). Views of leadership as relational recognize leadership "wherever it occurs" (Hunt and Dodge 2000) and do not fall into the common practice (Bedeian and Hunt 2006) of using the terms *leader* and *manager* interchangeably (Drath 2001; Hosking and Morley 1988; Murrell 1997; Rost 1991; Uhl-Bien 2005). Relational leadership also breaks down the distinction between leader and follower (Rost 1995). It sees leadership not as management, or managers and subordinates, but instead as an interactive process engaged in by *participants* (Hosking 1988; Hosking and Morley 1988), *collaborators* (Rost 1995), or *partners* (Graen and Uhl-Bien 1995; Uhl-Bien et al. 2000).

A third theme is the need to better understand the context in which leadership is embedded. Work on relational and collective self (Brewer and Gardner 1996; Ritter and Lord 2006; Van Knippenberg et al. 2004) recognizes that self-concepts are constructed in the context of interpersonal relationships and larger social systems.

Social identity theory of leadership (Hogg 2001) offers a framework for how group members, acting in relation, engage in social psychological processes that determine whether another will be recognized as a leader of the group (cf., Meindl 1995). Social constructionism sees leadership as embedded in context – person and context are interrelated social constructions made in ongoing localcultural-historical processes (Dachler 1988; Dachler and Hosking 1995; Hosking 2007). Moreover, network theory and extensions of LMX into networks recognize that dyadic relationships are part of a larger system of interacting relationships that comprise organizations and social systems (Balkundi and Kilduff 2005; Graen and Graen 2006; Uhl-Bien et al. 2000).

Despite these similarities, there are also key differences between these approaches (see Table 1). These differences lie primarily in the philosophical underpinnings and methodologies used to examine leadership. In relational constructionism, no attempt is made to raise one approach or perspective over others, nor is there any intention to suggest that there is *one true* variant of relational to constructionism (Hosking and Bouwen 2000). Rather, the ontological emphasis is on leadership as something that cannot be known independently and outside of the scientific observer – what is seen is the leadership reality as leadership observers have constructed it (Dachler 1988) (i.e., there are no leadership "truths," only multiple realities as constructed by

Table 1 Comparison of entity and relational perspectives

	Entity	Relational
Ontological assumptions	Realist (assumes an objective reality) • Views individuals in relationships as separate, independent bounded entities	Relational (assumes a social reality) • All social realities – all knowledge of self and of other people and things – are viewed as interdependent or co-dependent constructions existing and known only in relation
Approach to process	Cognitivist, Constructivist • Individuals performing internal cognitive operations (separable from external social influences) to make sense of and understand how things really are	Constructionist • Person and context are interrelated social constructions made in ongoing local-cultural-historical processes
Approach to methodology	Views relating as an individual act • These acts are reduced to one-way causal relations with feedback; therefore, the basic *unit of analysis is the individual* and studies are operationalized using individual-level variables	Assumes the *primacy of relations* • Focuses on communication as the medium in which all social constructions of leadership are continuously created and changed
View of leadership	Emphasizes the importance of interpersonal relationships • Focuses primarily on leadership in conditions of already "being organized"	Emphasizes the importance of "relating" and relatedness • Considers leadership as "a process of organizing"

participants and observers). In entity perspectives, it is assumed that there is an objective reality and the researcher's job is to uncover facts that reveal this reality; the ontological goal of knowing as completely as possible the real nature of leadership is answered through the authority of science (Dachler 1988).

As such, relational constructionism assumes a *relational ontology* (i.e., all social realities – all knowledge of self and of other people and things – are viewed as interdependent or co-dependent constructions existing and known only in relation, Hosking and Bouwen 2000). Entity perspectives adopt a *realist ontology*, viewing individuals in relationships as separate, independent bounded entities (e.g., Dachler and Hosking 1995; Gergen 1984). Moreover, relational constructionism theorizes processes as *historical and social co-ordinations*. Entity perspectives adopt a *cognitivist, constructivist* approach that theorizes processes as individuals performing "internal" cognitive operations (separable from "external" social influences) to make sense of and understand how things really are (Hosking and Bouwen 2000). In terms of methodology, relational perspectives assume the *primacy of relations* (Dachler and Hosking 1995) and therefore focus on communication as the medium in which all social constructions of leadership are continuously created and changed. Entity perspectives view relating as an individual act, reduced to one-way causal relations with feedback; therefore, the basic *unit of analysis is the individual* (Dachler 1988) and studies are operationalized using individual-level variables (e.g., surveys completed by individual respondents).

The difference in these approaches can be described as modern v. post-modern, but the point in illustrating these differences is not to set up a strict dichotomy or advocate one perspective over the other – in fact, quite the opposite. The intent is to highlight the key assumptions made by each approach, as well as their strengths and weaknesses, so that we can gain a broader understanding of the issues and opportunities that each has to offer. With a better understanding, we may be able to identify ways to advance new learning and new perspectives for the study of relational leadership.

For example, if we set aside for a moment the key ontological and epistemological differences between entity and relational perspectives (e.g., whether reality lies in an individual or in a socially constructed reality) and focus on an objective of enhancing understanding about relational leadership, we can see that the biggest practical difference between the two perspectives is in how they approach, or operationalize, *process*. Entity perspectives, although they refer to process (e.g., social exchange, role-making), *never really examine* it. Approaches to study to date have been static, in the sense that if they do address process (which is rare) these examinations are limited "snapshots" of relational realities as viewed through the perceptions and reported behaviors of respondents (most often using a few variables operationalized with survey questions) (e.g., Uhl-Bien and Maslyn 2003). Even with a greater number and more in-depth snapshots (e.g., longitudinal study), entity methodologies are limited in their ability to capture process, which requires a more dynamic examination of relational interactions as events emerge and unfold. Probably because of this, entity perspectives have done little to highlight the processes by which relationships develop to produce effective leadership – as Rousseau

(1998) said, we know little about what is inside the "black box" of leader-member exchange.

Relational perspectives focus purely on process in local-historical-cultural contexts, to the extent that it is difficult to engage in meaningful theory-building in the traditional sense of the word. As noted by Bradbury and Lichtenstein (2000), relational perspectives, which are dynamic approaches, are much harder to generalize. Therefore they require new standards of validity, reliability, and trustworthiness that are often uncomfortable to entity researchers. Moreover, relational perspectives can be seen as counter to attempts to produce a more unified theory of leadership: "One reason for this may be the inherently complex and psychological assumptions of interdependence and intersubjectivity" (Bradbury and Lichtenstein 2000: 561). Meeting the requirements of interdependence (a more complex understanding of causality) and intersubjectivity (e.g., a strong sense of personal identity) may be difficult for most leadership researchers who received little exposure to these kinds of issues and methods in their research training programs (Bradbury and Lichtenstein 2000: 561).

Without an understanding of the differing assumptions of these approaches and their associated methodologies, and with a continued "parting of the ways" or a failure of entity and relational perspectives to "speak to one another," we risk replicating the current state of understanding, thereby limiting our ability to advance knowledge regarding relational leadership. Therefore, I argue along with Bradbury and Lichtenstein (2000), that a laudable goal is to *gain a measure of integration across numerous methodologies*: "Both normal, multipersonal science and relational science are necessary to generate a more complete understanding of the world" (p. 562).

With this as a background, I now turn to a discussion of *Relational Leadership Theory*. I intend Relational Leadership Theory (RLT) to represent a new framework for leadership theory and research. The objective of RLT is to enhance our understanding of the relational dynamics – the social processes – that comprise leadership and organizing. The key question asked by RLT is: What are the relational (social) processes by which leadership emerges and operates? I contend that we have little understanding currently of these relational dynamics because the vast majority of our existing studies of leadership have neglected to focus on process (Hosking 1988; Hunt and Dodge 2000; Hunt and Ropo 1998; Ropo and Hunt 2000). Therefore, RLT is, at its core, a *process theory* of leadership.

In presenting "Relational Leadership Theory" as an overarching framework for the study of the relational processes of leadership, I hope to contribute to creating what Hosking describes as a "transitional space" that includes "diverse and perhaps radically different 'paradigms" (Kuhn 1970), "discourses" (Deetz 2000) or "intelligibility nuclei" (Gergen 1984)" (Hosking 2007) that, when considered relative to one another, can help illuminate key issues that need to be explored to increase our overall understanding of relational leadership.

Toward a Framework for Relational Leadership Theory

In the opening quote of this article, Hunt and Dodge (2000) refer to relational perspectives as recognizing leadership wherever it occurs, not restricted to a single or even small set of formal or informal leaders, and in its strongest form, functioning as a dynamic system embedding leadership, environmental and organizational aspects. Hunt (2004) describes these approaches as including social network analysis (Burt 1992), leader-member exchange (Graen and Uhl-Bien 1995), lateral and distributive approaches (Sayles 1964; Osborn et al. 1980), and social construction views (Dachler 1988). We see from the review above that, although these approaches can all be considered relational, what they mean by relational is quite different. Therefore, the purpose of this discussion is not to present a "unifying" framework, but rather to describe how these approaches can *engage* with one another to contribute to and advance a study of Relational Leadership Theory. By combining efforts and engaging more open dialogue and adaptive tension (Uhl- Bien et al. 2004), we hope to learn more about one of the most fundamental, but least understood, aspects of leadership: *the relational dynamics of leadership and organizing.*

Moreover, as indicated in the review above, Relational Leadership Theory is the study of both *relationships* (interpersonal relationships as outcomes of or as contexts for interactions) and *relational dynamics* (social interactions, social constructions) of leadership. These can be seen as representing the difference between leadership in the condition of "already being organized" versus the condition of leadership as "a process of organizing" (Hosking 1988). While historically the former has tended to focus less on process (and more on identifying associations between existing variables) and the latter more on process (though in local processes more than in broader contexts) (Hosking 1988), in the sections below I describe how process can be considered in both perspectives. Before I do this, I offer a brief definition of relational leadership and how it can be distinguished from other types of social interactions.

Relational Leadership Theory

Relational Leadership Theory is offered as an overarching framework for the study of the relational dynamics that are involved in the generation and functioning of leadership. Contrary to other studies of leadership, which have focused primarily on the study of leadership *effectiveness*, Relational Leadership Theory focuses on the *relational processes* by which leadership is produced and enabled. It does not define leadership as holding a managerial position, nor does it use the terms *manager* and *leader* interchangeably (cf., Bedeian and Hunt 2006; Hosking 1988). It sees leadership as able to occur in any direction (Rost 1991); in some variations, it may result in the breakdown of the distinction between who is leading and who is following

(Rost 1995), instead reflecting a mutual influence process (Hollander 1978; Graen and Uhl-Bien 1991; Uhl-Bien et al. 2000).

This is not to say that Relational Leadership Theory (RLT) precludes the study of manager-subordinate relationships. These relationships are still important to organizational functioning. However, Relational Leadership recognizes this as just one form of leadership – *managerial leadership* (cf., Uhl-Bien et al. 2004; Sjostrand et al. 2001) – and that other forms may be just as important (e.g., peer, network, upward, adaptive leadership). From a relational leadership perspective, "it is possible to see relationships other than those built from hierarchy... and to envision transformational phenomenon where the social change process occurs well outside the normal assumptions of command and control" (Murrell 1997: 39). Non-hierarchical relationships that are nurturing and supporting could be legitimized as means of influence, and thus forms of leadership (cf., Fletcher 2004; Gronn 2002; Murrell 1997; Pearce and Conger 2003; Seers 2004; Uhl-Bien 2003). This focus breaks away from the prevailing socially constructed notion that position in an organization is necessarily a reflection of leadership. It allows us to account for more of the social forces working to influence group leadership (Gronn 1999), and to view leadership responsibility as lying with the collective and not just the individual leader (Brown and Hosking 1986; Fletcher 2004; Marion and Uhl-Bien 2001; Murrell 1997).

Once we remove leadership from the study of managers, however, the challenge is: How do we identify whether the relational process is "really" leadership? There are multiple ways in which we could address this. One is to use an approach adopted by Dachler and Hosking who identify leadership as a modified form of "status" or influence. For example, as defined by Dachler (1988), relational leadership would address the processes by which: "(1) some social order is constructed; and (2) structurally differentiated groups emerge who proceed to perceive each other's 'qualifications' within constructed realities that become operative through the relationships inherent in or constitutive of social order"(p. 270). Hosking and Morley (1988) described leaders as those who consistently contribute certain kinds of acts to leadership processes. For example, participants are leaders when they: "(1) consistently make effective contributions to social order, and (2) are both expected and perceived to do so by fellow participants" (Hosking and Morley 1988). This is also consistent with Hogg's social identity theory of leadership. As described by Hogg (2005): "Leadership is a relational term – it identifies a relationship in which some people are able to persuade others to adopt new values, attitudes and goals, and to exert effort on behalf of those values, attitudes, and goals" (Hogg 2005: 53).

From this perspective, relational processes are leadership when the social influence that is generated contributes to the emergence of social order (i.e., emergent coordination) and new approaches, attitudes, goals, etc. (i.e., change). This perspective is consistent with the preceding review in which leadership was primarily described as some type of social influence relationship (e.g., Drath 2001; Hollander 1978; Graen and Uhl-Bien 2005; Rost 1991; Sayles 1964), as well as with views that see leadership as change (Bryman 1996). However, it differs in that it adds a perspective of *leadership as an outcome* (M.D. Mumford, personal communication,

February, 2005) – i.e., leadership is generated in social dynamics – rather than leadership as a formal (managerial) role that drives organizational processes.

Another, but perhaps more problematic, option is to predefine what a leadership relationship is, and then measure whether characteristics of that type of relationship are perceived by members in the relationship. This is the approach used in LMX theory and Graen's (2006) new version of LMX-MMX network leadership sharing theory (2006). Although this approach is valuable for identifying types of interpersonal relational contexts in which individuals operate, as House and Aditya (1997) point out, a problem with this approach is that it is too limiting to a specific type of relationship. In other words, although it tells us about LMX relationships (or MMX, which is LMX applied to a peer), we learn little about other types of relationships that may occur in leadership interactions. Additionally, for our purposes here, we learn little about relational processes.

Therefore, in the section below, I adopt an approach more consistent with the former, and offer a general definition of *relational leadership as a social influence process through which emergent coordination (i.e., evolving social order) and change (i.e., new values, attitudes, approaches, behaviors, ideologies, etc.) are constructed and produced.* This definition should be applicable to both entity and relational perspectives, since relating is a dynamic social process that can be seen as acts of individuals (operating in a context) *or* as social constructions of interacting relationships and contexts; it can be seen as either creating (i.e., "organizing" condition) or shifting (i.e., "organized" condition) organizational processes (i.e., social order and action).

Moreover, Relational Leadership Theory as I present it here is not a *theory* in the traditional sense of the word. It is an overarching framework for a variety of methods, approaches, and even ontologies that explore the relational dynamics of leadership and organizing. As described by Fairhurst and Putnam (2004), "The function of theory, as Deetz (1992: 74) purported, is conception not definition. In other words, theory should direct attention and focus rather than characterize the intrinsic nature of stable objects or mirror fixed attributes among them" (p. 8). Therefore, in the paragraphs below I attempt to direct attention and focus on potential questions that could be addressed by RLT, as well as describe some possibilities for how these can be tested considering the potential contributions of both entity and relational perspectives. In this discussion, I do not seek to identify whether entity or relational offers the "best" way to approach the study of relational leadership, but rather, how our perspectives will be informed if we view issues from multiple orientations (Fairhurst and Putnam 2004).

The discussion below is grounded in the following assumptions (cf., Hosking 1988; Hosking and Fineman 1990). First, leadership relationships are not restricted to hierarchical positions or roles. Instead relational leadership occurs throughout the organization: To study the leadership that occurs relationally is to "go more deeply into how human behavior is influenced at all levels" (Murrell 1997: 39). Second, leadership relationships are identified by interactive dynamics that contribute to emergence or direction of social order and action. Third, relational leadership, at a collective level, gets at the "whole process by which social systems change and...

the socially constructed roles and relationships developed that might be labeled leadership" (Murrell 1997: 39). Finally, all relationships occur in a context and this context is important to the study of relational dynamics (cf., Osborn et al. 2002).

Exploring Relational Dynamics

The focus of Relational Leadership Theory research is a better understanding of the relational dynamics – the social processes – that comprise leadership and organizing. Relational Leadership Theory sees leadership as the process by which social systems change through the structuring of roles and relationships (Fletcher 2004; Graen and Scandura 1987; Seers 2004; Senge and Kaeufer 2001; Uhl-Bien 2003, 2005). For example, as described by Murrell (1997):

> As leadership is shared and created jointly, so is the responsibility for structuring the organization... What this means is that people work together to define and develop their relationships not just as questions of influence and leadership, but also as questions of how to keep all of this moving and working together. How to... [work] becomes a question of how we relate to each other and work together. In answering this we lay out a structure... this structure becomes a product of the leadership relationships we envision as appropriate to our condition... [In this way] we become more consciously influencing the structure rather than only it influencing us. (p. 40)

Therefore, a key question asked by RLT is: How do people work together to define their relationships in a way that generates leadership influence and *structuring*? As noted in the quote, this question can be addressed from the standpoint of individual relationships (e.g., How do people work together to define their relationships?) and at a collective level (e.g., How do we keep all this moving and working together such that we become more consciously influencing the structure rather than only it influencing us?). In this way, relationships become both an "outcome" of investigation (i.e., How are leadership relationships produced?) and a context for action (i.e., How do relational dynamics contribute to structuring?).

Relationships as an Outcome As an outcome, the focus of investigation is on how leadership relationships are produced by social interactions. For example, relationships involve some type of connection or bond between an individual and another (a person, group, collectivity, organization, etc.). In some cases, social interactions produce these bonds, and in other cases they do not. However, we do not know why relational bonds form in some instances but not in others, or what factors contribute to formation of relational bonds. When social bonds (i.e., relationships) do result, they can be characterized as strong ties or weak ties (Granovetter 1973), as well as more positive or more negative in nature (Uhl-Bien and Maslyn 2003). Moreover, they can be motivated by instrumental or affective drives (cf., Kellett et al. 2002). Once formed, they provide a context for behaviour – they establish norms and expectations that serve as guidelines for future behavior. However, they remain dynamic, e.g., if norms are violated, the relationship is threatened and relationships can dissolve or re-form in positive or negative ways (Uhl-Bien et al. 2000). Interestingly, although there is much theorizing about how leadership relationships develop (Graen and Uhl-Bien 1991; Hogg 2001; Hollander 1964; Liden et al. 1997; Offstein et al. 2006; Uhl-Bien et al. 2000), we still know very little about these processes, and this is especially true if we expand our view of leadership beyond the manager-subordinate dyad.

Research addressing questions of how and why relational bonds develop as they do in leadership could adopt more of an entity perspective, a relational perspective, or a combination of the two. For example, research could examine *constructivist* concepts of how individuals' "internal" processes relate to how they understand and respond in the development of relationships within a larger context of social relations (an entity perspective). This work could continue the focus described above on social self-concept (relational and collective) (Brewer and Gardner 1996) and relational self-construal (van Knippenberg et al. 2004) as they function within relational processes, as well as consider how other variables identified as important antecedents in LMX research actually play out in relational dynamics (for reviews see Gerstner and Day 1997; Liden et al. 1997; Schriesheim et al. 1999; Uhl-Bien et al. 2000). Moreover, it could consider the role of *relational skills* in leadership development (Uhl-Bien 2003, 2005), exploring whether some individuals possess a greater understanding of how to more consciously manage exchange processes (e.g., testing and reciprocity) to develop more effective relationships in a broader range of relational situations (e.g., lower v. higher relational favorability) than others, and whether and how individuals' implicit theories of relationships play a role in relationship development processes (Uhl-Bien 2005).

Other research could adopt a constructionist perspective and examine the "skillful processes" of relationship development (Hosking 1988) – the interrelated social, cognitive, and political processes which reflect and effect differing values and interests of participants. As described by Hosking (1988), these processes involve and create interdependence and inequalities of influence. Leaders are those who make especially salient contributions, and are recognized as such because participants construe their influence as compatible with the means by which they seek to satisfy their own values and interests. Research on relationships from this perspective would focus on the sense-making activities of participants (Weick 1995), and investigate: (a) acts which influence social constructions (b) those who are perceived to make the most consistent and significant contributions, and (c) why they are perceived to do so (Hosking 1988). This represents a view of leadership as a political process in which different participants seek to further different, sometimes conflicting values and interests. Therefore, such research would consider values and interests of participants as important reflections of "participants' constructions of their pasts, presents, and futures, along with understandings of cause-effect relationships, the conditions for acceptance or rejection of influence attempts, and distributions of resources" (Hosking 1988: 154). These values and interests would be considered as central to participants' constructions of their social order and the terms in which they will "do business" (Hosking 1988) or engage in relationship development.

A pure entity approach could pursue a research program on models like that of Uhl-Bien et al. (2000) or Barry and Crant (2000), while a pure constructionist approach would adopt a post-modern discourse that "problematizes" leadership, e.g., assuming multiple realities and examining processes to consider how leadership relationships are variously constructed in different local-cultural-historical processes (Bryman 1996; Hosking 2007). A combined approach would take a static model like that of Uhl-Bien et al. (2000) (see Fig. 1 in their article) or Barry and Crant (2000) and "bring it to life" by operationalizing it with a richer methodology than using only surveys (and would examine broader relationships than just the manager-subordinate dyad). "Rich" discourse analysis methodologies are available in the communication literature (see Putnam and Fairhurst 2001, for a review) that can help "set in motion" the models by gathering information about the processes that occur among the interacting individuals (Fairhurst and Putnam 2004). Such techniques include sociolinguistics, conversation analysis, cognitive linguistics, pragmatics (including speech acts, ethnography of speaking and interaction analysis), semiotics, rhetorical and literary studies, critical discourse analysis, and post-modern studies (Fairhurst and Putnam 2004). One could also use a combination of theoretical modeling with qualitative approaches (Bryman 2004), grounded theory (Brown and Gioia 2002; Parry and Meindl 2002), case studies (Hunt and Ropo 1998; Ropo and Hunt 2000), etc.

Research could also examine the role of emotions in relational processes. Emotions play a key part in human interactions and dynamics (Ashkanasy et al. 2000; Humphrey 2002; Rafaeli and Worline 2001); therefore, future research could explore how various types of emotion are involved in leadership relationship development and, similarly, leadership emergence. As noted by Ashforth and Humphrey (1995), the literature on emotions is divided between the (a) social constructionist and symbolic interactionist and (b) naturalist and positivist views – perspectives which differ in the extent to which they see emotions as cognitively or socially mediated. These differences, consistent with those between entity and relational perspectives, imply different directions in terms of how relational leadership and emotions could be explored. The former suggests research directions that focus on how different emotions influence the way individuals perceive and interact with others in the process of interpersonal relationship development (e.g., an entity perspective), while the latter would explore how emotion is constructed and spread (i.e., emotional contagion) in the human interactions that take place in ongoing local-cultural-historical contexts.

Relational Dynamics as a Process of Structuring As a process of structuring, or organizing, the focus of investigation in Relational Leadership Theory would be on how relational interactions contribute to the generation and emergence of social order. In contrast to traditional leadership perspectives that view structure as the prescribed framework of the organization, directed by managerial leaders, research investigating Relational Leadership Theory as a process of structuring (Barley 1986; Fombrun 1986; Giddens 1984; Weick 2001) or organizing (Dachler and Hosking 1995; Hosking and Fineman 1990) would view structure as "patterned regularity of interaction," in which leadership can result from everyday practices that organizational members participate in to construct the very "rules" of organizing that they follow (Willmott 1981: 470; see also Hatch 1997; Sjostrand et al. 2001).

For example, structuration theory assumes that organizations bring people into regular interaction with one another, and these repeated interactions are the foundation of social order (Dachler and Hosking 1995; Hatch 1997). Although the repeated interactions generate an image that organization is solid and stable and that formal managerial leaders are "in charge" of events that occur around them (Sjostrand et al. 2001; Streatfield 2001), in reality, structures are highly dynamic and open to many small changes because they depend on the daily reproduction of the interaction patterns that constitute them: "If interaction patterns are disrupted or changed, then the social structure is opened to change" (Hatch 1997: 180). Since leadership is often considered as creating change in organizations (Bryman 1996), the implication of structuring is that leadership not only occurs through the managerial role, but also in the "disruptions" of daily interaction patterns that effect change in structure. These changes could be intentional or not intentional (i.e., "emergent," Uhl-Bien et al. 2004).

For example, Hosking (1988) describes how order is negotiated through a process of decision-making in which one or more participants conclude that the status quo "is changing, is likely to change, or is in need of change, and takes action on that basis" (p. 156). When this occurs, individuals interpret actual and potential events in relation to values and interests and in relation to beliefs about causal connections (i.e., relationships and networks) (Hosking 1988). As individuals make decisions about whether and how to approach changes to the status quo, the role of networking becomes important:

> The concept of "networking" here is used to refer to a major organizing activity, one which may make all the difference to whether or not changes in the *status quo* are understood and handled in ways that protect or further values and interests Networking helps participants to (a) build up their knowledge bases and other resources; (b) come to understand the processes through which they can promote their values and interests, and (c) translate their understandings into action. (Hosking 1988: 158–159)

Therefore, the networking of decision-makers is an important element in establishing the context for generation of social order. However, this conceptualization of networking differs from traditional social network research in that research in this area would not adopt a methodology that maps and identifies the contacts between people. Instead it would focus on the *dynamics* of relationships (weak and strong) and investigate how processes of exchange, influence, and associated values and interests play into these processes (Hosking 1988). It would examine the nature in which order is negotiated, both within and between groups, and explore what "counts" as leadership in contributing to this process.

Moreover, although structure is most apparent when interactions occur regularly, non-repetitive interactions and even *non-interactions* among particular groups or individuals may contribute to the social structure of the organization (Hatch 1997). We can see the importance of this in the example of a strategic reorganization in which top managers may decide to reorganize but the success of their change effort is fully reliant upon whether individuals within the organization decide to change their daily patterns of interaction (Hatch 1997). Traditional leadership theory has considered this likelihood, but has done so from the standpoint of resistance to change in which "subordinates" are noncompliant with directives from above. A structuring perspective sees the locus of leadership as not in the top managers and the compliance of followers but, rather, in the *interactions* that constitute the social structure (see also Weick 2001). Managerial leaders can attempt to influence these patterns of interaction, but they are only one set of players in the larger relational dynamic of structuring, and often their control is much more illusory than traditional leadership theory suggests (Sjostrand et al. 2001; Streatfield 2001).

In sum, the above examples are intended to illustrate some of the possibilities that can be considered by Relational Leadership Theory, but avenues for exploring relational leadership dynamics offer a wide variety of opportunities for future investigation. A critical factor to understand throughout this discussion, however, is that a key difference between relational leadership study and more traditional approaches is the recognition that leadership *is* relational, and cannot be captured by examination of individual attributes alone. Because of this, relational leadership, even when entity approaches are adopted, cannot be fully explained by more traditional leadership variables that do not regard relational context: "Influence in the abstract tells us little about the progress of the system represented by 'leader- with-followers-seeking-results'" (Hollander 1979: 162). For example, "Style is a *relational concept,* and fundamentally different from the idea of a trait because its effect and utility very much depend upon the *reaction of followers*" (Hollander 1979: 163). Therefore, variables that are used should truly capture a relational understanding, and methodologies should provide richer insight into *process* and context than has been offered by traditional leadership approaches.

Such methodologies can be found in Bradbury and Lichtenstein's (2000) review of relationality in organizational research. For example, relational leadership research may benefit from an understanding of participatory methods. These methods are "highly interpersonal, requiring direct communication between everyone involved in the project as to the goals, means, and outcomes of this research" (Bradbury and Lichtenstein 2000: 558). As such, they do not presume that the researcher *knows* the best design or the most appropriate issues to explore – rather the researcher and the organizational participants work in collaboration: "Participatory methods allow participants to cooperate in generating mutually defined projects that are accomplished through the interactions between researchers and subjects (Heron 1996). These projects often create social change in the process of research engagement.. ." (Bradbury and Lichtenstein 2000: 558).

Participatory methods include "insider/outsider research" (Bartunek and Louis 1996), "appreciative inquiry" (Cooperrider and Srivasta 1987), and "action science" (Argyris et al. 1985). In *insider/outsider research* the inside knowledge of a specific organization's practices is combined with a general knowledge of an organizational scholar; data are collected and analyzed in a fully collaborative effort between the insider and the scholar, and the result is model-driven understandings that can be better applied by organizational insiders (Bradbury and Lichtenstein 2000). *Appreciative inquiry* does not adopt the more traditional "problem-focused" orientation, as it can act as a constraint on human imagination and contribution to knowledge but, rather, posits that "we largely create the world which we later discover" (Bradbury and Lichtenstein 2000: 558). In this approach, the researcher enters the situation with an open mind and allows the issues to reveal themselves. *Action science* is based on consultative interactions between researcher and subjects where participants are encouraged to inquire into the set of assumptions and presuppositions that support their behaviors. "The goal is to create 'usable knowledge' (Argyris et al. 1985: ix) by articulating features of a science to inform how we might change the circumstances in which we live" (Bradbury and Lichtenstein 2000: 558). This approach posits that the generation and testing of propositions concerning the variables embedded in the status quo are a core concern to all.

Relational leadership exploring structuring would benefit from qualitative approaches that "uncover the invisible assumptions that generate social structures" (Bradbury and Lichtenstein 2000: 557). Overall, this type of work benefits from intensive ethnographic and interview-based methodologies (Barley 1986; Bradbury and Lichtenstein 2000; Cooren and Fairhurst 2004). Bradbury and Lichtenstein (2000) offer some examples, including Schein's model of organizational culture (which provides analytic methods for studying assumptions and beliefs that give rise to culture) and Barley's (1986) structurationist analysis (which combines qualitative ethnographic data with quantitative analysis of coded data to see how beliefs translate into tangible organizational systems and structures).

Finally, relational leadership might also explore the role of aesthetics in leadership processes (Grint 2005; Heron and Reason 2001; Ropo 2005; Strati 2000). As defined by Taylor and Hansen (2005), the study of aesthetics is concerned with knowledge that is created from sensory experiences, e.g., how one's thoughts, feelings and reasoning around their sensory experiences might inform their cognitions. Aesthetics can serve as a means for *connection* (Taylor and Hansen 2005), as patterns that connect mind and nature (Bateson 1979), or provide a sense of belonging to or being a part of a social group (Sandelands 1998). For example, aesthetics can be sensory reactions to leadership images (Jackson and Guthey 2007) – images that evoke a sense of connection to a depicted leader.

On a more personal level, Ropo (2005) describes aesthetic perspectives to leadership that include reactions to beauty and the presence of the living body (e.g., the body as a source of knowing, lived experiences, sensuous perceptions). It could also include senses evoked from the physical places and spaces in which humans encounter one another with emotions, multiple voices, listening, touching, and bodily presence (Ropo 2005). As applied to relational leadership, this perspective could focus on the aesthetic qualities of either the leader or the follower (i.e., an entity view), as well as consideration of how the relationship looks and feels – e.g., the extent to which it appeals to one's aesthetic sensibilities, both consciously and unconsciously (i.e., the relational view) (B. Jackson, personal communication, September, 2006).

Conclusion

Relationships – rather than authority, superiority, or dominance – appear to be key to new forms of leadership (Drath 2001). Yet, while relationships are at the heart of many of the new approaches emerging in the leadership literature, e.g., distributed (Gronn 2002), distributive (Brown and Gioia 2002), shared (Pearce and Conger 2003), post-heroic (Fletcher 2004), and complexity (Marion and Uhl-Bien 2001), we know surprisingly little about how relationships form and develop in the workplace. Moreover, investigation into the relational dynamics of leadership as a process of organizing has been severely overlooked in leadership research (Hosking 1988; Hosking and Fineman 1990).

The predominant approach to the study of relationships in leadership has been LMX theory. Although LMX informs us about the value of relationships, and provides a theoretical description of how dyadic relationships form, it has likely reached stage 3 of Reichers and Schneider's "evolution of concepts" framework (Hunt and Dodge 2000). As noted by Murrell (1997), the breakthrough in the LMX literature is in legitimizing a question of how the relationships of leaders and followers better explain or help direct leadership research. However, to contribute to understanding it would have to evolve into more sociological or social-psychology orientations and go beyond the limited focus on dyadic or leader-follower singular relationships (Murrell 1997). To do this, we need to morph what we have learned into a next stage of evolution – into a framework for the study of Relational Leadership Theory. We need to move beyond a focus on the manager-subordinate dyad or a *measure* of relationship quality to address the question of, what are the relational *dynamics* by which leadership is developed throughout the workplace?

Such an approach opens up the possibility for relational leadership as moving toward a more "postindustrial" model of leadership (Rost 1991) – one that is not hierarchical, can address various forms of relationships (not just dyadic and not just "leader-follower" relationships), focuses on relational dynamics (rather than a more static state of relational quality with antecedents and outcomes), and allows us to consider leadership as a process of structuring (Giddens 1984; Murrell 1997). Investigating relational leadership will require richer methodologies than over-reliance on cross-sectional survey data using limited measures (Bradbury and Lichtenstein 2000; Bryman 2004). It would allow us to consider *processes* that are not just about the quality of the relationship or even the type of relationship, but rather about the social dynamics by which leadership relationships form and evolve in the workplace. In this way, it moves leadership beyond a focus on simply getting alignment (and productivity) or a manager's view of what is productive, to a consideration of how leadership arises through the interactions and negotiation of social order among organizational members.

Acknowledgments The author would like to thank Russ Marion, Rebecca Grey, Bob Lord, George Graen, Brad Jackson, and four anonymous reviewers for their assistance and suggestions as this article was being developed. This article originally appeared in *Leadership Quarterly* 17 (2006: 654–676). Republished by permission of the journal and the author.

References

Abell, E. and S. Simons (2000). How much can you bend before you break: An experience of using constructionist consulting as a tool for organizational learning in the corporate world. *European Journal of Work & Organizational Psychology* 9(2):159–175.

American Heritage Dictionary (2000). *American Heritage Dictionary of the English Language*, 10th edn. Boston, MA: Houghton Mifflin Company.

Andersen, S.M. and S. Chen (2002). The relational self: An interpersonal social-cognitive theory. *Psychological Review* 109(4):619–645.

Argyris, C., R. Putnam and D. Smith (1985). *Action Science*. San Francisco, CA: Jossey Bass.

Ashforth, B.E. (1999). Leadership as an embedded process: Some insights from Sayles' *Managerial Behavior*. *The Leadership Quarterly* 10(1):21–24.

Ashforth, B.E. and R.H. Humphrey (1995). Emotions in the workplace: A reappraisal. *Human Relations* 48(2):97–125.

Ashkanasy, N.M., C. Hartel and W.J. Zerbe (eds.) (2000). *Emotions in the Workplace: Theory, Research and Practice*. Westport, CT: Quorum Books.

Balkundi, P. and M. Kilduff (2005). The ties that lead: A social network approach to leadership. *The Leadership Quarterly* 16(6):941–961.

Barley, S.R. (1986). Technology as an occasion for structuring: Evidence from observations of ct scanners and the social order of radiology departments. *Administrative Science Quarterly* 31(1):78–108.

Barry, B. and J.M. Crant (2000). Dyadic communication relationships in organizations: An attribution/expectancy approach. *Organization Science* 11(6):648–664.

Bartunek, J.H. and M. Louis (1996). Insider/Outsider Team Research. Thousand Oaks, CA: Sage

Bateson, G. (1979). *Mind and Nature: A Necessary Unity*. New York, NY: E.P. Dutton

Bedeian, A.G. and J.G. Hunt (2006). Academic amnesia and vestigial assumptions of our forefathers. *The Leadership Quarterly* 17(2):190–205.

Blau, P.M. (1964). *Exchange and Power in Social Life*. New York, NY: Wiley.

Borgatti, S.P. and P.C. Foster (2003). The network paradigm in organizational research: A review and typology. *Journal of Management* 29(6):991–1013.

Bouwen, R. and D.M. Hosking (2000). Reflections on relational readings of organizational learning. *European Journal of Work & Organizational Psychology* 9(2):267–274.

Boyd, N.G. and R.R. Taylor (1998). A developmental approach to the examination of friendship in leader-follower relationships. *The Leadership Quarterly* 9(1):1–25.

Bradbury, H. and B. Lichtenstein (2000). Relationality in organizational research: Exploring the "space between". *Organization Science* 11(5):551–564.

Brewer, M.B. and W. Gardner (1996). Who is this "we"? Levels of collective identity and self representations. *Journal of Personality & Social Psychology* 71(1):83–93.

Brower, H.H., F.D. Schoorman and H.H. Tan (2000). A model of relational leadership: The integration of trust and leader-member exchange. *The Leadership Quarterly* 11(2): 227–250.

Brown, H. and D.M. Hosking (1986). Distributed leadership and skilled performamce as successful organization in social movements. *Human Relations* 39(1):65–79.

Brown, M.E. and D.A. Gioia (2002). Making things 'click': Distributive leadership in an online division of an offline organization. *The Leadership Quarterly* 13(4):397–419.

Bryman, A. (1996). Leadership in organizations. In S.R. Clegg, C. Hardy and W. Nord (eds.) *Handbook of Organization Studies*. London: Sage Publications, pp. 276–292.

Bryman, A. (2004). Qualitative research on leadership: A critical but appreciative review. *The Leadership Quarterly* 13(4):397–419.

Burt, R.S. (1992). *Structural Holes: The Social Structure of Competition*. Cambridge, MA: Harvard University Press.

Cooperrider, D.L. and S. Srivasta (1987). Appreciative inquiry into organizational life. *Research in organizational change and development* 1:129–169.

Cooren, F. and G.T. Fairhurst (2004). Speech timing and spacing: The phenomenon of organizational closure. *Organization* 11(6):793–824.

Dachler, H.P. (1988). Constraints on the emergence of new vistas in leadership and management research: An epistemological overview. In J.G. Hunt, B.R. Baliga, H.P. Dachler and C.A. Schriesheim (eds.), *Emerging Leadership Vistas*. Lexington, MA: Lexington Books/ D.C. Heath and Co., pp. 261–285.

Dachler, H.P. (1992). Management and leadership as relational phenomena. In M.v. Cranach, W. Doise and G. Mugny (eds.), *Social Representations and Social Bases of Knowledge*. Lewiston, NY: Hogrefe and Huber, pp. 169–178.

Dachler, H.P. and D.M. Hosking (1995). The primacy of relations in socially constructing organizational realities. In D.M. Hosking, H.P. Dachler and K.J. Gergen (eds.), *Management and Organization: Relational Alternatives to Individualism*. Aldershot: Avebury, pp. 1–29.

Deetz, S. (1992). *Democracy in an Age of Corporate Colonization*. Albany, NY: State University of New York Press.

Deetz, S. (2000). Describing differences in approaches to organisation science. In P. Frost, R. Lewin and D. Daft (eds.), *Talking About Organisation Science*. Thousand Oaks, CA: Sage.

Drath, W. (2001). *The Deep Blue Sea: Rethinking the Source of Leadership*. San Francisco, CA: Jossey-Bass and Center for Creative Leadership.

Fairhurst, G.T. and L. Putnam (2004). Organizations as discursive constructions. *Communication Theory* 14(1):5–26.

Fletcher, J.K. (2004). The paradox of postheroic leadership: An essay on gender, power, and transformational change. *The Leadership Quarterly* 15(5):647–661.

Fombrun, C.J. (1986). Structural dynamics within and between organizations. *Administrative Science Quarterly* 31(3):403–421.

Foucault, M. (1977). *Discipline and Punish: The Birth of the Prison*. London: Allen and Lane.

Gergen, K.J. (1994). *Realities and Relationships*. Cambridge, MA: Harvard University Press.

Gergen, K. (1984). "An Introduction to Historical Social Psychology." *Historical Social Psychology*, 3:36.

Gerstner, C.R. and D.V. Day (1997). Meta-analytic review of leader-member exchange theory: Correlates and construct issues. *Journal of Applied Psychology* 82(6):827–844.

Giddens, A. (1984). *The Constitution of Society: Outline of the Theory of Structuration*. Berkeley, CA: University of California Press.

Graen, G. (2006). Post Simon, March, Weick, and Graen: New leadership sharing as a key to understanding organizations. In G. Graen and J.A. Graen (eds.), *Sharing Network Leadership*, vol. 4. Greenwich, CT: Information Age, pp. 269–279.

Graen, G. and J.A. Graen (2006). *Sharing Network Leadership*, vol. 4. Greenwich, CT:Information Age.

Graen, G.B., M.A. Novak and P. Sommerkamp (1982). The effects of leader-member exchange and job design on productivity and satisfaction: Testing a dual attachment model. *Organizational Behavior & Human Performance* 30(1):109–131.

Graen, G.B. and T. Scandura (1987). Toward a psychology of dyadic organizing. In B.M. Staw and L.L. Cummings (eds.), *Research in Organizational Behavior*, vol. 9. Greenwich, CT: JAI Press, pp. 175–208.

Graen, G. and M. Uhl-Bien (1991). The transformation of professionals into self-managing and partially self-designing contributors: Toward a theory of leadership-making. *Journal of Management Systems* 3(3):49–54.

Graen, G. and M. Uhl-Bien (1995). Relationship-based approach to leadership: Development of leader-member exchange (LMX) theory of leadership over 25 years: Applying a multi-level multi-domain perspective. *The Leadership Quarterly* 6(2):219–247.

Granovetter, M. (1973). The strength of weak ties. *American Journal of Sociology* 78:1360–1380.

Grint, K. (2005). *Leadership: Limits and Possibilities*. Basingstoke: Palgrave-Macmillan.

Gronn, P. (1999). *A realist view of leadership*. Paper presented at the Educational leaders for the new millenium – Leaders with soul, ELO-AusAsia On-line Conference.

Gronn, P. (2002). Distributed leadership as a unit of analysis. *The Leadership Quarterly* 13(4): 423–451.

Hatch, M.J. (1997). *Organization Theory: Modern, Symbolic, and Postmodern Perspectives.* Oxford: Oxford University Press.

Heider, F. (1958). *The Psychology of Interpersonal Relations.* New York, NY: Wiley.

Heron, J. (1996). Quality as primacy of the practical. *Qualitative Inquiry* 2(3):41–56.

Heron, J. and P. Reason (2001). The practice of co-operative inquiry: Research "with" rather than "on" people. In P. Reason and H. Bradbury (eds.), *Handbook of Action Research: Participative Inquiry and Practice.* London: Sage, pp. 179–188.

Hogg, M.A. (2001). A social identity theory of leadership. *Personality & Social Psychology Review* 5(3):184–200.

Hogg, M.A. (2005). Social identity and leadership. In D.M. Messick and R.M. Kramer (eds.), *The Psychology of Leadership: New Perspectives and Research.* Mahwah, NJ: Erlbaum, pp. 53–80.

Hollander, E.P. (1958). Conformity, status, and idiosyncrasy credit. *Psychological Review* 65: 117–127.

Hollander, E.P. (1964). *Leaders, Groups, and Influence.* New York, NY: Oxford University Press.

Hollander, E.P. (1978). *Leadership Dynamics: A Practical Guide to Effective Relationships.* New York, NY: Free Press

Hollander, E.P. (1979). The impact of Ralph M. Stogdill and the Ohio State leadership studies on a transactional approach to leadership. *Journal of Management* 5(2):157–165.

Hollander, E.P. (1992). The essential interdependence of leadership and followership. *Current Directions in Psychological Science* 1(2):71–75.

Hollander, E.P. (1995). Ethical challenges in the leader-follower relationship. *Business Ethics Quarterly* 5(1):55–65.

Hollander, E.P. and J.W. Julian (1969). Contemporary trends in the analysis of leadership processes. *Psychological Bulletin* 71(5):387–397.

Holmberg, R. (2000). Organizational learning and participation: Some critical reflections from a relational perspective. *European Journal of Work & Organizational Psychology* 9(2): 177–188.

Homans, G.C. (1961). *Social Behavior: Its Elementary Forms.* New York, NY: Harcourt, Brace, and World.

Homans, G.C. (1974). *Social Behavior: Its Elementary Forms*, Rev. edn. New York, NY: Harcourt Brace Jovanovich.

Hosking, D.M. (1988). Organizing, leadership, and skilful process. *Journal of Management Studies* 25(2):147–166.

Hosking, D.M. (2000). Ecology in mind, mindful practices. *European Journal of Work and Organizational Psychology* 9(2):147–158.

Hosking, D.M. and R. Bouwen (2000). Organizational learning: Relational-constructionist approaches: An overview. *European Journal of Work & Organizational Psychology* 9(2): 129–132.

Hosking, D.M., H.P. Dachler and K.J. Gergen (eds.) (1995). *Management and Organization: Relational Alternatives to Individualism.* Brookfield, CT: Avebury.

Hosking, D. and S. Fineman (1990). Organizing processes. *Journal of Management Studies* 27(6):583–604.

Hosking, D.-M. and I.E. Morley (1988). The skills of leadership. In J.G. Hunt, B.R. Baliga, H.P. Dachler and C.A. Schriesheim (eds.), *Emerging Leadership Vistas.* Lexington, MA: Lexington Books/D. C. Heath and Co., pp. 80–106.

Hosking, D.M. (2007). Not leaders, not followers: A post-modern discourse of leadership processes. In B. Shamir, R. Pillai, M. Bligh and M. Uhl-Bien (eds.), *Follower-Centered Perspectives on Leadership: A Tribute to the Memory of James R. Meindl* (pp. 243–264). Greenwich, CT: Information Age Publishing.

House, R.J. and R. Aditya (1997). The social scientific study of leadership: Quo vadis? *Journal of Management* 23:409–474.

Howell, J.M. and B. Shamir (2005). The role of followers in the charismatic leadership process: Relationships and their consequences. *Academy of Management Review* 30(1):96–112.

Humphrey, R.H. (2002). The many faces of emotional leadership. *The Leadership Quarterly* 13:493–504.

Hunt, J.G. (2004). What is leadership? In J. Antonakis, A.T. Cianciolo and R.J. Sternberg (eds.), *The Nature of Leadership*. Thousand Oaks, CA: Sage Publications, pp. 19–48.

Hunt, J. and G.E. Dodge (2000). Leadership déjà vu all over again. *The Leadership Quarterly Review of Leadership* 11(4):435–458.

Hunt, J.G. and A. Ropo (1998). Multi-level leadership: Grounded theory and mainstream theory applied to the case of general motors. In F. Dansereau and F.J. Yammarino (eds.), *Leadership: The Multiple-Level Approaches*. Westport, CT: JAI Press, pp. 289–328.

Ibarra, H., M. Kilduff and W. Tsai (2005). Zooming in and out: Connecting individuals and collectivities at the frontiers of organizational network research. *Organization Science* 16(4):359–371.

Jackson, B. and E. Guthey (2007). Putting the visual into the social construction of leadership. In B. Shamir, R. Pillai, M. Bligh and M. Uhl-Bien (eds.), *Follower-Centered Perspectives on Leadership: A Tribute to the Memory of James R. Meindl* (pp. 167–186). Greenwich, CT: Information Age Publishing.

Jacobs, T.O. (1971). *Leadership and Exchange in Formal Organizations*. Alexandria, VA: Human Resources Research Organization.

Jermier, J. (1993). Introduction – Charismatic leadership: Neo-weberian perspectives. *The Leadership Quarterly* 4(3-4):217–233.

Kark, R. and B. Shamir (2002). The influence of transformational leadership on followers' relational versus collective self-concept. *Academy of Management Proceedings*.

Katz, D. and R.L. Kahn (1978). *The Social Psychology of Organizations*. New York, NY: Wiley

Kellett, J.B., R.H. Humphrey and R.G. Sleeth (2002). Empathy and complex task performance: Two routes to leadership. *The Leadership Quarterly* 13(5):523–545.

Kilduff, M. and W. Tsai (2003). *Social Networks and Organizations*. London: Sage.

Klein, K.J. and R.J. House (1995). On fire: Charismatic leadership and levels of analysis. *The Leadership Quarterly* 6(2):183–198.

Krackhardt, D. (1999). The ties that torture: Simmelian tie analysis in organizations. *Research in the sociology of organizations* 16:183–210.

Kuhn, T.S. (1970). *The Structure of Scientific Revolutions*, 2nd edn. Chicago, IL: The University of Chicago Press.

Liden, R.C., R.T. Sparrowe, S.J. Wayne and G.R. Ferris (1997). Leader-member exchange theory: The past and potential for the future. In *Research in Personnel and Human Resources Management*, vol. 15. New York, NY/Greenwich, CT: Elsevier Science/JAI Press, pp. 47–119.

Likert, R. (1961). *New Patterns of Management*. New York, NY: McGraw-Hill.

Lipman-Blumen, J. (1996). *Connective Leadership: Managing in a Changing World*. New York, NY: Oxford University Press.

Lord, R.G., D.J. Brown and S.J. Freiberg (1999). Understanding the dynamics of leadership: The role of follower self-concepts in the leader/follower relationship. *Organizational Behavior and Human Decision Processes* 78:1–37.

Lord, R.G. and K.J. Maher (1991). *Leadership and Information Processing: Linking Perceptions and Performance*. Boston, MA: Unwin Hyman.

Marion, R. and M. Uhl-Bien (2001). Leadership in complex organizations. *The Leadership Quarterly* 12:389–418.

Meindl, J. (1995). The romance of leadership as a follower-centric theory: A social constructionist approach. *The Leadership Quarterly* 6(3):329–341.

Murrell, K.L. (1997). Emergent theories of leadership for the next century: Towards relational concepts. *Organization Development Journal* 15(3):35–42.

Offstein, E.H., R. Madhavan and D.R. Gnyawali (2006). Pushing the frontier of LMX research: The contribution of triads. In G. Graen and J.A. Graen (eds.), *Sharing Network Leadership*, vol. 4. Greenwich, CT: Information Age Publishing.

Osborn, R.N. (1999). Sayles' managerial behavior: Its impact on understanding leadership and nuclear power safety. *The Leadership Quarterly* 10(1):13–15.

Osborn, R.N., J.G. Hunt and L.R. Jauch (1980). *Organization Theory*. New York, NY: John Wiley.

Osborn, R.N., J.G. Hunt and L.R. Jauch (2002). Toward a contextual theory of leadership. *The Leadership Quarterly* 13:797–837.

Parry, K. and J. Meindl (eds.) (2002). *Grounding Theory and Leadership in Research: Issues and Perspectives*. Greenwich, CT: Information Age Publishing.

Pearce, C.L. and J.A. Conger (2003). *Shared Leadership: Reframing the Hows and Whys of Leadership*. Thousand Oaks, CA: Sage.

Phillips, A.S. and A.G. Bedeian (1994). Leader-follower exchange quality: The role of personal and interpersonal attributes. *Academy of Management Journal* 37(4):990–1001.

Putnam, L.L. and G.T. Fairhurst (2001). Discourse analysis in organizations. In F.M. Jablin and L. Putnam (eds.), *The New Handbook of Organizational Communication*. Thousand Oaks, CA: Sage, pp. 78–136.

Rafaeli, A. and M. Worline (2001). Individual emotion in work organizations. *Social Science Information* 40(1):95–123.

Ritter, B.A. and R.G. Lord (2006). *Leadership transference: The impact of previous leaders on follower performance*. Working Paper.

Ropo, A. (2005). *Aesthetic perspective to leadership*. Paper presented in a professional development workshop at the National Academy of Management Meeting, Honolulu, Hawaii.

Ropo, A. and J.G. Hunt (2000). Leadership and organizational change: Some findings from a processual grounded theory study. In J.A. Wagner III (ed.), *Advances in Qualitative Organizational Research*, vol. 2. Stamford, CT: JAI Press, pp. 169–200.

Rost, J.C. (1991). *Leadership for the Twenty-First Century*. London: Praeger.

Rost, J.C. (1995). Leadership: A discussion about ethics. *Business Ethics Quarterly* 5(1): 129–142.

Rousseau, D.M. (1998). LMX meets the psychological contract: Looking inside the black box of leader-member exchange. In F. Dansereau and F.J. Yammarino (eds.), *Leadership: The Multiple-Level Approaches (Contemporary and Alternative)*. Stamford, CT: JAI Press, pp. 149–154.

Sandelands, L.E. (1998). Feeling and Form in Social Life. Lanham, MD: Rowman and Littlefield.

Sayles, L. (1964). *Managerial Behavior: Administration in Complex Organizations*. New York, NY: McGraw Hill.

Schriesheim, C.A., S.L. Castro and C.C. Cogliser (1999). Leader-member exchange (LMX) research: A comprehensive review of theory, measurement, and data-analytic practices. *The Leadership Quarterly* 10(1):63–113.

Seers, A. (2004). Leadership and flexible organizational structures: The future is now. In G.B. Graen (ed.), *New Frontiers of Leadership*, vol. 2. Greenwich, CT: Information Age, pp. 1–31.

Senge, P. and K. Kaeufer (2001). Communities of leadership or no leadership at all. In S. Chowdhury (ed.), *Management 21c*. New York, NY: Prentice Hall, pp. 186–204.

Shamir, B. (1991). Meaning, self and motivation in organizations. *Organization Studies* 12(3): 405–425.

Shamir, B., R.J. House and M.B. Arthur (1993). The motivational effects of charismatic leadership: A self-concept based theory. *Organization Science* 4(4):577–594.

Simmel, G. (1950). *The Isolated Individual and the Dyad. The Sociology of Georg Simmel*. Glencoe, IL: Free Press, pp. 118–136.

Sjostrand, S.-E., J. Sandberg and M. Tyrstrup (eds.) (2001). *Invisible Management: The Social Construction of Leadership*. London: Thompson Learning.

Sparrowe, R. and R. Liden (1997). Process and structure in leader-member exchange. *Academy of Management Review* 22(2):522–552.

Sparrowe, R. and R. Liden (2005). Two routes to influence: Integrating leader-member exchange and social network perspective. *Administrative Science Quarterly* 50(4):505–535.

Stewart, R. (1999). Some observations concerning Sayles' managerial behavior. *The Leadership Quarterly* 10(1):17–20.

Stogdill, R.M. and A.E. Coons (1957). *Leader Behavior: Its Description and Measurement.* Columbus, OH: Ohio State University Press.

Stogdill, R.M., O.S. Goode and D.R. Day (1962). New leader behavior description subscales. *Journal of Psychology: Interdisciplinary and Applied* 54(2):259–269.

Strati, A. (2000). The aesthetic approach to organization studies. In H. Hopfl (ed.), *The Aesthetics of Organization.* London: Sage, pp. 13–34.

Streatfield, P.J. (2001). *The Paradox of Control in Organizations.* London: Routledge.

Taylor, S.S. and H. Hansen (2005). Finding form: Looking at the field of organizational aesthetics. *Journal of Management Studies* 42(6):1211–1231.

Tichy, N.M., M.L. Tushman and C. Fombrun (1979). Social network analysis for organizations. *Academy of Management Review* 4(4):507–519.

Turner, J.C., M.A. Hogg, P. Oakes, S. Reicher and M. Wetherell (1987). *Rediscovering the Social Group: A Self-Categorization Theory.* Oxford, UK: Basil Blackwell.

Uhl-Bien, M. (2003). Relationship development as a key ingredient for leadership development. In S. Murphy and R. Riggio (eds.), *The Future of Leadership Development.* Mahwah, NJ: Lawrence Erlbaum Associates Inc., pp. 129–147.

Uhl-Bien, M. (2005). Implicit theories of relationships in the workplace. In B. Schyns and J.R. Meindl (eds.), *Implicit Leadership Theories: Essays and Explorations.* Greenwich, CT: Information Age Publishing, pp. 103–133.

Uhl-Bien, M., G. Graen and T. Scandura (2000). Implications of leader-member exchange (LMX) for strategic human resource management systems: Relationships as social capital for competitive advantage. In G.R. Ferris (ed.), *Research in Personnel and Human Resource Management,* vol. 18. Greenwich, CT: JAI Press, pp. 137–185.

Uhl-Bien, M., R. Marion and B. McKelvey (2004). *Complexity leadership theory: Shifting leadership from the industrial age to the knowledge era.* Paper presented at the National Academy of Management Meeting, New Orleans, LA.

Uhl-Bien, M. and J.M. Maslyn (2003). Reciprocity in manager-subordinate relationships: Components, configurations, and outcomes. *Journal of Management* 29(4):511–532.

van Knippenberg, D., B. van Knippenberg, D. de Cremer and M.A. Hogg (2004). Leadership, self, and identity: A review and research agenda. *The Leadership Quarterly* 15(6):825–856.

Weick, K.E. (1995). Sensemaking in Organizations. Thousand Oaks, CA: Sage.

Weick, K.E. (2001). Making Sense of the Organization. Oxford: Blackwell.

Weierter, S.J.M. (1997). Who wants to play "follow the leader?" A theory of charismatic relationships based on routinized charisma and follower characteristics. The Leadership Quarterly 8(2):171–193.

Willmott, H. (1981). The structuring of organizational structure: A note. *Administrative Science Quarterly* 26:470–474.

Mary Uhl-Bien is BNSF Endowed Professor of Leadership at the TCU Neeley School of Business in Texas. Previously she held the Howard Hawks Chair in Business Ethics and Leadership at the University of Nebraska. She has also been a Visiting Scholar in Sweden, Spain, Portugal and Australia. Her current research focuses on complexity leadership theory, relational leadership and followership, and she has published widely in Leadership Quarterly. Her work on leadership theory is highly cited and she is a leading researcher and thinker in that area.

This Time from Africa: Developing a Relational Approach to Values-Driven Leadership

Mar Pérezts, Jo-Anna Russon, and Mollie Painter

Abstract The importance of relationality in ethical leadership has been the focus of recent attention in business ethics scholarship. However, this relational component has not been sufficiently theorized from different philosophical perspectives, allowing specific Western philosophical conceptions to dominate the leadership development literature. This paper offers a theoretical analysis of the relational ontology that informs various conceptualizations of selfhood from both African and Western philosophical traditions and unpacks its implications for values-driven leadership. We aim to broaden Western conceptions of leadership development by drawing on twentieth century European philosophy's insights on relationality, but more importantly, to show how African philosophical traditions precede this literature in its insistence on a relational ontology of the self. To illustrate our theoretical argument, we reflect on an executive education course called values-driven leadership into action, which ran in South Africa, Kenya, and Egypt in 2016, 2017, and 2018. We highlight an African-inspired employment of relationality through its use of the ME-WE-WORLD framework, articulating its theoretical assumptions with embodied experiential learning.

Keywords Critical leadership studies · Ethical leadership theory and education · Relationality · Ubuntu · Values-driven leadership

M. Pérezts
Emlyon Business School, Lyon, France

J.-A. Russon
School of Education, University of Nottingham, Nottingham, UK

M. Painter (✉)
Responsible and Sustainable Business Lab (RSB Lab), Nottingham Business School, Nottingham Trent University, Nottingham, UK

Gordon Institute of Business Science, University of Pretoria, Pretoria, South Africa
e-mail: mollie.painter@ntu.ac.uk

© The Author(s), under exclusive license to Springer Nature
Switzerland AG 2023
M. Painter, P. H. Werhane (eds.), *Leadership, Gender, and Organization*, Issues in Business Ethics 63, https://doi.org/10.1007/978-3-031-24445-2_8

167

Introduction

Research on ethical leadership development in Africa remains underdeveloped (Smit 2013). As such, a tacit assumption that Western approaches to leadership development suffice in supporting African leaders in their role as champions of values-driven business, may underpin both theory and practice within African and other non-Western contexts. Even more disturbingly, this absence may also reflect persistent colonial and neo-colonial biases in favour of Western philosophical. tradition in ethics education on the African continent (see Nkomo 2011; Murphy and Zhu 2012; Alcadipani et al. 2012; Smith 2013, for general discussions of these issues in management and research). In response to these risks, we will illustrate that there is much to be learned from the African context's diversity and richness in terms of underlying philosophical basis and empirical developments that could inform and enhance business ethics theory, practice and education more broadly. The creation of the *African Journal of Business Ethics* in 2005, and compilations of works like the virtual special issue on advancing business ethics research on Africa in the *Journal of Business Ethics* (Muthuri et al. 2017), and this volume are all important steps in this direction. They reflect a growing interest in the contributions that can originate in this part of the world (George et al. 2016; Kolk and Rivera-Santos 2016) which remain understudied; an interest also empirically visible through the burgeoning initiatives that have sprung worldwide from a variety of perspectives.

In this paper, we wish to further contribute to this growing body of work by focusing on African-inspired theoretical and pedagogical contributions to the area of ethical leadership development (Khoza 2006; Smit 2013), and more specifically to the importance of relationality in ethical leadership. Indeed, relational leadership is a rather recent issue both in general leadership studies (Cunliffe and Eriksen 2011), and in ethical and critical leadership studies (Maak and Pless 2006; Liu 2017; Rhodes and Badham 2018). However, relationality is a core feature and longer-standing concern of the African tradition of *Ubuntu*. Originating in southern Africa, this idea can be translated as "I am we; I am because we are, we are because I am" (Goduka 2000; Sulamoyo 2010). Under this principle, reality itself is understood relationally, in and by relationships. In the words of Nobel Peace laureate Desmond Tutu: others and community constitute "the very essence of being human. (…) It is not 'I think therefore I am'. It says rather 'I am human, therefore I belong, I participate, I share'" (Tutu 1999: 31). Within this conception, "The 'we' is an overarching notion that both supersedes and honours the individual identities within it" (Louw 2010, cited in Tavernaro-Haidarian 2018: 18).

Following recent works demonstrating the value of bringing together African and Anglo-American or other Western intellectual traditions, we believe there is an interesting opportunity to expand present theorizing on relational ethical leadership, this time from an African perspective. Several recent works have laid important foundations in this direction. For instance, Lutz (2009) suggested that the way Ubuntu philosophy places the community at the centre could help global management more adequately address issues pertaining to the common good. Woermann and Engelbrecht (2017) build on Ubuntu to conceptualize stakeholders as relation holders, once again insisting on the interconnections that knot human beings and communities together. Hoffmann and Metz (2017) demonstrate the value of bringing together African and Anglo-American intellectual traditions in their study of what the capabilities approach can learn from an Ubuntu ethic in the context of development theory. The capabilities approach emerged in the 1980s as an alternative approach to development and welfare economics, largely founded by Amartya Sen (1999) and Martha Nussbaum (2000). Hoffmann and Metz (2017) suggest that the more individualistic notions of freedom to realize one's valued human 'capabilities' are not in direct contrast to the communality of an Ubuntu ethic. Rather, they argue that an Ubuntu reading draws attention to the centrality of a relational ethic within the concept of capability and the relational properties of capabilities, and as such should inform new normative perspectives on capabilities. This application of Ubuntu to established conceptual approaches was also adopted by Tavernaro-Haidarian (2018) who draws on Ubuntu to frame a relational model of communication based on the premise that the interests of individuals and groups are 'profoundly bound-up', rather than incompatible. In Ubuntu, leadership is about mutuality and communal relationships based on harmony and fellowship. The centrality of consensus and communal relationships has implications for leadership, because from an Ubuntu perspective the leadership function becomes a process of learning for both 'facilitator' and 'participant'" (Blankenberg 1999: 46, in Tavernaro-Haidarian 2018). Drawing on the central Ubuntu idea that human interests are inherently bound-up and interrelated, we suggest that a core goal of ethical leadership is to work toward the greater good of others (Tavernaro-Haidarian 2018).

However, this burgeoning literature has had little crossfertilization with most of the ethical leadership and relational leadership literatures. Two explanations can be advanced for this. First, Western scholars can easily tend to see them as 'exotic' contributions whose theoretical relevance remains marginal in other contexts, as post-colonial theorists have argued (Ibarra-Colado 2006; Nkomo 2011; Alcadipani et al. 2012 among others). Second, most of these works offer theoretical or philosophical discussions of Ubuntu, but few explain how to translate the principles behind it into practice, thus undermining its empirical relevance in the eyes of many scholars who therefore remain largely unfamiliar with it.

Our paper seeks to address these two issues, firstly by establishing a theoretical dialogue among both traditions and proposing an African-rooted contribution to relational ethical leadership theory, and secondly by showing how this can effectively be put into practice through a pedagogical design. To do so, we draw on an executive education course called *values-driven leadership into action* (VDLA), which has run several times in South Africa, Kenya, and Egypt in 2016, 2017, and 2018. Taking its inspiration from the African context within which it was initiated, the course design presents several characteristics of interest for global business ethics scholars.

First, contrary to most research on business ethics in Africa which tends to focus on country or region-specific cases and surveys which indeed carry significant local insights (e.g. see the collection of Ike 2011; Kagabo 2011; Mawa and Adams 2011; Smurthwaite 2011; and the summary made by Rossouw 2011), VDLA purposefully takes a pan-African approach, where theoretical bases and participants come from a variety of countries, professions, sectors and backgrounds. From its inception, it has incorporated this multi-country, multi-stakeholder perspective, thus fostering rich conversations and contributing to its broader relevance. Second, the course takes an experiential learning approach, which displays the evocative power of a relational ontology rooted in Ubuntu. Third, the exercises developed in the course incorporate both African philosophical traditions such as Ubuntu and the continent's strength in story-telling, combining these with Western contributions, namely Mary Gentile's (2010, 2011, 2012, 2013) *'Giving Voice to Values'* (GVV) approach to pedagogy, which has been implemented across the globe in various cultural and emerging contexts such as India. The VDLA goes beyond GVV in its unique approach to developing relationality through its African experiential pedagogy and exercises tailored to exert this in the context of ethical leadership education.

The VDLA content evolved through the pilot phases into a unique three-day course that engages leaders across various sectors in a course that we believe illustrates a relational approach to values-driven leadership in a way which connects Western and African ontologies. It does so in two distinct ways: Firstly, theoretically, the course takes a relational accountability approach to actions on individual, group and societal levels through what it calls the ME-WE-WORLD framework. The VDLA starts with identifying the affective and relational roots of participants' personal normative beliefs, and proceeds to relate these beliefs to the role they and their organizations can play in addressing systemic societal issues. Secondly, methodologically, the course employs experiential techniques that connect participants, thereby putting Ubuntu philosophy into practice in ethical leadership education.

This paper is structured as follows. We begin by reviewing the literature on ethical leadership, and how recent contributions that include a relational perspective are both at a nascent stage and mostly inspired by Western ontologies and philosophies. Second, we outline a theoretical framework where the longer-standing tradition of Ubuntu can directly speak to the challenges of fostering a relational ethical leadership. To our knowledge, Ubuntu has not been employed in a practical setting on ethical leadership education. We illustrate our argument with the theoretical and experiential aspects of the VDLA course, particularly focusing on one of its key exercises: the 'dream-board exercise'. Thirdly, our discussion section will unpack the theoretical and methodological contributions of this African initiative to ethical leadership education and theory more broadly and will end by discussing potential avenues for pursuing these implications in the course's future occurrences both in African and Western settings.

Ethical Leadership and Relationality: A Review of the Literature

Relational Selves from the Perspective of Western Philosophy

In response to the various disillusionments with the disembodied, 'rational' calculating subject that Western thought inherited from the Enlightenment, poststructuralist philosophers in Europe offer us a more nuanced conception of our own subjectivity. They have contributed significantly to dismantling the subject-object distinction that lies at the heart of our ontologies and epistemologies. It took a while for scholars in organizational theory to start paying attention to the implications of these philosophers for business ethics (Ibarra-Colado et al. 2006; Ladkin 2006; Byers and Rhodes 2007; Jones 2007; Deslandes 2012; Painter-Morland 2012, 2013; Pérezts et al. 2015). In the past 10 years, several books have also appeared claiming to take this approach to the field of business ethics (Jones et al. 2006; Painter-Morland and Ten Ten Bos 2011).

In the European tradition, multiple philosophers offer us rich insights with regards to the relational dynamics that underpin our sense of selfhood. Scholars have drawn on multiple European philosophers, such as Deleuze (Painter-Morland 2012, 2013) Heidegger (Bakken et al. 2013; Blok 2014), Kierkegaard (Deslandes 2011a), Levinas (Bevan and Corvellec 2007), Pascal (Deslandes 2011b), Merleau-Ponty (Kupers 2013; Ladkin 2012), Henry (Faÿ and Riot 2007; Faÿ et al. 2010; Pérezts et al. 2015) and Ricoeur (Deslandes 2012) to help us understand what this relationality entails in the context of organizational life (Painter-Morland 2018).

To mention just one example, Merleau-Ponty's notion of the 'flesh' articulates the way in which our sensate, perceptive bodies are intertwined with the sensible world. This goes some way towards helping us understand what Cooper (2005: 1690) calls the 'interspace' between humans and their environment which emerges as the prime mover of human agency. Merleau-Ponty explains that perception is a two-way, dynamic and interactive process (Ladkin 2012). Thus, when I perceive another person, I am also aware that s/he can perceive me, and my perception is always already altered by this awareness. To articulate the qualitative experience that this constant interplay creates, Merleau-Ponty coined the term "percipient perceptibles". It allows us to understand the way in which others' perceptions of us are integrated within our self-concept and how it informs our own perceptive embodiment. This has inspired organizational theorists such as Ladkin (2012) to argue that we should not overlook the fact that without bodies, the perceptions that create the relational space for ethics would not be possible. This reconceptualization of agency from an embodied point of view has also allowed a reconsideration of the validity of assuming the existence of *homo economicus*, the calculating agent maximizing his or her self-interest, as the centre of organizational life. This critique has allowed a number of other alternative proposals to emerge: *homo reciprocans, homo ludens, homo ecologicus*, etc. (Painter-Morland 2018).

Critical reflections on ethical approaches that make the transcendental subject the locus of action, also extends to justice-theories. In his analysis of the conceptions of justice that inform organizational ethics, Rhodes (2011) highlights that the most prominent contemporary theory that informs our thinking is that of John Rawls, also described as the 'justice as fairness' approach. This approach to justice argues that the relations between people and organizations should be arranged to ensure the fair distribution of rights, duties and benefits among all involved. The principle of justice as fairness lies at the heart of social contracts, and as such, it assumes the existence of calculating individual subjects negotiating for their own benefit. In articulating a poststructuralist response to prominent justice-theories that are designed to avoid some getting more than others (pleonexia), Rhodes (2011) draws on Levinas to reframe the locus of agency from the individual self who is trying to negotiate his/her fair share, towards the 'Other', whose existence demands an ethical response, even when self-interest or legal obligation may not dictate it (Rhodes 2012). In this way, a Levinasian approach to ethics is decidedly relational in a way that Rawlsian principles are not.

Overall, the European poststructuralist tradition has not had a very strong influence on American approaches to business ethics thus far, with most textbooks exclusively drawing on Anglo-American analytic philosophy. There has however been a growing awareness that though European philosophy is helpful in informing decision-making models such as utilitarianism and deontology, it often falls short in terms of inspiring values-driven action and leadership, as we will discuss hereafter.

Ethical Leadership and Relationality

The connection between ethics and leadership is longstanding and the role that individual leaders can play in facilitating ethical action is well documented. When ancient political philosophers, from both East and West advised and reflected on the power figures of their time, they were already theorizing on the leader and leadership with a deep sense of the responsibility and ethics behind it (Prastacos et al. 2012). More recently, the ethical aspects of leadership have been defined in terms of strong or exemplary personality traits, making them worthy of their followers, sometimes almost in a religious sense (Grint 2010). The notion of servant leadership for instance also shares this quasi-religious terminology of serving; the leader being in the service of followers in order to humbly develop them and provide them with guidance (van Dierendonck 2011). In a recent paper, Walton (2018: 109) shows leaders' 'positive deviance' in insisting on their organizations' divestment in fossil fuel investments can be extremely influential in terms of energizing a broader group of individuals and institutions towards supporting sustainability agendas. The mission-alignment between individual leaders and the decisions and actions taken by their organizations is central to them acting as catalysts for change. Others have noted how our reflected and portrayed 'best self' (Roberts et al. 2005) is both "an anchor and a beacon, a personal touchstone of who we are and a guide for who we can become" (2005: 712), thereby implying that the organization can propel or hinder each person's 'best', i.e. their strengths and contributions. However, such conceptions focus on the individual figure of the leader, somewhat neglecting that leaders are only leaders in and through the relationships that bind them with followers.

Towards a More Relational Conception of Leadership

More process-oriented approaches stress the fact that individual leaders do not lead in isolation, shifting the attention from the individual leader as the unit of analysis to the web of leadership connections, and the processes and practices by which these are constructed, maintained or challenged (Crevani et al. 2010). Some have advanced the importance of conceiving these processes as processes of relationality (Fairhurst and Uhl-Bien 2012) and coined the notion relational leadership (Uhl-Bien 2006; Cunliffe 2009). The importance of *relationality* and its dialectics, paradoxes, and dilemmas are well established in organization studies and critical leadership studies (Cooper 2005; Collinson 2005, 2014; Cunliffe and Eriksen 2011). Yet its reception in the field of 'relational leadership' still reveals certain distinct impasses.

Most importantly, the literature continues to grapple with seemingly incommensurable paradigms, which Uhl-Bien and Ospina (2012) describe as the tension between 'entity' perspectives and 'constructionist' perspectives. The former is positioned as closer to the 'objectivist' epistemological position, whereas the latter is portrayed as 'subjectivist'. The underlying distinction between 'objective' and 'subjective' echoes other problematic binaries such as 'facts' versus 'values', 'reason' versus 'emotion', 'mind' versus 'body', 'hard' systems versus 'soft' systems etc. Such distinctions have been challenged from the perspective of contemporary continental philosophy and sociology (Painter-Morland 2013), resulting in a relational ontology that describes 'identity' as an emergent product of the interrelation of individuals with others, i.e. other persons, but also animate and inanimate entities (Painter-Morland and Deslandes 2017). From this perspective, leaders' sense of 'direction' goes beyond the relationship between leaders and followers, and much further than their mutual constructions of each other. Here we follow Painter-Morland and Deslandes (2017) in arguing that embodied processes of habituation, physical and virtual organization, discursive practices all conspire to create certain relational constraints, which are not mere 'subjective' constructions.

Furthermore, recently Rhodes and Badham (2018) for instance have argued that failing to acknowledge the power embedded in the relations between leaders and followers is a major shortcoming of relational ethical leadership, since it can result in the seeming incommensurability of the ethical demands that a relational ethic in leadership implies. The contribution of Levinasian ethics (e.g. Bevan and Corvellec 2007), places this embodied tension of incommensurability in the foreground, thereby speaking directly to the lived experience of participants who might face difficult leadership situations where ethics—and their ability to lead and act ethically—are compromised. Drawing on the relational phenomenology of Michel Henry, Pérezts et al. (2015) have argued that it is in the inter-corporeal and embodied connections that a team and its ethical leader can build an *esprit de corps* and find the strength to collectively fight the pressure to behave unethically in complex business situations.

Such relations imply dependability and accountability between individuals, thereby infusing relational leadership with a particular attention to ethics in this ongoing process (Maak and Pless 2006; Painter-Morland 2008a; Cunliffe and Eriksen 2011). Values-driven leadership emerges from the relational orientation that emerges as sensing, perceptive bodies enter into complex sets of inter-relations. Out of these inter-relations, feelings, cognitions, meanings, as well as communities, artefacts, structures and functions are constantly being created, questioned, recreated and renegotiated (Kupers 2013). New values, behaviours and social dynamics emerge and are continually renegotiated. In transitional periods, one can witness 'inter-leadership' within which the transitional dimensions of selves, agents, cultures and systems are complexly interconnected (Kupers 2013).

Leadership Development and Education

One specific contribution to values-driven leadership is Mary Gentile's (2010, 2011, 2012, 2013) Giving Voice to Values (GVV), which was influential in the design of the VDLA course, as described later in the paper. GVV has become a well-established approach to values-driven leadership development (Gentile 2013), with multiple applications worldwide. It starts from the premise that whilst many individuals in organizations may know what the right thing to do is, they often simply think it is impossible to take this action. Instead of focusing on ethical decision-making and the dilemma discussions that traditional business ethics curricula usually focus on, it is a 'post-decision making' tool aimed at action: "once you know what you believe is right, how can you get it done, effectively?" (Arce and Gentile 2015: 537). Additionally, it is profoundly relational in its methodology in that it focuses on mapping all the parties involved and identifying their stakes in the problem, as well as arguments to work with some or against others in getting the right thing done. Finally, it aims at empowering individuals and equipping them with a set of tools to work their way through the conflicting situations they are bound to encounter.

Following what we saw in the previous section, these insights on the self as a relational being have been slow to filter through to the leadership literature, with the first major text exploring the construct of relational leadership published in 2012 (Uhl-Bien and Ospina 2012). Articles drawing on European philosophy to rethink leadership have also been limited in number (Ladkin 2012; Rhodes 2012; Painter-Morland and Deslandes 2014; Blom and Alvesson 2015; Bouilloud and Deslandes 2015). We believe that African traditions have a much longer tradition of acknowl-edging relationality and embodied subjectivity that shirks subjectobject dualisms, and that much can be learnt from its implications for leadership development. We also suggest that the VDLA course draws on this kind of relational ontology, and that it is important to articulate the contribution that African philosophy makes to understanding such an ontology, and to highlighting its practical implications.

An African-Inspired Theoretical Framework for Relational Ethical Leadership

"A concept like Ubuntu cannot be understood in a monolithic way. It can be compared to a river that breaks into tributaries and forms many islands around which its water flows and later converges and forms one big river." (Kgatla 2016: 2).

Ubuntu, Relationality and Ethics

While pertaining to the southern part of the African continent originally, numerous works have stressed that the essence of relationality behind Ubuntu is both historical and diffused and cannot be said to be country or region specific. For instance, McDonald (2010) considers it an 'African worldview' and Nussbaum characterizes Ubuntu as "an underlying social philosophy of African culture" and one of "the inspiring dimensions of life in Africa" (2003: 1). This is why in the introduction we mentioned that relationality is a core feature and longer-standing concern of such African philosophical traditions preceding some of the Western preoccupations with ethical relational leadership, by grounding interconnectedness in a relational ontology of the self. While Western Cartesianism has favoured placing the individual in the foreground, almost independently of everyone and everything else, Ubuntu stresses "an I/we relationship as opposed to the Western I/you relationship with its emphasis on the individual" (Chilisa 2012: 21; cf. Tutu 1999). The individual does not exist independently from the collective whose interests lie above those of the individual, who is in turn bound by the community in its human essence (McDonald 2010). Fundamentally, Ubuntu "…addresses our interconnectedness, our common humanity and the responsibility to each other that flows from our deeply felt connection" (Nussbaum 2003: 1). As such, it offers a relational approach to morality and ethics grounded in harmony, and brings a different ethos to Western approaches, which prioritise utility, autonomy and capability (Metz 2014).

As suggested by the opening quote of this section, although the general spirit behind Ubuntu is relatively simple to understand, it is far from being simplistic. Four elements need to be noted here. To begin with, as McDonald reminds us:

> there is no easy or direct translation to English, and there are unresolved debates about its ontological status. Morphologically, Ubuntu is a Nguni term, with phonological variants in many African languages, including umundu in Kikuyu, imuntu in Kimeru, bumuntu in kiSukuma, vumuntu in shiTsonga, bomoto in Bobangi, and gimuntu in kiKongo (Kagame 1976, as cited in Kamwangamalu 1999: 25). For Ramose (2002a: 230), it is critical to see the word as 'two words in one', consisting of the prefix ubu- and the stem ntu-, evoking a dialectical relationship of being and becoming. In this sense, ubu- and ntu- are 'two aspects of being as a one-ness and whole-ness', with ubuntu best seen as a dynamic interplay between the verb and the noun rather than a static or dogmatic state of thinking (2010: 14).

The key words here are 'one-ness' and 'whole-ness' and the conception that being is both relational and dialectical, i.e. it cannot be understood solely by one of these aspects, but as intricately linked, as two sides of the same coin.

If we go into a more detailed conception, Praeg (2017) points to two different ways of framing Ubuntu. First, as African Humanism (see for example Metz 2014), which speaks of the core values of friendliness, love and harmony, and the moral quest to 'do the right thing' towards unity (Praeg 2017). Second, Ubuntu can be described as African Communitarianism, which contains a 'dark' side that is political, and can also include violence, discipline, coercion and persuasion in the pursuit of unity and the common good, with significant implications for post-colonial moral theorizing (Praeg 2017: 295). Tavernaro-Haidarian (2018) deals with the challenge of the 'communitarian' aspect by viewing Ubuntu as an ideal theory rather than its historic or anthropological iterations, concluding that the significant value of Ubuntu can be its role in evolving society in a forward-looking manner. We draw on this approach, whilst recognizing that the communitarian aspect also has important implications for values-driven leadership in practice, and thus cannot be ignored.

Third, besides theoretical complexity, one must be careful not to oversimplify the historical construction and current reach of Ubuntu thought. For instance, Stacy (2015) and Praeg (2017) provide useful insights on the divergent framings of Ubuntu. Firstly, as a pre-colonial, historical and cultural African logic of interdependence among a visible (perhaps tribal) community; disrupted by colonialism and the hegemony of individual liberalism. Secondly, Ubuntu, as an abstract post-colonial philosophical construct, that is both influenced by, and influences major discourses (e.g. on human rights) and everyday politics, particularly in South Africa. The potential of Ubuntu as an emancipatory concept, particularly in South Africa has been discussed by various African academics (see for example McDonald 2010; Praeg 2014; Stacy 2015). For instance, McDonald (2010) discusses how the philosophy and language of Ubuntu have been appropriated by market ideologies in post-apartheid South Africa but suggests that the transformative nature of Ubuntu beliefs and practice can reinvigorate the discourse of socialist/anti-capitalist movements. Furthermore, Praeg (2017) argues that it is a common mistake in many Western approaches to Ubuntu to neglect its political dimensions and assumptions rooted in its complex historical construction:

> ...thinking Ubuntu is a political act before it becomes an epistemological, ontological or ethical answer to anything; that by thinking Ubuntu we are implicitly doing politics long before we get to do what we explicitly aim to do, namely to explore epistemology, ontology or ethics. (Praeg 2017: 294).

Finally, and linked to what has just been said, Ubuntu thinking is far from being an idealistic conception devoid of considerations of power. It is infused with the desire to reconcile ambiguous and conflicting situations. Here again, it offers a relational perspective on these issues. Rather than a conflictual approach of right or wrong, or 'power to' or 'power over', Ubuntu offers relational notions of power that can counteract the I/you dichotomy, providing a space for collaboration and deliberation where power is inclusive, and grows between people (Tavernaro-Haidarian 2018: 27, 35). It is in this regard, that an Ubuntu ethic also moves beyond the kind of Rawlsian 'justice-as-fairness' principles that we discussed earlier. Where Rawlsian justice requires of us to negotiate fair distribution of benefits and duties between distinct parties, an Ubuntu orientation disrupts a view of the self which allows us to pit one person or party's interests against another.

Furthermore, Western ways of thinking and constituting knowledge have largely been characterized by a binary either/or logic (for a recent exception see the paradox theory literature, and its application for resolving business ethics dilemmas and contradictions, e.g. Pérezts et al. 2011). In contrast, an Ubuntu orientation refuses to submit to binary alternatives and mutually exclusive solutions, "Our affairs and realities can be thought of as bound-up, complementary and open-ended, encouraging a vast diversity of views and voices. Commonalities and overlaps can be found and emphasized and related social action enabled" (2018: 37).

Ethical Relational Leadership from an African Perspective

As mentioned earlier, the area of ethical leadership development has been identified by African scholars as a key priority in business education and development in the region (Khoza 2006; Smit 2013; Hoffmann and Metz 2017). In their paper on comparative leadership styles, and drawing on some of their earlier works in managing organizations in Africa, Blunt and Jones (1997) made an early call to not underestimate the risks of neo-colonialism and acknowledge the limits of leadership theories originated in the global West when applied to emerging contexts, including Africa (cf. also Nkomo 2011; Smith 2013). While Ubuntu is not explicitly mentioned by Blunt and Jones, they do highlight how leadership in Africa is characterized by "the importance of family and kin networks (… and that) social networks (are) crucial to provide individual security" (1997: 19). Drawing on the elements reviewed in the preceding paragraphs, we shall now attempt to derive implications for rethinking ethical relational leadership from this perspective.

Swanson (2007) conceptualizes Ubuntu as a collectivist philosophy, linking affective, relational and moral elements in the idea of 'humble togetherness', particularly applied in a pedagogical context. This proposal can directly contribute to leadership conceptualized not as strength and other highly masculine stereotypes, but as humility, and the relationality of levels that bind an individual to others, linking it to the pursuit of the idea of the 'common good' on a global scale (Lutz 2009; Tavernaro-Haidarian 2018). From this perspective, leadership is built around the idea of relatedness, and harmony between leaders and followers in a constant process of learning-by doing (Hoffmann and Metz 2017; Tavernaro-Haidarian 2018).

Four Principles of Ethical Relational Leadership from an African Perspective

Aiming to build on such works, and believing in the value of bringing such insights to a broader audience, we shall now take this opportunity to expand present theorizing on relational ethical leadership. We outline what we view as four potential principles of ethical relational leadership, this time from an African perspective: interdependence, relational normativity, communality and understanding unethical leadership essentially as a failure to relate.

1. *Interdependence* The fulfilment of the self (the leader) is understood as interdependent with the care and welfare of others. The Ubuntu world view "I am because we are" is relational, and thus the Ubuntu ethic would situate the core of ethical leadership and the freedom of individual leaders as being bound up interdependently with others (Hoffmann and Metz 2017). The ethical value of leadership within this frame of thought is rooted in relationships between people, rather than just the individual:

   > An Ubuntu ethic is unambiguous about freedom: it is in large part a form of interdependence with others, a kind of 'freedom to' relate in a certain way that is distinct from the negative liberty of 'freedom from' the interference of others (Hoffmann and Metz 2017: 158).

2. *Relational normativity* An African perspective on ethical relational leadership has a normative element. In defining humanity or humanness as a bind to others and a drive towards restoration and peace, it carries an inescapable normative imperative: "Ubuntu as a concept that epitomizes humanness is ever seeking restoration, healing, peace and life to all" (Kgatla 2016). Furthermore, this imperative also explicitly addresses issues about inequality that remain pervasive in the African context (Murove 2014). Material inequality then appears as an implicit element of relationality, which mirrors the normative aspect of Ubuntu to strive for the betterment not only of the self, but of the world that self is bound to.

3. *Communality* is central. Community relationship is valued for its own sake. It is about social network and ties, rather than a defined community, it is a communal relationship of fellowship and harmony (Metz 2014). This communality is about relationality and interdependence that places communal interests above individual interests (McDonald 2010). Here too, the various levels can connect to make ethical leadership engage relationally between the self and the community embedded in mutual relationships of fellowship and harmony.

4. *Unethical leadership as a failure to relate* Reflecting on relationships at the heart of morality and justice in the Ubuntu ethic, Hoffmann and Metz (2017) summarize this as "wrongdoing is essentially a failure to relate", the fact of being closed to others and the world, what others have called ethical blindness or myopia. This fourth dimension complements the prior three by adding a negative definition to what ethical relational leadership is not under this theoretical framework.

In order to make these ideas more concrete, we shall now unpack how this theoretical framework can be deployed in practice and translated effectively into action and ethical leadership development, rooted in an African-inspired relationality.

How the VDLA Course Unpacks Relational Ethical Leadership Genesis and Aims of the VDLA

The Values-Driven Leadership in Action (VDLA) executive course was developed as part of the third author's role in facilitating the design of an executive development course on behalf of an international NGO, as a service to African Business Schools. Three of the corporate members of this NGO (company X, X and X, not disclosed here for blind review) identified talent development in Africa as a major priority. Together they sponsored a curriculum development workshop in December 2015, the initial pilot phases (2016–2017), train-the-trainer courses (2017 and 2018), and an on-going quality-assurance process. Through a process of co-creation with faculty members from eight African business schools, a draft curriculum for an executive development course on ethical African leadership evolved. Mary Gentile was part of the initial curriculum development workshop, sharing her GVV approach with participants, and facilitating discussion about its relevance in the African context. In the meantime, various international grants have been sought to continue the programme and fulfil its mission, which is to "build leadership capacity for ethical and sustainable business on the African continent" (programme description).

Relying on a series of theoretical tools drawing on various philosophical traditions and ongoing reiteration in practice, the course has evolved into a unique integrative design to help participants put values-driven leadership into action. One of its key components is what is called the ME-WEWORLD framework (see Fig. 1). As far as we know, no scholarly rationale has been presented for this multi-level integrative ME-WE-WORLD framework, although this terminology has been used in the past by large corporations, such as the Coca-Cola Company when discussing sustainability and social value (Perez 2012; ECCBC 2018).

We believe that a more rigorous conceptualization of this MEWE-WORLD framework, based on how it is used in practice (in particular through the dream-board exercise explained hereafter), will not only strengthen its application, but also allow us to use it as a critical tool to reflect on corporate practice and inform contextually relevant approaches to values-driven business on the African continent. It is important to stress that 'Africa' should not be treated as a homogenous whole (cf. Nkomo 2011), and that its rich diversity of traditions should be reflected in the various iterations of the course as it is employed in different contexts.

The employment of this ME-WE-WORLD framework occurred spontaneously as part of the evolving curriculum with African faculty suggesting it as a helpful model to frame training on leading ethical and sustainable businesses on the continent. Other experiential learning exercises were also identified, as is described elsewhere (references removed for blind review). For the purposes of this paper, we would specifically like to develop the ME-WEWORLD 'dream-board' exercise by articulating its theoretical assumptions in and through a reflection on its employment in practice.

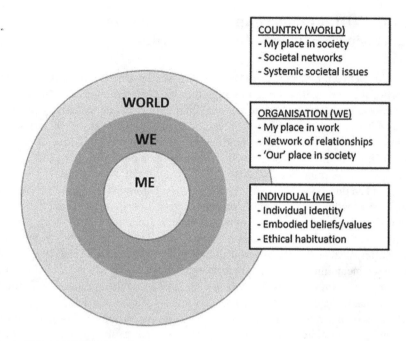

Fig. 1 VDLA ME-WE-WORLD framework

Theorizing from the Dream-Board Exercise

To be clear, it is important to acknowledge that the practice of using the dream-board came first, and the theoretical reflection that we offer here, after the fact. It was during the third pilot of the course material in Egypt that the facilitator (one of the authors) intuited that it could be helpful to create a 'dream-board' for the group to articulate and name their hopes and dreams on three levels: individual (ME), organizational (WE) and country (WORLD). As mentioned by Smith (2013: 214), "naming the world" is important and performative. Where this intuition came from, the facilitator can only explain in retrospect. Having run two pilots at that stage, she felt that a more experiential and interactive approach was needed to make the ME-WE-WORLD framework more meaningful to participants.

An important factor may also have been the challenge of sustaining group energy and attention after lunch on the first day of the training. Her goal was to engage the participants on an affective level and trigger positive aspirations within the group, rather than merely focusing on Africa's problems. Again, echoing Smith's insights for decolonizing methodologies and research: "In all community approaches, pro-cess- that is methodology and method- is important. In many projects, process is far more important than the outcome. Processes are expected to be respectful, to enable people, to heal and to educate" (2013: 218). Since she has always used anonymous post-it notes to great effect to animate confidential group participation, she impro-vised the dream-board exercise on the spot.

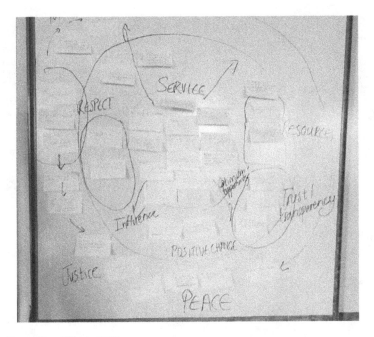

Fig. 2 Dream-board Egypt 2017

She drew three concentric circles on a white-board (see Fig. 2), with ME being the inner circle, and the organization and the world in expanding circles around it. Each participant was then given three post-it notes and asked to use these to anonymously write down three dreams, i.e. one for her/him as individual, one for his/her organization, and one for the 'world', here defined as their own country, i.e. Egypt. This exercise was also conducted a year later in Kenya (Fig. 3). By articulating their dreams, participants locate themselves (ME) within a network of relationships including personal and professional ones (WE), and more broadly (WORLD) (see Figs. 1, 2, and 3). None of the subjective (ME) level issues can be disconnected from the other two, meaning that they are always relationally constructed and experienced.

In what follows, we highlight some of the emerging insights regarding the role of relationality in ethical leadership that emerged from the dream-board exercise, reflecting on both African and European philosophical perspectives (Table 1 summarizes the themes arising from the dream-board exercise). We follow our four principles of ethical relational leadership derived from our review of Ubuntu outlined in the previous section.

1. *Interdependence* In the dream-board exercise, at the individual level, each participant conceptualizes herself or himself in the sense that they 'dream for themselves'. These dreams were often intensely personal, but even as such, dreams of "contentment", making "positive change" or having "positive impact" and "peaceful" relationships indicate a desire for harmony with others and one's

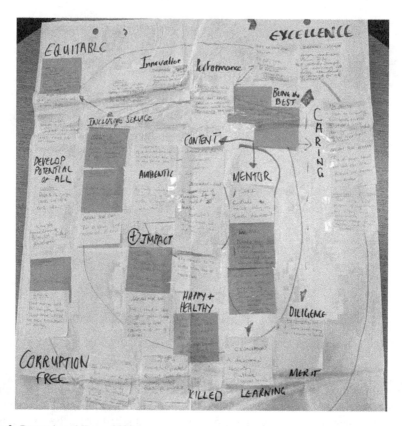

Fig. 3 Dream-board Kenya 2018

Table 1 VDLA dream-board exercise—themes emerging

ME	WE	WORLD (Egypt)[a]
VDLA cohort: Egypt 2017 Dedication to community and societal service, Be an agent of change, Inspire others to lead change in their world, Cooperation, influence	Care for the marginalised, Integrity, Catalyst for change, Industry leader/growth, Social impact	Tolerance, No extremism, Equality, respect and acceptance, Peace and justice, transparency, Education
VDLA cohort: Kenya 2018 Authentic, Contentment, Happy and healthy, impact on society, Self-actualisation, Fulfilment	Impact on society, Being the best—Success—a Centre of excellence, Innovation A learning organization, Responsive to societal needs, merit, Develop new leaders	Equitable, Governance and accountability, Excellence (be the best), care and respect, corruption free, Develop the potential of all citizens

[a] The VDLA Egypt in 2017, took place 3 days after the attack on a Sufi Mosque in Egypt's Sinai Peninsula which killed over 300 people. This may have underpinned an overarching focus on peace and tolerance in the 'WORLD' element of the Dream-Board for the Egyptian participants

environment.[1] More specifically, service to others, especially to younger genera-
tions, and dreams related to leading transformational societal change were prominent. The relational ontology of the self that is operative here certainly reflects
some of the poststructuralist insights discussed above, but we believe that the
African notion of Ubuntu may offer another conceptual angle to understand the
agency of values-driven leaders on the African continent. Reflecting on some of
the key principles of Ubuntu may help us gain more depth in understanding the
capacities for moral agency that African leaders possess. From this perspective,
the details of lives in relation to others lie at the heart of moral agency. As outlined by Metz (2014) and more recently Hoffmann and Metz 2017) they prize
relationships to the point that they seek to sustain them by closely linking very
personal aspects, elements of one's history, self-understandings, one's aspirations as well as one's fears, and understanding the sharing of these as the basis
for more harmonious relationships.

2. *Relational normativity* The African approach to ethics is neither particularly
   principled, nor prescriptive. Hoffmann and Metz go as far as stating that no
   "prominent African thinker seeks to offer an algorithm by which to apply ethical
   values and principles" (2017: 158). Reflecting Mary Gentile's GVV approach,
   the normativity that guides action is relationally defined, with a sense of 'how
   can *we* get the right thing done'? What we see emerging from the dream-boards
   is not dreams of 'freedom from' (someone or something), but rather the desire
   for harmonious interdependence. The way in which individual interest is
   reframed in terms of being 'bound-up' with groups is central to Ubuntu philosophy. However, this desire for harmonious interdependence does not rule out the
   presence of factors such as the importance of competitiveness, excellence and
   on-going innovation in organizational contexts that may pit individuals and
   groups against one another. This duality was evident in the dream-board exercise
   with participants dreams for their organization's related to both care and societal
   impact, intertwined with dreams of being a "catalyst for change", the "Best in
   class/leader of industry" and being a "centre of excellence for Africa".

Many of the practices taking place at the organizational level tend to disrupt relationality, for instance by encouraging competitive behaviours in individual incentive plans. This creates certain ethical challenges that the training can highlight,
particularly the gaps between the various levels represented in ME-WE-
WORLD. From the perspective of Ubuntu philosophy, organizing and competing
can be framed in more humanitarian notions of relationality which can bring a different ethos to Western priorities of utility, autonomy and capability (Metz 2014).
The Ubuntu ethic of prizing relationships draws attention to individual's histories,
self-understandings and aspirations in a normative sense, because this provides the
basis for seeking insight on how relations can be more harmonious or less conflictual (Metz 2014).

---

[1] We should however also acknowledge that "retiring rich by a seashore" was also mentioned!

Rethinking these organizational values from a relational point of view emerges as an important imperative. The content of the dream-boards echoes Painter-Morland's (2007) argument that relational responsiveness allows us to argue that organizations should not only be concerned with accountability *for* past mistakes or future disasters, but to proactively be accountable *towards* various stakeholders. Somewhat echoing what Woermann and Engelbrecht (2017) call the Ubuntu challenge to business, i.e. to conceive stakeholders as "relation holders". The challenge may indeed be to reframe the organizational discourse from a relational perspective to be more in line with the dreams that exist on individual level, and in terms of societal needs. Currently, the way in which organizations function and the terminology that they use often denies or underemphasizes relationality.

3. *Communality* The VDLA course seeks to empower African leaders to solve complex ethical dilemmas in society. A sense of community and complex dilemmas was present at all levels of the ME-WE-WORLD framework in the dream-board exercises. This was reflected in dreams at the individual level to serve and care for the community, but the organization was also seen as a potential agent of transformation, with dreams such as "Catalyst of positive change", "become an academy for youth empowerment", "be a centre of excellence for Africa", and "Impactful solutions in the health sector". Themes around tolerance, equality, acceptance, and opportunities for all reflected the Ubuntu ethic of communal harmony in dreams for society as a whole.

By drawing on community relationality, partnerships and systemic levers for change can be identified at the individual, organizational and societal levels. In the VDLA these 'levers for change' are presented as a 'Toolkit for moral practice' and incorporate various tools ranging from listening skills in an organizational setting, to external tools such as reporting and transparency mechanisms. This approach reflects an Ubuntu ideal of non-competitive consensual models of decision-making and agreement for change. Rather than make the individual the sole agent, the approach that is suggested is systemic and 'communal' in nature. An Ubuntu ethic favours "dialog and public deliberation in order to determine the right way forward", and resolutions to complex dilemmas are dependent on communal discourse and deliberation, as opposed to solitary reflection (Hoffmann and Metz 2017: 158). Consequently, an Ubuntu based framing of the organization as a community in relation to other communities challenges the ethic of competition and success by giving space for the consideration of how an organization may contribute to the pursuit of greater equality or unity.

4. *Unethical leadership as the failure to relate* From the perspective of African philosophy, unethical leadership emerges when one's connection to others are severed through individualist behaviour and personal greed, many examples of which unfortunately exist across the continent. Western consumerism and growth aspirations have created materialist ambitions and competitive attitudes that seem to be perpetuated by corporate rhetoric around competitiveness, innovation and profit margins within organizations. Results from the Global Survey on

Business Ethics showed that the overarching theme for Sub-Saharan Africa was 'ethical management and leadership', with 'corporate governance', 'ethics management' and 'the prevention of corruption and corporate misconduct' the most popular areas of focus for teaching and training (Rossouw 2011: 88). Could it be that corporate values are in need of a relational overhaul?

The VDLA seeks to empower African leaders to confront such challenges, and aspires to transformational change in individuals, their organizations and society. This was particularly evident in the dream-board in the WORLD (COUNTRY) dimension:

> "No discrimination on the basis of race, gender; nationality for refugees and stateless persons"; "Peace through good accountability of governments; transparency for government performance"; "To become a country where resources are equitably distributed through governance, accountability and transparency."
>
> "I dream of a country that feeds [and] protects its citizens while allowing them to fully explore their human potential".

From an Ubuntu perspective the unethical failure to relate, conversely suggests that relationality can challenge systemic ethical failures such as corruption and mismanagement. This has significant implications for ethical leadership theory and development.

VDLA in Practice

The dream-board demonstrates the applicability of relationality and Ubuntu in a practical setting, involving African leaders from business, government and non-profits. However, it is also appropriate to note resultant impacts in practice among VDLA participants. This is something we have been able to track due to the establishment of the Research on Ethical African Leadership Network (REAL-Network) in May 2018. The REAL-Network was established for the explicit purpose of (a) sustaining VDLA engagement (e.g.: through monthly video calls), and (b) to track ongoing application of VDLA. Not all VDLA alumni choose to engage with the REAL-Network, but Table 2 highlights the case of six VDLA participants who have stayed engaged and have gone on to use the VDLA in various ways.[2]

Four VDLA alumni delivered bespoke VDLA training either within their organization or to target groups within their community or sector. One small business owner began the process of preparing a tender for delivering VDLA workshops to several government departments, and one academic was able to gain funding as a

---

[2] In each cohort of 15–20 participants, around 10% have remained particularly active, pursuing their engagement by becoming certified trainers and/or by organizing workshops with VDLA methodologies within their own organizations. The six mentioned in Table 2 belong to this top 10%.

Table 2 Post-workshop VDLA engagement

	VDLA workshop	Participant nationality	organization type	Post-workshop VDLA engagement
P1	November 2017	Egyptian	NGO/non-profit	Develop and deliver VDLA training for a community project, Become a certified VDLA facilitator, Co-facilitate the design and delivery of a local VDLA three-day workshop
P2	November 2017	Egyptian	Corporate	Deliver a VDL seminar at their organization's annual regional gathering, Become a certified VDLA facilitator, Co-facilitate the design and delivery of a local VDLA three-day workshop
P3	June 2018	South African	Non-profit	Become a certified VDLA facilitator, Design and organize a series short VDLA workshops for managers and professionals within their sector
P4	June 2018	Nigerian	Small business owner	Become a certified VDLA facilitator, Engage with local government departments about holding VDLA workshops, Prepare a tender for delivering VDLA workshops to several government departments
P5	November 2016	South African	Academic	Become a certified VDLA facilitator, Support research engagement with the VDLA, Gain research funding as a result of collaboration with VDLA alumni from other countries
P6	June 2018	South African	Healthcare professional	Become a certified VDLA facilitator, Design and organize sector based mini VDLA workshops

result of connections with VDLA participants from other countries, forged via the REAL-Network.

In November 2018, we asked REAL-Network members whether engagement with particularly 'problematic' stakeholders was more likely, less likely or remained the same as a result of their attendance at a VDLA course. They were also asked to reflect on why they answered as they did. Out of 18 respondents, three did not answer the question, one stated: "remained the same" and the remaining 14 stated "more likely". Reasons given included "Yes, because of interaction and the nurturing of trust" [Respondent (R) 18]; "I believe after the course I started to think differently that we can always live our values and that it is not a question of the 'what' but the 'how'" [R4]; "understand the more likely motivation of other stakeholders" [R11]. Many of the reasons given highlight the primacy of aspects of relationality to overcome challenges in engaging with other stakeholders. For example, one respondent stated "Values driven leadership amongst other seeks to come out with business solutions that can take into account interests of others" [R16]. Whilst anecdotal, this further illustrates the value of African perspectives on relationality which situates a failure to relate as a core feature of unethical leadership.

The dream-board illustrates how VDLA participants can locate themselves and their dreams for their organization and their world in the ME-WE-WORLD framework during a training programme. Similarly, we see how VDLA alumni demonstrate further engagement with the ME-WE-WORLD framework at various levels. In relation to the ME for example, by becoming certified VDLA trainers, by seeking to empower others (WE) with VDLA principles and citing aspects of relationality as central to engaging with difficult stakeholders (WE) and/or (THE WORLD). Our reflection on this VDLA exercise demonstrates how the amalgamation of Western and African conceptions of leadership development can identify principles for values driven leadership in action: interdependence; relational normativity; communality, and the framing of unethical leadership as the failure to relate. The theoretical and practical implications for ethical leadership theory and development are considered in the remainder of this paper.

Discussion and Contributions to Ethical Leadership Theory and Development

Our paper presents an empirically illustrated theoretical proposal for rethinking ethical relational leadership from an African perspective. This has been identified as a key area for developing business ethics training in African settings (Ike 2011; Rossouw 2011; Smit 2013), particularly in the face of numerous critiques on the impact of business ethics education in fostering moral development (Catacutan 2013).

In doing so, we have strived to address two shortcomings.

First, the fact that Western scholars have often treated non-Western epistemologies, ontologies and experimentations as marginal. Such a Western bias has largely contributed to an epistemic domination, long denounced by post-colonial theorists. In contexts such as Africa, including other voices and developing management education programmes rooted in local ontological and epistemological sensibilities can help fight the risk of epistemic coloniality (Ibarra-Colado 2006; Murphy and Zhu 2012). Such initiatives, being theoretically and methodologically informed from the South, become "a significant site of struggle between the interests and the ways of knowing of the West, and the interests and ways of resisting of the other" (Smith 2013: 31). Furthermore, such programmes can help spread their contributions in the reverse direction, from South to North, further challenging many of the underlying assumptions that undermine taking ethical concerns seriously and effectively in management education (Nkomo 2011; Painter-Morland 2015). Second, while some notable exceptions discussed earlier in this paper do exist, they often offered theoretical or philosophical discussions of Ubuntu, while nevertheless lacking actionable guidelines to translate its principles into concrete managerial and leadership practice.

This paper responds to these two issues, firstly by establishing a theoretical dialogue among both traditions and proposing an African-rooted contribution to relational ethical leadership theory, and secondly by showing how this can effectively be put into practice through a pedagogical design of the VDLA. In fact, instead of one-directionally 'applying' certain theoretical ideas, the practice of experiential learning methods that draw on relational techniques enabled us to articulate the potential theoretical conversation between Western and African ontologies. As such, it allowed us to reveal an intimate interaction between theory and practice in a way that defies the binaries which still plague 'applied philosophy'.

We shall now discuss some of the most relevant contributions and outline some avenues for pursuing this line of research. Most importantly, we believe our proposed theoretical framework as illustrated by the VDLA course offers interesting insights to pursuing ethical relational leadership theory, this time from an African perspective. Thus, we add to emerging attempts to make connections between African philosophies such as Ubuntu and global management theory and leadership (e.g. Lutz 2009; Prozesky 2009). While relational leadership (Uhl-Bien 2006; Cunliffe 2009) continues to develop, both in general leadership studies (Cunliffe and Eriksen 2011), and in ethical and critical leadership studies (Maak and Pless 2006; Liu 2017; Rhodes and Badham 2018), relationality is a core feature. We believe that everyday practice in the African context precedes much of this theorization. We have attempted to show how its insights can help overcome some of the dichotomies of Western ontologies (mind/body, me/you) by offering a stronger relational reading, thereby more closely knitting together the subjective, intersubjective and collective levels, by means of the exercises playing out on the different ME-WE-WORLD levels.

Some leadership scholars have offered important insights into the way leaders provide direction in organizations. Instead of unilaterally 'directing' the behaviours of others, 'enabling' leadership entails disrupting existing patterns, encouraging novelty and then making sense of whatever unfolds (Plowman et al. 2007: 342). As a counteracting force, a basic life goal of African philosophy and Ubuntu is to realize human excellence, through community and honouring harmonious relationships (Metz 2014). We suggest that Ubuntu challenges the unethical *failure to relate* by calling leaders in a relational-normative sense to see oneself as an integral part of the whole, working to achieve the good of all, pursuing cooperative creation and distribution of wealth (Metz (2014), drawing on the Nigerian philosopher Segun Gbadegesin and the Kenyan philosopher Professor D. A. Masolo).

Furthermore, the dream-board statements presented in the previous section could easily be dismissed as fanciful and seemingly unattainable when confronted with systemic challenges such as inequality, exclusion, discrimination, corruption and unaccountable power. Yet, the importance of service to others that emerges from the dream-board also flies in the face of many Western 'strong-man' conceptions of leadership. It parallels what European scholars have recently termed 'weak management', which is characterized by hospitality, fragility and putting the 'Other' at the heart of management (Deslandes 2018). From a leadership development perspective, the VDLA course is, in a very concrete manner (e.g. through experiential exercises such as the dream-board), creating a relational space where relationality can unfold. This relationality has *agency*, which shapes everyone and everything in its ambit. From this perspective, relational accountability becomes key to the process by which responsible and sustainable business practices emerge (Painter-Morland 2007, 2008a, b, 2012; Painter-Morland and Deslandes 2015). If this process of relational accountability fails, we may also argue that it is a result of impoverished or corrupted relational space. The space of the VDLA course itself is a space for relational engagement for facilitators as well. As detailed above, the dream-board exercise and other elements have emerged as embodied improvisations, because on the one hand the safe communal space was created to allow for such improvisations and engagement on a personal level by the facilitator. On the other, the main objective was precisely to maintain the relationality among the group, an aspect that we suggest is central to empowering values-driven leadership in action.

More broadly, we have sought to contribute to the business ethics as practice perspective (Clegg et al. 2007; Painter-Morland 2008b), by focusing on the practicality of implementing values-driven leadership. Rhodes and Badham (2018) recently concluded that ethical irony is one way of approaching this. We suggest that VDLA is an alternative approach which maybe more directly 'applicable' in the sense that it infuses relationality into each of the steps of the course. Moreover, in an African context, it provides an overarching theoretical framework that integrates inputs both from Western and African traditions. Namely, Mary Gentile's *Giving voice to values* (GVV) is woven into the VDLA course in a unique way. The basic GVV premise, which has found rather positive echoes among African participants on the VDLA course, is that "most people want to bring their *whole* selves to work and therefore to act on their values" (Gentile 2011: 306, emphasis in original). This holistic, rather than compartmentalized view of the self is a key component for fostering relationality, yet it is often undermined by Western injunctions of 'leaving one's ethics at the door' when entering the workplace, a point which is often instilled very early in management education (Giacalone and Promislo 2013).

The dream-board constitutes a first springboard to dream different, to imagine alternative states of the world, in order to then be able to re-script our own rationalizations of why the world is as it is, and seemingly cannot be changed.

On a more political level, Ubuntu philosophy emphasizes inclusive deliberation, rather than 'power over' (Tavernaro-Haidarian 2018: 27, 35), and by adopting a critical perspective (in a political sense, such as that advocated by Praeg 2017), Ubuntu can be a vehicle for questioning the relations of power that systematically exclude people (Stacy 2015). For Metz (2014) the value in this approach lies in what Ubuntu can contribute to debates on the ideal distribution of political power, both nationally and internationally in mechanisms such as the United Nations. In a consideration of what a progressive form of Ubuntu socialism might bring to society, McDonald (2010) suggests that whilst small Ubuntu-inspired victories can contribute to change, a more comprehensive vision of transformation is required, with democratic, consultative processes of change from above and below. Such inclusive notions of power and relationality have significant implications for the promotion of valuesdriven leadership that contributes to transformational societal change in Africa and beyond.

The ME-WE-WORLD framework provides a way of directly addressing Giacalone and Thomson's (2006) critique of how business school curricula tends to promote an organization-centred worldview and its profit interests, instead of a human-centred worldview. Our proposed theoretical framework fosters concern for an interconnectedness, or 'togetherness' (Swanson 2007) of the different levels, thereby challenging the organization-centeredness of mainstream management education. The organization is still there, and as the figures above illustrate, it remains a key player, but it is viewed as part of a holistic system, amidst other stakeholders (Brinkman and Sims 2001). Such a shift away from an organization-centric perspective, Giacalone and Thomson (2006) argue, could help integrate a vision of the self (identification) and a view of others and the world (inspiration) that triggers their motivation.

Additionally, let us not forget that identification and inspiration are two of the key elements of leadership. It is in this regard that our analysis offers insights that could deepen and extend our understanding of post-heroic approaches to leadership such as transformational leadership (Burns 1978; Bass 1990; Bass and Riggio 2006; McCleskey 2014). Some applications of transformational leadership have been criticized as narrow and managerialist, and often ineffective because it fails to take account of systemic pressures (Currie and Lockett 2007). Our analysis would suggest that its failure may lie in its continuing reliance of individualist assumptions, i.e. a central, strong individual lies at the heart of the 'transformation' that takes place in organizations and in the lives of followers. Embracing a more radically defined relational ontology would allow one to view 'leading' as a relational response that requires systemic change and fundamentally shift the focus away from individual leaders towards understanding relational dynamics.

Conclusion

We set out to show how theorizing relationality from the African philosophical tradition of Ubuntu can bring new insights to Western philosophical perspectives on relationality in the context of ethical leadership development. We have presented an African-rooted contribution to relational ethical leadership theory and demonstrated how this can effectively be put into practice through a particular pedagogical design of the VDLA. Consequently, this paper provides an important African contribution, which can help counteract the dominance of Western philosophical conceptions in leadership development literature, in particular its individualist and organization-centeredness. There are of course limitations to our contribution, our theorizing on African-inspired relationality draws on one particular example of an Ubuntu-inspired leadership course. Nonetheless, the centrality of Ubuntu-inspired notions of interdependence, normative relationality, and communality brings a fresh perspective, particularly when unethical leadership is framed as the failure to relate.

This demonstrates firstly, how values-driven leadership discourse can be reframed from a relational perspective in a way that is more in line with the dreams that exist on the individual level for ourselves, our organization and our society. Secondly, we have also shown how the practice of embodied experiential learning through programmes such as the VDLA, can provide a space for vocalizing relational aspirations as a catalyst for values-driven leadership in action. In the process, examples and useful exercises emerged that highlight how practicing Ubuntu could transform the way in which leadership development takes place. As a basic tenet of African philosophy and ethics, Ubuntu suggests that a basic life goal should be to realize human excellence, which can only be done if living communally with others, honouring harmonious relationships (Metz 2014).

Much remains to be done to establish the both the theoretical and societal impact of Ubuntu-inspired relational practices in terms of preventing unethical behaviour in various contexts. It is in this regard that our study is only the first step in articulating the relationship between Western and African ontologies from a theoretical perspective. A more fine-grained conceptual analysis of the points of divergence and overlap would be required. In terms of studying the impact of Ubuntu-inspired leadership development in practice, a lot more data will need to be gathered in various contexts. The fact that up to now the VDLA has been focused on small-group experiential learning, limits the numbers of respondents to our ongoing investigations on impact. There are however plans to scale the programme, also by means of digitalization, which would potentially allow us to add quantitative data to what at this stage is limited to qualitative assessments of impact.

What seems clear, is that it is surely time for African notions of relationality to be more central in our theorizing and practical outworking of values-driven leadership, by bringing the whole self to the workplace and developing ethical relational—and holistic—forms of leadership. Further interdisciplinary research might explore the interdependencies and mutually enriching aspects of both Western and African traditions, drawing on anthropological and sociological insights, as well as perspectives from behavioural economics, to develop a nuanced understanding of agency. It would also be important to explore how this African perspective connects to other voices from the South and other emerging economies, in order to understand how relational forms of leadership may foster more sustainable business models that serve social interests. Fostering relational accountability among our leaders in the way we develop management education may be the key to finding new ways of approaching the purpose of business as such.

References

Alcadipani, R., Khan, F., Gantman, E., & Nkomo, S. 2012. Southern voices in management and organization knowledge. *Organization* 19 (2): 131–143.

Arce, D. G., & Gentile, M. 2015. Giving voice to values as a leverage point in business ethics education. *Journal of Business Ethics* 131: 535–542.

Bakken, T., Holt, R., & Zundel, M. 2013. Time and play in management practice: An investigation through the philosophies of McTaggart and Heidegger. *Scandinavian Journal of Management* 29 (1):13–22. https://doi.org/10.1016/j.scaman.2012.09.003.

Bass, B. M. 1990. From transactional to transformational leadership: Learning to share the vision. *Organizational Dynamics* 18 (3): 19–31.

Bass, B. M., & Riggio, R. E. 2006. *Transformational leadership* (2nd ed.). New York: Psychology Press.

Bevan, D., & Corvellec, H. 2007. The impossibility of corporate ethics: For a Levinasian approach to management ethics. *Business Ethics: A European Review* 16(3): 208–219.

Blankenberg, N. 1999. In search of real freedom: Ubuntu and the media. *Critical Arts, 12*(2), 42–65.

Blok, V. (2014). Being-in-the-world as being-in-nature: An ecological perspective on being and time. *Studia Phaenomenologica* 14: 215–235.

Blom, M., & Alvesson, M. 2015. All-inclusive and all good: The hegemonic ambiguity of leadership. *Scandinavian Journal of Management* 31 (4): 480–492.

Blunt, P., & Jones, M. L. 1997. Exploring the limits of western leadership theory in East Asia and Africa. *Personnel Review* 26 (1/2): 6–23.

Bouilloud, J., & Deslandes, G. 2015. The aesthetics of leadership: Beau geste as critical behaviour. *Organization Studies* 36 (8): 1095–1114.

Brinkman, J., & Sims, R. R. 2001. Stakeholder-sensitive business ethics teaching. *Teaching Business Ethics* 5 (2): 171–193.

Burns, J. M. 1978. *Leadership*. New York: Harper Collins.

Byers, D., & Rhodes, C. 2007. Ethics, alterity, and organizational justice. *Business Ethics: A European Review* 16 (3): 239–250. https://doi.org/10.1111/j.1467-8608.2007.00496.x

Catacutan, R. 2013. Education in virtues as goal of business ethics instruction. *African Journal of Business Ethics* 7 (2): 62–67.

Chilisa, B. 2012. *Indigenous research methodologies*. Thousand Oaks: Sage.

Clegg, S. R., Kornberger, M., & Rhodes, C. (2007). Business ethics as practice. *British Journal of Management* 18 (2): 107S122.

Collinson, D. 2005. Dialectics of leadership. *Human Relations* 58 (11): 1419–1442.

Collinson, D. 2014. Dichotomies, dialectics and dilemmas: New directions for critical leadership studies? *Leadership* 10 (1): 36–55.

Cooper, R. 2005. Peripheral vision: Relationality. *Organization Studies* 26 (11): 1689–1710.

Crevani, L., Lindgren, M., & Packendorff, J. 2010. Leadership, not leaders: On the study of leadership as practices and interactions. *Scandinavian Journal of Management* 26 (1): 77–86.

Cunliffe, A. L. 2009. The philosopher leader: On relationalism, ethics and reflexivity—A critical perspective to teaching leadership. *Management Learning* 40 (1): 87–101.

Cunliffe, A., & Eriksen, M. 2011. Relational leadership. *Human Relations* 64: 1425–1449.

Currie, G., & Lockett, A. 2007. A critique of transformational leadership: Moral, professional and contingent dimensions of leadership within public services organizations. *Human Relations,* 60 (2): 341–370.

Deslandes, G. 2011a. Indirect communication and business ethics: Kierkegaardian perspectives. *Business and Professional Ethics Journal* 30 (3): 307–330.

Deslandes, G. 2011b. In search of individual responsibility: The dark side of organizations in the light of Jansenist ethics. *Journal of Business Ethics* 101: 61–70. https://doi.org/10.1007/s10551-011-11736.

Deslandes, G. 2012. Power, profits, and practical wisdom: Ricoeur's perspectives on the possibility of ethics in institutions. *Business and Professional Ethics Journal* 31(1): 1–24. https://doi.org/10:5840/bpej20123111.

Deslandes, G. 2018. Weak theology and organization studies. *Organization Studies*. https://doi.org/10.1177/0170840618789209.

ECCBC. 2018. 'ME WE WORLD—Sustainability—ECCBC'. Retrieved August 30, 2018 from http://www.eccbc.com/en/sustainability/me-we-world.

Fairhurst, G. T., & Uhl-Bien, M. 2012. Organizational discourse analysis (ODA): Examining leadership as a relational process. *Leadership Quarterly* 23 (6): 1043–1062.

Faÿ, E., Introna, L., & Puyou, F. R. 2010. Living with numbers: Accounting for subjectivity in/with management accounting systems. *Information and Organization* 20 (1): 21–43.

Faÿ, E., & Riot, P. 2007. Phenomenological approaches to work, life and responsibility. *Society and Business Review* 2 (2): 145–152.

Gentile, M. 2010. *Giving voice to values: How to speak your mind when you know what's right.* New Haven: Yale University Press.

Gentile, M. 2011. A faculty forum on giving voice to values: Faculty perspectives on the uses of this pedagogy and curriculum for values-driven leadership. *Journal of Business Ethics Education* 8: 305–307.

Gentile, M. C. 2012. Values-driven leadership development: Where we have been and where we could go. *Organization Management Journal* 9 (3): 188–196.

Gentile, M. 2013. *Educating for values-driven leadership: Giving voice to values across the curriculum.* NY: Business Expert Press.

George, G., Corbishley, C., Khayesi, J., Haas, M., & Tihanyi, L. 2016. Bringing Africa in: Promising directions for management research. *Academy of Management Journal* 59 (2): 377–393.

Giacalone, R. A., & Promislo, M. D. 2013. Broken when entering: The stigmatization of goodness and business ethics education. *Academy of Management Learning and Education* 12 (1): 86–101.

Giacalone, R. A., & Thomson, K. R. 2006. Business ethics and social responsibility education, shifting the worldview. *Academy of Management Learning and Education* 5 (3): 266–277.

Goduka, I. N. 2000. Indigenous/African philosophies: Legitimizing spirituality centred wisdoms within academy. In P. Higgs, N. Vakalisa, T. Mda, & N. Assie-Lumumba (Eds.), *African voices in education.* Landsdowne: Juta and Co Ltd.

Grint, K. 2010. The sacred in leadership: Separation, sacrifice and silence. *Organization Studies* 31: 89–107.

Hoffmann, N., & Metz, T. 2017. What can the capabilities approach learn from an ubuntu ethic? A relational approach to development theory. *World Development* 97: 153–164.

Ibarra-Colado, E. 2006. Organization studies and epistemic coloniality in Latin America: Thinking otherness from the margins. *Organization* 13 (4): 463–488.

Ibarra-Colado, E., Clegg, S. R., Rhodes, C., & Kornberger, M. 2006. The ethics of managerial subjectivity. *Journal of Business Ethics* 64 (1): 45–55.

Ike, O. 2011. Business ethics as a field of teaching, training and research in West Africa. *African Journal of Business Ethics* 5: 89–95.

Jones, C., (Ed.). 2007. Special issue: Levinas, business, ethics. Business Ethics: A European Review 16 (3): 196–321.

Jones, C., Parker, M., & Ten Bos, R. 2006. *For business ethics.* Abingdon: Routledge.

Kagabo, L. 2011. Business ethics as field of training, teaching and research in francophone Africa. *African Journal of Business Ethics* 5 (2): 74–80.

Kgatla, S. T. 2016. Relationships are building blocks to social justice: Cases of biblical justice and African Ubuntu. *HTS Teologiese Studies/Theological Studies* 72 (1): a3239. https://doi.org/10.4102/hts.v72i1.3239.

Khoza, R. 2006. *Let Africa lead: African Transformational leadership for 21st century business.* Johannesburg: Vesubuntu Publishing.

Kolk, A., & Rivera-Santos, M. 2016. The State of research on Africa in business and management: Insights from a systematic review of key international journals. *Business and Society* 56 (7): 1–22.

Kupers, W. M. 2013. Embodied inter-practices of leadership. *Leadership* 9: 335–357.

Ladkin, D. 2006. When deontology and utilitarianism aren't enough: How Heidegger's notion of 'dwelling' might help organisational leaders resolve ethical issues. *Journal of Business Ethics* 65 (1): 87–98.

Ladkin, D. 2012. Perception, reversibility, "flesh": Merleau-Ponty's phenomenology and leadership as embodied practice. *Integral Leadership Review* 12 (1): 1–13.

Liu, H. 2017. Reimagining ethical leadership as a relational, contextual and political practice. *Leadership* 13 (3): 343–367.

Louw, D. J. 2010. Power sharing and the challenge of ubuntu ethics. paper presented at the forum for religious dialogue symposium of the research institute for theology and religion at the University of South Africa, January 2010, Pretoria, South Africa.

Lutz, D. 2009. African Ubuntu philosophy and global management. *Journal of Business Ethics* 84 (3): 313–328.

Maak, T., & Pless, N. M. 2006. Responsible leadership in a stakeholder society: A relational perspective. *Journal of Business Ethics* 66: 99–115.

Mawa, M., & Adams, J. 2011. Business ethics as field of teaching, training and research in East Africa. *African Journal of Business Ethics* 5 (2): 66–73.

McCleskey, J. A. 2014. Situational, transformational, and transactional leadership and leadership development. *Journal of Business Studies Quarterly* 5 (4): 117–130.

McDonald, D. A. 2010. Ubuntu bashing: The marketisation of 'African values' in South Africa. *Review of African Political Economy* 37 (124): 139–152.

Metz, T. 2014. Harmonizing global ethics in the future: A proposal to add south and east to west. *Journal of Global Ethics* 10 (2): 146–155. https://doi.org/10.1080/17449626.2014.931875.

Murove, M. F. 2014. Ubuntu. *Diogenes* 59 (3–4): 36–47. https://doi.org/10.1177/039219 2113493737.

Murphy, J., & Zhu, J. 2012. Neo-colonialism in the academy? AngloAmerican domination in management journals. *Organization* 19 (6): 915–927.

Muthuri, J. N., Amaeshi, K., Adeleye, I., & Luiz, J. 2017. Business ethics in Africa: Virtual special issue of journal of business ethics. *Journal of Business Ethics*.

Nkomo, S. M. 2011. A postcolonial and anti-colonial reading of 'African' leadership and management in organization studies: Tensions, contradictions and possibilities. *Organization* 18 (3): 365–386.

Nussbaum, M. 2000. *Women and development: The capability approach*. Cambridge: Cambridge University Press.

Nussbaum, B. 2003. African culture and Ubuntu: Reflections of a South African in America. *World Business Academy Perspectives* 17 (1): 1–12.

Painter-Morland, M. J. 2007. Redefining accountability in a network society. *Business Ethics Quarterly* 17 (3): 515–534.

Painter-Morland, M. 2008a. Systemic leadership and the emergence of ethical responsiveness. *Journal of Business Ethics* 82: 509–524.

Painter-Morland, M. 2008b. *Business ethics as practice: Ethics as the everyday business of business*. Cambridge: Cambridge University Press.

Painter-Morland, M. J. 2012. Rethinking responsible agency in corporations: Perspectives from Deleuze and Guattari. *Journal of Business Ethics* 101 (10): 83–95.

Painter-Morland, M. J. 2013. The relationship between identity crises and crises of control. *Journal of Business Ethics* 114: 1–14.

Painter-Morland, M. J. 2015. Philosophical assumptions undermining responsible management education. *Journal of Management Development* 34 (1): 61–75.

Painter-Morland, M. J. 2018. The role of continental philosophy in business ethics research. In E. Freeman (Ed.), *Research approaches in business ethics*. Cambridge: Cambridge University Press.

Painter-Morland, M., & Deslandes, G. 2014. Gender and visionary leading: Rethinking 'vision' with Bergson. *Deleuze and Guattari. Organization* 21 (6): 844–866. https://doi.org/10.1177/1350508413488636.

Painter-Morland, M. J., & Deslandes, G. 2015. Rethinking authenticity and accountability—Facing up to the conflicting expectations of media leaders. *Leadership*. https://doi.org/10.1177/1742715015578307.

Painter-Morland, M. J., & Deslandes, G. 2017. Reconceptualizing CSR in the media industry as relational accountability. *Journal of Business Ethics*. https://doi.org/10.1007/s10551-016-3083-0.

Painter-Morland, M. J., & Ten Ten Bos, R. (2011). *Business ethics and continental philosophy*. Cambridge: Cambridge University Press.

Perez, B. 2012. Sustainability for me, we and the world: The CocaCola Company. Retrieved August 30, 2018, from https://www.coca-colacompany.com/stories/sustainability-for-me-we-andthe-world.

Pérezts, M., Bouilloud, J. P., & Gaulejac, V. 2011. Serving two masters: The contradictory organization as an ethical challenge for managerial responsibility. *Journal of Business Ethics* 101: 33–44.

Pérezts, M., Faÿ, E., & Picard, S. 2015. Ethics, embodied life and esprit de corps: An ethnographic study with anti-money laundering analysts. *Organization* 22 (2), 217–234.

Plowman, D. A., Solansky, S., Beck, T. E., Baker, L., Kulkarni, M., & Travis, D. V. 2007. The role of leadership in emergent, selforganization. *Leadership Quarterly* 18 (4): 341–356.

Praeg, L. 2014. *A report on Ubuntu*. Pietermaritzburg: UKZN Press.

Praeg, L. 2017. Essential building blocks of the Ubuntu debate; or: I write what I must. *South African Journal of Philosophy* 36 (2): 292–304. https://doi.org/10.1080/02580136.201 6.1261442.

Prastacos, G. P., Wang, F., & Soderquist, K. E. (Eds.). 2012. *Leadership and management in a changing world: Lessons from Ancient East and West Philosophy*. New York: Springer.

Prozesky, M. 2009. The Scott/Harker Model of ethical business leadership in the light of an African understanding of human existence. *African Journal of Business Ethics* 4 (1): 1–4.

Rhodes, C. 2011. Organisational justice. In M. J. Painter-Morland & R. Ten Bos (Eds.), *Business Ethics and Continental Philosophy*. Cambridge: Cambridge University Press.

Rhodes, C. 2012. Ethics, alterity and the rationality of leadership justice. *Human Relations, 65*(10), 1311–1331. https://doi.org/10.1177/0018726712448488.

Rhodes, C., & Badham, R. 2018. Ethical irony and the relational leader: Grappling with the infinity of ethics and the finitude of practice. *Business Ethics Quarterly* 28 (1): 71–98.

Roberts, L. M., Dutton, J. E., Spreitzer, G. M., Heaphy, E. D., & Quinn, R. E. 2005. Composing the reflected best-self portrait: Building pathways for becoming extraordinary in work organizations. *Academy of Management Review* 30 (4): 712–736.

Rossouw, G. J. 2011. The state of business ethics as a field of teaching, training and research in Sub Saharan Africa. *African Journal of Business Ethics* 5 (2): 96–102.

Sen, A. 1999. *Development as freedom*. New York: Anchor Books.

Smit, A. 2013. Responsible leadership development through management education: A business ethics perspective. *African Journal of Business Ethics* 7 (2): 45–51.

Smith, L. T. 2013. *Decolonizing methodologies: Research and indigenous peoples*. London: Zed Books Ltd.

Smurthwaite, M. 2011. Business ethics as field of training, teaching and research in Southern Africa. *African Journal of Business Ethics* 5 (2): 81–88.

Stacy, D. (2015). Ubuntu Versus ubuntu: Finding a philosophy of justice through obligation. *Law and Critique, 26:* 305–312.

Sulamoyo, D. 2010. "I am because we are": Ubuntu as a cultural strategy for OD and change in sub Saharan Africa. *Organization Development Journal* 28 (4): 41–51.

Swanson, D. M. (2007). Ubuntu: An African contribution to (re)search for/with a 'humble togetherness'. *Journal of Contemporary Issues in Education* 2 (2): 53–67.

Tavernaro-Haidarian, L. 2018. *A relational model of public discourse: The African philosophy of Ubuntu*. Oxon: Routledge.

Tutu, D. (1999). *No future without forgiveness*. NY: Doubleday.

Uhl-Bien, M. 2006. Relational leadership theory: Exploring the social processes of leadership and organizing. *The Leadership Quarterly* 17 (6): 654–676.

Uhl-Bien, M., & Ospina, S. M. (2012). *Advancing relational leadership research. A dialogue among perspectives*. Charlotte, NC: Information Age Publishing.

van Dierendonck, D. (2011). Servant leadership: A review and synthesis. *Journal of Management* 37 (4): 1228–1261.

Walton, A. A. 2018. Fossil fuel divestment: The power of positively deviant leadership for catalyzing climate action and financing clean energy. In S. L. Steffen, J. Rezmovits, S. Trevenna, & S. Rappaport (Eds.), *Evolving leadership for collective wellbeing: Lessons for implementing the United Nations sustainable development goals* (pp. 101–120). Bingley: Emerald Publishing Limited.

Woermann, M., & Engelbrecht, S. 2017. The Ubuntu challenge to business: From stakeholders to relationholders. *Journal of Business Ethics.* https://doi.org/10.1007/s10551-017-3680-6.

Mar Pérezts is currently an Associate Professor of Philosophy and Organization, and member of OCE Research Center at Emlyon Business School, in Lyon, France. Originally from Mexico, she graduated from the Ecole Normale Supérieure d'Ulm in Philosophy and won the FNEGE-AIMS best dissertation award for the ethnography of a banking compliance team. She been a visiting scholar in several universities abroad (University of Alberta (Canada) with a grant from the CEFAG-FNEGE; University of Leipzig (Germany), Scuola Supériore Sant'Anna di Pisa (Italy), University of Nottingham Trent (UK) with a Visiting Fellowship Grant from the British Academy), and Università di Trento (Italy). Her work has been published in leading academic journals such as *Organization Studies; Journal of Business Ethics; Gender, Work and Organization; Organization*, and the *European Management Journal*.

Jo-Anna Russon is a Senior Research Fellow in the School of Education, University of Nottingham, UK. Her research resides within the field of business and development studies in two key areas. First, the relationship between the private sector and development, particularly in the context of UK foreign aid and corporate social responsibility in sub-Saharan Africa. Jo-Anna is currently co-leading an ESRC funded project on the role of consultants and contractors in UK aid. The second area spans the disciplines of business, development and education. Current research includes projects working with lecturers in technical and vocational education in South Africa and community-led skills development initiatives in Uganda.

Mollie Painter currently heads up the Responsible and Sustainable Business Lab (RSB Lab), a Research Centre within Nottingham Business School, Nottingham Trent University, UK and is an Extraordinary Professor at the Gordon Institute of Business Science, University of Pretoria. Her research is focused on business ethics, CSR, sustainability and responsible leadership. She has held academic positions in South Africa, the USA, the UK, and Slovenia. . She also serves as co-Editor-in-Chief of *Business Ethics Quarterly*. Between 2015 and 2020, she held the Coca-Cola Chair of Sustainability at IEDC-Bled in Slovenia.

Corporate Social Responsibility and Multi-Stakeholder Governance: Pluralism, Feminist Perspectives and Women's NGOs

Kate Grosser

Abstract The corporate social responsibility (CSR) literature has increasingly explored relationships between civil society and social movements, including non-governmental organizations (NGOs), and corporations, as well as the role of NGOs in multi-stakeholder governance processes. This paper addresses the challenge of including a plurality of civil society voices and perspectives in business–NGO relations, and in CSR as a process of governance. The paper contributes to CSR scholarship by bringing insights from feminist literature to bear on CSR as a process of governance, and engaging with leaders of women's NGOs, a group of actors rarely included in CSR research. The issues raised inform contributions to the CSR literature relating to the role of women's NGOs with regard to the gender equality practices and impacts of corporations, and with respect to defining the meaning and practice of CSR. The paper frames marginalized NGOs as important actors which can contribute to pluralism, inclusion and legitimacy in CSR as a process of governance. It identifies several key barriers to the participation of women's NGOs in CSR, and concludes by making suggestions for future research, as well as practice.

Keywords Corporate social responsibility · Pluralism · Gender equality · NGOs · Inclusive governance · Legitimacy

Introduction

Research into the organizing of corporate social responsibility (CSR) has explored business–civil society relations extensively, including the role of activists and non-governmental organizations (NGOs) in their relationships with individual corporations, and with multi-stakeholder governance processes (Brown et al. 2000; Den Hond and De Bakker 2007; De Bakker and Den Hond 2008; Rasche et al. 2013;

K. Grosser (✉)
RMIT University, Melbourne, VIC, Australia
e-mail: kate.grosser@rmit.edu.au

© The Author(s), under exclusive license to Springer Nature
Switzerland AG 2023
M. Painter, P. H. Werhane (eds.), *Leadership, Gender, and Organization*, Issues
in Business Ethics 63, https://doi.org/10.1007/978-3-031-24445-2_9

Burchell and Cook 2013; Scherer and Palazzo 2007, 2011). The 'political CSR' literature draws upon Habermas (1974) to establish the particular political significance of the participation of civil society associations, movements and NGOs as "the core actors in the process of democratic will formation" (Scherer and Palazzo 2007: 1107) within CSR deliberative processes. Here it is argued that "NGOs – at least partly – compensate for the shrinking power of the nation-state vis-à-vis transnationally operating corporations" (p. 1108). At the same time political, and other, CSR scholars alert us to the value and significance of difference, and the importance of including a plurality of perspectives in processes that define legitimate norms and practices concerning business–society relations (Scherer and Palazzo 2007, 2011; Gilbert and Rasche 2007). NGOs, it is argued, help to bring a plurality of perspectives, and particularly the interests of the less powerful, to business regulation and new governance systems (Braithwaite and Drahos 2000). However, the extent to which we are actually seeing a plurality of perspectives represented, and in particular those of traditionally marginalized populations, through NGO participation in CSR has not been much discussed in the literature.

CSR research has focused on activists and NGOs working on environmental issues (Hoffman 1999) as well as labour rights and human rights (Vogel 2008), but rarely those working on gender equality. Meanwhile, development and feminist scholars have highlighted the failure of much CSR practice to incorporate the voices and concerns of poorer and traditionally marginalized groups and stakeholders (e.g., Coleman 2002; Newell 2005; Grosser and Moon 2005a, b; Marshall 2007; Grosser 2009; Banerjee 2011). Bostrom and Hallstrom (2010) note that differences in the material resources of NGOs limit their participation in transnational processes of standard development, and thus their ability to influence the content of the resulting standards. Therefore, the issue of which types of NGOs might currently be marginalized with respect to CSR processes deserves some attention. Little empirical research in CSR explores this issue. My paper addresses this gap in the literature with reference to women's NGOs in particular.

In defining CSR, it is important to note that although 'a leitmotiv of wealth creation progressively dominates the managerial conception of responsibility' (Windsor 2001: 226), CSR is now much less about business practices alone (i.e., corporate centred), and much more about the combination of self, social, governmental and multi-stakeholder regulation of corporations with respect to their social and environmental impacts and implications (McBarnet et al. 2007; see also Moon et al. 2011; Gond et al. 2011; Rasche et al. 2013). In this context, as new standards for corporate responsibility emerge and become institutionalized, CSR has been described as "a multi-actor and multi-level system of rules, standards, norms and expectations" (Levy and Kaplan 2008: 438), involving a highly political deliberation process that "aims at setting and resetting the standards of global business behavior" (Scherer and Palazzo 2008: 426).

In line with these perspectives, this paper discusses CSR as a multi-stakeholder process of governance involving business government and civil society, and in particular NGOs. We have witnessed the emergence of new multi-stakeholder governance processes and initiatives at the global level (e.g., Ethical Trading Initiative,

UN Global Compact, Global Reporting Initiative, UN Guiding Principles on Business and Human Rights), as well as at the national and local levels, in the context of CSR. These now influence the policies and practices of corporations—multinational and local alike, through the institutionalization of new standards, rules, norms and expectations (Slager et al. 2012). Such multi-stakeholder initiatives involving NGOs as well as business, and sometimes government, have become significant sites of business regulation (Vogel 2008). Indeed, Vogel (p. 269) argues that these non-state market driven governance systems "offer the strongest regulation and potential to socially embed global markets". Moreover, the literature suggests that "social movement activity appears to be most influential at the agenda-setting stage – i.e. shaping which issues actors view as important and debate" (De Bakker et al. 2013: 582). With reference to corporate ethical/CSR codes of conduct, Doh and Guay (2004: 7) confirm "that NGOs achieve the greatest impact ... when they intervene early in the code development process" (emphasis added). These arguments would seem to lend some urgency to the issue of participation by marginalized, including women's, NGOs in multi-stakeholder CSR processes.

Gender equality, defined by the Council of Europe (1998: 7) as 'an equal visibility, empowerment and participation of both sexes in all spheres of public and private life', is increasingly acknowledged as a key issue in CSR practice, with reference to the business case for gender, diversity and inclusion and women's/human rights (Grosser and Moon 2005a, b, 2008; UN Global Compact Women's Empowerment Principles; Global Reporting Initiative; Ethical Trading Initiative; FTSE 4 Good, Kilgour 2007). Gender equality is also recognized for the fact that it is integral to addressing other core CSR agendas, as evidenced by the feminisation of poverty (Habermas 1998), gender analysis with regard to environmental degradation (Marshall 2007) and long-standing recognition of gender equality as a key to development (Millennium Development Goals). Moreover, feminist CSR scholars have highlighted how

> issues of inclusion and exclusion, of scrutiny of the power to define and contribute to the debate become critical if this is to be an opportunity for the realisation of some new reality, a process of co-creation of something other than business-as-usual. (Coleman 2002: 22. See also Marshall 2007)

Thus, as new standards and new processes of regulation and governance relating to corporations and their responsibilities to society are developed and institutionalized, "The ability of various parties to engage effectively... becomes crucial" (Bebbington et al. 2007: 360).

My paper begins to explore issues of marginalization and inclusion with reference to women's NGOs and CSR. The literature to date suggests that women's NGOs may be somewhat absent from CSR processes (Kilgour 2007; Grosser and Moon 2005a, b), but little research has explored these suggestions with reference to women's NGOs themselves. Thus, my paper adds to the literature on gender and CSR, which to date has addressed gender issues relating to the workplace (Grosser and Moon 2005a, b, 2008), the supply chain and value chain (Barrientos et al. 2003; Hale and Opondo 2005; Pearson 2007), the community (Newell 2005) and CSR leadership (Marshall 2007), but rarely with respect to the involvement of NGOs in CSR.

The extensive literature on social movements, and particularly NGOs, organizational change and CSR (Brown et al. 2000; Den Hond 2010; De Bakker et al. 2013) discusses how NGOs influence companies through adversarial campaigns as well as collaborative partnerships. Research explores different NGO engagement strategies, sometimes placing these in the context of broader strategies for social change adopted by NGOs (Den Hond and De Bakker 2007; Burchell and Cook 2013; De Bakker et al. 2013). The CSR literature also explores how NGOs try to bring about wider 'field-level' change. One way they do this is by working with leading companies to drive up standards. In addition, they "try to affect the coercive, normative, or cognitive institutional pressures in the field – for instance, by lobbying with public authorities and business associations for regulation or standards, or by raising public awareness" (Den Hond and De Bakker 2007: 916) including through participation in multi-stakeholder governance initiatives (e.g., Den Hond and De Bakker 2007; De Bakker and Den Hond 2008). Thus, Doh and Teegen (2002: 665), among others, argue that NGOs have "assumed a particularly prominent role in influencing the interaction between business and governments over the terms of international business rules, norms, and practices". Following these themes in the literature on NGOs and CSR, my paper explores both the relationships that women's NGOs have with individual companies, and their engagement with wider CSR multi-stakeholder governance processes. With regard to the latter I investigate the extent of, and possible barriers to participation by women's NGOs.

The overarching goal of this paper is to bring feminist perspectives to bear on CSR as a multi-stakeholder process of governance wherein NGOs have been identified as significant actors. In so doing, first I highlight insights from feminist literature on CSR, and NGOs, which reveals the need to include women's NGOs in governance processes. I then explore the views of leaders in women's NGOs regarding CSR, in order to begin the process of including their perspectives in debates about CSR. Thus, the paper contributes empirically to the CSR literature by engaging with leaders of women's NGOs, a group of actors rarely included in CSR research. The findings from the empirical research inform contributions to CSR scholarship relating to the role of women's NGOs with regard to the gender equality practices and impacts of corporations, and with respect to defining the meaning and practice of CSR as it relates to gender equality in particular. A significant debate has emerged in the literature on business–NGOs relations concerning the risks of possible co-optation of NGO agendas by business, as in 'a de-radicalisation of the movements and a diluting of issues to accommodate them within the established political order' (Burchell and Cook 2013: 742). However, Burchell and Cook (2013) also show how social movements, of which NGOs are a part, actively contest the meaning, language and interpretation of CSR and responsible business practice. Building on these insights, my paper begins to explore CSR as a contested definitional domain with reference to gender issues, and the role of NGOs working on gender equality. Finally, the paper frames marginalized NGOs as important actors which can contribute to pluralism, inclusion and legitimacy in CSR as a process of governance.

The paper proceeds by first outlining the feminist underpinnings of the research, followed by a description of the methods used in this study. Next I report the research outcomes as they relate to how women's NGOs define CSR and view the field, the relationships they have with individual companies, and finally their engagement with wider CSR multi-stakeholder governance processes. I then discuss the research outcomes. Key issues to emerge here include the importance of cross-sector collaborations between gender experts and activists within corporations and NGOs; the role women's NGOs are beginning to play with respect to redefining the meaning of CSR; and the challenge of access to funding for marginalized NGOs to participate in CSR as a process of governance. I note the main limitations of the paper, and conclude with suggestions for future research, as well as practice.

Feminist Perspectives on CSR and NGOs

There is a growing acknowledgement of gender equality in CSR practice and research, but more often with reference to women on corporate Boards, and as managers, than those on the margins of organizations. Moreover, there is little evidence in the literature of engagement between business managers and civil society experts on gender equality (Kilgour 2007; Grosser and Moon 2008; Grosser et al. 2008). An emerging feminist CSR literature explores gender issues in global supply chains (Barrientos et al. 2003; Pearson 2007; Prieto-Carron 2008; Hale and Opondo 2005); social reporting and CSR benchmarking (Grosser and Moon 2005a, b, 2008); specific CSR initiatives (Kilgour 2007); CSR and sustainability leadership (Marshall 2007); and stakeholder relations (Grosser 2009). Feminist scholars have also called for attention in CSR to women's reproductive labour (Pearson 2007), and begun to debate CSR as a political process of participation and governance (Coleman 2002; Kilgour 2007; Marshall 2007; Grosser 2011). Recent scholarship analyses CSR and gender issues from an institutional perspective (Karam and Jamali 2013). A small number of studies relating to corporate supply chains in developing countries have documented some benefits arising from participation by women's NGOs in CSR code development (e.g., Hale and Opondo 2005; Pearson 2007). However, beyond noting the lack of participation by women's NGOs in the UN Global Compact (Kilgour 2007), little research has addressed the involvement of women's NGOs in new processes of voluntary regulation involving non-state actors and CSR. This is despite the fact that gendered organization scholars argue that the mobilization of women's movement groups agitating for change from outside organizations are "essential to success" in efforts to change inequality regimes (Acker 2006: 456).

Meanwhile, drawing upon the work of Gilligan (1982), feminist ethics scholars have highlighted the importance of including women's voices, not just their rights to equal treatment in the workplace, in debates about business– society relations. Derry (1997: 29) argues that "Ethics particularly business ethics – must address sexism by incorporating the concept of listening. Only by learning to listen will ethical theorists be able to formulate theories that increase understanding and recognition of women" and other marginalized voices. On this point, Marshall (2007: 173) asks "Where are… women's voices in CSR?" practice as well as research. She addresses this point with respect to CSR leadership. Here I contribute to this debate by exploring women's voices in CSR as represented by women's NGOs.

The CSR literature discusses 'the associations citizens form, such as NGOs, movements, or civil society networks … in order to advocate their causes in a broader public context' (Scherer and Palazzo 2007: 1107). Regarding NGOs in particular, Bostrom and Hallstrom (2010: 37–38) describe these as 'not-for-profit organizations, usually with voluntary members or participants. NGOs are part of global or local civil societies'. Den Hond (2010: 173) identifies NGOs as 'a highly diversified set of organizations that are independent from the state and formally organized on a non-profit basis. Among them are activist or advocacy NGOs, concerned with some specific policy issue area, such as human rights or environmental protection.' Broad social protest movements are often deemed to be the precursor to NGOs (Doh and Guay 2006), and in this context Maddison and Partridge (2007: 79) argue that 'women's NGOs … are generally understood as being constitutive components of the women's movement.' As such they 'generally fall into two categories; those concerned with the broad sweep of issues and concerns that are implicated in the pursuit of gender equality, and those organisations with a more specialised focus and expertise, for example in areas such as reproductive rights, education or childcare'.

Feminist research on NGOs identifies a lack of gendered perspectives, and the marginalization of women's voices and concerns from mainstream NGO agendas. International law scholars, for example, observe that "the agendas of NGOs are not necessarily produced with greater democracy or transparency than the agendas of individuals or states" (Charlesworth and Chinkin 2000: 89). Indeed, "civil society is not necessarily hospitable to women's interests. In many ways, international civil society tends to reflect the existing power imbalances in the nation state system" (Charlesworth and Chinkin 2000: 169). According to these authors, even in 'progressive' NGOs, women and their concerns tend to be marginalized, where widespread racism and sexism is observed in many environmental movements for example. The marginalization of gender issues by development NGOs is similarly noted in the gender and development literature (e.g., Bhattacharjya et al. 2013). Thus, while numerous CSR scholars frame NGOs as providing a voice for less powerful groups (Scherer and Palazzo 2007; O'Dwyer et al. 2005), NGOs can also play a part in excluding marginalized peoples (Squires 2005). Newell (2005: 453) points out that

> poorer sections of communities are often underrepresented in, or left out altogether, from processes of constructing and implementing 'soft' regulation (not legally binding) and self-regulation, even when cited as the intended beneficiaries. This is either because they are not identified as a legitimate stakeholder group in the way an NGO or trade union might be, or

because the assumption, often misplaced, is that those bodies will act as adequate intermediaries for the representation of poorer groups' concerns. Work on the design of codes of conduct in the horticulture sector, for example, suggests that the concerns of the poorest seasonal and temporary women workers are often not dealt with by such tools.

Charlesworth and Chinkin (2000: 169) argue therefore for "the importance of women taking an active role in international civil society" including developing theoretical underpinnings for the role of women's social movements in the creation of international law. This argument supports my attention to the issue of participation by women's NGOs in new CSR related multi-stakeholder processes of regulation and governance.

With reference to women's NGOs themselves, feminist literature addresses the role of women's NGOs in government policy making (e.g., Maddison and Partridge 2007; Squires 2005), in organizational change (e.g., Acker 2006; Yancey-Martin 2006), in international law (Charlesworth and Chinkin 2000) and with respect to multilateral economic institutions (O'Brien et al. 2000) for example. Charlesworth and Chinkin identify a lack of participation by women's NGOs in international law making. Along similar lines, O'Brien et al. (2000) comment on the limited ability of women's social movements and organizations to participate in and influence international economic policy making at the World Bank. However, the literature on women's movements and NGOs rarely comments on engagement with private sector organizations, or CSR, even in debates about feminist antiglobalization activism (Maiguashca 2011). Rather, this literature reveals a long-standing and ongoing focus by women's social movements and NGOs on government as the actor with whom to collaborate when it comes to trying to address gender change (Maddison and Partridge 2007; Squires 2005; Molyneux 1998). Above I noted initial findings regarding the relative absence of women's NGOs from CSR processes. These observations were derived with reference to the absence of women's NGOs in the UN Global Compact (Kilgour 2007), and from other standard setting initiatives in the field (Grosser and Moon 2005a, b). However, Burchell and Cook (2013: 747) argue that "Too little research focuses on the activities and strategies of the movements themselves". Thus, my paper explores the issue of women's NGO participation in CSR from the perspectives of leaders in these organizations.

The literature on women's NGOs reveals that they are often poorly funded and resourced as compared to other parts of civil society, as are women's advocacy networks generally, which impacts their ability to influence debates (Maddison and Partridge 2007; Charlesworth and Chinkin 2000; O'Brien et al. 2000; Burgess 2011). It is also argued that women's NGOs may lack skills in economic analysis and related policy areas (O'Brien et al. 2000). A further challenge identified is the relative lack of interest in gender equality, as opposed to environmental and other issues, at the World Bank for example, which may contribute to the exclusion of women's NGOs from the dialogue (O'Brien et al. 2000). These debates suggest an exploration of women's NGO participation in CSR is timely. Next I turn to my research methods before describing my findings.

Methods

This research was designed to be an inductive, qualitative study with the goal of unearthing rich description about the nature of women's NGO interactions with CSR. Eleven semi-structured interviews were carried out with leaders in 10 national women's NGOs, 8 in the UK and 2 in Australia. These countries were chosen because I had previously interviewed company managers about gender equality and CSR in these locations, and identified what seemed to be a lack of engagement between business and women's NGOs. My methods followed those of O'Dwyer et al. (2005) whose research involved eight semi-structured interviews with leaders of five leading environmental NGOs and three social NGOs in Ireland. Like them, and in line with qualitative research more generally (Bourdieu 1982), my "primary objective did not involve a quest to generalise the perceptions gained" but rather to "gain detailed insights surrounding these perceptions by exploring in-depth how and why they came to be held" and "the contextual influences on their formulation" (O'Dwyer et al. 2005: 19). This "required some form of access to in-depth knowledge of these individuals' lived experiences in their roles as NGO leaders" (pp. 19–20).

Context

Scholars have increasingly engaged with NGO leaders in attempts to contribute analysis that "provides a voice on emerging CSD[1] developments" (O'Dwyer et al. 2005: 16) to marginalized non-managerial stakeholders, whose perspectives, they argue, have "been largely ignored" (p. 14). In this paper, I do not claim to 'provide a voice' to leaders in women's NGOs, but I do seek to hear their views, and to help ensure that these are heard in wider debates about business–society relations. Given that women's movements and associated NGOs are "primarily organized to advance women's gender specific concerns" (Molyneux 1998: 224), my interviews focused on the role women's NGOs play in encouraging business to address gender equality issues in particular.

Prior to interviews, I explored the websites of each NGO and took detailed notes relating to the issues they work on, as well as their key partners, campaigns and strategies. The NGOs included advocacy organizations campaigning for gender equality, service organizations providing services to women (e.g., women's refuges), and women's membership organizations offering education, skill-sharing and socializing opportunities. As these functions often overlap many of the NGOs played more than one of these roles. In addition, all the NGOs in this study are to some extent campaigning organizations. Some are also 'umbrella' organizations, which collectively represented over 600 regional and local women's NGOs. Most, but by no means all, described themselves as feminist organizations. They work on

---

[1] Corporate Social Disclosure.

employment issues including equal pay, flexible working, job segregation, pensions, ethnic minority women's issues and racism, dismissal due to pregnancy, childcare, sexual harassment, and young women's access to decent work. Within and beyond the workplace they also address domestic violence, pornography, prostitution, human trafficking and other forms of violence against women, poverty, health, education, homelessness, drug abuse, ex-offenders, the intersection between discrimination based on sex and age, supporting young mothers, the criminal justice system, the environment and women's political representation.

Interviewees

I chose to interview leaders in national NGOs due in part to the impracticality of interviewing many different local and regional NGOs, and the fact that, where an NGO has several regional branches, decisions about strategy and policy are often made centrally. My initial sample was influenced by my previous involvement in feminist practice, whereby I had worked with, and alongside, several national women's NGOs in my work on gender equality policy in the UK, and thus had access to leaders in several NGOs. Thereafter, I used a snowball technique (Corley and Gioia 2004), asking each interviewee for recommendations as to other women's NGO leaders who could provide insights on my research topic. I also approached other leading national women's NGOs in each country for interviews, all of which granted interviewee access.

All my interviewees were women and the roles they played within their organization included that of Director, General Secretary Chief Executive, Executive Officer, Chair, Chairman, Head of Policy, Head of Development, and Corporate Relations Manager. They thus included leaders, as well as senior managers taking leadership in areas related to my research, and which the leaders thought would be the best people in their organizations to address the interview topic. Interviews were anonymous; thus, I have not named the interviewees or their organizations. However, I have numbered each interviewee and identified their roles so that the variety of speakers is evident, as well as the number of different perspectives on each topic (see Table 1 below).

Seven of the interviews were carried out face-to-face, and four were done by telephone for reasons of convenience to the interviewees. All but one were recorded and transcribed. The interview length was, on average 1 h, and provided a data set for analysis of around 110,000 words.

Data Analysis

I coded my data using a grounded theory (Glaser and Strauss 1967; Charmaz 2006) approach which was informed by my literature review and at the same time involved letting concepts emerge from the data (Glaser 1992) and searching for

Table 1 Interviewees roles in women's NGOs

Interviewee numbers	Interviewee roles
Interviewee 1	Director, UK advocacy NGO
Interviewee 2	Head of Development, UK advocacy NGO
Interviewee 3	Corporate Relations Manager, UK service providing NGO
Interviewee 4	Chief Executive, UK service providing NGO
Interviewee 5	Executive Officer, Australian service providing NGO
Interviewee 6	Head of Policy, UK service providing NGO
Interviewee 7	Chair, Australian advocacy NGO
Interviewee 8	Recent Chair, UK advocacy NGO
Interviewee 9	Director of an umbrella UK advocacy NGO
Interviewee 10	General Secretary, UK women's membership NGO
Interviewee 11	National Chairman, UK women's membership NGO

"common and distinct conceptualizations for multiple observations across a data set" (Locke 2008: 103). While a number of the key themes emerging from my interviewees related directly to issues in the extant CSR literature on NGOs, a number of new themes also emerged. These themes appear novel to the extent that they either 'don't seem to have adequate theoretical referents in the existing literature', or that they '"leap out" because of their relevance to a new domain' (Gioia et al. 2013: 20), in this case the debate about gender and CSR. Following Corley and Gioia (2004), information about how I moved from first order data to more aggregate conceptualizations is provided in Table 2 below.

Research Outcomes

This section presents the research outcomes from my interviews with leaders of, and senior managers in, national women's NGOs in the UK and Australia. I start by noting how CSR is conceptualised by my interviewees before going on to explore the extent to which their organizations are involved in collaboration with individual corporations. I then address the issue of their wider involvement in multi- stakeholder CSR governance processes.

Understandings of CSR

CSR is a highly contested concept (Gond and Moon 2012). Thus, I begin by noting comments from my interviewees with respect to how they perceive, define and understand CSR, in order to contextualize the more detailed research findings that follow.

Table 2 Data structure

First order data	Second order themes	Wider themes and aggregate dimensions
Advocacy NGO describes beginning to engage with corporates in attempt to encourage regulatory compliance and improve practice Service providing NGOs describe engaging with corporations in search of new sources of funding and campaign support	Reasons for beginning to engage with corporates	New NGO strategies re gender equality. CSR as regulatory compliance and beyond compliance with respect to gender issues
Gender Equality Forum: collaboration between UK advocacy NGO and gender experts/feminists in six large corporations, to advance gender equality in the companies involved Sexism in the City: UK advocacy NGO and gender experts/ feminists in three large corporations campaign to end use of pornography in the workplace, and of lap-dancing clubs for business entertainment Long-term collaboration between UK service providing NGO working on domestic violence and Anita Roddick, Founder of the Body Shop. Campaigns in 26 countries Collaboration of UK service providing NGO working on domestic violence with Opportunity Now, Business in the Community (UK) Long-term collaboration between Australian service providing NGO and women leaders in business nationally, providing core funding, contacts and advice	Cross-sector collaboration between gender experts and feminists within large corporations and leaders in women's NGOs	Feminist tempered radicals in business as possible mediators between civil society gender equality issues/ experts and corporations
Gender Equality Forum (UK advocacy NGO and gender experts/feminists in six large corporations) addresses new gender workplace issues, e.g., discrimination against ethnic minority women Sexism in the City campaign addresses routine use of pornography in the workplace, and use of lap-dancing clubs for business entertainment Raising domestic violence as a workplace issue for corporate members of Business in the Community (UK) Young mothers and employment campaign by UK service NGO, getting corporates involved	Women's NGOs contesting/expanding the meaning of CSR/ responsible business with respect to gender equality (rather than being coopted)	Marginalized voices in CSR
Women's NGOs are poorly funded and resourced relative to other types of NGOs Traditional focus on government as driver of change on gender equality Engagement with business not on feminist agendas traditionally/many women's NGOs lack relationships with business people Lack of information about CSR Scepticism	Barriers to participation by women's NGOs in CSR governance processes	Marginalized NGOs with respect to CSR multi-stakeholder governance initiatives. Pluralism, inclusion and legitimacy in CSR

Some interviewees expressed frustration with limited conceptions of CSR which define it primarily as philanthropy.[2] One described CSR as "fluffy" and weak. According to this interviewee, the corporate managers she collaborates with find that equality issues are taken more seriously when given independent strategic priority within a business, rather than being located within a CSR mandate. Therefore, engagement with CSR does not look like a useful strategy to this interviewee. Other interviewees also described limited perceptions of the scope and scale of CSR practice, defining it loosely with reference to business discretionary behaviour (see also discussion of scepticism below).

However, others conceptualise CSR much more broadly, describing it in terms of core business operations and impacts upon societal stakeholders. One interviewee described CSR as an important contemporary paradigm shift in the way markets view profit generation, via a move to considering the triple bottom line, and the intersection of business and human rights.

Several interviewees see CSR as an alternative regulatory compliance process when it comes to equalities law, and as a process of business accountability. Some described CSR in wider governance terms. For example, one said:

> So…to me, [CSR is] about … creating … forms of governance for private sector organizations which recognises their broader responsibilities and broader role in terms of … social justice, in terms of environmental justice …and how that can impact on … communities … It's about …both unleashing …a broader social role and a transformational role [for business] but [it's] also about them recognising their responsibilities to the communities in which they operate. (emphasis added) (Interviewee 1)

Many of my interviewees regard discrimination, and gender equality, as a CSR issue. Yet, despite these broad definitions, and locating gender issues within the field, most of my interviewees described their organizations as little engaged with the CSR movement. This is an important finding in itself, and is explored below with respect to reasons for lack of engagement by women's NGOs in CSR as a process of governance. However, prior to this, I discuss women's NGO relations with individual companies.

Women's NGO Relations with Individual Companies

Several of my interviewees described engagement with individual companies. Of these, only one was an advocacy NGO. This UK organization directly engaged in ongoing collaboration with leading corporations specifically to address gender equality within these businesses. The NGO ran a pioneering programme of work with managers from a small group of leading companies (various sectors) to improve corporate equality and diversity strategies and outcomes. The programme involved publication by the NGO of several 'Think pieces' on core gender equality in the

---

[2] This point was made particularly by Australian interviewees.

workplace issues, and a series of Gender Equality Forum meetings to discuss the issues raised therein with managers. The NGO hoped "to begin to really challenge the people who we see as already leading the field, to take a further step... and in a sense, respond to their desire to be challenged." The Director of this NGO (Interviewee 1) described being approached by business people for advice about how to further improve gender equality practice, being asked "well what's our new framework [for] turning the dial up?... Shall we just keep on turning the [same] dial up or are we actually doing the wrong thing?". In light of opportunities for cross-sector collaboration the NGO aimed to provide "a safe space for [corporate managers] to begin to have the kind of arguments that they're going to have to have internally if they're wanting to up the ante in terms of getting.. change to happen." The project included sharing expertise, "stimulating debate and giving them the tools to move forward". It was also a new fundraising venture for the NGO, but the Director emphasised that this was not the main reason for the development of the programme. The focus was on commonly noted workplace equality issues such as equal pay, job segregation and women on Boards. However, the NGO raised additional issues that are not routinely addressed by corporate gender/diversity managers, such as the experience of ethnic minority women in the workplace, thereby helping to expand corporate gender equality agendas.

Doh and Guay (2006), among others, have suggested that where government enforcement mechanisms are under-resourced and ineffective, NGOs have begun to regard collaboration with business as a way of encouraging regulatory compliance. Interviewees in this NGO supported this suggestion with respect to gender equality in particular. The Director said

> There are ... some simple pragmatic reasons why we're [doing this programme of work], mostly to do with the closure of the EOC[3]... and the perception of Opportunity Now[4] as being very unchallenging .... we've always worked at policy level but ...we now have one of the best legislative frameworks in Europe but some of the poorest performers... for a women's rights organization, that clearly demarcates to us that we need to shift the focus, or rather add to our kind of armoury [for] pressuring change, practice change as well as policy change. So it's very much the beginning of a journey for us, in terms of how we work to encourage practice change with some of the private sector.

The Head of Development in this same NGO (Interviewee 2) said

> if ultimately we are about women's rights in the UK, it's going to take a lot more than policy and legislative change to actually get closer to achieving women's rights. So part of our new vision ... is going to be about influencing how legislation gets translated back into practice.

Thus, these interviewees indicate that their engagement with a small group of leading companies was part of a wider strategy for field-level change by the NGO, supporting findings from Den Hond and De Bakker (2007). To this end, the NGO

---

[3] Equal Opportunities Commission.

[4] Opportunity Now is the gender equality programme of Business in the Community (UK). It has a membership of approximately 360 employers, half of which are private sector companies, and administers a gender equality benchmarking programme.

involves public sector organizations in the dialogue with corporations on gender equality "because.. there's a lot of learning that can be done to and fro" between sectors, particularly with regard to disseminating best practice to supplier companies. According to one interviewee, some private companies have become good at this. In effect, this small NGO had set up a multi-stakeholder forum aimed at improving business practice relating to gender equality in the UK. This is an important point given that most of the CSR literature on multi-stakeholder initiatives describes those initiated by business or government. However, interviewees from this NGO were critical of the weakness of CSR initiatives on gender equality, such as Opportunity Now, and did not describe their work with the private sector with reference to CSR.

Through another campaign this same NGO was further re-defining the agenda with respect to gender equality in the business community. The campaign involved collaboration with three large corporations (including British Telecom and Barclays Wealth) to challenge sexist workplace practices in financial services companies in the City of London. The focused was on the gender equality impacts of lap-dancing clubs used in corporate entertainment, and the display of pornography in the workplace. Thus, once again this NGO was helping to expand the agenda with regard to responsible business and gender issues.

My research finds that women's service-providing NGOs are also building relationships with corporates but with a different set of primary objectives than the advocacy NGO. The focus here is on opening up new sources of funding, as government funding shrinks and gaining company support to advance gender equality campaigns both in and outside business. Two UK interviewees described the CSR agenda as particularly useful for these purposes. One said that in her role as Corporate Relations Manager (Interviewee 3), "it's quite handy to have the diversity agenda fitting in with the skills and apprenticeship [issues in] our campaign, and wanting to better women's opportunities". The Chief Executive of another NGO (Interviewee 4) said "CSR broadly [is useful] because ... when we've made approaches to companies, it's given us a hook. That's the most important thing, plain and simple really... that's what it's done, given us a legitimisation for approaching them". This suggests that as CSR rhetoric extends to gender issues, it can become a resource for women's NGOs.

The Corporate Relations Manager quoted above described how corporates use NGOs such as hers to gain CSR credentials. However, both these interviewees felt that when it comes to collaboration with charities corporate managers are much more interested in engaging with, and supporting, NGOs working on environmental issues than those addressing gender equality. The Corporate Relations Manager (Interviewee 3) suggested that part of the problem is that "Our brand isn't big enough" to be useful to corporates. However, the Executive Officer of another Australian based NGO (Interviewee 5) said "if companies are doing work on.. anti-discrimination.. and CSR, it's not what they make ads about... they make ads about ...making bio-fuel, and the fact that ...[they have a] commitment to not fund environmentally-damaging projects". Thus, these interviewees felt that environmental credentials are more important to companies than gender credentials when it comes to CSR. This finding echoes O'Brien et al.'s (2000) assertion with regard to World Bank–NGO collaboration, and suggests that business interests in social movement agendas, in the context of CSR, may offer more potential as a resource for some NGOs than others.

Despite this, the Executive Officer (Interviewee 5) who commented on the preference to address environmental issues in corporate public image making, also described how having personal relationships with corporate representatives can help overcome this obstacle. One businesswoman's involvement with her NGO has brought hugely significant funding to the organization for core program work over a 10-year period, helping to break their dependence upon government funding. In her experience, some companies particularly want to support women's organizations and their projects. Another interviewee supported this emphasis on key relationships with business leaders. As Chief Executive of a service-providing NGO working on domestic violence (Interviewee 4), she explained that before 2000 their funding came mostly from trusts and government. They began working with companies in the mid-1990s, gradually gaining private sector sponsorships, including for service delivery. Explaining that few other women's NGOs had alliances with corporates at that time: "the biggest company ... for really taking a stand, standing way out from the crowd ... has been [the] Body Shop". In collaboration with this company, the NGO campaigned in the 1990s for improved legislation on domestic violence, which they achieved: "we had postcard campaigns, which they [the Body Shop] delivered". This was innovative in that it was much more than just a funding opportunity: "That was through Anita's [Roddick's] interest ... because Anita was a feminist and it was through her interest in women's human rights ... that's how the Body Shop [a UK leader in CSR] first did any work on these issues at all".

Such long-term collaboration with a leading women's NGO illustrates ways in which feminist, activist, women leaders in business, and in the field of CSR, contribute to gender equality. Through this collaboration The Body Shop helped run a Stop the Violence in the Home campaign in 26 countries, facilitating a much wider campaign reach than would otherwise have been possible, and providing a new source of income for the NGO. The company gained positive reputation as a result, and the NGO was then able to engage several other corporates in support of their campaign. Drawing upon the new focus on gender issues in CSR, and in order to reach a larger number of companies, in 2003 the NGO undertook a project in collaboration with the CSR organization Business in the Community's gender equality program, Opportunity Now. Together, they produced over a thousand copies of a CD-Rom on domestic violence as a workplace issue, which went out to many companies and local authorities. Thus, this NGO both utilized the CSR gender agenda, and expanded it, to incorporate domestic violence as an issue which impacts upon workforce productivity, and where companies can make a difference through workplace programmes, as well as by supporting charities.

These findings point to the importance of individual cross-sector relationships at the managerial level, between gender experts and feminist activists, a theme not explored a great deal in the CSR literature on business–NGO relations. Indeed, the Head of Policy in another service-providing NGO noted that lack of involvement in businesswomen's networks by many women's NGOs was a problem, because good relationships with people in business can facilitate dialogue on key gender equality issues. Moreover, this interviewee argued that "the responsibility for engagement is not just about women's organizations having to go to the source but also about the mountain coming to Mohammed, so to speak" (Interviewee 6). This raises issues for corporate and CSR professionals with respect to reaching out to marginalized stakeholders and NGOs, facilitating their participation in stakeholder processes, and covering the costs involved in bringing their expertise to the table (see discussion of funding below).

Women's NGO Engagement with CSR Multi-Stakeholder Governance Processes

According to my interviewees, the national women's NGOs in this study are rarely engaged with the CSR movement or involved in CSR multi-stakeholder processes that are defining and developing new norms, standards and practices relating to business social responsibilities. Nor do these NGOs scrutinize corporate CSR reports, or attempt to directly hold companies to account for their gender equality impacts. Several interviewees said that they do not identify corporations in their organizational/campaign strategy. Some described debating Norway's requirement for 40% females on corporate Boards, and other issues relating to the private sector, but their work still focuses on getting the government to address these issues. The Director of a leading women's advocacy umbrella organization in the UK with a membership including many smaller women's NGOs believed that none of these organizations were directly engaging in CSR initiatives. In Australia, interviewees explained that corporate accountability could not be a priority for them at the moment because "The national [women's] movement is just coming back onto its feet after a period of struggle and what [my employers] really want is a clear policy advocacy voice and they define that primarily in governmental terms" (Interviewee 5). Another in Australia said "I've tried for years to get [women's organizations] interested in [this agenda] and there's just a total lack of interest in it" (Interviewee 7). Yet another (UK) interviewee reflected upon this lack of engagement and considered it odd: "it's weird isn't it because it (CSR) is such a ... big hot topic in itself" (Interviewee 3).

In exploring why women's NGOs are little engaged with CSR initiatives, and multi-stakeholder governance processes in particular, several key issues emerged in interviews. One of the most important of these is that, as suggested in the literature, there is still a primary focus among women's NGOs on government as the driver of change. The majority of my interviewees regard it as a government responsibility to hold companies to account on gender equality issues, through a range of different mechanisms. Interestingly, despite lack of reference to CSR, several interviewee comments reflected debates about the changing role of government, and "the government of self-regulation" (Gond et al. 2011), in the CSR literature. For example, one argued "Government through its procurement process needs to be driving that process of change, in terms of that [social] accounting system ... that should happen through proper procurement" (Interviewee 1).

A small number of interviewees explained how their focus is gradually moving away from an exclusive engagement with government, and towards engagement with companies. The Director of one advocacy NGO said

> Because the women's sector is so small in the UK, [and because] we had relatively good relationships with the government at a point [we worked at policy level and legislative level, and] ... I think we were right to do that, ... [that] was where we had most impact for ... [the] human resource that we could expend. But ... we've now got this situation where, partly as a result of our campaigning with others, we've got a very good legislative framework [but] practice is very poor. So [now we're] extending our change mechanisms and making sure we build the resource in order to be able to do that. [It's] also about working in a changing political climate where [having] policy impact is becoming much less easy. ... we're just getting less bang for our buck at policy level now... So ... that drives the change as well.
> (Interviewee 1)

It is interesting to note that the issue of funding, not often addressed in the CSR literature on business–NGO relations, emerged time and again in my interviews (see also previous section). This reflects observations about severe resource constraints in the literature on women's NGOs. Several, interviewees explained the failure of their organizations to participate in CSR initiatives as due to a chronic lack of resources whereby women's NGOs have too much to do and very limited budgets, leaving them no time to engage in another whole new area of work as represented by CSR. Interviewees from advocacy NGOs described "very resource-constrained times" (Interviewee 6), being "dramatically under-funded" as compared to other areas of the voluntary sector (Interviewee 2), and having "enough on our plates" (Interviewee 8). The Head of Policy from a service providing NGO described a

> struggle with ... trying to engage women's organizations in the policy-making that will eventually affect their service users and their funding. When it comes to a choice of having to deal with a service user who's turned up on your doorstep with just the clothes she's standing in, or come into a half-day meeting that is quite frankly unlikely to amount to anything ... or if it does, it'll be years away. ... there's just no contest. And understandably so... So it's about us finding other ways to enable that engagement.... it's definitely on our agenda [private sector accountability], it's just ... it seems like a bit of a luxury. ... we've got to really focus where the money is, which is really local government.[5] (Interviewee 6)

The Director of a national umbrella NGO which services many smaller women's NGOs explained that, partly because of funding constraints "the whole women's agenda, [is] very divided, fund[ed] in sectors, in discrete ... chunks, which actually precludes a more ... intellectual and ... cohesive argument and discussion"

---

[5] This interviewee described how privatisation has led to a situation whereby women's service-providing NGOs which had traditionally been supported by government grants, now have to bid for contracts, to provide domestic violence shelters for example, against private companies that can undercut their prices, and that often have little knowledge and experience in the field of gender equality and domestic violence.

(Interviewee 9). Lack of funding also means that women's NGOs are not well placed to take on new issues, or provide expertise to other sectors. The Head of Development at an advocacy NGO explained that "part of the reason that a lot of businesses and a lot of practitioners aren't speaking to the women's sector [is] because the women's sector's just not equipped to advise or [doesn't] have the capacity to advise" (Interviewee 2).

A new emerging issue in this respect is that, as state funding for NGOs shrinks, and the NGOs working on gender and other equality issues seek new sources of revenue from the private sector, the NGOs, according to one of my interviewees, perceive a challenge inherent in taking a critical position towards their funders: "Something that we need to think about is that dichotomy in itself, to build a relationship and to hold them to account at the same time?" (Interviewee 3). The Corporate Relations Manager at this service-providing NGO regarded this problem as a further disincentive to involvement by her NGO in corporate accountability initiatives. This point relates to fears of NGO co-optation evident in the CSR literature (Burchell and Cook 2013). However, the General Secretary of a very large UK women's membership NGO (Interviewee 10) emphasised that her organization guards its independence very carefully when working with corporates. They tend to engage, and get sponsorship for specific, one-off projects with private sector companies rather than seeing themselves as on-going partners.

Lack of information was also deemed a barrier to participation by women's NGOs in CSR governance processes. The Director of one umbrella NGO confessed

> I didn't even know that [companies] had such things as … stakeholder groups that they consulted with and stuff like that, …and I mean we're one of the big women's organizations and we are not [informed]… So there is a huge gap, even for an organization like us that actually does realise the importance of [these issues]. (Interviewee 9)

One of the barriers identified was a lack of corporate transparency: "it's difficult to get straightforward, clear information on what the private sector is up to" (Interviewee 8).

A related issue again concerned relationships with people in business, where two interviewees said that, despite some important exceptions, on the whole women's NGOs lack the necessary relationships with business leaders to facilitate constructive engagement with CSR processes. One said: "I think most people involved in working in women's organizations don't come from private business backgrounds, don't have any real knowledge or expertise in that field and wouldn't know how to begin" (Interviewee 8). The Director of an umbrella advocacy NGO argued "I just don't think there's a sufficient level of consciousness about what the issues are … [or that] everyone's got that awareness yet of what their role is" (Interviewee 9). Commenting on the fact that engagement with business has not traditionally been on the feminist agenda, the Executive Officer of one service-providing NGO in Australia explained that there are "the professional women's organizations that were interested in advancing individual women, and then there were the feminist organizations that were very different" (Interviewee 5). The Chair of an Australian advocacy NGO added

I think it's a generational thing... a lot of the older feminists just don't ... get it and a lot of them came out of the left, so they can't see any reason that you should be talking about business... people who cut their teeth in the Labour Party ... or in the Communist Party in many cases, ... You try and talk to them about reforming business and they go 'Uh?'. (Interviewee 7)

This interviewee felt that things would improve with the next generation.

In similar vein, several interviewees gave a general scepticism about business and its approach to gender equality as a reason to stay away from the CSR agenda. For example, one from a women's membership NGO said: "there's more important issues that affect women, the family, the home, the environment...we're not going to get anywhere anyway, so why waste our time?" (Interviewee 11). In response to hearing that corporations don't appear to experience pressure from NGOs to disclose more about gender equality issues another asked: "if they did, would it make a difference?" (Interviewee 3). The Director of an umbrella NGO said: "if we can't even get [effective reporting] happening in the public sector with a duty [to do so], what hope have we got elsewhere?" (Interviewee 9). Finally, the Head of Development in an advocacy NGO regarded involvement with CSR as dependent in part on the "re-branding [of] CSR ... so it's not still perceived as very fluffy" (Interviewee 2).

My finding that the women's NGO sector appears to be relatively uninvolved in CSR processes may also be because these NGOs are overlooked by the CSR 'industry'. Several interviewees suggested a need for some sort of capacity building for women's organizations on CSR issues in order to help them access funds and play a role in defining business responsibilities, and holding companies to account with regard to gender equality. Finally, the Executive Officer of an Australian service providing NGO (Interviewee 5) noted that internationally the women's movement has focused a great deal on human rights issues, framing gender equality as a human right. This suggests that the new business and human rights agenda might help women's NGOs to engage with CSR in the future.

Discussion

My findings suggest that engagement with business is emerging as a relatively new strategy for women's NGOs which have traditionally focused on government as the primary driver of gender change in organizations. It seems that women's NGOs may have continued to focus on government perhaps for longer than some other social movements and NGOs (e.g., environmental NGOs). This may be partly because government has played such a key role with respect to gender equality through legislative change in the two countries where NGOs in this study are based. However, while beginning to engage with individual companies, many women's NGOs still lack relationships with people in business, and women's NGOs appear to be little engaged in wider CSR governance processes, supporting suggestions in the literature on gender and CSR (Kilgour 2007; Grosser and Moon 2005b).

With regard to NGO strategies for engagement with individual companies, one women's advocacy NGO in this study engages in dialogue, and collaborates in practice, with a small group of leading companies to help advance their gender equality strategies. The reason given for this engagement fits well with the CSR literature that explains NGO engagement with business as a way of encouraging regulatory compliance (Doh and Guay 2006), and my study extends this theory to the field of gender equality regulation. The same NGO simultaneously, and in collaboration with businesses, runs a more adversarial campaign that challenges other corporations to improve their workplace practices with respect to issues beyond regulation, such as pornography in the workplace and the use of lap-dancing clubs for business. Thus, while often discussed in instrumental terms by business, my study illustrates how CSR with respect to gender equality is beginning to be viewed by NGOs as a process of regulatory compliance, and one that also moves beyond compliance, fitting with wider theories of CSR (Crane et al. 2008). Moreover, my findings help illustrate how the either/or discussion with respect to NGO dialogue and adversarial campaigns relating to corporate practice is far too simplistic (Burchell and Cook 2013). Women's NGOs adopt a range of strategies in their new engagements with corporations.

The outcomes of my research also add to the debate about possible co-optation by business of social movement agendas, and social movement agency in CSR (Burchell and Cook 2013). Specifically, my paper illustrates how, while the use of language relating to gender equality by business in the context of CSR may be viewed as an appropriation of social movement language (Burchell and Cook 2013), it can also be used as a resource for women's NGOs. Meyerson and Kolb (2000) argue that narratives that are explicit about gender issues are an important success factor for advancing gender equality within organizations in projects that attempt to advance the dual agenda of profit maximization and gender equality. In as much as companies adopt rhetoric relating to gender equality in efforts to instrumentalize this agenda for reputational and profit making purposes (Gherardi 1995), my research shows that women's NGOs can also draw upon such rhetoric as a resource, or hook, upon which to hang their appeals for funding and support for gender equality campaigns. However, my study suggests that this strategy may be limited by a relative lack of focus on gender equality, as compared to environmental issues, by corporations in their CSR programmes.

If we regard CSR as a contested definitional domain, my interviews show how some women's NGOs, through their engagement with company practice, are contesting the meaning of CSR, albeit from the margins. They are beginning to redefine responsible business with respect to gender equality, expanding this agenda to include issues of domestic violence, pornography and corporate entertainment as a workplace practice for example. Indeed, an emerging agenda has since become evident that re-frames CSR from a women's NGO perspective as "Corporate Sexual Responsibility" (Swedish Women's Lobby 2013). Guerard et al. (2013) view the relationship between social movements and corporations as 'a series of framing contests'. Feminist literature on strategic framing has focused on efforts by women's movements and gender experts to influence government gender equality agendas (Pollack and Hafner-Burton 2000; Walby 2005), but not much investigated this process with respect to attempts to engage with, and influence, corporations. My paper suggests that women's NGOs are beginning to strategically frame their agendas in their emerging corporate engagement strategies, and, in the process, to redefine CSR.

My research also contributes to the literature on business–NGO relations in the context of CSR by raising two further issues that have been little discussed therein to date. The first of these concerns the significance of cross-sector relationships between individual corporate and NGO managers. The research presented here reveals examples of important collaboration between corporate managers and women's NGO leaders as feminists. In theorizing this finding, I turn to Marshall's (2007) discussion of tempered radicals in CSR. Tempered radicals are "people who work within mainstream organizations and professions and want also to transform them" (Meyerson and Scully 1995: 586) for example, promoting diversity. Marshall (2007) discusses Anita Roddick as a feminist tempered radical in CSR. Through interviews in this study I find that, via a relationship with a key national women's NGO working on domestic violence, Anita Roddick was able to utilize the resources and reach of the Body Shop to make a major contribution to the campaign against domestic violence, and to gain reputational advantage for the Body Shop in the process. My interviewees provide evidence that other managers in business have also sought help from a women's advocacy NGO in efforts to advance gender equality in their companies (see discussion of the Gender Equality Forum above). I find the concept of tempered radicals useful in this regard in that it seems to help explain such cross-sector collaborations, which, according to my interviewees, can play a key role in driving change. Indeed, these relationships may mediate the success or failure of NGO engagements with corporations.

The other issue raised by my interviewees that is little discussed in the CSR literature is that of NGO funding. Several interviewees from service providing NGOs described approaches to individual companies based on a need to find a new source of funding as government funding for NGOs shrinks. Moreover, there was a suggestion by one of these interviewees that this need for funding was a reason not to be visibly challenging corporate gender equality practice, or pushing for accountability and transparency on this issue. My study therefore raises new questions regarding how NGOs might be coopted by business agendas through their need for financial support. It may be that the funding issue is so important to my interviewees because a number of them come from service providing NGOs, which do not appear to be discussed as much as advocacy NGOs in the CSR literature. However, service-providing NGOs are also involved in advocacy work on gender equality, and are important stakeholders with regard to the social impacts and responsibilities of corporations. Furthermore, my interviewees from advocacy NGOs similarly raised the funding issue.

Funding also appears to be significant with regard to women's NGO participation in, and contribution to, wider CSR multi-stakeholder governance processes. Given the central importance assigned in much of the CSR literature to the role of NGOs in CSR governance, the question of how these actors are funded to

participate is a very important one. Yet this issue is little discussed in the CSR literature, beyond a managerial perspective (Husted 2003), an omission which may be
due in part to a focus on those actors that are already present at the table in CSR
initiatives (e.g., Gilbert and Rasche 2007). Exploring marginalized and absent
stakeholders, as this paper does, raises the issue of NGO access to financial
resources, and places this at the centre of the debate. The literature on women's
NGOs suggests that lack of resources constrains the ability of these organizations to
participate and influence the agenda with regard to international law, and international economic institutions, for example. My research suggests that this is true also
with respect to CSR, supporting Bostrom and Hallstrom's (2010) assertion that differences in the material resources of NGOs mediates their ability to participate in
processes of standard development relating to social and environmental issues in
business. The impact of public sector cuts on funding for women's NGOs in the UK
and Australia points towards a possible intensification of this problem in the current
economic climate (Women's Resource Centre 2013; Maddison and Partridge 2007).

The literature on women's NGOs, and on those representing other marginalized
populations (e.g., Nanz and Steffek 2004), suggests that it is not only additional
resources that are needed, but also capacity building. My study supports this argument, pointing to lack of information about CSR as a barrier to participation by
women's NGOs. This is significant because "Making global governance public presupposes that relevant political information is made available to interested stakeholders" (Nanz and Steffek 2004: 333). Lack of participation in CSR governance
will limit the extent to which women's NGOs will be able to articulate their agendas
therein, challenge the possible co-optation of feminist agendas for instrumental
business interests (Gherardi 1995; Fraser 2013), and contribute to social regulation
through global governance systems (Vogel 2008). However, my research has also
unearthed one national multi-stakeholder Gender Equality Forum in the UK, established by a women's NGO and involving business as well as government representatives in efforts to advance field-level change. This raises questions about the extent
to which marginalized groups may perhaps bypass mainstream CSR governance
processes and establish alternative ones. Further research involving marginalized
NGOs and communities will be important in advancing our understanding in this
respect.

More broadly, my paper raises concerns about marginal voices and legitimacy in
CSR. The need to include NGOs which represent the voices of traditionally marginalized stakeholders in CSR multi-stakeholder initiatives is an issue closely linked to
their legitimacy and their effectiveness. Attempts to establish legitimacy with
respect to CSR governance often make reference to pluralism and inclusiveness
(Scherer and Palazzo 2007; Gilbert and Rasche 2007). Coupland (2005: 355) argues
that CSR "invokes legitimacy from beyond the boundaries of an organization", as
companies describe their CSR activities as a response to societal expectations.
Palazzo and Scherer (2006: 71) argue that legitimacy "involves organizations in
processes of active justification vis-a-vis society rather than simply responding to
the demands of powerful groups". In the feminist organizational studies literature,
Martin (1993) argues for measuring legitimacy, as in a sense of justice, and asserts

the need to test this empirically with attention to the viewpoints of members of disadvantaged groups, who may not agree that something is legitimate or just. Charlesworth and Chinkin (2000) argue that we should insist on equal participation of women in the international legal system and its institutions as a condition of their legitimacy. Thus, research suggesting the absence or marginalization of diverse stakeholder perspectives, including those of women's NGOs, as evidenced in this paper, raises important questions about pluralism in CSR, and the legitimacy of new multi-stakeholder CSR governance processes. This is an area where much further research is needed.

Conclusions

Feminist scholars have noted the importance of including knowledge from the margins in organizational research (Calas and Smircich 1997). The political CSR literature has highlighted the importance of including a plurality of perspectives in processes that define legitimate norms and practices concerning business–society relations. That literature has also emphasized the importance of NGOs in this regard (Scherer and Palazzo 2007). My paper contributes to this stream of research by framing NGOs representing marginalized populations as important actors in CSR as a process of governance. With a focus on gender issues, and acknowledgement of increasing reference to gender equality in the context of CSR, my paper contributes empirically to the literature by engaging with leaders of women's NGOs, a stakeholder group not often considered in CSR research. Research on business–NGO relations has informed my investigation as to engagement by women's NGOs with individual companies, and with wider CSR multi-stakeholder governance processes that aim to bring about field-level change.

The meaning, definition, scope and purpose of CSR are not fixed, but rather are open for contestation (Brammer et al. 2012). One of the reasons to include traditionally marginalized voices and perspectives is that they raise new issues that may help to advance theory as well as practice. This study contributes to the literature by showing how, through collaboration with managers in individual corporations, some of whom may be described as tempered radicals (Meyerson and Scully 1995), as well as through public campaigns, a small number of women's NGOs are beginning to contest the meaning, definition and scope of CSR with respect to gender equality. However, it seems that the new gender equality issues that these women's NGOs bring to the field may well not be effectively represented in wider multi-stakeholder governance processes that are setting new norms and standards for the business community. This is because, according to my interviewees, the women's NGOs in this study rarely participate in CSR as a wider process of governance.

My paper makes a contribution to research, as well as practice, through identifying some of the barriers to participation in CSR as a process of governance by women's NGOs. In particular, I have highlighted the importance of funding and capacity building. Commitments to inclusive CSR practice will, I conclude, have to be adequately resourced in order to be effective. Specifically, resources will need to be allocated to acquiring the expertise of NGOs working with marginalized populations, and on equality issues, in recognition of the fact that this expertise is an important resource for the creation and operation of inclusive, and by implication legitimate, governance. Without such funding, so called 'inclusive' multi-stakeholder CSR governance will almost certainly remain an empty promise despite the best of intentions on the part of CSR practitioners. Moreover, as noted in my introduction to this paper, consideration of gender equality is material to the effectiveness of CSR initiatives which address other key issues such as poverty reduction, environmental degradation and development. I would suggest that CSR organizations (including multi-stakeholder initiatives) will need to reach out to women's NGOs, and to other marginalized groups. It seems that it will not be sufficient simply to fund the participation of such NGOs in CSR processes, important though this is, because chronic lack of time and resources means that they are not able to effectively build capacity and engage with new CSR agendas and organizations. One way to overcome this barrier might be to commission such NGOs as experts to inform the development of CSR tools and practice, in particular those whose claims to legitimacy rest on notions of inclusivity.

Beyond the suggestions made above, future research on the role of tempered radicals in business, and particularly feminist tempered radicals, would, I believe, enhance our understanding of how cross-sector collaborations involving business and NGOs might help advance gender equality in society. Further research involving NGOs representing marginalized communities will also be important in bringing out new issues, and enhancing theory development in CSR. In particular, further research is needed on how to ensure greater participation by such NGOs in CSR governance processes.

I regard the main limitation of this study to be the fact that it explores participation in CSR governance processes by women's NGOs from the UK and Australia only. Women's NGOs in the global South have played a leading role in challenging globalization (e.g., Mohanty 2002). Further research is needed which explores the participation in CSR of women's NGOs from a number of different countries, and particularly from developing countries. Moreover, Squires (2005: 375) warns of the dangers of "focusing on particular organizations as representative of women's views". She argues that women's NGOs can help bring "group perspectives from outside the existing policymaking elite" into the policy arena. However, these NGOs can also serve to "reify group identities, obscuring both intra-group divisions and inter-group commonalities" (p. 375). Referring to the intersections of inequality based on sex, race and class, and other differences, she argues for involving diverse social groups in dialogue, and in deliberative processes generally, in order to include not just women's perspectives, but "complex equality (which recognizes diversity)" (p. 384). Furthermore, as noted by Banerjee (2010), many marginalized populations do not have established NGOs to represent them, thus research on inclusions in CSR governance will need to continue to extend beyond the role of NGOs.

The aim of this paper has been to contribute to a wider research agenda addressing pluralism, diversity and inclusion in new governance systems involving non-state actors, including NGOs. The paper specifically brings feminist perspectives. It has explored the role of women's NGOs with regard to the gender equality practices and impacts of corporations, and with respect to defining the meaning of CSR. A new debate has been emerging among feminist scholars about whether feminism has become 'capitalism's handmaiden' and been co-opted by neoliberal agendas, and how to reclaim it (Fraser 2013). Despite the limitations noted above, I consider that women's NGOs have an important role to play in ensuring that companies, and multi-stakeholder governance initiatives, are held accountable with respect to the gender equality rhetoric that has been taken up in the field of CSR. The participation of women's NGOs will be important in helping to ensure that such rhetoric is translated into forms of practice that are beneficial not just to corporations, but to a wide range of civil society actors.

Acknowledgments I would like to thank Jeremy Moon (Copenhagen Business School), Michael Humphreys (Durham University), Lauren McCarthy (Nottingham University Business School), Dorothea Baur, and three anonymous reviewers at Journal of Business Ethics for useful comments on earlier drafts of this paper.

References

Acker, J. (2006). Inequality regimes: Gender, class, and race in organizations. Gender and Society, 20, 441–464.

Banerjee, S. B. (2010). Governing the global corporation: A critical perspective. Business Ethics Quarterly, 20, 265–274.

Banerjee, S. B. (2011). Voices of the Governed: Towards a theory of the translocal. Organization, 18, 323–344.

Barrientos, S., Dolan, C., & Tallontire, A. (2003). A gendered value chain approach to codes of conduct in African horticulture. World Development, 31, 1511–1526.

Bebbington, J., Brown, J., Frame, B., & Thomson, I. (2007). Theorizing engagement: The potential of a critical dialogic approach. Accounting, Auditing and Accountability Journal, 20, 356–381.

Bhattacharjya, M., Birchall, J., Caro, P., Kelleher, D., & Sahasranaman, V. (2013). Why gender matters in activism: Feminism and social justice movements. Gender and Development, 21(2), 277–293.

Boström, M., & Hallström, K. (2010). NGO power in global social and environmental standard setting. Global Environmental Politics, 10(4), 36–59.

Bourdieu, P. (1982). Leçon sur la Leçon. Paris: Editions de Minuit.

Braithwaite, J., & Drahos, P. (2000). Global business regulation. Cambridge, MA: Cambridge University Press.

Brammer, T., Jackson, G., & Matten, D. (2012). Corporate Social Responsibility and institutional theory: New perspectives on private governance. Socio-economic Review, 10, 3–28.

Brown, L. D., Khagram, S., Moore, M. H., & Frumkin, P. (2000). Globalization, NGOs and multisectoral relations. In J. S. Nye & J. D. Donahue (Eds.), Governance in a globalizing world. Washington, DC: Brookings Institution Press.

Burchell, J., & Cook, J. (2013). CSR, co-optation and resistance: The emergence of new agonistic relations between business and civil society. Journal of Business Ethics, 115, 741–754.

Burgess, G. (2011). The uneven geography of participation at the global level: Ethiopian women activists at the global periphery. Globalizations, 8(2), 163–177.

Calas, M. B., & Smircich, L. (1997). Feminist inquiries into business ethics. In A. Larson & E. Freeman (Eds.), Women's studies and business ethics towards a new conversation (pp. 50–79). New York: Oxford University Press.

Charlesworth, H., & Chinkin, C. (2000). The boundaries of international law. Manchester: Manchester University Press.

Charmaz, K. (2006). Constructing grounded theory. A practical guide through qualitative analysis. London: Sage Publications.

Coleman, G. (2002). Gender, power and post-structuralism in corporate citizenship. Journal of Corporate Citizenship, 5(Spring), 17–25.

Corley, K., & Gioia, D. (2004). Identity ambiguity and change in the wake of a corporate spin-off. Administrative Science Quarterly, 49, 173–208.

Council of Europe. (1998). Gender mainstreaming: Conceptual framework, methodology and presentation of good practice. Council of Europe. EG-s-Ms (98) 2 Feb.

Coupland, C. (2005). Corporate social responsibility as argument on the web. Journal of Business Ethics, 16, 355–366.

Crane, A., McWilliams, A., Matten, D., Moon, J., & Siegel, D. (Eds.). (2008). The Oxford handbook of corporate social responsibility. Oxford: Oxford University Press.

De Bakker, F. G. A., & Den Hond, F. (2008). Introducing the politics of stakeholder influence: A review essay. Business and Society, 47, 8–20.

De Bakker, F., Den Hond, F., King, B., & Weber, K. (2013). Social movements, civil society and corporations: Taking stock and looking ahead. Organization Studies, 34, 573–593.

DenHond, F. (2010).Reviewessay: Reflections on relationships between NGOs and corporations. Business and Society, 49, 173–178.

Den Hond, F., & De Bakker, F. G. A. (2007). Ideologically motivated activism: How activist groups influence corporate social change activities. Academy of Management Review, 32, 901–924.

Derry, R. (1997). Feminism: How does it play in the corporate theatre? In A. L. Larson & R. E. Freeman (Eds.), Women's studies and business ethics towards a new conversation. New York: Oxford University Press.

Doh, J., & Guay, T. (2004). Globalization and corporate social responsibility: How nongovernmental organizations influence labor and environmental codes of conduct. Management International Review, 44, 7–30.

Doh, J., & Guay, T. (2006). Corporate social responsibility, public policy, and NGO activism in Europe and the United States: An institutional-stakeholder perspective. Journal of Management Studies, 43, 47–73.

Doh, J., & Teegen, H. (2002). Nongovernmental organizations as institutional actors in international business: Theory and implication. International Business Review, 11, 665–684.

Fraser, N. (2013). Fortunes of feminism: From state-managed capitalism to neoliberal crisis. London: Verso.

Gherardi, S. (1995). Gender, symbolism and organizational cultures. London: Sage Publications.

Gilbert, D. U., & Rasche, A. (2007). Discourse ethics and social accountability—The ethics of SA 8000. Business Ethics Quarterly, 17, 187–216.

Gilligan, C. (1982). In a different voice. Cambridge, MA: Harvard University Press.

Gioia, D., Corley, K., & Hamilton, A. (2013). Seeking qualitative rigor in inductive research: Notes on the Gioia methodology. Organizational Research Methods, 16(1), 15–31.

Glaser, B. (1992). Basics of grounded theory research. Mill Valley, CA: Sociology Press.

Glaser, B., & Strauss, A. (1967). The discovery of grounded theory: Strategies of qualitative research. London: Wiedenfeld and Nicholson.

Gond, J. P., Kang, N., & Moon, J. (2011). The government of self-regulation: On the comparative dynamics of corporate social responsibility. Economy and Society, 40(4), 640–671.

Gond, J. P., & Moon, J. (2012). Corporate social responsibility in retrospect and prospect: Exploring the life-cycle of an essentially contested concept. In J. P. Gond & J. Moon (Eds.), Corporate social responsibility: A reader. New York: Routledge.

Grosser, K. (2009). CSR and Gender Equality: Women as stakeholders and the EU sustainability Strategy. Business Ethics: A European Review, 18, 290–307.

Grosser, K. (2011). Corporate social responsibility, gender equality and organizational change: A feminist perspective. Unpublished Doctoral Dissertation, University of Nottingham, Nottingham.

Grosser, K., Adams, C., & Moon, J. (2008). Equal Opportunity for Women in the Workplace: A study of corporate disclosure. Research Report. London: Association of Chartered and Certified Accountants.

Grosser, K., & Moon, J. (2005a). Gender mainstreaming and corporate social responsibility: Reporting workplace issues. Journal of Business Ethics, 62, 327–340.

Grosser, K., & Moon, J. (2005b). The role of corporate social responsibility in gender mainstreaming. International Feminist Journal of Politics, 7, 532–554.

Grosser, K., & Moon, J. (2008). Developments in company reporting on workplace gender equality?: A corporate social responsibility perspective. Accounting Forum, 32, 179–198.

Guerard, S., Bode, C., & Gustafsson, R. (2013). Turning point mechanisms in a dualistic process model of institutional emergence: The case of the diesel particulate filter in Germany. Organization Studies, 34, 781–822.

Habermas, J. (1974). Theory and practice. London: Heinemann Educational Books Ltd.

Habermas, J. (1998). The inclusion of the other: Studies in political theory. Cambridge, MA: MIT Press.

Hale, A., & Opondo, M. (2005). Humanising the cut flower chain: Confronting the realities of flower production for workers in Kenya. Antipode, 37, 301–323.

Hoffman, A. (1999). Institutional evolution and change: Environmentalism and the US chemical industry. Academy of Management Journal, 42, 351–371.

Husted, B. (2003). Governance choices for corporate social responsibility: To contribute, collaborate or internalize? Long Range Planning, 16, 481–498.

Karam, C., & Jamali, D. (2013). Gendering CSR in the Arab Middle East: An institutional perspective. Business Ethics Quarterly, 23(1), 31–68.

Kilgour, M. A. (2007). The UN Global Compact and substantive equality for Women: Revealing a 'well hidden' mandate. Third World Quarterly, 28, 751–773.

Levy, D. L., & Kaplan, R. (2008). Corporate social responsibility and theories of global governance: Strategic contestation in global issue arenas. In A. Crane, A. Mcwilliams, D. Matten, J. Moon, & D. Siegel (Eds.), The Oxford handbook of corporate social responsibility. Oxford: Oxford University Press.

Locke, K. (2008). Grounded theory. In R. Thorpe & R. Holt (Eds.), The Sage dictionary of qualitative management research. London: Sage Publications.

Maddison, S., & Partridge, E. (2007). How well does Australian democracy serve Australian women? In The democratic audit of Australia. School of Social Sciences, The Australian National University.

Maiguashca, B. (2011). Looking beyond the spectacle: Social movement theory, feminist anti-globalization activism and the praxis of principled pragmatism. Globalizations, 8(4), 535–549.

Marshall, J. (2007). The gendering of leadership in corporate social responsibility. Journal of Organizational Change Management, 20, 165–181.

Martin, J. (1993). Inequality, distributive justice, and organizational illegitimacy. In K. Murnighan (Ed.), Social psychology in organizations: Advances in theory and research (pp. 296–321). Englewood Cliffs, NJ: Prentice-Hall.

McBarnet, D., Voiculescu, A., & Campbell, T. (2007). The new accountability. Cambridge, MA: Cambridge University Press.

Meyerson, D. E., & Kolb, D. M. (2000). Moving out of the 'Armchair': Developing a framework to bridge the gap between feminist theory and practice. Organization, 7, 553–571.

Meyerson, D. E., & Scully, M. A. (1995). Tempered radicalism and the politics of ambivalence and change. Organization Science, 6(5), 585–600.

Mohanty, C. T. (2002). "Under Western Eyes" revisited: Feminist solidarity through anticapitalist struggles. Signs, 28 (2 (Winter)), 499–535.

Molyneux, M. (1998). Analysing women's movements. Development and Change, 29, 219–245.

Moon, J., Crane, A., & Matten, D. (2011). Corporations and citizenship in new institutions of global governance. In C. Crouch & C. MacLean (Eds.), The responsible corporation in a global economy. Oxford: Oxford University Press.

Nanz, P., & Steffek, J. (2004). Global governance, participation and the public sphere. Government and Opposition, 39, 314–335.

Newell, P. (2005). Citizenship, accountability and community: The limits of the CSR agenda. International Affairs, 81, 541–557.

O'Brien, R., Goetz, A. M., Scholte, J. A., & Williams, M. (2000). Contesting global governance. Cambridge, MA: Cambridge University Press.

O'Dwyer, B., Unerman, J., & Bradley, J. (2005). Perceptions on the emergence and future development of corporate social disclosure in Ireland. Accounting, Auditing and Accountability Journal, 18, 14–43.

Palazzo, G., & Scherer, A. (2006). Corporate legitimacy as deliberation: A communicative framework. Journal of Business Ethics, 66, 71–88.

Pearson, R. (2007). Beyond women workers: Gendering CSR. Third World Quarterly, 28, 731–749.

Pollack, A., & Hafner-Burton, E. (2000). Mainstreaming gender in the European Union. Journal of European Public Policy, 7(3), 432–456.

Prieto-Carron, M. (2008). Women workers, industrialization, global supply chains and corporate codes of conduct. Journal of Business Ethics, 83, 5–17.

Rasche, A., De Bakker, F., & Moon, J. (2013). Complete and partial organizing for corporate social responsibility. Journal of Business Ethics, 115(4), 651–663.

Scherer, A. G., & Palazzo, G. (2007). Toward a political conception of corporate responsibility: Business and society seen from a Habermasian perspective. Academy of Management Review, 32, 1096–1120.

Scherer, A., & Palazzo, G. (2008). Globalization and corporate social responsibility. In A. Crane, A. Mcwilliams, D. Matten, J. Moon, & D. Siegel (Eds.), The Oxford handbook of corporate social responsibility. Oxford: Oxford University Press.

Scherer, A., & Palazzo, G. (2011). The new political role of business in a globalized world: A review of a new perspective on CSR and its implications for the firm, governance, and democracy. Journal of Management Studies, 48(4), 899–931.

Slager, R., Gond, J. P., & Moon, J. (2012). Standardization as institutional work: The regulatory power of a responsible investment standard. Organization Science, 33(5–6), 763–790.

Squires, J. (2005). Is mainstreaming transformative? Theorizing mainstreaming in the context of diversity and deliberation. Social Politics, 12, 366–388.

Swedish Women's Lobby. (2013). http://sverigeskvinnolobby.se/wpcontent/uploads/2013/08/Flyer-CSW-2-2.pdf.

Vogel, D. (2008). Private global business regulation. Annual Review of Political Science, 11, 261–282.

Walby, S. (2005). Gender mainstreaming: Productive tensions in theory and practice. Social Politics, 12(3), 321–343.

Windsor, D. (2001). The future of corporate social responsibility. International Journal of Organizational Analysis, 9, 225–256.

Women's Resource Centre. (2013). The impact of public spending cuts on women's voluntary and community organisations in London. London: Women's Resource Centre.

Yancey-Martin, P. (2006). Practicing gender at work: Further thoughts on reflexivity. Gender, Work and Organization, 13(3), 254–276.

Kate Grosser is a Senior Lecturer at RMIT University (Melbourne) School of Management, and Co-Director of RMIT's Business and Human Rights Centre. She has pioneered research that critically engages with Corporate Social Responsibility (CSR) theory and practice from feminist perspectives, including new scholarship on gender, business and human rights. She is particularly interested in the contribution of feminist theories; CSR as a process of governance; and the role of feminist social movements. Her work appears in, among others: *Business Ethics Quarterly; Journal of Business Ethics; Organization; Gender, Work and Organization; Business Ethics: A European Review*. She sits on the Distinguished Advisory Board at *Gender, Work & Organization*, and has a strong focus on research engagement and impact, having acted as advisor to the UN Working Group on Business and Human Rights, and numerous other international and national bodies.

Empowering Women through Corporate Social Responsibility: A Feminist Foucauldian Critique

Lauren A. McCarthy

Abstract Corporate social responsibility (CSR) has been hailed as a new means to address gender inequality, particularly by facilitating women's empowerment. Women are frequently and forcefully positioned as saviours of economies or communities and proponents of sustainability. Using vignettes drawn from a CSR women's empowerment programme in Ghana, this conceptual article explores unexpected programme outcomes enacted by women managers and farmers. It is argued that a feminist Foucauldian reading of power as relational and productive can help explain this since those involved are engaged in ongoing processes of resistance and self-making. This raises questions about the assumptions made about 'women' and what is it that such CSR programmes aim to 'empower' them 'from' or 'to'. Empowerment, when viewed as an ethic of care for the Self, is better understood as a self-directed process, rather than a corporate-led strategy. This has implications for how we can imagine the achievement of gender equality through CSR.

Keywords Gender · Empowerment · Corporate social responsibility · Foucault · Feminism

Introduction

Feminism is enjoying a resurgence in popular culture (Koffman and Gill 2013), and feminism's goals of gender equality and equity appear to be mirrored in a growing number of corporate social responsibility (CSR) programmes and policies which claim to empower women in businesses' value chains (Cornwall and Anyidoho 2010; Coleman 2010). These policies contain phrases such as 'Empower a woman and you feed a community'; 'Gender economics is smart economics' and 'Women are our most valuable untapped resource', echoed throughout international bodies

L. A. McCarthy (✉)
University of Massachusetts Amherst, Amherst, MA, USA
e-mail: lauren.mccarthy@rhul.ac.uk

225

M. Painter, P. H. Werhane (eds.), *Leadership, Gender, and Organization*, Issues in Business Ethics 63, https://doi.org/10.1007/978-3-031-24445-2_10

such as the United Nations (UN), The World Bank and within national government policy (Prügl 2015; Roberts 2015). The potential for 'empowered' women to contribute to social, economic and environmental sustainability is a well-worn rhetoric in development circles, now imported into CSR (Cornwall and Anyidoho 2010). Accordingly, businesses such as Coca-Cola, Vodafone, Walmart, H&M, General Mills, and many others, are engaging in 'women's empowerment' projects as part of their CSR efforts in value chains (ICRW 2016). After many years of inattention to gender in CSR in scholarship and practice (Marshall 2011; Spence 2016), women's empowerment through CSR is now an established facet of international development (Grosser et al. 2016; ICRW 2016).

The focus on women as carriers of global development and sustainability is related to the longstanding debate within business ethics, particularly within *Business Ethics Quarterly,* about whether there are 'feminine' ethics (Dobson and White 1995), how they are related to feminist ethics (Derry 1996; Liedtka 1996), and how such ethics might be observed in women and men within organisations (Burton and Dunn 1996; Wicks et al. 1994; Wicks 1996). In particular, feminist ethics, with its focus on relationality and cooperation, has been positioned as cultivating more socially responsible business (Wicks et al. 1994; Wicks 1996), with women (although not exclusively) exuding a power to change the world for the better (White 1992). To this end, recent corporate attention on empowering women in value chains, particularly in the global South, mirrors these early approaches to feminism, business ethics and social change. As I will argue, this adoption of some of the (mis)assumptions of feminist ethics into CSR programmes is not without concern.

CSR is defined here as a set of practices and policies enacted by private businesses with the ostensible aim of first, limiting negative impacts of businesses (doing no harm), and second, contributing to society through activities that benefit people and planet (Gond and Moon 2011). While business remains a dominant actor within this phenomenon, it is worth stressing that other organisations are relevant (and powerful) to the context, including governments, non-governmental organisations (NGOs), civil society, and the 'beneficiaries' of CSR practices themselves (Gond and Moon 2011; Grosser 2009). The diversity of 'gendered' CSR practices is reflected in an increased awareness of women in the global South as salient stakeholders (Karam and Jamali 2013) and investment in women's empowerment programmes,[1] which are often forms of multi-stakeholder initiatives or public-private partnerships involving corporations, NGOs, governments and funding bodies such as the IMF (Bexell 2012; ICRW 2016). These new configurations of governance, with respect to women and CSR, are beginning to be addressed in scholarship (Bexell 2012; Roberts 2015). Yet there remain few studies on the operationalisation of 'gendered' CSR in the form of women's empowerment programmes (Tornhill 2016a). 'Gendered' CSR makes explicit tensions over

---

[1] According to one study in 2016 over 31 million USD was invested in 31 corporate women's empowerment programmes (ICRW 2016).

'imposing' cultural changes from lead companies in the global North, onto men and women in the global South (Adanhounme 2011; Khan and Lund-Thomsen 2011).

   The overall aim of this article, therefore, is to explore the concept of women's empowerment as a relevant, yet contested concept for business ethics and CSR scholars. In its current usage within CSR, empowerment entails a discourse of caring, cooperative women 'lifting themselves and others out of poverty' (WEP 2013) through individual micro-entrepreneurship enterprises, facilitated by business (Roberts 2015). This is very different from the original women's and civil rights movement's conceptualisation, where empowerment is a socio-political process, and where shifts in power are central to change, for individuals *and* across social groups (Batliwala 2007). Examining this disjuncture, and providing windows into the realities of CSR empowerment programmes, I offer two vignettes taken from research in the Ghanaian cocoa value chain. Here, the subject positions that a women's empowerment discourse creates for the men and women involved is contrasted with the embodied, gendered experiences of Ghanaian farmers and cooperative workers.[2] To explore why the discourse fails to live up to the reality I turn to feminist Foucauldian ideas of gender, power and freedom.

   Deconstructing the term 'women's empowerment' indicates two broad conceptual concerns: gender and power. In this article I draw on a conceptualisation of gender not just as a social construction, practice or performance, but as a process which encapsulates all of these dimensions of human existence (Linstead and Pullen 2005; Pullen 2006; Pullen and Knights 2007). Inspired by the writings of Foucault and by feminist thinkers who have applied this work to gender theory (e.g. Grosz 1994), Linstead and Pullen (2005: 292) argue that 'Gender is not the construction or outcome of a performance but is immanent within those performances making them productive of new molecular connections in the meshwork of identity.' This translates into an understanding of gender as something fluid, and an ongoing process of self-making (Butler 2004; Linstead and Brewis 2004). This is important in relation to the notion of 'women's empowerment' since it problematises the idea of 'women' or 'woman' as a static category of identity, role or even performance. The rhetoric of a hierarchal binary between men and women has previously been deconstructed by feminist organisational scholars studying leadership (e.g. Acker 1990; Bowring 2004), but this scrutiny has not yet fallen on the assumptions made about the men and women involved in CSR programmes.

   In speaking of 'empowerment' it is necessary to explore what is meant by 'power' (Hardy and Leiba-O'Sullivan 1998). I take inspiration from Michel Foucault (1978, 1980, 1982, 1986, 1994) and the ways his work has been interpreted by many feminist scholars in relation to gender (Butler 1997; Hayward 2000; McNay 1992; Pullen 2006; Sawicki 1991). Power is relational (power is everywhere and enacted

---

[2] In this article, I mainly explore women's resistance and interaction with women's empowerment programmes, since so much of the focus within these CSR interventions is on women *per se*. However, men are also key actors within this story, as they engage with, or affect, the outcomes of empowerment programmes as well. The particular role of men within women's CSR empowerment projects is a ripe area for future research.

by all), and productive (a site of ongoing negotiation over meaning) (Foucault 1986, 1982). In particular, Foucault's later works (1982, 1985; 1986; 1994; 1987) present an intriguing picture of the role of the individual in power relations, and how individuals create their own 'conditions of freedom' within strategic games of power play (Crane et al. 2008). Opposed to theories which treat women as a homogenous group, with fixed identities labouring under patriarchal structures, post-modern feminist scholars have drawn upon Foucault's theory of power due to its potential for human agency, resistance and alternative understandings of gendered power relations (Butler 2004; Kelan 2010; Kondo 1990; McNay 1992; Pullen 2006; Sawicki 1991). As this article aims to show, applying a feminist Foucauldian understanding of power and gender to CSR in the global South, specifically in relation to the outcomes of CSR women's empowerment projects, contributes an alternative perspective on what is fast-becoming a CSR 'fashion'. It reignites a conversation within *Business Ethics Quarterly* regarding how feminist approaches might see women as individuals, yet also recognise the relational, interconnected nature of systems of gender inequality and power in which CSR initiatives take place (Derry 1996).

I therefore provide two contributions to CSR theory regarding development initiatives with this article. First, I contribute to the study of gender, business ethics and CSR by unpacking the notion of 'women's empowerment' in corporate-led programmes in the global South. I contrast the current discourse that surrounds women's empowerment alongside accounts of the 'beneficiaries' and champions of these programmes acting in unexpected or paradoxical ways. Women become synonymous with gender and with static roles as carer, mother and entrepreneur. Their 'innate power' is co-opted into a business case narrative which requires women to remain in these roles. Yet and as I show in my vignettes, women (and men) may resist these positions and contribute to unintended programme outcomes.

Second, I contribute to theory on women's empowerment and CSR by accounting for such paradoxical outcomes through feminist Foucauldian theory on power and freedom. I explain how the concepts of 'subjectivation' and freedom are useful for exploring the meaning of empowerment for CSR and business ethics scholars. These concepts stress the recursive relationship between human beings, power relations and social change, and emphasise how individuals constantly negotiate and resist 'gender' (Butler 2004; McNay 2000), thus problematising the notion of 'women's' empowerment. Further, a feminist Foucauldian reading of freedom, which presents human beings as 'subjects' who are both 'free' and 'constrained' within power relations (Crane et al. 2008; Foucault 1987; Hayward 2000; Hirschmann 2002) is best understood as a process in which workers' *own* capability for struggle and resistance is paramount (Foucault and Deleuze 1977). Again, this challenges prior articulations of feminine/feminist ethics as focused on women as a group, and ethics lying in the collective (Dobson and White 1995; White 1992), and the manifestation of this in CSR practice. Instead, I argue, the current focus of businesses striving to 'empower women' through CSR may not always be possible, or indeed, welcome, when freedom is better understood as self-making, and the female and male 'beneficiaries' of CSR reconceptualised as active agents therein.

The article is structured as follows: I first introduce the phenomenon of CSR women's empowerment programmes. I explore the concept of empowerment, highlighting four ways in which the current narrowing of a neoliberal approach to empowerment fails to live up to the original concept's ideal. I then introduce my own research on CSR women's empowerment, entailing a case study from the Ghanaian cocoa industry. I draw on two vignettes to illustrate the ways in which CSR women's empowerment programmes in the global South are often more complex and problematic than the narrative around them allows for. Following this, I use a feminist Foucauldian lens to answer two pertinent questions relating to the vignettes, and CSR and women's empowerment more generally: why might women resist empowerment efforts, and what do corporations seek to 'empower' these women from or to? I finish with a discussion on what a feminist Foucauldian lens on women's empowerment adds to theoretical approaches to CSR and business ethics, particularly around the notion of 'freedom', and suggest some ways in which businesses may wish to rethink their gender equality efforts.

Women's Empowerment Through CSR

Can CSR programmes be a vehicle for women's empowerment? This question is not easily answered, since divergent opinions exist regarding how female emancipation can be won (Prügl 2015), and empirical evidence on how marginalised people (such as women workers) experience CSR remains scarce (Ansari et al. 2012). Yet the ubiquitous 'business case' for women's empowerment persists (e.g. Coleman 2010; Pellegrino et al. 2011). This narrative of women's empowerment has been well-recounted by others (Koffman and Gill 2013; Wilson 2011), so I only introduce it briefly here. The logic follows that if girls are empowered through education (cf. Nike's The Girl Effect)[3] or empowered as adults within value chains (cf. Coca-Cola's 5by20)[4] then women's 'entrepreneurial potential' will be 'unleashed', creating more sustainable business, and 'helping families and communities prosper' (Coca-Cola 2012). It is argued that women, as mothers, carers and community-influencers can provide routes out of poverty not just for themselves but for families, communities and even nations (World Bank 2011).

---

[3] The Girl Effect is a campaign and development programme, created and launched at Davos in 2009 by The Nike Foundation and partners include the United Nations. In 2015 it became an NGO in its own right. Through awareness raising and training it seeks to empower girls in developing countries, 'as co-creators of new solutions' to global poverty (girleffect.org)

[4] In 2010 Coca-Cola pledged to economically empower five million women in their value chain by 2020. Working with partners such as Care (an NGO), the 5by20 initiative seeks to 'unleash the entrepreneurial spirit' of women through skills & microfinance training (http://www.coca-colacompany.com/sustainabilityreport/we/womens-economic-empowerment.html#section-empowering-5-million-women-by-2020)

The World Economic Forum argues that women's 'advancement' can help tackle 'five global problems of: demography, leadership, food security and agriculture, sustainability and scarcity, and conflict' (WEF 2013: 3). Coleman (2010) compiles evidence for the business benefits of investing in women's empowerment, citing initiatives by Nike, Unilever and the World Bank, and supported by consultancy reports (e.g. Pellegrino et al. 2011) and NGOs (e.g. Oxfam 2012). Behind the slogans there are some compelling empirics, for example, on how increasing women's empowerment can lead to increased productivity on farms (Coles and Mitchell 2011) or how empowered women are more likely to send their children, especially girls, to school (Quisumbing et al. 2004). There is also growing evidence that increasing women's empowerment leads to national economic growth (Duflo 2012; World Bank 2011). Yet the evidence that links this to organisational performance is relatively scant in comparison to the strength of the rhetoric (ICRW 2016). Furthermore, impact assessments of women's empowerment within value chains reveal mixed results (Rohatynskyj 2011; Tornhill 2016a, b), with unsurprisingly, corporate-sponsored evaluations yielding positive results (e.g. Yeager and Goldenberg 2012).

All of this is not to say that an evidence-base for businesses engaging in women's empowerment is not valuable, but that the rhetoric of a business case has potentially eclipsed the reality. Cornwall, Harrison and Whitehead (2007) write of 'gender myths and feminist fables' within the gender and development sector. I contend that these are being incorporated non-reflexively into the CSR lexicon, especially regarding the business case for women's empowerment. Furthermore, concern has been raised over the moral legitimacy of businesses to engage in global governance (Bexell 2012; Switzer 2013) and the appropriateness of CSR activity as a means to promote gender equality: activity that stands accused of strengthening businesses' power in the global economy (Pearson 2007). Corporate-led women's empowerment efforts, with Nike's *The Girl Effect* advertisements the most heavily critiqued, is argued to position girls and women as 'productive and contented workers in colonial enterprises' (Wilson 2011: 316), "lifted out" of history and politics to be recast as individual entrepreneurial subjects' (Koffman and Gill 2013: 90). The structural and institutional factors which mean women continue to face multiple economic, social and political inequalities are conveniently erased from the twenty-first century, neoliberal narrative of women's empowerment (Cornwall 2007; Koffman and Gill 2013; Roberts 2015; Wilson 2011).

Many feminist analyses of women and/or gender with relation to business' role in society would find this co-optation of women's empowerment unsurprising, given the complicity of capitalism, and more recently the advent of CSR, with a patriarchal system where historically men have 'power over' women (Pearson 2007; Elson and Pearson 1981). Thus, the question of whether business- and CSR- can empower women within systems where they are already being exploited appears to be redundant. Numerous empirical studies make this point, such as cases which document the beating and sexual harassment of women workers by male supervisors in Kenyan flower value chains (Hale and Opondo 2005), or less overtly the 'gender-blindness' of CSR codes of conduct, and auditing, which do not recognise the specific needs of women workers and effectively shut out their concerns from regulatory structures of power (Barrientos et al. 2003).

Women employed in value chains can earn better incomes, learn new skills, and gain confidence and autonomy (Maertens and Swinnen 2010). Thus, to argue that market economies always work against women is misleading, but the *quality* of work affects to what extent employment can considered 'empowering' (Kabeer and Mahmud 2004). Generally, women's work continues to be under-valued in both status and pay (Pearson 2007), and leaves few economic options, as women continue to juggle the 'triple shift' of paid work, housework and care work (Waring 1988). Many thus question the concept of 'choice' regarding women's employment within the value chains where CSR is found (Wilson 2011). Are women free to turn down a low-paid, unsafe job when their options are thus limited (Drebes 2014)? Over the last forty years a significant body of work has shown how women have been a disposable resource for business (Pearson 2007), with the illusion of personal economic choice keeping industries stocked with workers (Reiman 1987). Interestingly, the rise in female employment witnessed in the Middle-East is often predicated on new economic opportunities for business (Karam and Jamali 2013), whilst other aspects of equality, such as sexual freedom, remain untouched (Syed and Van Buren 2014). The gap between economic, and social and political equalities, and the role of CSR in addressing this, is thus pertinent to the question of empowerment.

The Concept of Empowerment

It therefore pays to interrogate some of the assumptions behind these dichotomous positions: those who claim women's empowerment is possible through CSR, and those who critique both the method (CSR programmes) and the agent (business). Before turning to my own accounts of women's empowerment in the cocoa value chain, let us explore what 'empowerment' is taken to mean in both approaches. According to the World Bank, empowerment is 'the process of enhancing an individual's or group's capacity to make purposive choices and to transform these choices into desired actions and outcomes' (World Bank in Cornwall et al. 2008: 3). CSR women's empowerment programmes most often focus on the individual woman as an entrepreneur (Wilson 2011), i.e. on economic empowerment, aiming for the specific outcome of wealth accumulation (Cornwall et al. 2007; Kabeer 1999; Roberts 2015). This is usually facilitated by an intervention, led by an NGO or by a company, which provides training or microfinance. Power is therefore viewed as something someone 'has' (Lukes 1974) and women's empowerment is achieved when their innate 'power within' (tied to their identity as women) (Cornwall 2007) is drawn out by an external party, such as a business or NGO.

In contrast to this entrepreneurial framing of empowerment, Rowlands (1995) defines empowerment as:

The process by which people, organisations or groups who are powerless (a) become aware of the power dynamics at work in their life context, (b) develop the skills and capacity for gaining some reasonable control over their lives, (c) exercise this control without infringing upon the rights of others and (d) support the empowerment of others in the community. (McWhirter 1991 in Rowlands 1995: 103)

There are four points pertinent to this broader definition of empowerment that are worth considering in application to CSR. The first is that empowerment is best understood as an ongoing process (Kabeer 1999) with many cyclical 'stages' involved (Summerson-Carr 2003). Even here, however, the concept of a process can be co-opted into a series of steps that external parties, such as companies, can enact to achieve employee or stakeholder empowerment (Hardy and Leiba-O'Sullivan 1998). The problem is that as a cyclical, messy process empowerment takes time and can fail more often than succeed- a frustration that few NGOs can manage and budget for (Cornwall et al. 2007, 2008) and that few corporations can understand given business' short-term focus on results (Mena et al. 2010).

Second, empowerment is about power in that it is a *socio-political* process (Batliwala 2007) during which people become aware of power relations and then exercise some control over these (Rowlands 1995; Freire 1970). This process, however, can unfold for different people at different times and in different ways, complicating the notion of a 'tidy' process of social change (Cornwall 2007). As I argue in the remainder of the article, however, assuming that the 'beneficiaries' of women's empowerment programmes are 'powerless' (McWhirter 1991 in Rowlands 1995: 103) is problematic since it presupposes a particular understanding of power as something 'held' by one group (often men, and/or the ruling class) over another (often women, and/or the poor). This echoes a recurring problem with the conceptualisation of power and agency in much CSR and development literature (Drebes 2014).

Third, whilst economic empowerment (wealth accumulation and control of finance) is one aspect of empowerment, and economic resources, in the form of equal pay for example, are closely related to other forms of power, it is by no means indicative of empowerment as a whole (Cornwall 2014; Kabeer 1999) and presents problems in how to measure and evaluate women's empowerment (Mena et al. 2010). Many indicators are overly reliant on economic measures, or the representation of women in different roles and occupations (Cornwall et al. 2007; Kabeer 1999), a problem also observed in evaluations of organisational diversity (Ahonen et al. 2014). For example, a recent report which claims to explore 'how women may thrive' in the workplace turns out to simply measure women's representation in different top management roles (Mercer 2016). Focusing on 'counting the women' is just one basic indicator of gender in organisations, and has very little to do with empowerment in a fuller sense (Kabeer 1999).

Fourth, empowerment involves groups of people, or individuals within society acting not just as individual 'entrepreneurs' but as social beings in cohort with others (Batliwala 2007; Cornwall et al. 2008). This echoes discussions of relationality in business ethics and stakeholder theory, where the isolation of traditional leadership (Liu 2015; Painter-Morland 2008; Uhl-Ben 2011), especially around business ethics and accountability (Freeman and Liedtka 1997; Painter-Morland 2006), has been critiqued for ignoring the social ties that bind us. This chimes with the critique of a neoliberal notion of empowerment which treats women as atomised entities. Empowerment, however, whilst entailing an internal process of self-awareness, or consciousness-raising, requires *others*. It is difficult for groups of marginalised people to make changes to their lives working alone, especially when those groups are implicated in profit-driven, transnational value chains (Freire 1970; Summerson-Carr 2003). Conversely whilst often women are forced to work in groups during CSR empowerment programmes (Tornhill 2016a), as we explore in the next sections this raises questions about which women, in which groups, and why we assume they 'should' work together (Cornwall 2007; Yuval-Davis 1994).

Problematising Empowerment: Insights from Ghana

I here introduce vignettes from my own research into this area. Over the last four years I have been involved in evaluations and studies around a women's empower-ment programme within the Ghanaian cocoa value chain. This programme involves a British company which makes chocolate from cocoa; a Ghanaian cocoa coopera-tive which buys the cocoa from smallholder farmer members; a British NGO partner which advises on the programme; and hundreds of individual Ghanaian cocoa farm-ers.[5] Since 2013 I have collected data on this partnership and the programme, through document analysis, observations in the field, group discussions, and in-depth unstructured interviews and participant-led drawing (McCarthy and Muthuri 2016).[6]

The initial research project involved the production of 48 participant drawings, over 80 hours of observations, 23 in-depth interviews with staff and women farmers, and analysis of 120 internal and external documents relating to the programme. Here I present two vignettes drawn from this larger body of empirical work. Vignettes 'are stories generated from a range of sources including previous research findings. They refer to important factors in the study of perceptions, beliefs and attitudes' (Hughes 1998: 381). Thus, my goal is not to provide evidence for an empirical paper, but rather to provide accounts as windows into other worlds

---

[5] The cooperative was founded to collectivise smallholder cocoa farmers to bring them further up the value chain. Cocoa is grown on small plots of land by farmers, who then decide who to sell their produce to. Members of the cooperative receive a Fairtrade price for their cocoa, as well as benefits such as a free cutlass and the benefit of local social initiatives such as health clinics and training.

[6] Participant-led drawing was used to address sensitive, and culturally contextual concepts such as 'gender' and 'inequality', beyond the verbal. This was a means of trying to find another way of 'hearing' workers' 'voice' and addressing some of the power imbalances between researcher and researched in global South settings (McCarthy and Muthuri 2016).

(Humphreys 2005; VanMaanen 1988), particularly those relating to the complex, processual and unpredictable nature of empowerment and power. Indeed, Foucault uses vignettes in his discussions of philosophy (1977a), and they are particularly favoured within feminist research (Ramazanoglu and Holland 2002). Chaudhry (2009), in her ethnographic study into gendered violence in India, explains that vignettes allow her to adopt a 'dialogic' approach to research, involving the embedding of direct quotations from participants, an indirect re-telling of their stories and opinions, and a unique means of embracing reflexivity into interpretation of the social world. Following this method (e.g. Chaudhry 2009; VanMaanen 1988) my two vignettes are written in the first-person present tense to try and capture the unfolding of surprising and unexpected beliefs and behaviour of some of the women I encountered within a CSR women's empowerment programme. They illustrate some of the common problems regarding focusing on women's empowerment within a CSR context, echoed in empirical studies (e.g. Cornwall 2007, 2014; Koffman and Gill 2013; Switzer 2013; Tornhill 2016a, b). They enable me to identify salient assumptions regarding gender and CSR practices, and to start to pose questions around the unexpected ways in which CSR women's empowerment programmes play out. The vignettes provide a means of connecting the messiness of what I, and my participants, experienced in Ghana with the often-complex theories of feminist Foucauldians.

Cocoa, a non-indigenous crop, was introduced to Ghana by British colonisers and immediately positioned as a 'male crop' (Doss 2002).[7] Colonisation also introduced 'Western' norms regarding gender, especially around marriage, divorce and work (Clark 1994; Duncan 2010). These imported social rules have, over time, mixed with the varied regional cultures' different social roles for women and men (Clark 1994). For example, the Asante ethnic group[8] (which many of those in my study belonged to) is matrilineal,[9] with women famously dominating market places and trading, partially because they were forced out of the cash-crop cocoa boom (Clark 1994). In terms of gender relations, Clark (1994: 107) notes that within Asante culture there is a culture of individuation, 'a value of personal autonomy and dignity', which means that women and men are used to working separately and dividing their assets and income. To some extent, Ghanaian women have greater freedoms than women in other Sub-Saharan African countries (Baden et al. 1994). Yet women are still expected to provide unpaid care work (often without men's

---

[7] Crops become ascribed with gendered social norms about who should grow and sell them. Cocoa, as a cash crop, is seen as being appropriate work for male farmers, but less for women. Crops grown for domestic subsistence are labelled as 'women's crops' (Doss 2002).

[8] Ghana has over 100 ethnic groups. The Asante (sometimes written as Ashanti) are found mainly in central Ghana.

[9] Land inheritance law and customs in Ghana vary by region, and are complex. For example, elder women in the Asante culture decide alongside village chiefs to whom land will be passed to, but the practice is that land usually goes to sisters' sons, meaning land ownership in general remains male-dominated (Barrientos and Bobie 2016; Quisumbing et al. 2004).

help), and unpaid labour on the farm, while men are the main (and often sole) decision-makers on the farm and at home (Clark 1994).

Within cocoa farming it is only in recent years that women could own their own land and engage in the industry (Clark 1994). Men continue to dominate cocoa land-ownership (only 20% of registered cocoa farmers are women), which impacts upon women's ability to produce crops, sell them in their own name, and join cooperatives (Barrientos and Bobie 2016). The low numbers of female cocoa landowners belie the findings of my case study, and many others (see Barrientos and Bobie 2016), which show that women perform nearly half of all cocoa work required on farms. Yet women farmers face challenges in terms of getting access to land, fertilisers, pesticides, training, loans and labour (Barrientos 2013; Barrientos and Bobie 2016).

Within this context the background of the vignettes is thus: The businesses, alongside a supporting NGO, have engaged in a women's empowerment programme for over twenty years. The programme had been mutually designed and instigated by the three partnership organisations, with initial help from an external international women's NGO. They aim to economically, socially and politically empower farming women in the cooperative. This first took the form of leadership training, and affirmative recruitment for Ghanaian women in the cooperative structure, and later, craft-based income training. Originally conceived as part of a microfinance project, the craft-based projects (typically making batik, soaps, notebooks, jewellery or growing vegetables for the market) began with a 'pooling' model: women would form business and savings groups together to share resources and receive a small revolving loan from the cooperative, which was encouraged to be used for craft-based micro-businesses, echoing many microfinance models (Hudon and Sandberg 2013). Women were to work in groups, which established a system of peer-scrutiny, encouraging women to pay back loans and into the communal 'pot' (Mayoux 1999). The model also reflected the wider aims of the Ghanaian organisation, which being a cooperative, and as stated in their mandate, operated on principles of democracy, sharing and 'fairness'. Women were positioned as central to this ideal as they 'hold the community together, they hold the society together' (Interview with Coop staff member, 2013). I was repeatedly told by UK and Ghanaian management how women were more loyal to the cooperative than men were, and how through the women's empowerment programme they would 'market' the cooperative to other women.

In 2013 an evaluation using surveys, group discussions and participatory drawing workshops revealed that whilst the numbers of women in decision-making positions in the cooperative had grown, and some of those women reported feeling more confident, the economic empowerment programmes were not creating wealth for women (McCarthy and Muthuri 2016). The reasons for this included low uptake of training opportunities, variable quality in products for sale, a lack of markets for products, and a consequent high 'dropout' rate of women. The evidence showed that women's time is taken up by unpaid care work and substantial unpaid cocoa farming tasks, leaving no time for honing additional new skills and craft production. Thus, women dropped out of groups, failed to market and sell their produce, and reported that they were struggling with tasks: 'You know as women we are challenged. We are taking care of the home and everything else!' (Female farmer, focus group, 2013). In the vignettes below I offer insights into the research which begins to challenge some of the assumptions of much CSR theory which positions those in the global South as needy but thankful 'beneficiaries' (Drebes 2014), and women as compliant, cooperative agents of development (Cornwall 2007).

Vignette 1: Unexpected Resistance

It's a hot, dry day as I arrive in Ghana and meet Ama and Shirley, Ghanaian local women, who have worked for over ten and three years respectively as gender managers on the women's empowerment programme at the cooperative. In a meeting room with my co-researcher, our research assistants, translator, and other cooperative staff we discuss how we will organise the programme evaluation and workshops. I immediately like the way Ama and Shirley humourously square up to reticent colleagues in our initial research meeting who are either unenthused by the women's empowerment projects, or are sceptical about the need to carry out research. They are both educated about, and have plentiful experience of working on gender and development issues. They are also the only female managers in the whole cooperative, which reflects the extremely male-dominated environment of cocoa suppliers.

The next day we begin carrying out interviews with local farming women. I am impressed with the ways in which both Ama and Shirley talk about empowerment and encourage the women we talk to. They enthuse about the need to hear from the women farmers themselves. I'm looking forward to starting the workshops out in the rural areas. However, over the next few days, Ama begins to withhold research funds. She avoids meetings and leaves Shirley trying to organise the rest of the research team. On two separate days, we are seriously delayed because Ama locks away the materials we need for fieldwork (such as paper and pens for drawing, and the cash for petrol). Another staff member whispers that they have not received any payment for the extra days they have worked whilst we are doing research: is this another delaying tactic from Ama? I email the NGO and chocolate company back in London and it's clear that this kind of resistance have taken place before: 'She's a bully... but she gets things done' (Interview with UK business manager, 2013). I want to speak to Ama and ask her what is going on, but she avoids my calls and we don't see her again during the fieldwork.

It's two weeks later and I am discussing the results of the evaluation with Shirley. As we go through some of the visual data from the workshops with farmers, we talk about the low uptake of craft training and more worryingly, how women are reporting very little, to no, income from the projects. Shirley continues to argue for craft-based training, despite this. I suggest that perhaps it would be better to help farming women to become better cocoa farmers, but she shakes her head. She maintains that the programme should open a shop: 'A shop would give us internal funding... so we will be able to sustain the programme.' Shirley's main concern seems to be to preserve the programme, rather than thinking about the aims of the programme itself. Pushing away/resisting the idea of farming training, as an alternative to crafts-training, Shirley comments that: 'We should find something for the women to **also** do, that they have... financial independence' (Interview with Shirley, 2013, my emphasis). I note in my observations journal that the farming women who are part of the empowerment programme are referred to by some cooperative staff as 'wives of farmers', and that in nearly all meetings with village-level members questions are directed to (and always answered by) male farmers. Women appear to exist *outside* the core business of cocoa farming. Economic empowerment through craft or small-scale agro-entrepreneurship is 'in', and empowerment through more inclusive cocoa farming is 'out', despite women already being cocoa farmers, and this seeming to have more potential as a lucrative livelihood stream.

As I sit with my co-researcher on the last evening of our visit to Ghana, we reflect on the different ways in which Ama and Shirley were resisting. My co-researcher posits that perhaps Ama and Shirley, struggling in a male-dominated organisation, fear for their jobs and thus stick with what they know best. Yet it had been made clear at the beginning that the gender programme would require more work and that their jobs were safe (indeed, Ama was eventually offered a leading role in a new, externally funded women's empowerment project) (Correspondence with NGO, 2015). We are taken aback by the resistance these two influential women had exercised. Perhaps job protectionism was one aspect, but why would they try to scupper changes to the programme? Why are they so wedded to the idea of craft-based training, despite their own experiences, and now, as the evaluation shows that this approach isn't working?

Vignette 2: All for One and None for All

Spring is in the air as I approach the offices of the NGO partner, in London, a few weeks after my return from Ghana. The purpose of our meeting is to discuss the somewhat disappointing results of the women's empowerment programme evaluation. As well as running workshops with the farmers in Ghana, I've interviewed several on-the-ground staff at the cooperative, and therefore feel I have garnered a few additional insights into what is happening in the cocoa value chain, but need to understand further the results from the NGO manager's experience.

Settling in the office with coffee, I ask Olivia, the British NGO manager responsible for overseeing the programme, if I can take a look at the documentation around the setting up of the women's empowerment programme. It is clear that the initial plans stipulated for women to work in groups. Yet when talking to women during workshops I found little evidence of them working collectively, preferring to work alone. I had asked some women why this was the case, but they did not want to explain. As British professionals, their refusal is puzzling to us because the risks associated with setting up microbusinesses- alone- are higher, and thus many of these women are unable to save alone to engage in enterprise. Trying to understand what is happening on the ground, and putting aside our own expectations, I turn to years of evaluation reports. I read about conflicts within groups around repayments of loans and where profit from the communal 'pot' would be spent (when, or if, there would be any) and how for some time now women farmers have reported back to the organisation that they do not like working in groups, preferring to work alone (Internal Documentation, dated 2002). As noted above this reflects local culture. I tell Olivia how Shirley is now struggling to manage women's expectations: 'A lot of women came and requested individual loans, but the programme is not about loans, but that's what the women think… It's getting out of hand' (Interview with Shirley, 2013). Women are beginning to lose interest in the programme, which they say demands too much from them (Focus group, 2013). The women don't want to work together, but working alone means they do not have the money to invest in their businesses, and they appear to become despondent. Olivia is concerned, because there is no more money for loans or individual financial support.

On a more positive note, I point out that there are encouraging statistics for the number of women moving into decision-making roles in the cooperative. For example, some women who had leadership training to become cocoa buyers, or cooperative leaders said in the workshops that they 'feel that anything a man can do, I can also do' (Interview with woman farmer and cooperative leader, 2013). I do, however, have to tell Olivia that there are concerns amongst the board members that this is only empowering a certain kind of farming woman: 'some of the stronger farmers marginalised the weaker ones' and 'some of the really strong women from lower classes, and backgrounds, got one-by-one picked off and side-lined' by other women (Interview with board member, 2013). Olivia sighs, and agrees that this is a problem, and that 'it would be a mistake to say that the men outdid the women, ostracised them over there and took their jobs. But it wasn't like that.' She tells me about attending an annual Fairtrade meeting in Ghana, where farmers are asked to decide on how to share the Fairtrade premium out amongst themselves. Olivia says that last year there was 'an almost mass-riot' with farmers 'standing up, shaking their fists' (Conversation with Olivia, 2013) and demanding their individual portion of profit. She adds that 'it's not just men- it's the women too'.

I leave the NGO office thinking about how the evaluation and insights gathered from farmers and staff members, problematises some of the deep assumptions made about cooperation, collaboration, and women in CSR empowerment projects. Farmers enact 'everyday resistance' (Scott 1985) against the discourses of cooperation and collaboration, so common to women's empowerment narratives. Olivia and I wonder how we will write up the findings: Can the relative success of the social and political empowerment of some women farmer leaders be called empowerment, when those very same farmers re-create the gendered power relations which keep other women poorer, in a lower status and in continued inequality in comparison to their male colleagues? Did the programme make a mistake in assuming that the farmers were willing to cooperate?

Re-Thinking Empowerment in CSR: Feminist Foucauldian Insights

The vignettes introduced above present a complex picture of empowerment in Ghana, showing how people (in this case women) reject, resist and behave in ways counterintuitive to CSR and development narratives. There are numerous economic explanations for such behaviour, relating to the amount of time women spend in unpaid care work in the home and in cocoa farming, for example, such that they do not have spare time for entrepreneurial activities. Moreover, paid work in cocoa farming can be more lucrative than craft work (given the right support). However, as noted above, empowerment is not simply an economic concept. Thus, in this section I add to, and move beyond such explanations to use Foucault's later works, and in particular his concepts of 'subjectivation', and 'freedom as an ethic of care for one-self' to explore and better understand why these individuals might have reacted to CSR women's empowerment in the ways described in the vignettes. I draw upon later Foucault because it presents alternative readings of the 'power' in empowerment, and the agency and resistance of individuals therein (Crane et al. 2008; Drebes 2014; Knights and Vurdubakis 1994; Skinner 2012). I apply feminist interpretations of Foucault's work which have been especially fruitful for understanding the construction of men and women's subject positions in society (Pullen 2006).[10] In the next two sections I first ask 'why are women resisting empowerment?' before moving to a more conjectural discussion on 'what is it that we mean when we seek to 'empower' women in CSR anyway'?

Why Are Women Resisting Empowerment?

As noted earlier, 'gendered' CSR almost always chooses to focus on women (Bexell 2012; Prügl 2015; Tornhill 2016a), and frequently pushes women to work in groups, collaborating for the good of other women and/or families (Switzer 2013; Wilson 2011). The business case for women's empowerment turns on the assumption that since women are often mothers, carers, and involved in community work, and are supposed to have better interpersonal skills than men, they will cooperate with each other for the common good (ICRW 2016; WEF 2013). In both my vignettes, however, we see women confounding assumptions of women as (a) communal and (b) compliant. In Vignette 2, despite a cultural barrier to women becoming leaders in the cooperative, some achieved this, to then enact that role in their

---

[10] However, it is important to acknowledge that feminist interpretations of Foucault's work have been controversial. Some have picked up on his masculinist tendencies in language (Grimshaw 1993; McNay 1992) and perhaps more troublingly, what has been termed his 'sexist' genealogy of sex and ethics, which focuses on free men in Greek antiquity, and thus erases the embodied experiences of those enslaved and/or female (Grimshaw 1993).

own manner by 'marginalising' and 'resisting, dividing and ruling' (Interview with board member, 2014) other women. This is not unique to CSR, or Ghanaian contexts, but echoes studies which demonstrate the problems of essentialising women's 'nature' (e.g. Wajcman 1998). In Vignette 1, Ama and Shirley resisted and rejected change to be anything but compliant. That the women in these stories don't act in 'ladylike' ways or in line with the discourse of 'caring, sharing' women, or that sometimes their behaviour may seem 'irrational' or counterintuitive to outsiders does not subtract from their demonstrable agency in this situation. Understanding why this might be requires reconsidering what power is, how it is manifest, and what it means for women's empowerment in CSR in the global South.

Feminist scholars have found Foucault's middle period of writings (e.g. 1977a), useful when exploring power relations (Pullen 2006). Foucault's focus was on language and ideas and how over time discourses come to create 'technologies of power' which are enacted upon the subject. This power is insidious, similar to an understanding of power as something subconscious, but it is exercised by all rather than owned by one social group (Foucault 1986), meaning it cannot be 'overthrown' (Cooper 1994: 437). Indeed, one contribution of Foucauldian thought to the study of business ethics is the role of subjects themselves in the creation and re-creation of power relations (Crane et al. 2008). Power in this reading is not necessarily negative, but can be productive:

What makes power hold good, what makes it accepted, is simply the fact that it doesn't only weigh on us a force that says no; it also transverses and produces things, it induces pleasure, forms knowledge, produces discourse (Foucault 1977b: 120).

Thus, in this reading the notion of empowering the 'powerless' is complicated: for example, women working in the cocoa value chain in Ghana take part in power relations and for that reason may recreate the conditions of their own inequalities, for example, by choosing to work alone rather than pool resources. Further, Ama and Shirley, and other women, were perhaps driven to act in unexpected ways because they were women in a male-dominated organisation. The discourses at play within the Ghanaian cocoa industry still place men as cocoa farmers, managers and leaders. Ama and Shirley's fight to achieve management positions within the Ghanaian cooperative suggests high stakes, and that perhaps if they had been men their story would not played out in the same way. Yet it is clear in the vignette that Ama and Shirley are not simply conduits for 'patriarchy', but 'multiple selves whose lives are shot through with contradictions and creative tensions' (Kondo 1990: 224). They are individuals raised in Ghana in traditional gender roles, working with Western feminist concepts translated into their daily working lives and up against competing expectations from farmers, managers and their own families. Ama and Shirley (re)produced gendered power relations in complex ways: I argue that they were neither 'powerful' nor 'powerless', but an active part of both states.

Foucault's later work (i.e., the last two volumes of *The History of Sexuality* (1978; 1986 and 1980; 1982; 1994), holds further clues here. His attention shifted from technologies of power (on the individual e.g. patriarchy) to 'technologies of the self' or subjectivation (1994) (Crane et al. 2008). These, 'permit individuals to effect by their own means, or with the help of others, a certain number of operations on their own bodies and soils, thoughts, conduct and way of being' (Foucault 1994: 225) to 'not only set themselves rules of conduct, but also seek to transform themselves, to change themselves in their singular being' (Foucault 1985: 10–11). I argue that Foucault's concept of subjectivation helps us to understand why women like Ama and Shirley resist, or farmers reject 'traditional' female roles as they 'actively fashion their own identities' (McNay 2000: 9), including gender identities, within specific cultures:

I am interested... in the way in which the subject constitutes himself in an active fashion, by the practices of the self, these practices are nevertheless not something that the individual invents by himself. They are patterns that he finds in his culture and which are proposed, suggested and imposed upon him by his culture, his society and his social group (Foucault 1987: 11).

Thus, Ama and Shirley, who both wish to promote gender empowerment, approach this from a hybrid identity of middle-class Ghanaian business professionals, and engage in practices of the self with multiple intersectional identities: of ethnicity, gender and class. This can intensify the 'self-policing' and conflict that subjects may experience in the subjectivation process (O'Grady 2004). We might argue, then, that this conflict is one reason why they insisted on continuing to focus on micro-entrepreneurship, whilst rejecting women's (proven) active role in cocoa farming. Cocoa's positioning as a 'man's crop' in Ghana means that women farmers continue to be seen as 'helpers', rather than legitimate farmers in their own right, despite increased female land ownership. Paradoxically, Ama and Shirley's insistence on traditional crafts as empowerment modes appears to undo the gender equality progress made for women working in cocoa in Ghana. A feminist Foucauldian lens, however, suggests new ways to interpret why they behaved in this way.

These vignettes viewed through the lens of feminist Foucauldian theory, confront the idea of gender as universal, structural and essentialist (Cooper 1994: 439) since gender is an 'ongoing process, a becoming' during subjectivation (Skinner 2012: 906; Butler 1997). Women and men take the different subject positions drawn for them and mold, create and re-create their own selves. As McNay (2000: 6) argues, in reimagining the role of the self in creating gendered power relations, it is necessary to consider that 'individuals may respond in unanticipated and innovative ways which may hinder, reinforce or catalyse social change.' In this way, subjectivation is intricately linked to resistance (Foucault 1982; Knights and Vurdubakis 1994) and often gender resistance (Butler 2004; 1997; Cooper 1994; Kondo 1990; McNay 2000).

Resistance can be corporeal (such as Ama locking away materials) (Grosz 1994), or discursive (arguing for craft-based empowerment only) (Butler 1997). Some of the farming women in Vignette 2 resisted corporeally, through physical protest and refusing terms at the Fairtrade meeting, while other women leaders resisted discursively, when they turned to 'bullying', 'marginalising', and individualism. What this shows us is how gendered power relations are tightly tied to local cultural context. For example, despite a continued push from the cooperative and

NGO for craft-based, economic empowerment projects, some women farmers in Vignette 1 resisted these, often because they had no time for such projects in what were already busy lives involving cocoa farming as well as significant amounts of unpaid work. When they did sign-up for the projects, they often resisted taking part in group savings and loans models. This may be explained by the value of individuation within Asante culture (Clark 1994). In these ways women farmers resisted 'in complex ways to partly overturn the dominant order… but also to partly support it' (Pullen and Simpson 2009: 582). By desiring their autonomy, and refusing to take part in group activities, these women farmers were on one hand agentic, refusing to conform to project specifications imposed from outside their own culture. Furthermore, the small number of women leaders who marginalised other women also engaged in resistance, challenging the 'development myth' of cooperative, caring women (Cornwall et al. 2008). Yet the almost universal approach to CSR and women's empowerment is to treat 'women' as a homogenous group based on sex categories (Ahonen et al. 2014; Cornwall 2014; Yuval-Davis 1994). In reality, women and men create their own gender identities in a multiplicity of ways (Linstead and Pullen 2005), including through resistance.

Debates around 'gender myths and feminist fables' (Cornwall et al. 2007) and the nature of women are also found in theories of relationality in business ethics (Borgerson 2007; Painter-Morland 2006, 2008). Relational theory argues that human development is optimised through cooperation and support (Fletcher 1998), with women performing the necessary caring roles particularly well (Uhl-Ben 2011). Held (1993) has argued for a form of feminine 'power to' which celebrates women's care and collaboration, a view shared in feminist ethics, ethics of care and feminist stakeholder approaches (Burton and Dunn 1996; Liedtka 1996; White 1992; Wicks et al. 1994). Such perspectives are echoed in arguments for women-led CSR leadership (Marshall 2011), small-business responsibility (Spence 2014) and relational leadership (Liu 2015; Uhl-Ben 2011). Whilst some approaches stress that socialisation, positioned as the cause of difference in men and women's behaviour, allows for shifts in gender stereotypes (e.g. Uhl-Ben 2011; Werhane and Painter-Morland 2011), critics have expressed concern over the essentialism or reductionism that a focus on difference has created (Derry 1996). Socialisation is often framed as structural and rigid, especially when it comes to static gender roles (McNay 2000). This narrative of gender difference has eclipsed the nuance of feminist ethics (Borgerson 2007), like the gender and development rhetoric (Cornwall 2007). This narrowing of ideas around gender and feminism can be damaging to gender equality since it reifies differences between men and women in ways that serve to replicate existing power relations (Grimshaw 1993; McNay 2000). However, it is not my intention to enter into a debate about feminist ethics or an ethic of care in this article, but rather to point out that a similar over-simplification of the social construction of gender roles (Borgerson 2007; Uhl-Ben 2011) has occurred in the CSR women's empowerment discourse.

My vignettes, viewed through a Foucauldian understanding of power, illustrate how women are individuals, and act as such, but within a system of power relations which 'constrains and enables' actors who push at the boundaries of possibility

(Hayward 2000: 12; Foucault 1982). As active constituents of their own worlds, the women leaders 'marginalising' other women, or women farmers rejecting programmes, are seizing empowerment opportunities- just not in ways CSR managers may wish for (Cooper 1994; Pullen 2006; Sawicki 1991). Seeing power relations in this way is important for exploring 'empowerment' because it means that women, in particular, are moved out of the category of 'victim' and afforded agency, meaning that 'despite large scale gender inequalities, women are not just passive dupes of patriarchal structures of domination' (McNay 1992: 82). It means that women are recognised as individuals, and not simply symbolic of relational skills, collaboration or care.

How Is Women's Empowerment in CSR 'Empowering'?

A feminist Foucauldian lens upon CSR women's empowerment programmes highlights some of the paradoxes at play within this recent management phenomenon. Foucault elucidates how women (and men) 'self-make' themselves, often through resistance. This helps us to better understand why it is that women in the vignettes acted in ways counterintuitive to Western, CSR-based notions of development. Are these women who reject empowerment projects, or assumed gender roles, 'empowered' when they do this? Or do we need to rethink what the term means? In this section I use Foucault's later work (1985, 1986, 1987) to ask 'what is it that women's empowerment in CSR contexts is actually aiming to do'? What is it that women are being empowered 'from' or 'to'?

Since power is understood to be an ongoing, relational element of human subjectivation, so too can freedom be perceived as an ongoing process inextricably linked to our everyday existence (Amigot and Pujal 2009; Crane et al. 2008; Foucault 1987). This is very different from a liberal approach to freedom, which we are more familiar with, where human beings require 'freeing from' one state of being in preference for another (Berlin 1958). In contrast, Foucault (1987) regards freedom as 'the ability to participate actively and purposefully in power relations' (Crane et al. 2008: 304). Therefore, 'Foucault's conception of personal freedom... is never an absolute state, or an end point in a liberation struggle, but rather a defining characteristic of what it is to be human' (Crane et al. 2008: 303). Women's empowerment is thus more complicated than 'freeing them to' acquire wealth, or practice care, or 'freeing them from' patriarchal control. Instead, as Foucault (1985, 1986, 1987) theorises in his exploration of sexuality in Greek antiquity, freedom is related to 'an ethics of care for the self', which enable individuals 'to give oneself the rules of law, the techniques of management, and also the ethics, the *ethos*, the practice of the self, that will allow these games of power to be played with the minimum of domination' (Foucault 1987: 12). Freedom is rooted within the individual's search for an internal ethics, in a constant interplay of power relations within the self (Foucault 1987). 'In short, one must abandon the political calculus of domination and liberation' (Rose 1999: 95). To paraphrase Rose (1999: 65), a Foucauldian approach to CSR and women's empowerment questions how women and men in value chains are 'defining and acting towards themselves in terms of a certain notion of freedom?' This then raises the question as to what extent women can 'acquire' *for themselves*-knowledge, practices of the self and ethics to be 'free?'

My vignettes illustrate the subjectivation process (which we can consider as an internal process) *and* the often difficult (external) contexts in which women and men co-construct their own freedoms, in this case in the context of a gendered cocoa industry, material poverty and a well-meaning, yet ineffective, CSR intervention (Amigot and Pujal 2009; Hirschmann 2002; O'Grady 2004; Pullen 2006). Even within constrained contexts such as these, from a Foucauldian perspective, women managers and farmers are 'free', since they take an ethic of care of themselves, symbolised by their resistance and engagement in power relations within the empowerment programme itself (Crane et al. 2008). This freedom, however, does not reflect how freedom and empowerment are usually understood, since there may be very few immediate material benefits or changes arising from such a process (Hirschmann 2002).

Thus, a feminist Foucauldian approach moves away from existing notions of feminist and care ethics which often position women as instrumental to other's 'freedom' e.g. as more ethical managers (e.g. Liedtka 1996; White 1992), or which perceive 'freedom' as lying in individuals' capacity to exercise care for others (e.g. Held 1993). This is because Foucault theorises that freedom lies in the capacity to choose an ethic of care *for oneself*. Rather than care being understood as behaviour directed externally, to others' needs, 'care is better treated as a disposition or attitude that may be incorporated into one's own freely chosen rules of conduct, where respect for one's own and others' freedom is the fundamental principle' (Syballa 2001: 79). This important distinction does not undermine the importance of caring for others, which also remains part of Foucault's *ethos* (O'Grady 2004; Syballa 2001) but it legitimises thinking, talking and working with women as individuals, and not as a homogenous mechanism for societal, business or national growth. Situating 'freedom' within an ethic of care for oneself signals returning to women as individuals, but not atomised individuals, since they are always interacting, and in relation to, each other. Furthermore, whilst an ethic of care for oneself does focus on individual subjects, it does not remove them from historic, societal, economic or cultural limits (Syballa 2001). In this way, we better understand gender inequality as a multi-level phenomenon: corresponding to and interlinked between individuals, groups and society, and 'empowerment' related to an individual recognising the capacity to choose different pathways, even when these pathways might seem 'irrational' to onlookers unaware of the complexities of others' lives.

The vignettes, however, demonstrate how 'freedom' with regard to CSR women's empowerment has been sold as individual women becoming entrepreneurs (Cornwall 2007; Roberts 2015). This single example is symbolic of a much larger shift towards the 'empowered, self-made (wo)man' narrative in management, development and CSR (Batliwala 2007; Hardy and Leiba-O'Sullivan 1998; Tornhill 2016b). This narrative encapsulates technologies of consumption illustrated within women's base of the pyramid schemes (e.g. in Unilever's Project Shakti; Prügl

2015) and technologies of therapeutics illustrated in 'self-actualisation' training (e.g. in Coca-Cola's 5by20 initiative; Tornhill 2016b), which conceptualise 'freedom as autonomy' (Rose 1999). This view champions freedom as lying solely in the capacity to please oneself (Rose 1999). This is arguably at the heart of CSR and women's empowerment, given that it focuses on empowerment as a lone endeavour, unrelated to the structural elements of gender inequality, and targeted almost exclusively on personal wealth accumulation (Roberts 2015; Switzer 2013). In Vignette 2, women's 'group' work was ultimately addressed at women as individual wealth-generators, a far-cry from the original conceptualisation of women's groups for consciousness-raising purposes (Batliwala 2007). It becomes clear that such atomistic framing of societal problems such as gender inequality, and the individualistic 'solutions' offered through CSR women's empowerment programmes, are inadequate on both moral (Rose 1999) and practical grounds (Batliwala 2007).

Finally, despite the subjectivation and resistance I have shown occurring at the intersections of women's empowerment programmes and CSR in the global South, the neoliberal framing of 'freedom' (Amigot and Pujal 2009) remains one of corporations 'empowering' women on their behalf. This falls into Foucault's concern with 'the indignity of speaking for others' (Deleuze and Guattari 1977 in Foucault and Deleuze 1977: 209) when power's diffuse nature requires marginalised women to lead *their* struggle with *their* own forms of action. Yet once again, we must be aware that individuals may respond with 'passivity' within power relations (Foucault and Deleuze 1977: 216). Women may respond in ways that are not in line with the 'rational', neoliberal discourse of freedom, or empowerment. Since human subjects are involved in the creation of their own freedoms, they have both the potential to provoke or limit their own version of self-mastery. I conclude by exploring what these paradoxical positions mean for practice and for future theorising on gender, CSR and empowerment.

Concluding Remarks

Programmes to enable the empowerment of women have become a feature of many CSR policies. Yet there are several myths associated with the term 'empowerment' which are tied to misunderstandings around the concepts of 'power' and 'gender'. For many, women's empowerment translates to 'empowering women'. This linguistic slip is crucial, for it positions the main agents of empowerment as outside of the women themselves: be they NGOs, governments or companies; and depicts women as objects onto which empowerment is 'done'. This formulation chimes with the criticisms levied at other CSR development initiatives (Drebes 2014; Khan and Lund-Thomsen 2011) which tend to cast those in the global South as 'voiceless, powerless victims' or 'beneficiaries'. Banerjee (2010: 272) points out that much CSR scholarship neglects to look 'at the demand side of the CSR equation' and the choices, agency and resistance of respective workers and communities.

I therefore contribute to theories on CSR and development by showing how men and women can resist CSR, generally, and women's empowerment programmes, in particular, in unexpected ways and with seemingly paradoxical responses. I have argued that a Foucauldian conceptualisation of power relations as pervasive and relational: not 'held' by anyone or enacted 'against' anything, but existing in relationships between human subjects (Foucault 1982, 1986) is helpful. Specifically, the feminist Foucauldian attention to subjectivation and freedom (Butler 1997; McNay 1992, 2000; Sawicki 1991) offers nuanced insights into the complex power relations at play in contexts of CSR women's empowerment. Chiefly, since inequalities are tied up in power relations that all individuals are involved in producing, individuals can 'craft themselves' (Kondo 1990), challenging and resisting gender roles in numerous ways, some of which may appears puzzling to outsiders.

The article also highlights two important aspects of the CSR and women's economic empowerment myth: first, that entrepreneurship discourses are rarely 'just about gender', but include ethnicity, class and nationhood which entwine in a mesh of hybrid identities (Calás and Smircich 2006). Therefore, the story is more complicated than the global North holding power over the global South, but demonstrates the complex playing out of post-colonial history within CSR (Drebes 2014), where 'new subjectivities of transnationalism' proliferate in gendered ways (Calás and Smircich 2006: 321). Second, it demonstrates how CSR women's empowerment projects, if they continue to pursue narrow objectives of entrepreneurship, can further marginalise women from mainstream value chains (e.g. by pushing women into craft-based, rather than cocoa-based, work). This raises questions as to what extent CSR for women's empowerment is desirable, when managers (in all locations) ignore local contexts and thus re-create gendered and racialised 'difference'. Thus, future research and theory building might wish to adopt an intersectional approach to CSR and business ethics, in order to pay better attention to individuals' lives along the intersections of their experience: gender, ethnicity, disability, class and other categories.

Further, an exploration of what 'freedom' means in relation to empowerment highlights that a corporate adoption of the term is far from the Foucauldian concept of freedom that exists when individuals are able to engage in an ethic of care with themselves (Foucault 1985, 1986, 1987). Like recent criticisms of diversity initiatives (Ahonen et al. 2014) and rule-based CSR codes of conduct (Crane et al. 2008), empowerment programmes which utilise universal means and goals do not allow for the processual, personal nature of freedom, or how those who CSR aims to help are both provider and provided for, subject and object. Since the workers at the 'receiving' end of programmes will likely respond to and produce their own forms of power, gender and freedom, CSR for women's empowerment would require subverting assumptions about who and what 'women' are (Cornwall 2007). The continual recasting of women as a synonym for gender, the conflation of sex and gender, and the 'development myth and feminist fable' of women saving the world in sisterhood are legion (Cornwall et al. 2007; Koffman and Gill 2013; Switzer 2013). Echoing early concerns with the essentialism contained within misunderstandings of 'feminine' and feminist ethics (Derry 1996), women in the global

South are continuously positioned as saviours of others because of their sex. Indeed, there is no escape from the confines of this fixed gender identity because the identity itself has been co-opted as a strategy for 'empowerment'. This means a concern over inequalities has moved away from an understanding of gender as an embodied, discursive, social construct and back towards a fixed identity. Future theorising on the role of women and men in CSR should once more scrutinise how these categories are constructed and construed within research. CSR in practice, and as a theory, risks becoming useless if the core problems it wishes to improve, such as gender inequality, are ill-understood.

This is not to dissuade corporate social responsibility focus on gender inequalities. Business recognition of the importance of gender inequality and marginalised female stakeholders in their organisations and wider value chains is a step in the right direction. My concern is with the narrow framing of CSR as a vehicle for gender equality through 'women's empowerment programmes'. Echoing concerns of others (Roberts 2015; Tornhill 2016b; Wilson 2011), I would ask whether businesses enacting CSR can support 'empowerment' in its fullest sense, when that requires stepping back and allowing men and women to enact their own forms of freedom? Rose (1999: 97) calls for 'ways of organizing our concern for others that did not seek to set them free – relations of obligation, of commitment, perhaps evoking an older sense of care.' In relation to CSR programmes, this may mean moving beyond an enterprise-based idea of empowerment that relies upon women and men becoming better consumers or entrepreneurs to be 'empowered' or 'developed.' It would mean framing women's empowerment less as a business, or national, opportunity and more as an 'obligation' for business and governments. The current focus on 'empowering women' through CSR has eclipsed a wider, and perhaps more crucial conversation on mainstreaming gender equality throughout all dimensions of a business, and into market economies. As in the Ghanaian case here, a concerted effort to challenge the assumptions around cocoa as a 'male crop', by targeting training and resources at women farmers for example, would be one means of 'gendering' the business' CSR. Further, businesses could engage in championing reproductive autonomy, safety from violence, freedom of association, and childcare provision, through their own operations and through partnership or lobbying. To promote gender equality, all these actions would be good places for businesses to start, whilst being cautious in not 'speaking for others' (Foucault and Deleuze 1977) and inadvertently recreating inequalities as shown here.

A practical solution to some of these problems in CSR and women's empowerment may be closer attention to 'what women [and men] really want,' to borrow a cliché. First, the inclusion as men within gender equality efforts is key, since they remain influential actors within organisations, industries and households (Cornwall 2014). Men and masculinities need to be brought into conversations around equality and empowerment, not just 'in the field' but also as potential 'elite allies' within CSR management (Grosser et al. 2016). A key benefit of taking a feminist Foucauldian approach has been that it moves away from binary understandings of gender (i.e. a focus on women only) to exploring how human individuals take part in power relations, in relation to each other and the consequences this has for certain groups of people (Pullen 2006). Moving beyond a 'woman only' approach to empowerment and incorporating men as also having responsibility for social change would be a welcome development.

Second, we continue to know very little about people's hopes, desires and experiences within CSR initiatives (Ansari et al. 2012; Banerjee 2010) and issues of gender and power are known to effect stakeholder engagement efforts (Grosser and Moon 2005; Grosser 2009) as well as impact assessments (Barrientos et al. 2003). Participatory methods may offer innovative ways in which to get closer to individuals' experiences, meaning-making and intentions, as the onus lies on *in-situ* understandings, processes and the participation of women and men who are ostensibly at the heart of CSR programmes (McCarthy and Muthuri 2016). Happily, the women's empowerment programme in this Ghanaian case has now incorporated a more reflexive approach to gender inequality, beginning literacy classes open to both sexes, and considering how men might be brought into projects (McCarthy and Muthuri 2016).

Ultimately, since power and freedom are deeply connected to the Self, the potential for change, through CSR, may lie in starting from the position that empowerment and its processes come from within ourselves as individuals and 'how we relate to ourselves and others' (Crane et al. 2008: 315). 'Freeing' women from poverty, or inequality, through CSR empowerment programmes may become problematic when we make assumptions about what women need to be 'freed' from, or how this should be done. Facilitating reflection, space for discussion and women and men workers' own desires, should be a goal for research and practice.

Acknowledgements Thanks to Jean-Pascal Gond, Charlotte Karam, Jeremy Moon, Judy Muthuri and Laura Spence, who have helped develop and refine previous iterations of this paper. The author would like to acknowledge the support of the Velux Chair for Corporate Sustainability at Copenhagen Business School during the writing of this article. Thank you to the handling editor, Kate Grosser, and the four anonymous reviewers for detailed and developmental comments and suggestions. Finally, thanks to the women involved in the study for their time and insight.

References

Acker, J. 1990. Hierarchies, jobs, bodies: A theory of gendered organizations. *Gender & Society,* 4(2): 139-158.

Adanhounme, A.B. 2011. Corporate social responsibility in postcolonial Africa: Another civilizing mission? *Journal of Change Management,* 11(1): 91-110.

Ahonen, P., Tienari, J., Meriläinen, S., & Pullen, A. 2014. Hidden contexts and invisible power relations: A Foucauldian reading of diversity research. *Human Relations,* 67(3): 263-286.

Amigot, P., & Pujal, M. 2009. On power, freedom, and gender: A fruitful tension between Foucault and feminism. *Theory & Psychology,* 19(5): 646-669.

Ansari, S., Munir, K., & Gregg, T. 2012. Impact at the 'Bottom of the pyramid': The role of social capital in capability development and community empowerment. *Journal of Management Studies,* 49(4): 813-842.

Baden, S., Green, C., Otoo-Oyortey, N., & Peasgood, T. 1994. Background paper on gender issues in Ghana. BRIDGE development-gender report, No. 19. Brighton, UK: Institute of Development Studies.

Banerjee, S.B. 2010. Governing the global corporation: A critical perspective. *Business Ethics Quarterly*, 2(2): 265–274.

Barrientos, S. (2013). *Gender production networks: Cocoa-sustaining cocoa-chocolate sourcing from Ghana and India.* Brooks World Poverty Institute working paper, No. 186. Manchester, UK: University of Manchester.

Barrientos, S., & Bobie, A.O. 2016. *Promoting gender equality in the cocoa-chocolate value chain: Opportunities and challenges in Ghana.* GDI Working Paper 2016-006. Manchester, UK: University of Manchester.

Barrientos, S., Dolan, C., & Tallontire, A. 2003. A gendered value chain approach to codes of conduct in African horticulture. *World Development*, 31(9): 511–1526.

Batliwala, S. 2007. Taking the power out of empowerment: An experiential account. *Development in Practice,* 17(4/5): 557-565.

Berlin, I. 1958. Two concepts of liberty. In I. Berlin *Four essays on liberty*. Oxford: Oxford University Press.

Bexell, M. 2012. Global governance, gains and gender: UN–business partnerships for women's empowerment. *International Feminist Journal of Politics*, 14(3): 389-407.

Borgerson, J. L. 2007. On the harmony of feminist ethics and business ethics. *Business and Society Review*, 112(4): 477-509.

Bowring, M. A. 2004. Resistance is not futile: Liberating Captain Janeway from the masculine-feminine dualism of leadership. *Gender, Work & Organization*, 11(4): 381-405.

Burton, B., & Dunn, C. 1996. Feminist ethics as moral grounding for stakeholder theory. *Business Ethics Quarterly*, 6(2): 133–148.

Butler, J. 1997. *Excitable speech: A politics of the performative*. New York and London: Routledge.

Butler, J. 2004. *Undoing gender*. London and New York: Routledge.

Calás, M.B., & Smircich, L. 2006. From the 'Woman's point of view' ten years later: Towards a feminist organization studies. In S.R. Clegg, C. Hardy, T.B. Lawrence, & W.R. Nord (Eds.) *The SAGE Handbook of Organization Studies*. 284-346. Thousand Oaks, CA: SAGE.

Chaudhry, L.N. 2009. Forays into the mist: Violences, voices, vignettes. In A.Y. Jackson & LA. Mazzei (Eds.) *Voice in qualitative inquiry: Challenging conventional, interpretive and critical conceptions in qualitative research*. 137-164. London & New York: Routledge.

Clark, G. 1994. *Onions are my husband: Survival and accumulation by West African market women*. Chicago: University of Chicago Press.

Coca-Cola Company. 2012. *Sustainability Report 2011/2012*. At: http://www.coca-colacompany. com/sustainabilityreport/we/womens-economic-empowerment.html#section-empowering-5-million-women-by-2020. Accessed: 8th April 2017.

Coleman, I. 2010. The global glass ceiling. *Foreign Affairs*, 89(3): 13-20.

Coles, C., & Mitchell, J. 2011. *Gender and agricultural value chains and practice and their policy implications*. Rome: Food and Agriculture Organization.

Cooper, D. 1994. Productive, relational and everywhere? Conceptualising power and resistance within Foucauldian feminism. *Sociology*, 28(2): 435–454.

Cornwall, A. 2007. Myths to live by? Female solidarity and female autonomy reconsidered. *Development and Change*, 38(1): 149–168

Cornwall, A. 2014. *Women's empowerment: what works and why?* WIDER Working Paper No. 2014/104. Helsinki: World Institute for Development Economics Research.

Cornwall, A., & Anyidoho, N.A. 2010. Introduction: Women's empowerment: Contentions and contestations. *Development,* 53(2): 144–149.

Cornwall, A., Harrison, E., & Whitehead, A. 2007. Gender myths and feminist fables: The struggle for interpretive power in gender and development. *Development and Change,* 38(1): 1–20.

Cornwall, A., Gideon, J., & Wilson, K. 2008. Introduction: Reclaiming feminism: Gender and neoliberalism. *IDS Bulletin*, 39(6): 1–9.

Crane, A., Knights, D., & Starkey, K. 2008. The conditions of our freedom: Foucault, organization and ethics. *Business Ethics Quarterly*, 18(3): 299–320.

Deleuze, G. & Guattari, F. 1977. *Anti-Oedipus: Capitalism and Schizophrenia*. London: Penguin Classics.

Derry, R. 1996. Toward a feminist firm. *Business Ethics Quarterly*, 6(1): 101–109.

Dobson, J., & White, J. 1995. Toward the feminine firm: An extension to Thomas White. *Business Ethics Quarterly*, 5(03): 463-478.

Doss, C.R. 2002. Men's crops? Women's crops? The gender patterns of cropping in Ghana. *World Development*, 30(11): 1987–2000.

Drebes, M. 2014. Including the 'Other': Power and postcolonialism as underrepresented perspectives in the discourse on corporate social responsibility. *Critical Sociology*, 42(1): 105-121.

Duflo, E. 2012. Women empowerment and economic development. *Journal of Economic Literature*, 50(4): 1051–1079.

Duncan, B.A. 2010. Cocoa, marriage, labour and land in Ghana: some matrilineal and patrilineal perspectives. *International African Institute*, 80(2): 301-321.

Elson, D., & Pearson, R. 1981. "Nimble fingers make cheap workers": An analysis of women's employment in third world export manufacturing. *Feminist Review*, 7(1): 87–107.

Fletcher, J. K. 1998. Relational practice: A feminist reconstruction of work. *Journal of Management Inquiry*, 7(2): 163.

Foucault, M. 1977a. *Discipline and Punish*. Middlesex, UK: Penguin.

Foucault, M. 1977b. Truth and power. In J. D. Faubion, (Ed.) *Power. Essential works of Foucault 1954-1984, Volume 3*. 111-133. London: Penguin.

Foucault, M. 1978. *The history of sexuality volume 1: The will to knowledge*. Harmondsworth, UK: Penguin.

Foucault, M. 1980. *Power/knowledge: Selected interviews and other writings 1972-7*. Brighton, UK: Harvester Press.

Foucault, M. 1982. The subject and power. *Critical inquiry*, 8(4): 777–795.

Foucault, M. 1985. *The history of sexuality volume 2: The use of pleasure*. Harmondsworth, UK: Penguin.

Foucault, M. 1986. *The history of sexuality volume 3: The care of the self*. New York: Vintage.

Foucault, M. 1987. The ethics of the concern of the self as a practice of freedom. An interview translated by J.D. Gauthier. In J. Bernauer & Rasmussen, D. (Eds.) *The Final Foucault*. 1-20, London & Cambridge, Mass: MIT Press.

Foucault, M. 1994. Technologies of the self. In P. Rabinow (Ed.) *Michel Foucault: Ethics: Subjectivity and Truth. The essential works of Michel Foucault 1954-1984. Volume 1*. 223-254. London: Penguin.

Foucault, M. & Deleuze, G. 1977. Intellectuals and power. In D. Bouchard (Ed.) *Language, counter-memory, practice*. 207-217. Ithaca: Cornell University Press.

Freeman, R.E., & Liedtka, J. 1997. Stakeholder capitalism and the value chain. *European Management Journal*, 15(3), 286-296.

Freire, P. 1970. *Pedagogy of the oppressed*. New York: Herder and Herder.

Gond, J-P., & Moon, J. 2011. Corporate social responsibility in retrospect and prospect: Exploring the life-cycle of an essentially contested concept. In J-P. Gond & J. Moon (Eds.), *Corporate social responsibility: A reader. Volume 1*. 1-28. London and New York: Routledge.

Grimshaw, J. 1993. Practices of freedom. In C. Ramazanoglu (Ed.) *Up Against Foucault: Explorations of some tensions between Foucault and feminism*. 51-72. London and New York: Routledge.

Grosser, K. 2009. Corporate social responsibility and gender equality: women as stakeholders and the European Union sustainability strategy. *Business Ethics: A European Review*, 18(3): 290–307.

Grosser, K., & Moon, J., 2005. The role of corporate social responsibility in gender mainstreaming. *International Feminist Journal of Politics*, 7(4): 532–554.

Grosser, K., McCarthy, L. & Kilgour, M.A. 2016. (Eds.) *Gender equality and responsible business: Expanding CSR horizons.* Saltaire, UK: Greenleaf.

Grosz, E. 1994. *Volatile bodies: Toward a corporeal feminism.* Minneapolis, IN: Indiana University Press.

Hale, A., & Opondo, M. 2005. Humanising the cut flower chain: Confronting the realities of flower production for workers in Kenya. *Antipode*, 37(2): 301–323.

Hardy, C., & Leiba-O'Sullivan, S. 1998. The power behind empowerment: Implications for research and practice. *Human Relations*, 51(4): 451-483.

Hayward, C.R. 2000. *De-Facing power.* Cambridge: Cambridge University Press.

Held, V. 1993. *Feminist morality: Transforming culture, society, and politics.* Chicago, Illinois: Chicago University Press.

Hirschmann, N.J. 2002. *The subject of liberty: Toward a feminist theory of freedom.* Princeton and Oxford: Princeton University Press.

Hudon, M., & Sandberg, J. 2013. The ethical crisis in microfinance: Issues, findings, and implications. *Business Ethics Quarterly*, 23(4): 561-589.

Hughes, R. 1998. Considering the vignette technique and its application to a study of drug-injecting and HIV risk and safer behaviour. *Sociology of Health and Illness*, 20(3): 381- 400.

Humphreys, M. 2005. Getting personal: Reflexivity and autoethnographic vignettes. *Qualitative Inquiry*, 11(6): 840-860.

ICRW. 2016. *The business case for women's economic empowerment: An integrated approach.* Washington, D.C.: ICRW.

Kabeer, N. 1999. Resources, agency, achievements: Reflections on the measurement of women's empowerment. *Development and Change*, 30(3): 435-464.

Kabeer, N., & Mahmud, S. 2004. Globalization, gender and poverty: Bangladeshi women workers in export and local markets. *Journal of International Development,* 16(1): 93–109.

Karam, C.M., & Jamali, D. 2013. Gendering CSR in the Arab Middle East: An institutional perspective. *Business Ethics Quarterly*, 23(1): 31–68.

Kelan, E.K. 2010. Gender logic and (un)doing gender at work. *Gender, Work & Organization*, 17(2): 174–194.

Khan, F. R., & Lund-Thomsen, P. 2011. CSR as imperialism: Towards a phenomenological approach to CSR in the developing world. *Journal of Change Management*, 11(1): 73-90.

Knights, D., & Vurdubakis, T. 1994. Foucault, power, resistance and all that... In J. M. Jermier, D. Knights, & W. R. Nord (Eds.) *Resistance and power in organizations.* 167–198. London and New York: Routledge.

Koffman, O., & Gill, R. 2013. 'The revolution will be led by a 12-year-old-girl': Girl power and global biopolitics. *Feminist Review*, 105: 83-102.

Kondo, D.K. 1990. *Crafting selves: Power, gender, and discourses of identity in a Japanese workplace.* Chicago: Chicago University Press.

Liedtka, J. M. 1996. Feminist morality and competitive reality: A role for an ethic of care? *Business Ethics Quarterly*, 6(2): 179–200.

Linstead, A., & Brewis, J. 2004. Editorial: Beyond boundaries: Towards fluidity in theorizing and practice. *Gender, Work and Organization*, 11(4): 355-362.

Linstead, S., & Pullen, A. 2005. Fluid identities and un-gendering the future. In A. Pullen & S. Linstead (Eds.) *Organization and Identity.* 242-269. London: Routledge.

Liu, H. 2015. Reimagining ethical leadership as a relational, contextual and political practice. *Leadership*: 1-24. DOI:https://doi.org/10.1177/1742715015593414.

Lukes, S. 1974. *Power: A radical view.* (2005th edition). Basingstoke, UK: Palgrave Macmillan.

Maertens, M., & Swinnen, J. 2010. *Are African high-value horticulture supply chains bearers of gender inequality?* Rome: The World Bank.

Marshall, J. 2011. En-gendering notions of leadership for sustainability. *Gender, Work & Organization*, 18(3): 263–281.

Mayoux, L. 1999. Questioning virtuous spirals: Microfinance and women's empowerment in Africa. *Journal of International Development,* 11(1): 957-984.

McCarthy, L., & Muthuri, J. N. 2016. Engaging fringe stakeholders in business and society research: Applying visual participatory research methods. *Business & Society*: 1-43. DOI: 0007650316675610.

McNay, L. 1992. *Foucault and feminism: Power, gender, and the self.* Boston: Northeastern University Press.

McNay, L. 2000. *Gender and agency: reconfiguring the subject in feminist and social theory.* Cambridge, UK: Polity Press.

Mena, S., de Leede, M., Baumann, D., Black, N., Lindeman, S., & McShane, L. 2010. Advancing the business and human rights agenda: Dialogue, empowerment, and constructive engagement. *Journal of Business Ethics*, 93(1): 161-188.

Mercer. 2016. *When women thrive: Global report 2016.* New York: Mercer.

O'Grady, H. 2004. An ethics of the self. In D. Taylor & K. Vingtnes (Eds.) *Feminism and the final Foucault.* 91-117. Illinois: Illinois University Press.

Oxfam. 2012. *Gender equality: It's your business.* Oxford: Oxfam International.

Painter-Morland, M. 2006. Redefining accountability as relational responsiveness. *Journal of Business Ethics,* 66(1): 89-98.

Painter-Morland, M. 2008. Systemic leadership and the emergence of ethical responsiveness. *Journal of Business Ethics,* 82(2): 509-524.

Pearson, R. 2007. Beyond women workers: Gendering CSR. *Third World Quarterly*, 28(4): 731–749.

Pellegrino, G., D'Amato, S., & Weisberg, A. (2011). *The Gender dividend: Making the business case for investing in women.* New York: Deloitte.

Prügl, E. 2015. Neoliberalising feminism. *New Political Economy,* 20(4): 614-631.

Pullen, A. 2006. Gendering the research self: Social practice and corporeal multiplicity in the writing of organizational research. *Gender, Work and Organization*, 13(3): 277-298.

Pullen, A., & Knights, D. 2007. Editorial: Undoing gender: Organizing and disorganizing performance. *Gender, Work & Organization*, 14(6): 505-511.

Pullen, A., & Simpson, R. 2009. Managing difference in feminized work: Men, otherness and social practice. *Human Relations*, 62(4): 561–587.

Quisumbing, A. R., Payongayong, E. M., & Otsuka, K. 2004. *Are wealth transfers biased against girls? Gender difference in land inheritance and schooling investment in Ghana's Western region.* Washington, D.C.: The World Bank.

Ramazanoglu, C., & Holland, J. 2002. *Feminist methodology: Challenges and choices.* London: SAGE.

Reiman, J. 1987. Exploitation, force, and the moral assessment of capitalism: thoughts on Roemer and Cohen. *Philosophy & Public Affairs*, 16(1): 3-41.

Roberts, A. 2015. The Political Economy of "Transnational business feminism". *International Feminist Journal of Politics*, 17(2): 209-231.

Rohatynskyj, M. 2011. Development discourse and selling soap in Madhya Pradesh, India, *Human Organization*, 70(1): 63-73.

Rose, N. 1999. *Powers of freedom: Reframing political thought.* New York: Cambridge University Press.

Rowlands, J. 1995. Empowerment examined. *Development in Practice*, 5(2): 101-107.

Sawicki, J. 1991. *Disciplining Foucault: Feminism, power and the body.* New York and London: Routledge.

Scott, J.C. 1985. *Weapons of the weak: Everyday forms of peasant resistance.* New Haven, USA: Yale.

Skinner, D. 2012. Foucault, subjectivity and ethics: towards a self-forming subject. *Organization*, 20(6): 904–923.

Spence, L.J. 2014. Small business social responsibility: Expanding core CSR theory. *Business & Society*, 55(1): 23-55..

Spence, L.J. 2016. The obfuscation of gender-awareness and feminism in CSR research and the academic community: An essay. In K. Grosser, L. McCarthy, & M. A. Kilgour (Eds.), *Gender Equality and Responsible Business: Expanding CSR Horizons*. 16-30. Saltaire, UK: Greenleaf.

Summerson Carr, E. 2003. Rethinking empowerment theory using a feminist lens: The importance of process. *Affilia*, 18(1): 8-20.

Switzer, H. 2013. (Post)feminist development fables: The Girl Effect and the production of sexual subjects. *Feminist Theory*, 14(3): 345–360.

Sybylla, R. 2001. Hearing whose voice? The ethics of care and the practices of liberty: a critique. *Economy and Society*, 30(1): 66-84.

Syed, J., & Van Buren, H. 2014. Global business norms and Islamic views of women's employment. *Business Ethics Quarterly*, 24(2): 251-276.

Tornhill, S. 2016a. The wins of corporate gender equality politics: Coca-Cola and female micro-entrepreneurship in South Africa. In K. Grosser, L. McCarthy, & M. A. Kilgour (eds.), *Gender Equality and Responsible Business: Expanding CSR Horizons*. 185-202. Saltaire, UK: Greenleaf.

Tornhill, S. 2016b. "A bulletin board of dreams": corporate empowerment promotion and feminist implications. *International Feminist Journal of Politics*: 1-17. https://doi.org/10.1080/1461674 2.2016.1190214

Uhl-Ben, M. 2011. Relational leadership and gender: From hierarchy to relationality. In P.H. Werhane & M. Painter-Morland (Eds.) *Leadership, Gender, and Organization*. 75-108. Heidelberg, London, NY: Springer.

VanMaanen, J. 1988. *Tales of the Field*. Chicago: Chicago University Press.

Wajcman, J. 1998. *Managing Like a Man: Women and Men in Corporate Management*. Cambridge, UK: Polity Press.

Waring, M. 1988. *If Women Counted: A New Feminist Economics*. London: Macmillan.

Werhane, P.H., & Painter-Morland, M. 2011. Editors' introduction. In P.H. Werhane & M. Painter-Morland (Eds.) *Leadership, Gender, and Organization*. 65-66. Heidelberg, London, New York: Springer Dordrecht.

White, T. 1992. Business, ethics, and Carol Gilligan's "two voices." *Business Ethics Quarterly*, 2(1): 51-61.

Wicks, A.C. 1996. Reflections on the practical relevance of feminist thought to business. *Business Ethics Quarterly*, 6(4): 523-531.

Wicks, A.C., Gilbert Jr., D.R., & Freeman, R.E. 1994. A feminist reinterpretation of the stakeholder concept. *Business Ethics Quarterly*, 4(4): 475–497.

Wilson, K. 2011. 'Race', gender and neoliberalism: changing visual representations in development. *Third World Quarterly*, 32(2): 315–331.

World Bank. 2011. *World development report 2012: Gender equality and development*, Washington, D.C.: The World Bank.

World Economic Forum (WEF). 2013. *Five challenges, one solution: Women. Global agenda council on women's empowerment 2011 – 2012*. Geneva: WEF.

Yeager, R., & Goldenberg, E. 2012. HERproject women's health program delivers real business returns. *Global Business and Organizational Excellence*, (January/February): 24–36.

Yuval-Davis, N. 1994. Women, ethnicity and empowerment. *Feminism & Psychology*, 4(1): 179-197.

Lauren A. McCarthy is an Assistant Professor of Legal Studies and Political Science at the University of Massachusetts Amherst. She holds a PhD and MA in Political Science from the University of Wisconsin-Madison and a BA from the College of Social Studies at Wesleyan University. Her research focuses on the relationship between law and society in Russia, police and other law enforcement institutions, and human trafficking. She teaches courses on law and society, comparative law, Russian politics, human rights, human trafficking, and sports and justice. Her recent book, *Trafficking Justice: How Russian Police Use New Laws, from Crime to Courtroom* published by Cornell University Press explores how Russian law enforcement agencies have implemented laws on human trafficking.

Women Leaders in a Globalized World

Patricia H. Werhane

Abstract This article will defend a very simple thesis. In a diverse globalized world with expanding economic opportunities, pandemic risks such as the global COVID-19 virus, and the Black Lives Matter movement, we will need to revisit and revise our mindsets about free enterprise, corporate governance, and most importantly, leadership. That we can change our mindsets and world view is illustrated by studies of primate behavior, in particular, the Forest Troop savanna baboons, and the kind of leadership necessary in a global political economy, even given the pandemic, is, interestingly often exemplified by women.

Keywords Globalization · Leadership · Women leaders · Systems thinking

Introduction

According to Robert Sapolsky, a leading expert in the study of primates, until fairly recent it was thought that "[c]ertain species seemed simply to be that way they were, fixed produces of the interplay of evolution and ecology, and that was that" (Sapolsky 2006: 105). This was a conclusion thought particularly applicable to primates, and in his work to baboons. As he writes:

> Hierarchies among baboons are strict, as are their consequences. Among males, high rank is typically achieved by a series of successful violent challenges...Male baboons, moreover, can fight amazingly dirty, [and]...the victorious male is to subject the other to a ritualized gesture of dominance.... A baboon group, in short, is an unlikely breeding ground for pacifists. ...[P]rimate species with some of the most aggressive and stratified social systems have been seen to cooperate and resolve conflicts? but not consistently, not necessarily for

---

This is a substantially revised version of the paper originally published in the first edition of this book, *Leadership, Gender and Organization*. See Werhane 2007, 2011.

P. H. Werhane (✉)
Center for Professional Responsibility, Gies College of Business, University of Illinois, Chicago, IL, USA

© The Author(s), under exclusive license to Springer Nature Switzerland AG 2023
M. Painter, P. H. Werhane (eds.), *Leadership, Gender, and Organization*, Issues in Business Ethics 63, https://doi.org/10.1007/978-3-031-24445-2_11

benign purposes, and not in a cumulative way that could lead to some fundamentally non-Hobbesian social outcomes.... At least that was the lesson until quite recently. (Sapolsky 2006: 108)

In the early 1980s, "Forest Troop," a group of savanna baboons studied by Sapolsky contracted tuberculosis. The dominant (Alpha) males in the troop who had foraged at a garbage dump and had prevented the rest of the troop from entering the dump, died. "The result was that the Forest Troop was left with males who were less aggressive and more social than average, and the troop now had double its previous female-to-male ratio."(Sapolsky 2006: 115) As a result, and this still persists after 20 years, in this troop "there remained a hierarchy among the Forest Troop males, but it was far looser than before....aggression was [and is] less frequent, ...[a]nd rates of affiliative behaviors, between males, and between males and females has soared." (Sapolsky 2006: 115) Even when male newcomers from other [presumably aggressive] savanna baboon troops join the Forest Troop (a common practice among baboons to prevent genetic inbreeding) these males are "socialized into nonaggressive behavior pat terns."...in other words, new males find out that in this Forest Troop, things are done differently and they adapt accordingly. According to Sapolsky, this sort of behavior, until documented by careful study, would have been thought of as "nearly as unprecedented as baboons sprouting wings" (Sapolsky 2006: 115).

This article will defend a very simple thesis. In a diverse globalized world with expanding economic opportunities, pandemic risks such as the global COVID-19 virus, and the Black Lives Matter movement, we will need to revisit and revise our mindsets about free enterprise, corporate governance, and most importantly, leadership. That we can change our mindsets and world view is illustrated by studies of primate behavior, in particular, the Forest Troop savanna baboons, and the kind of leadership necessary in a global political economy, even given the pandemic, is, interestingly often exemplified by women.

The Globalized Planet

In the first iteration of this paper (Werhane 2007) I pointed out that by 2007, the date of its publication, "globalization has now shifted into warp drive..." (Wright 2005) That is, free enterprise has not only infiltrated most of the corners of the earth, but jobs, ideas, goods, and services, like the internet, are now global. This is not simply that one's telephone, computer, and flight information are outsourced to many other parts of the world, or that a chat room is accessed by people from all parts of the globe. An X-ray taken in a Chicago hospital is likely to be sent electronically to a physician in India to be read and analyzed. Cell phones have infiltrated the poorest and most remote regions of the planet. In Thomas Friedman's words, "the world [of the 21st century] is flat" (Friedman 2005: 213).

Today, in 2020, most global organizations are now embedded in complex adaptive sets of global political, economic, and cultural relationships and networks. What we once called 'externalities' have become part of a mainstream of interrelated networked global systems in which businesses and other organizations operate. This conclusion is widely understood and accepted today, although has been redefined after the COVID-19 pandemic. Many countries including the United States are now reconsidering their massive outsourcing, although this may be impossible to reverse and deglobalization may only be an aspiration. For example, Medtronic, who makes ventilators for COVID patients, reminded us recently that these machines have more than 1000 parts, many of which are sourced from at least 14 countries (Schlesinger 2020: 1).

This phenomenon of economic globalization means that one cannot outsource underpaid labor, product or service quality, issues of diversity, nor disregard cultural or religious differences, or even corporate social responsibilities. If, for example, the clothes we wear are made under subhuman labor conditions as defined in the country of origin, one cannot dismiss that as someone else's problem. It is ours. This is what we have learned from the pandemic and the global spread of the Black Lives Matter movement, which began in the United States. The world is very small, and economic largesse, poverty and disease are no longer merely externalities. Cultural differences are not just opportunity costs even when one is operating in remote and poor regions. These differences have to do with human relationships, with cultural conflicts as well as consensus, and one cannot ignore them.

As we now experience the Blacks Lives Matter movement, begun in the United States, (now a global outcry), this is in part, a result of economic globalization as well as the internet and social media. In particular, it illustrates the failure of global free enterprises and many political economies to imagine a global pandemic and multi-diverse, multi-gendered organizations whose leaders as well as employees reflect equally this diversity and account for the spread of disease.

But what does globalization have to do with women, and women corporate leaders in particular? Let us begin with the data. Women have been in management training and in MBA programs in significant numbers since the 1970s, and by 2020, 92% of all US based companies have at least one woman in senior management (Grant Thornton 2019). However, in 2020 there were merely thirty-seven women CEOs in the U.S. Fortune 500 publicly held companies, three of whom were "women of color" (Asians), none of whom were Afro-American. In 1995 there were no women in the largest global companies so this is an improvement, but not matching the numbers of women, 50% of the global population (of whom consistently at least 35% have been in MBA programs since the 1970s), and globally, at least 50% of all university graduates are women (Hirchliffe 2020; Grant Thornton 2019). There are now 25% women on corporate boards in the United States, much improved since the 1990s, but still not an equitable number, given the equal level of education of men and women (Hirchliffe 2020).

Globally the data on women leaders is varied. According to the latest study by Grant Thornton, in 2018, fully 29% of all companies globally had at least one woman in senior management, although globally only 15% of the CEOs were women. Eastern Europe leads in the number of women in senior management, 32%, and Latin America has the lowest number, 25% (Grant Thornton 2019). At this rate it may take until the next century, 2100, to see a gender balance in corporate leadership. This is despite the fact that, according to a number of the studies, see for example, Blumberg 2018 "A profitable firm at which 30 percent of leaders are women could expect to add more than one percentage point to its net margin compared with an otherwise similar firm with no female leaders." (Blumberg 2018: 1).

It is easy to speculate why this is the case and to complain about discrimination, unequal opportunities and treatment, glass ceilings, etc. Rather than taking on these complaints however, we will use this data as background to argue that in a transforming global economy, leadership styles we see exemplified in women, best fit the kind of global governance most appropriate for an ever-changing world.

Prevailing and Worn-out Mindsets

The late Ghoshal (2005) contended that a series of what he calls 'worn-out mindsets" (Ghoshal 2005: 83) dominate (and still dominate) management and managerial thinking, at least in North America and the United Kingdom. These mindsets, he contends, have a pernicious effect of contaminating management teaching, literature, and practice in ways that are both false and dangerous. Some of the most popular include notions from agency theory that describe individuals as primarily individual rational utility maximizers where self-interest and opportunistic behavior drive management decision-making. Such managers, of course, cannot be trustworthy on their own, thus one needs to spell out principal-agency relationships, wherein managers must be placed in carrot-stick relationships so as to insure that they pursue the proper corporate aim, which should be a preoccupation to maximize shareholder value. This model often perpetuates a hierarchical reward-punishment management focus, rules-based compliance, and reward (i.e., pay) for performance. The result, Ghoshal concludes, is the following: "Combine agency theory with transaction costs economics, add in standard versions of game theory and negotiation analysis, and the picture of the manager that emerges is...the ruthlessly hard-driving strictly top-down, command-and-control focused, shareholder-value-obsessed, win-at-any-cost business leader" (Ghoshal 2005: 85).

Ghoshal clearly (and I suspect, deliberately) exaggerates the state of management education and management performance. In most management education today, a teams-approach is a prevailing model for forward-thinking education. Stakeholder theory has challenged the preoccupation merely with shareholder profits (not only in academia but in many companies as well), and 'stakeholder' language permeates annual corporate reports. Still, there remains a not insignificant focus on managerial and company self-interest and principal-agent issues and an at least implicit preoccupation with profit maximization as a primary goal, goaded by the demand for quarterly performance, all of which affect management activities. There are still multinational and global companies that think about cultural difference merely as opportunity costs, and there remains a tendency to define 'human resources' as human capital, similar to natural resources. The relatively new Sarbanes Oxley legislation in the United States has created a climate of rule-governed compliance rather than principles-governed mentalities that preempt corporate mission statements and values-based decision-making.

Why do these mindsets matter? As I have argued at length elsewhere (e.g., Werhane 1999): "Our conceptual scheme(s) mediate even our most basic perceptual experiences." (Railton 1986: 172) Our views of the world, of ourselves, of our culture and traditions, and even our values orientations are social constructions. These points of view or mental models are socially learned, they are incomplete, and sometimes distorted, narrow, single-framed. Nevertheless, all experiences are framed, ordered and organized from particular points of view. Sometimes these models become self-fulfilling, that is, "reality [is] how we see and feel events, not events as they appear objectively, because we are not objective" (Nin 1971: 91). Mental models, function on the organizational and systemic levels as well as in individual cognition (Senge 1990). As a result, sometimes, we imagine we are trapped within an organizational culture that creates mental habits that preclude creative thinking. Ghoshal's point is that management education and practice traps us in false mental models, which, he concludes, are absurdities, and "[a]bsurdities in theory lead... to dehumanization of practice" (Ghoshal 2005: 85). Worse, even if these alleged "absurdities" in management practices are viable in United States companies for creating economic value-added in this country, they do not work well in global environments for companies working across various cultures and ingrained but alien traditions.

But because our mindsets are socially constructed frameworks, they are just that...frameworks that can be changed. Since all experience is modeled—whatever those experiences are about-- their content cannot be separated from the ways we frame that content (Werhane 1999). The good news however, is that because they are learned incomplete social constructions, our mental models or mindsets are revisable both at the individual and organizational levels, just as the Forest Troop, when challenged by new circumstances, changed what appeared to be innate genetically imprinted behavior patterns.

Challenging "Worn-out Mindsets"

In this collection we include a seminal article by Janet Borgerson who challenges the alleged dominance of self-focused self-interest in market transactions. According to Borgerson, feminist theory "challenges the dualism of self versus other, or individual versus community—in which the discrete existence of each element is linked to conceptions of autonomy—becomes a question of relationships between self and other and responsibilities of self to the other, and vice versa, in particular contexts. That is, feminist ethical theory attempts to account for intersubjectivity, or interrelations between moral agents even as the boundaries between these become blurred" (Borgerson 2007: 478). In an earlier piece Virginia Held proposes that the self is not merely autonomous but is always interconnected with and constituted by our social context and relationship to and with others (Held 1990). Thus, by these accounts, self-interest is partly, if not wholly constituted by our social relationships.

To fill out this idea, we go back to the writings of the "father" of free enterprise, Adam Smith. Smith begins his first book, *The Theory of Moral Sentiments*, with the following:- "How selfish soever man may be supposed, there are evidently some principles in his nature, which interest him in the fortune of others, and render their happiness necessary to him, though he derives nothing from it except the pleasure of seeing it.... The greatest ruffian, the most hardened violator of the laws of society, is not altogether without it" (Smith 1759; 1976, I.i.I.I). Smith argues that human beings by nature are both self-interested and interested in others. Human beings are not merely motivated by their own interests, but also have interests in maximizing the well-being of others, or at a minimum, not inflicting more pain. This is not merely sentimentalism, according to Smith. While all my interests are mine, in the obvious sense that they originate in myself, I am not the only object of these interests. Thus, rational beings have genuine interests in others, as well as themselves as objects of concern and aggrandizement. Our own self-interest is not always the primary motivating force, and even so, being self-interested is not necessarily bad so long as one is not merely selfish and unconcerned with how one's actions affect others. Agency theory, then, may exaggerate the importance of monitoring principal-agent relationships in every case, because at least some managers will be interested in the firm and its well-being for its own sake despite their own personal gains or losses.

If we ignore Smith's analysis of self-interest, and continue to predict or propose that we all are or should be self-interested (in the sense of being primarily interested in outcomes for ourselves as rational utility maximizers), this perspective affects our thinking about what constitutes or should constitute 'good management' as well as our own behavior. If we promulgate that mindset, it will become reality.

But this worn-out mindset or collection of mindsets is just that, worn-out. Two recent movements in commerce have challenged that. In 2019 the Business Roundtable, an influential American busines organization, revised its commitment to placing shareholder value as the first priority. In its revision of its "Statement on the Purpose of a Corporation," the Roundtable declared:

> companies should serve not only their shareholders, but also deliver value to their customers, invest in employees, deal fairly with suppliers and support the communities in which they operate.... Major employers are investing in their workers and communities because they know it is the only way to be successful over the long term. These modernized principles reflect the business community's unwavering commitment to continue to push for an economy that serves all Americans. (Business Roundtable 2019)

In another ongoing movement to which some major companies have committed, Conscious Capitalism, declares that it "supports a global community of business leaders dedicated to elevating humanity through business. We provide mid-market executives with innovative and inspiring experiences designed to level-up their business operations and collectively demonstrate capitalism as a powerful force for good when practiced consciously" (consciouscapitalism.org) (Conscious Capitalism 2019).

These two declarations illustrate that there are many successful companies that are not focused merely on profit maximization while ignoring their other stakeholders. What is intriguing is that what is called for in our present global political economies and with the transnational companies that operate in vast numbers of countries, is exactly what the feminist thinkers, in particular Held, Ciulla, and Borgerson propose. A feminist approach to leadership that focuses on local contexts, interrelationships, the specific cultural norms and emotional contexts in which an organization proposes to operate, fits global operations more successfully that a "one size fits all" management style applied to every business context with a preoccupation only on profits. This calls for a paradigm shift as counterevidence to Ghoshal's critique.

Three Overlapping Paradigm Shifts: Stakeholder Theory, Systems Thinking and Feminist Leadership

Rethinking Stakeholder Theory

Rather than focus merely on returns for shareholders, stakeholder theory argues, in brief, that companies have obligations to create value added for all their primary stakeholders, usually listed as shareholders, employees and managers, customers, suppliers, and the communicates in which the company operates. The argument is based on instrumental and rights-based arguments. From an instrumental point of view, stakeholder well-being is a necessary component for creating stakeholder value-added. Companies cannot operate without taking into account various stakeholders, because their activities, survival and prosperity depends, in different ways, upon these stakeholders just as these groups of individuals and organizations depend on the corporation for their well-being. From a more rights-based perspective, the company and its stakeholders are all individuals or groups of individuals and they exist in mutual reciprocal relationships with each other. Thus, those relationships are of equal value, and shareholders do not take priority (although they are equal participants) just because of fiduciary obligations created by their capital input. Fig. 1 illustrates at least one version of this theory (Freeman 2002).

There are at least two questions about this wheel and-spoke depiction of stakeholder relationships and corporate governance, both of which the "father" of modern stakeholder theory, RE. Freeman, acknowledges, (see Freeman 1984, 2010). First, the central preoccupation of this graphic is always on the corporation. The depiction of stakeholders with the corporation in the center draws our primary attention to the company and then to its relationships with its stakeholders. This creates a mental model that implicitly prioritizes the corporation while the other stakeholders appear like satellites circling the company rather than as equal players, despite claims to the contrary. It is also an abstract model - names and faces of the stakeholders remain anonymous and the depiction of each remains vague. Although stakeholder relationships are relationships between sets of individuals, the diagram does not depict these relationships as such. (See McVea and Freeman 2005 on the importance of "names and faces" in stakeholder relationships).

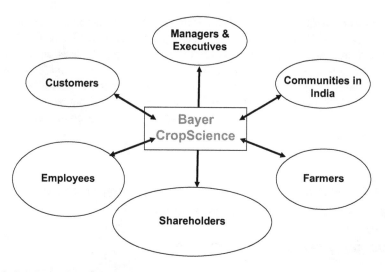

Fig. 1 Standard stakeholder map

Let me illustrate with an example. Suppose we are trying to depict the vast array of interrelationships of an MNC such as the large German pharmaceutical Bayer (Fig. 1). A few years ago the German pharmaceutical Bayer purchased an Indian company CropScience that grew and harvested flax seeds, a product that Bayer needed for some of its chemical production (Subramanian et al. 2010). Bayer had operated in India for almost 100 years but had never dealt with rural communities. In this instance it turned out that there was a long tradition in the various Indian villages growing flax seeds that children as young as 6 years old would harvest the seeds. These children thus often fell behind in school, and eventually dropped out. But part of Bayer's corporate mission was a general principle never to hire or condone child labor. So, Bayer was faced with the option of either pulling out of this market or coming up with a solution that satisfied local farmers as well as Bayer's mission, and at the same time respecting these centuries-old traditions that were part of the social goods of these communities—all while upholding Bayer's own principle of never condoning child labor in any of its operations. (Notice that Bayer's principled approach to child labor is also intertwined with its more utilitarian interests in these flax seeds and a pragmatic aim to try to solve this problem that would satisfy all of these seemingly conflicting norms.)

Because of its economic power, Bayer could have imposed the requirement of forbidding the use of child labor in these farms. Or it could have simply accepted this practice as part of rural Indian culture and tradition. But instead Bayer approached the problem with the kind of nuanced appreciation of the local complex relationships and traditions. Bayer tried to understand the local system through the eyes of a "local" participant and to envision a solution that would both work on the ground and satisfy their larger corporate mission. Bayer initially paid the farmers supplements for hiring adult harvesters, and subsidized families who depended on the children's wages for their family income. As it turned out, the adult workers were more efficient harvesters, so farmers were more satisfied, as well. Then, it worked with local Indian educators to provide remedial education for the children so that the children could return to school and succeed, without falling behind. Thus, Bayer has its flax seeds, children receive education, and all parties are satisfied with the outcome without feeling morally compromised (Subramanian et al. 2010).[1]

To accomplish all of this, Bayer had to rethink itself and its relationships with various stakeholders. One way to trigger such rethinking is to reimagine a stakeholder map with the rural farm children in the middle (Fig. 2). Still, it is uncertain whether this approach adequately depicts the myriad of interrelationships that Bayer must take into account as a global corporation operating in a variety of environments including farmers in rural India. And why should any particular stakeholder be featured in the center, if, as the theory suggests, each has equal, although not identical, rights and responsibilities. Figure 3 better depicts Bayer and Bayer CropScience's context. What it suggests, further, is that in a global economy, a systems approach is perhaps a more adequate way of thinking about corporate governance.

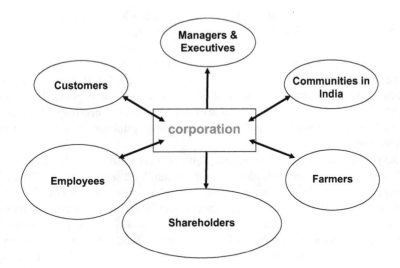

Fig. 2 Corporate stakeholder map

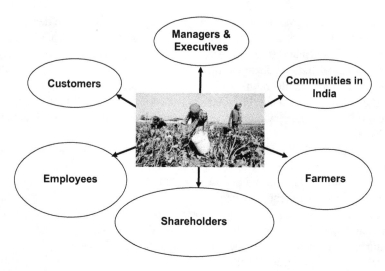

Fig. 3 Revised stakeholder map

Systems and Systems Thinking[2]

A rationalist autonomous model, even if one brackets what Ghosal called a flawed theory that we are all individual rational utility maximizers, does not adequately take into account the embeddedness of each of us in a complex array of relationships. With the ever-expanding globalization of media, the internet, and commerce an over-individualist account of human behavior belies the fact that we live within, communicate and interact with a set of interrelated complex systems. The global spread of the COVID-19 virus demonstrates this interconnectivity. A systems approach is a necessary ingredient to leadership thinking in today's global environment.

"A system is a complex of interacting components together with the networks of relationships among them that identify an entity and/or a set of processes" (Laszlo and Krippner 1998: 51). "A truly systemic view of considers how a set of individuals, institutions and processes operates in a system involving a complex network of interrelationships, an array of individual and institutional actors with conflicting interests and goals, and a number of feedback loops" (Wolf 1999: 1675). A systems approach presupposes that most of our thinking, experiencing, practices and institutions are interrelated and interconnected. Almost everything we can experience or think about is in a network of interrelationships such that each element of a particular set of interrelationships affects some other components of that set, and the system itself, and almost no phenomenon can be studied in isolation from other

---

[2]This section is taken from a slightly revised version of an earlier paper. See Werhane 2002. See also Werhane 2019.

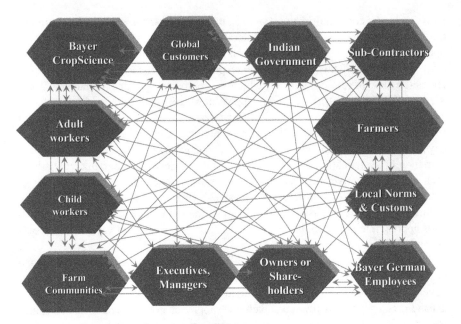

Fig. 4 Stakeholder systems networks (Werhane 2008: 470)

relationships with at least some other phenomenon. Systems are connected in ways that may or may not enhance the fulfillment of one or more goals or purposes: they may be micro (small, self-contained with few interconnections), mezzo (within health care organizations and corporations), or macro (large, complex, consisting of a large number of interconnections). Corporations are mezzo-systems embedded in larger political, economic, legal, and cultural systems. Global corporations are embedded in many such systems. These are all examples of "complex adaptive systems," a term used to describe open interactive systems that are able to change themselves and affect change in their interactions with other systems, and as a result are sometimes unpredictable (Plsek 2001). What is characteristic of all types of systems is that any phenomenon or set of phenomena that are defined as part of a system have properties or characteristics that are, altered, lost or at best, obscured, when the system is broken down into components. For example, in studying corporations, if one focuses simply on its organizational structure, or merely on its mission statement, or only on its employees or customers, one obscures if not distorts the interconnections and interrelationships that characterize and affect that organization in its internal and external relationships.

Since a system consists of networks of relationships between individuals, groups, and institutions, how any system is construed and, how it operates, affects and is affected by individuals. The character and operations of a particular system or set of systems affects those of us who come in contact with the system, whether we are individuals, the community, professionals, managers, companies, religious communities, or government agencies. An alteration of a particular system or corporate operations within a system (or globally, across systems) will often produce different kinds of outcomes. Thus, part of moral responsibility is incurred by the nature and characteristics of the system in which a company operates (Emanuel 2000; Werhane 2002). Adopting a systems approach Mitroff and Linstone in their book, *The Unbounded Mind*, argue that any organizational action needs to be analyzed from what they call a Multiple Perspective method. Such a method postulates that any phenomenon, organization, system or problems arising from or within that phenomenon of system should be dealt with from a variety of disparate perspectives, each of which involves different world views where each challenges the others in dynamic exchanges of questions and ideas (Mitroff and Linstone 1993, Chap. 6). Returning to the Bayer CropScience example, the model in Fig. 3 illustrates a systems approach to this complex operation that takes into account various stakeholders and different but equal constituents.

Returning to the thinking of Held and Borgerson from Part I of this collection, a systems approach is by and large a feminist approach. Feminist theorists argue that ethics entails relationships between individuals, and by analogy, between individuals and organizations. A revised stakeholder approach coupled with systems thinking captures that element of human experience and thus that dimension of ethical thinking. In what follows, I shall describe one study of leadership that may give us fresh insights into how one should lead in a global business environment.

An Alternative View of Leadership in a Global Economy

Until recently it was common in the leadership literature to define leaders as the heads of hierarchical organizations. "In a hierarchical organization, leaders organize subordinates into a pyramid-like structure. At the lowest level, less-experienced employees take direction from supervisors and managers at higher levels. Communication typically flows from the top to the bottom. Most decisions tend to be made by leaders at the top with little or no input from employees at lower levels". But many large, medium and small organizations have tried to abandon such structured hierarchies. In a global multicultural economy where interactions are across cultures and often between managers from various cultures and perspectives, this leader/follower model is outdated. As Joanne Ciulla articulates it:

> leadership is not a one person or a position. It is a complex moral relationship, based on power and influence, trust, obligation, commitment, emotion, and some vision or goal based on what the leader or the leader and followers think is desirable or good. The leader/leadership relationship can be moral or immoral. They may think unethical things such as discrimination or genocide are good. The leader or leaders may manipulate or use coercion on followers. [G]ood leadership has to be both ethical and effective. An incompetent ethical leader and a competent unethical leader are both problematic. (Ciulla 2020)

In this model, leadership is interactive, dynamic, and entails a set of mutually inter-relational processes between leaders and managers, where each participant contrib-utes to the vision and progress toward excellence in performance and change in the company. The most effective global leaders are and will be those who are not only visionary, but who are used to working with a diverse population collaboratively rather than in a traditional leadership-follower dynamic. This sort of leader thinks and acts across cultures, just as in the United States marketplace we think and act across state borders, without thinking about those borders as "borders" at all.

The vision and goals these leaders share with their managers are not merely per-sonal aspirations or derived from a particular nationality, religion, or ethnic origin. Rather, these are, or should be, evolving shared corporate goals, developed from managerial interactions that at the same time take into account cultural differences. Thus, in a globalized economy, many of the operative mindsets in management may need reconception. A systems approach to corporate governance is one viable approach to global management and calls for thinking carefully about what we expect of global business leaders managing in multiple environments. While there are no definitive "recipes" for this, it might be useful to examine some models of leadership that are less hierarchical and that do not depend on a traditional leader/ follower relationship.

In a recent study of global women leaders in four non-North American countries (India, Japan, Jordan, and the United Kingdom (UK)K) Regina Wolfe and I traced the leadership styles and milieus of each of these leaders within their country's legal and cultural contexts. As one can imagine, each woman faced different but almost overwhelming challenges as a women leader in predominantly patriarchal cultures. Even women in the UK, where one would expect gender equality and equal oppor-tunity, we found that in fact, male dominance (particularly in commerce) still pre-vails. For example, in 2020 only 2% of CEOs in the FTSE 250 are women.

What we discovered in studying these women leaders, despite their extraordi-narily different backgrounds, was that each of them was prepared for leadership. They were well-educated and never imagined that they could not lead.[3] Each was fearless and undaunted by cultural mores that were antithetical to their positions, and male counterparts who had not imagined that a woman could be successful. Most worked in sectors of their political economy where there were few other women. Each took on projects that seemed impossible for anyone to achieve. But not one woman sacrificed her basic values and belief system. Each tried to create their own style without giving up who they were as women. And every woman we studied mentored other women in their field so that those relationships were nour-ished (Wolfe and Werhane 2017).

Most of the women in our study appear to be flexible, adapting and readapting themselves to new and changing situations. They exhibit what James MacGregor Burns once called "transforming leaders." (Burns 1978: 1) Burns defines

---

[3] This is in contrast to a 2004 study of American women leaders cited in the first edition of this book where many of the women leaders were not prepared beforehand to lead. See Werhane et al. 2007.

transforming leadership as "a relationship of mutual stimulation and elevation that converts follows into leaders and may convert leaders into moral agents....[This] occurs when one or more persons engage with others in such a way that leaders and followers raise one another to higher levels of motivation and morality" (Burns 1978: 3). One of the distinctive and characteristic features of these particular women in leadership positions is their ability to engage in interactive leadership relationships with their managers and employees and a determination to empower others. Many spoke of building value added in their organizations through a participatory inclusive style of leading their employees as colleagues rather than as subordinates or followers. Indeed, the terms "subordinate" and "follower" seldom surfaced in the interviews we conducted. Unlike leaders in hierarchically structured organizations, these women do not view their authority as a matter of power. They do not think of themselves as persons in superior positions of formal authority even when they find themselves in leadership positions in traditionally hierarchically ordered organizations.

We find these models for global leadership encouraging. Now let us consider a current example: Mary Barra, the first female CEO of General Motors (GM), one of the largest auto manufacturers in the world. Between 1002 and 2014 GM was manufacturing the Chevrolet Cobalt (one of their best-selling automobiles), eventually selling over 2.6 million of these cars. However, problems with the ignition switch were detected in its Chevrolet Cobalt as early as 2002. But despite hundreds of injuries and at least 32 fatalities from this failure[4] and thousands of complaints, the Company said it was a "customer convenience problem," (Valukas 2014: 2) To redesign the switch properly and recall the Cobalt would have been very costly (Valukas 2014: 8), since they eventually produced and sold 2.6 million of them. (Fletcher 2014). Was this simply negligence; was there a preoccupation with profitability, or was it protection of the Chevrolet brand as a "safe" option? At GM, time and time again from 2002 to 2014, despite overwhelming evidence of the dangers of ignition switches on the Cobalt and other models as well as engineering questions, management did not think this was serious enough to warrant recalls or redesign the switch (Valukas 2014: 1–8).

GM was likely driven by goals of efficiency and productivity, all values we teach in business schools. These are ordinarily fine goals. But management did not consider the means: the human beings who drove these autos and were in mortal danger. In 2014 GM underwent a leadership change, and for the first time, on January 15, 2014, a woman, Mary Barra, became CEO. Almost at once she publicly addressed the faulty ignition switch issue. In February of 2014 she hired an outside firm, Jenner and Block, to investigate and help the company address this issue. A thorough investigation was initiated by Barra using a former US attorney, Anton Valukas with Jenner and Block, a study that is now publicly available (see Valukas 2014). In brief, the investigation concluded that for several years of production,

---

[4] The actual number of fatalities has not been calculated accurately, in part because of deaths from airbag failures and other mechanical malfunctions as well. Recently the *Wall Street Journal* (September 5, 2020) reported that there were over 120 deaths. (Colins 2020)

most of the ignition switches were defective and that customers were not notified of the lethal defect. All of this was made public by Ms. Barra. GM notified federal safety regulators about the ignition switch recall that would affect 778,000 cars. It would eventually grow to cover all 2.6 million cars globally (Isidore 2014). Despite this scandal, GM's sales rose during 2014 (Feloni 2018).

According to a report by Richard Feloni, "Mary Barra said the recall crisis of 2014 forever changed her leadership style....{According to this report] Barra said the experience taught her to be impatient about solving problems and to encourage employees and managers to be transparent with each other....[S]he accelerated this impatience she had with arbitrary rules and processes that restricted employees and their managers. She [aimed] to dismantle the decades-old culture that resulted in employees not voicing concerns and then committees dismissing concerns when they did arise..." (Feloni 2018: 3).

Was this dramatic change at GM due to the fact that Barra was a woman? Perhaps, and it is her leadership style that reflects feminist thinking—the idea of being transparent and values-driven, and flexible when she faced the ignition switch challenge.

There are some valuable lessons to be learned from the Wolfe-Werhane study and from Mary Barra--some leadership skills, style, and values-orientation that, I would argue, fit well in a flattened world not merely governed by self-interest, preoccupation with shareholder value added, and a mindset that considered different cultural settings are merely opportunity costs.

Some of the leaders in this study appear to be what Northouse and others have called "adaptive leaders." That is, they have happened to be at the right place at the right time with talents that matched the situation (Northouse 2018, Chap. 11). More of the women in our study, however, appear to be situational leaders, adapting and readapting themselves to new and changing situations (Northouse 2018, Chap. 11). Indeed, some of these women actively pursued change working to reengineer their organizations or starting new entrepreneurial ventures.

Their interactions with managers and employees are seldom transactional exchanges of rewards or demotions for superior or inferior performance. Rather, they saw leadership as an ongoing process, envisioning themselves as team leaders, as inspirational rather than directive, as participative rather than hierarchical, working to coordinate and balance their interests and those of their employees, and transforming these into shared corporate goals. This is usually translated into forms of interactive and participatory leadership that empowers employees while achieving corporate ends. Thus, as Joanne Ciulla argues, leadership is thought of as a two-way interaction where both managers and employees are motivated and sometimes even changed (Ciulla 2020). As a result, these women were not afraid of hiring or working with managers and other professionals who were smarter or more capable than they, nor of seeking out and encouraging their successors. Values-based leaders create or propound values for their instrumental worth, and they align their employees and shareholders to accept and work for those values.

The women we studied by and large were what we would call ethical leaders. They literally practiced the leadership style they "preached," working to embody their personal values in their professional and social lives. Ethical leadership goes even further in at least three ways. Ethical leaders assume that personal, professional and organizational values are congruent. The values embedded in the organizational mission and direction are worthwhile- not only instrumentally, but for their own sake. They are community or global standards that have moral worth even if the company in question fails to achieve them. An ethical leader, under this rubric, not only embodies her personal, professional and organizational values (and expects the same from her employees and managers, shareholders, and the organization), but continually tests these values against societal norms, organizational consistency and outcomes (Freeman et al. 2005). Finally, most of the leaders we studied in this small sample seem to care more about the sustained success of their organization than their own legacy, but the women we studied were not humble. They had achieved success; they were very proud of that and of their capabilities as business leaders. This was not because they were women, but because they had created and embodied a viable and successful leadership style that worked well in diverse environments.

Global Leadership in the Twenty-First Century

Ciulla defines global leadership as "a process by which [diverse groups of people] are empowered to work together synergistically toward a common vision and common goals..." Given the thesis that the world is flat, and the argument that I made, it follows that global leaders must be multicultural systems thinkers, if not by background, at least by the leadership skills they exhibit. In such a world, one must be adaptable to new situations, flexible, inclusive and collaborative, or failure is inevitable. At the same time, some time ago according to Nancy Adler, "the CEO of a global company cannot change her message for each of the countries and cultures in which her company operates. Global leaders, unlike domestic leaders, address people worldwide....a fundamental distinction is that global leadership is neither domestic nor multidomestic: it focuses on cross-cultural interaction. Thus, global leaders must articulate and communicate a vision which, in and of itself, is global... and compelling to people from around the world" (Adler 1997: 175). In a globalized world, too, transparency and trust are crucial, because there are virtually no secrets anyway. Such leaders must be visionary and open-minded because they are challenged with new ideas, some worthwhile, others less so, every day in every encounter. A hierarchical model of leader/follower is not ideal in global companies, simply because the diversity of cultures and challenges requires collaboration and team effort across many traditional barriers and religious divides. Ideally, the best global leaders are not merely values-driven but are what we have called "ethical leaders," who embody their values in all that they do and promote. These are all characteristics of the women we studied.

Conclusion

The Forest Troop savanna baboons were challenged by changes in the male-female population that allowed the less dominant males to be sought after as mates. That phenomenon, in turn, changed the social relationships and culture of this troop. By analogy, the globalized world has changed the dynamics of local and multinational business. This new world requires dramatic behavioral and social modifications in managerial leadership- not merely for economic reasons, or to attack pandemics, but also to face and address the demands of diversity and real equality of opportunities. These global challenges can be taken on by women and men who adapt the leadership style and values we found in women leaders we studied. It is to a company's peril to ignore this way of leading and to ignore the possibility of women as well as men leading the major global organizations in this new century.

References

Adler, N.J. (1997). Global Leadership; Women Leaders. *Management International Review* 37, 171-196.

Blumberg, Y. (2018). Companies with more female executives make more money—here's why. Make It. [online]. CNBC. Available at: https://www.cnbc.com/2018/03/02/why-companies-with-female-managers-make-more-money.html [Accessed July 21 2020].

Borgerson, J. (2007). On the Harmony of Feminist Ethics and Business Ethics. *Business and Society Review* 12, 477-509.

Burns, J. M. (1978). *Leadership*. Harper Collins Publishers, New York.

Business Roundtable. (2019). Business roundtable redefines the purpose of a corporation to Promote an Economy That Serves All Americans. Business Roundtable. Available at: https://www.businessroundtable.org/business-roundtable-redefines-the-purpose-of-a-corporation-to-promote-an-economy-that-serves-all-americans [Accessed July 30 2020].

Ciulla, J. (2020). *Pioneers in Business Ethics*. University of Illinois Video Project transcription.

Colins, M. (2020). Boss Talk: Steering GM Through Tumultuous Times. *Wall Street Journal* [online]. Dow Jones Institutional News. Available at: http://search.proquest.com/docview/2440324505/ [Accessed July 15 2020].

Conscious Capitalism. (2019). *Conscious capitalism* [online]. Available at: www.consciouscapitalism.org [Accessed July 25 2020].

Emanuel, L. (2000). Ethics and the Structures of Health Care. *Cambridge Quarterly* 9, 151-168.

Feloni, R. (2018). GM CEO Mary Barra said the recall crisis of 2014 forever changed her leadership style. *Business Insider* [online]. Available at: https://markets.businessinsider.com/news/stocks/gm-mary-barra-recall-crisis-leadership-style-2018-11-1027725818 [Accessed July 25 2020].

Fletcher, M. (2014). GM CEO: 15 Fired over Ignition Switch Recalls. Washington Post [online]. Available at: https://www.washingtonpost.com/business/economy/gm-ceo-15-fired-over-ignition-switch-recalls-probe-shows-pattern-of-failures-no-coverup/2014/06/05/2dc575bc-ecb8-11e3-9f5c-9075d5508f0a_story.html [Accessed July 25 2020].

Freeman, R. E. (2002). Stakeholder Theory of the Modern Corporation. In T. Donaldson, P.H, Werhane and M. Cording (eds.), *Ethical Issues in Business*, 7th edition, (pp. 38-49). Prentice Hall, Upper Saddle River, NJ.

Freeman, R. E., Martin. K, Parmar, B., Cording, M.P. and Werhane, P.H. (2005). *Leading Through Values and Ethical Principles*. In R. Burke (ed.), Inspiring Leaders, (pp. 149-174). Routledge, London/New York.

Freeman, R.E. (1984; 2010). *Strategic Management: A Stakeholder Approach*. Cambridge University Press, Cambridge.

Friedman, T. L. (2005). *The World is Flat*. Farrar, Strauss and Giroux, New York.

Ghoshal, S. (2005). Bad Management Theories are Destroying Good Management Practices. *Academy of Management Learning and Education* 4, 75-91.

Held, V. (1990). Feminist Transformations of Moral Theory. *Philosophy and Phenomenological Research* 1, 321-44.

Hirchliffe, E. (2020). *The Number of Female Eos in the Fortune500 hits an all-time record. Fortune* [online]. Available at: https://fortune.com/2020/05/18/women-ceos-fortune-500-2020/ [Accessed July 30 2020].

Isidore, C. (2014). *What did Mary Barra know about the GM recall, and when did she know it? CNNMoney* [online]. Available at : https://money.cnn.com/2014/11/10/news/companies/barra-recall/index.html [Accessed July 15 2020].

Laszlo, A. and S. Krippner. (1998). Systems Theories: Their Origins, Foundations and Development. In J. Scott (ed.), *Systems Theories and a Priori Aspects of Perception*, (pp. 47-74). Elsevier, Amsterdam.

McVea, J.F. and Freeman, R.E. (2005). A Names-and-Faces Approach to Stakeholder Management: How Focusing on Stakeholders as Individuals Can Bring Ethics and Entrepreneurial Strategy Together. *Journal of Management Inquiry*. 14, 57-69.

Mitroff, I. and Linstone, H. (1993). The Unbounded Mind. Oxford University Press, New York/Oxford.

Nin, A. (1971). *Diaries of Anais Nin: 1944-1947*, Vol. IV. Harcourt, New York.

Northouse, P. (2018). *Leadership: Theory and Practice*. 8th edition. Sage Publications, Thousand Oaks, Ca.

Plsek, P. (2001). Redesigning Health Care with Insights from the Science of Complex Adaptive Systems. In *Crossing the Quality Chasm: A New Health System for the 21st Century*, (pp. 309-323). National Academy Press, Washington, DC.

Railton, P. (1986). Moral Realism. *Philosophical Review* 95, 168-175.

Sapolsky, R. M. (2006). A Natural History of Peace. *Foreign Affairs* 85, 104-120.

Schlesinger, J. (2020). How the Coronavirus Will Reshape World Trade. *Wall Street Journal*, 20–21, 1-10.

Senge, P. (1990). *The Fifth Discipline*. Doubleday, New York.

Smith, A. (1759; 1976). *The Theory of Moral Sentiments*. Oxford University Press, Oxford.

Subramanian, S., Dhanaraj, C. and Branzei, O. (2010). *Bayer CropScience in India: A, B values and strategy*. Richard Ivey School of Business Foundation. Case #910M62-PDF-ENG.

Thornton, G. (2019). *Women in business: building a blueprint for action*. Grant Thornton [online]. Available at: https://www.grantthornton.global/globalassets/global-insights%2D%2D-do-not-edit/2019/women-in-business/gtil-wib-report_grant-thornton-spreads-low-res.pdf [Accessed July 30 2020].

Valukas, A.R. (2014). *Report to board of directors of General Motors company regarding ignition switch recalls- Jenner & Block tech rep. Autosafety* [online]. https://www.aieg.com/wp-content/uploads/2014/08/Valukas-report-on-gm-redacted2.pdf [Accessed July 30 2020].

Werhane, P.H. (1999). *Moral Imagination and Management Decision-Making*. Oxford University Press, New York.

Werhane, P.H. (2002). Moral Imagination and Systems Thinking. *Journal of Business Ethics* 38, 33-42.

Werhane, P.H. (2007). Women Leaders in a Globalized World. *Journal of Business Ethics* 74, 425-435. Rpt in P.H. Werhane and M. Painter-Morland (eds.), Leadership, Gender and Organization, (pp.33-48). Dordrecht. Netherlands.

Werhane, P.H. (2008). Mental Models, Moral Imagination and Systems Thinking in the Age of Globalization. *Journal of Business Ethics* 78, 463-474.

Werhane, P. 2011. "Women Leaders in a Globalized World." In Painter-Morland and Werhane, eds., *Leadership, Gender and Organization*. Dordrecht: Springer Nature.

Werhane, P.H. (2019). *Embedded Leadership. Ethical business leadership in troubling times.* Elgar, London.

Werhane, P.H., Hartman, L., Archer, C., Englehardt, E. and Pritchard, M. (2013). *Obstacles to Ethical Decision-Making.* Cambridge University Press, Cambridge.

Werhane, P.H., Posig, L., Gundry, L., Ofstein, L. and Powell, E. (2007). *Women in Business.* Praeger, Westport CT.

Wicks, A., Werhane, P.H., Elms H. and Nolan, J. (2021). Spheres of Influence: A Walzerian Approach to Business Ethics. *Journal of Business Ethics.* Forthcoming.

Wolf, S. (1999). Toward a Systemic Theory of Informed Consent in Managed Care. *Houston Law Review* 35, 1631-1681.

Wolfe, R. and Werhane, P.H. (2017). *Global Women Leaders.* Elgar Publishers, Cheltenham UK.

Wright, R. (2005). *Reading Between the Lines: The Incredible Shrinking Planet. What Liberals can Learn from Thomas Friedman's New Book.* Slate [online]. Available at: http:// www.slate. com/id/2116899 [Accessed: October 23 2006].

Patricia H. Werhane, Professor Emerita, was formerly Ruffin Professor of Business Ethics at Darden School of Business, University of Virginia and later the Wicklander Chair in Business Ethics at DePaul University. Currently, a Fellow at the Center for Professional Responsibility at the Gies College of Business at the University of Illinois, she is the author or editor of over 30 books and over 100 articles, most prominently in business ethics. She was the founding editor of *Business Ethics Quarterly* and is the Executive Producer of a video series on founding thinkers in business ethics and corporate responsibility.

Index